# The History of the Navy of the United States of America

# CLASSICS OF NAVAL LITERATURE

## JACK SWEETMAN, SERIES EDITOR

This series makes available new editions of classic works of naval history, biography, and fiction. Each volume is complete and unabridged and includes an authoritative introduction written specifically for the Naval Institute Press. A list of titles published or currently in preparation appears at the end of this volume.

# The History of the Navy of the United States of America

James Fenimore Cooper

With a new introduction by Edward L. Beach

Naval Institute Press
Annapolis, Maryland

Naval Institute Press
291 Wood Road
Annapolis, MD 21402

One-volume abridged edition originally published in
1846.

Library of Congress Cataloging-in-Publication Data

Cooper, James Fenimore, 1789–1851.
    The History of the Navy of the United States of
    America / James Fenimore Cooper ; with an
    introduction by Edward L. Beach.
        p. cm.—(Classics of naval literature)
    Originally published: Philadelphia : Thomas,
    Cowperthwait & Co., 1846.
      ISBN 1-55750-231-5
      1. United States. Navy—History.    2. United States—
    History, Naval.    I. Title.    II. Series.
VA56 .C66 2001
359'.00973—dc21                                    00-054625

Printed in the United States of America on acid-free
paper ∞

08 07 06 05 04 03 02 01    9 8 7 6 5 4 3 2
First printing

# Introduction

## An Appreciation of James Fenimore Cooper's *History of the Navy of the United States of America*

One of the things I'm fond of saying about my childhood is that I read many of the books in Father's library entirely to pieces lying on my stomach on our living room rug. Only seven or eight years old at the time, today I can own up to this malfeasance with little guilt, but the books were badly mistreated, and I've wondered how Dad could have let me get away with it. One of them was by James Fenimore Cooper, far better remembered for his famous novels *Deerslayer* and *The Last of the Mohicans*, less well known as author of the book the reader is presently holding in his or her hands: *The History of the Navy of the United States of America,* the first useful survey of America's naval experience. The book was published in two volumes in 1839, then revised and abridged—and reduced to a single more manageable volume—by Cooper himself. My father's edition was printed in 1846. In deserved penance for having so damaged this treasured book, it now stands beautifully rebound on my own shelves. It was from there that it sprang to current republication in the Naval Institute Press's Classics of Naval Literature series.

Devotees though they may be, aficionados of the Cooper novels about our frontier days have all remarked that his text is sometimes turgid. In writing he was a perfectionist, and it shows, sometimes too much. Readers will perhaps wish he had written in a more modern time, forgetting that the calendar controls more than dates alone. And yet, in spite of its occasional old-fashioned language, Cooper's *History of the Navy* holds a surprising command of the nautical vernacular— surprising, that is, until one learns that he had been a merchant sailor and then a midshipman in our navy, resigned his commission before the War of 1812 at the demand of his future father-in-law, and regretted the move the rest of his life. How things might have turned out had Cooper remained in the naval service cannot be guessed, but the indications are that he missed the swell of the wave and the roar of great guns, and made up for their absence in his life by writing about them with heart and verve. *The History of the Navy* is far from his only nautical work, but it was the one over which he labored longest. To him our Navy owes much of its appreciation of the War of 1812.

It is well also to keep in mind that in the first half-century of our existence we were at least as much involved on the sea as on the land and, the War of 1812 aside, that the years from 1830 to 1850, during which Cooper's history first appeared (he began work on it in the 1820s), were among the most tumultuous in our early naval annals. Those two decades would have been far better recorded, far more thoroughly studied, had they not been so overshadowed only a few years later by the great tragedy of the Civil War.

In 1835 the rebellion of Texas against Mexico took place, and in 1842 occurred the infamous mutiny on the tiny recruit training brig *Somers*. In 1845 the newly formed Republic of Texas applied for and was accepted into the Union of the United States. This brought on our war with Mexico (1845–

46), and then the huge Mexican Cession comprising the states of California, Nevada, Colorado, Utah, New Mexico, and Arizona. Combined with other influences, such as the discovery of gold and the salubrious climate of our West Coast, the accumulation of these events created probably the third most important era of our early history, rivaled only by our Revolution and the Civil War, and now, in a completely different way, by the Second World War.

A significant omission in my 1846 copy of Cooper's history, however, is any mention at all of the tragedy of the tiny recruit training brig *Somers*, which occurred in 1842, and had a tremendous effect on our Navy. The ship's mentally unstable captain, Alexander Slidell Mackenzie by name, unlawfully executed three of his crew (an eighteen-year-old midshipman and two senior enlisted men) on charges of planning to mutiny. Although Cooper brought events down to the present in 1841, when he abridged his history, and later also revised his unabridged edition, he did not take advantage of any of these subsequent reprintings to include the *Somers* story, or any comment about it. Perhaps he had the idea, as he occasionally stated in other contexts, that his history should be a repository of fact, not an exposition of controversies. Nonetheless, in 1853, two years after Cooper's death, a version of the *Somers* affair, taken "from the author's manuscripts, and other authentic sources," was included in a reprint of his history—but it is tame stuff in comparison to Cooper's elsewhere published denunciations of Mackenzie. Although the quoted line is from the title page, students of Cooper's life and works believe it is hardly likely to have been lifted from anything he wrote.

After returning the *Somers* to New York with its dreadful tale, Mackenzie was tried by general court-martial and acquitted (though not "most fully and most honorably" so). A national furor resulted. Cooper, already renowned as an author and independent idealist, arrayed himself strongly with those holding that neither naval nor civilian law had been properly observed, and that the correct charge should have been murder in the first degree. The Navy had hitherto held that the proper way to train recruits and young officers was by "the school of the ship," but the revelation of the despotic power of a misguided captain, ranging at his sole discretion from flogging to the death penalty, created so much indignation in the minds of so many prominent people—Cooper being among the foremost—that the final result, three years later, was creation of the U.S. Naval Academy in the old Fort Severn grounds at Annapolis, Maryland.

Not a word is devoted to this subject in the revised *History of the Navy* that Cooper published in 1846. Despite his deep concern over the "mutiny," particularly in view of his forthright and public position in the ensuing controversy in 1842 and 1843, this occasions surprise. Another noteworthy omission is any reference in the text to a promise he appears to have made in his preface. There he writes, "a powerful and combined attempt has been made to injure both the book and the author, in connexion [*sic*] with his account of the Battle of Lake Erie"—and he continues his denunciation for the entire following two-thirds of the preface. But despite diligent search, nowhere in the book is there a hint of what the dispute was about. I was much more than seven years old when I made this interesting discovery; Cooper may simply have lost sight of what he wrote in the preface to his 1846 edition, but in his later revision of his original history he inserted only a lengthy footnote to refute assertions that he wished "to add to the reputation of Captain Elliott at the expense of that of Captain Perry."

The accepted history of the important battle fought on Lake Erie in September 1813 is greatly to the credit of Perry, the young commander of the U.S. fleet. His second-in-command, Jesse Duncan Elliott, older than Perry but of a lesser rank, is today considered a malcontent who held back from combat, hoping Perry would fall early so that Elliott could have the glory of turning defeat into victory. In the controversy that developed immediately afterward, Cooper seems initially to have supported Elliott, in spite of his personal dislike of the man, partly on the ground that no member of our naval "model society of gentlemen" would ever do anything dishonorable, but this favorable attitude waned over the years. In the meantime, Cooper and Mackenzie became literary rivals. Each wrote a travel book about England, but Mackenzie had cultivated the friendship of noted author Washington Irving, and his narration of his travels received better reviews. After the first edition of Cooper's history appeared, in 1839, Mackenzie (who had married into the powerful, Newport-based, Perry clan of Rhode Island) published a biography of Oliver Hazard Perry in which he publicly disputed Cooper's version of the Battle of Lake Erie. Cooper retaliated strongly, in 1843, with *The Battle of Lake Erie*, and turned the whole business into personal hatred in 1844 when he came out with an elaborate and devastating review of Mackenzie's court-martial over the *Somers* affair. In time he was disabused of his notion about the high quality of Elliott's motivation, but was never reconciled with Mackenzie, whom he evermore despised.

Robert D. Madison, a professor in the Department of English at the present-day U.S. Naval Academy, to whom I owe understanding of this fairly tortuous explanation, feels that Cooper, holding an impracticably altruistic ideal of self-government, expected members of this model society invariably to act with ideal self-abnegation. His history, twenty years in composition, was intended not only to describe warfare at sea but also to extol naval officers as in fact greater than life. To him they were, or should be, manifestations of perfection in democracy, i.e., in the newly minted American character. In spite of their earlier disagreements, as noted, Cooper even initially supported Mackenzie in the *Somers* controversy, but turned bitterly against him when he came to see the incident as simple murder, committed by an obsessed tyrant who had come into more authority than he could handle.

The 1846 edition of *The History of the Navy* contained numerous woodcut engravings of some of the battles of the War of 1812, many of which are faithfully reproduced in the present edition. In my youth, however, I recall being somewhat concerned that the ships all looked the same except as to number of masts and arrangement of sails. During following years, in spite of Dad's careful tutelage as to their construction, I was never able to correlate the appearance of the hulls as shown in the old, painstakingly drawn, engravings published in Cooper. To me most of them resembled the *Constitution*—and similar criticism may be levied at nearly all the contemporary artists of the period.

Cooper was, of course, a novelist, a writer of dramatic historical fiction by vocation, and it was in this medium that he made his greatest mark on our culture as author of two American classics. His single voyage as a ship's boy in a merchant vessel, and his two years of naval service, gave him love for the sea but no particular pedigree for it, and his detailed descriptions of naval action must therefore be seen not only from the viewpoint of their literary quality but also their accuracy, which means their sources. Evident to anyone with a maritime background is that he must have had total access, not only to the official logs and reports of the actions narrated, but to routine general records as well. His history contains compendiums of ships' names and rates (by number of guns though not necessarily their sizes), long lists of their commanders, and enough tedious information from official documents to put any reader to sleep. He also goes sometimes into considerable detail as to action taken (or inaction, as the case may be) and, on the plus side, nowhere is this more evident than in his lengthy narration of Commodore Isaac Chauncey's campaign against Sir James Yeo of the Royal Navy on Lake Ontario.

It is, however, only fair to point out that the Great Lakes became in truth the most significant area of combat during the War of 1812, that the principal contest lay over control of the two southernmost and smallest of the lakes, and that although neither side exhibited striking initiative, except in swiftly building powerful warships out of nearby green timber, the outcome of the arduous and lengthy campaign was one of the most enduring and friendly boundaries between nations that has ever existed. Had either Chauncey or Yeo been able to send a message like Perry's triumphant, "We have met the enemy and they are ours," the possible result might have been similar also. After Perry's victory on Lake Erie, General William Henry Harrison, later president of the United States for a month, called Perry to his staff as a reward for the victory, advanced into Canada toward Toronto, and defeated the Canadian defenses. Had Chauncey made it possible for Harrison to continue his advance eastward along the northern shore of Lake Ontario and maybe beyond, up the St. Lawrence River, it is reasonable to suggest that the American dream of those days of capturing Canada, which we tried during the Revolutionary War, might have come true in 1813.

The opposite might also have taken place. Had Yeo been victorious, the Second War for American Independence might have turned into a disaster involving loss of much of our Midwest, and possibly some of New England too. Cooper avoids this tangle of conjecture, and it is just as well. Neither of these things happened. Both shores of the St. Lawrence River, and the northern borders of the Great Lakes, remained Canadian, and never have two nations been better friends. Any conquest of Canada will be through the growing effects of natural economics, our mutual power grid, the extraordinary explosion of communications that computer technology has brought us, and the friendly resolution of mutual problems. It is even on (quiet) record that there have been a number of armed invasions of Canada, and vice versa, by police officers in hot pursuit of suspected criminals, or even only of speeding cars, and in every case the police of the other side cooperated fully. Both nations drive on the same side of the street, and are thus one in yet another of the ways that really matter.

But to return to James Fenimore Cooper. His *History of the Navy* is extraordinary, not only in its meticulous reconstruction of nearly every move made by Chauncey and Yeo, but also in his description of every ship the two rivals built, and how they used them. Their final flagships, for example, were considerably bigger, and carried more and bigger guns, than our revered *Constitution*. The biggest warships on either side in the War of 1812 were on the smallest of the Great Lakes, Ontario, and both sides had work well along on two huge line-of-battle ships, designed to carry more than one hundred guns each—that, like the rest of the two opposing fleets, never would have been able to leave that relatively tiny body of water. Henry Eckford, shipbuilder extraordinary for Chauncey, and the Brown brothers, Noah and Adam, for Perry on Lake Erie, deserve tremendous credit for these accomplishments—and truth to tell, Sir James must have had pretty good builders of his own, for the British, too, knew well the importance of the Great Lakes.

It is evident that Cooper received much assistance, not only in research but also in more esoteric Navy matters, from Chauncey, with whom he was well acquainted and whom he repaid in the way he wrote about him. His book quotes frequently from the voluminous reports the Commodore continually made to Secretary of the Navy Hamilton and his successor, Jones. Since Chauncey enjoyed full support from both of the Navy secretaries, and from the Congress, it's evident that the importance of his arena of action was not only understood, but his handling of it approved. Novelists and historians naturally love combat, most especially when it can be the source of daring deeds among tall masts, great white sails, heavy black cannon, and beautiful, uninhibited women. Truth is more prosaic. Isaac Chauncey and Sir James Yeo are too often dismissed as "birds of a feather who would build but not fight." One should also consider what might have happened if either one had decided to risk all for personal glory. History is not generally reversible.

Of Chauncey, Cooper has the following to say: "No officer of the American Navy ever filled a station of the responsibility and importance of that which Commodore Chauncey occupied; and it may be justly questioned if any officer could have acquitted himself better, of the high trust that had been reposed in him. He commanded the profound respect of the vigilant, bold, and skillful [sic] commander to whom he was opposed, and to the last, retained the entire confidence of his own government."

Chauncey, in assisting Cooper, did something for us that a number of persons have remarked on without full appreciation and understanding. Near the end of the War of 1812, in fact after a treaty of peace had been signed in Europe but before receipt of the news across the Atlantic, our famous old frigate *Constitution*, dubbed *Old Ironsides*, now sentimentally preserved in Boston where she was built, fought and captured two ships at once: the small frigate *Cyane*, and the new large sloop of war *Levant*. During the battle, fought at night, Captain Charles Stewart so brilliantly handled his larger and heavier ship that he actually raked both of his antagonists at the same time by suddenly swerving between them, firing heavy broadsides in both directions and then, to their amazed dismay, immediately duplicating the feat by backing all his sails and sailing his big ship backward for another set of two-directional raking broadsides. But let Cooper describe it (see page 423), remembering that the information and initial enthusiasm were Chauncey's:

The sea now being covered with an immense cloud of smoke, and it being now moonlight, Captain Stewart ordered the cannonading to cease. In three minutes the smoke had blown away, when the leading ship of the enemy was seen under the lee-beam of the *Constitution*, while the sternmost was luffing, as if she intended to tack and cross her wake. Giving a broadside to the ship abreast of her, the American frigate threw her main and mizzen topsails with topgallant sails set, flat aback, shook all forward, let fly her jib-sheet, and backed swiftly astern, compelling the enemy to fill again to avoid being raked. The leading ship now attempted to tack, to cross the *Constitution*'s fore-foot, when the latter filled, boarded her fore-tack, shot ahead, forced her opponent to ware [*sic*] under a raking broadside, and to run off to leeward to escape from the weight of her fire.

Father made sure I fully savored that passage, and here, essentially, Cooper ends his active history. He terminates the book, however, by some later detail that, in effect, dates it a little better in time. He refers to "a recent law" (1841) and to construction of "the following two-decked ships . . . all of (which) have been used on foreign stations. . . ." He goes on to mention the 120-gun *Pennsylvania* as having recently been launched (she made only one voyage in her entire career), lists the numbers of officers in various ranks in the "new navy," and concludes the volume with the comment that "there is no longer any question concerning the expediency of the republic's maintaining a powerful marine." With this sentiment, I cannot but agree.

Edward L. Beach

BATTLE OF LAKE ERIE.

# PREFACE.

THIS work has been reduced in size, and conse-quently in cost, by omitting that portion of th' original matter which it is thought will have the least interest with the general reader. The original descriptions of the battles, attacks, chases, &c., have been retained, nearly verbatim, and the narrative is unbroken. Wherever there has been any alteration, in this respect, it has been made with a view to improvement. The opportunity has been taken, also, to introduce a little new matter, and to correct a few errors. Some faults of style, and many errors of the press, have been corrected. In a word, in the author's opinion, this reduced work has all the value or interest which may belong to the original, the documents and more elaborate reasoning excepted. As a mere narrative, he thinks the abridgment will be found to have the most attraction.

A powerful and combined attempt has been made to injure both the book and the writer, in connexion with his account of the Battle of Lake Erie. As to the final decision of the world on this subject, the author feels no concern; but he will take this occasion to say, that the man who makes up his mind on such a subject, without looking for evidence, is guilty equally of weakness and injustice; and as for those who do inquire into the testimony, who collate and consider it, as he has himself done, the author has no apprehensions concerning their decision. His assailants are fast refuting themselves; for, not satisfied with contradicting each other, as has already been done in fifty instances, they are contradicting their own witnesses, and their own statements. The moment is near when a full review of the whole matter will be laid before the public, in which these facts will be made apparent to any reader who will take the trouble to peruse it. It is not difficult to deceive the world for a time; and this is done so much the more easily, when passion, prejudice, and clamour conspire to aid the effort; but public opinion never fails to take ample vengeance for the mistakes into which it has fallen even by its own negligence and compliance. The victims are those who have been so ignorant of the power of truth as to act under the delusion of hoping to smother it, in an age like this, and on a question that can excite party feeling only for a day.

# CONTENTS.

1 *

# CONTENTS.

## CHAPTER VI.

## CHAPTER VII.

## CHAPTER VIII.

## CHAPTER IX.

## CHAPTER X.

## CHAPTER XI.

# CONTENTS.

# CONTENTS.

# CONTENTS.

## CHAPTER XXV.

## CHAPTER XXVI.

## CHAPTER XXVII.

## CHAPTER XXVIII.

## CHAPTER XXIX.

## CHAPTER XXX.

## CHAPTER XXXI.

# CONTENTS.

# CONTENTS.

## CHAPTER XXXIX.

## CHAPTER XL.

## CHAPTER XLI.

## CHAPTER XLII.

## CHAPTER XLIII.

## CHAPTER XLIV.

## CHAPTER XLV.

# CONTENTS.

## CHAPTER XLVI.

## CHAPTER XLVII.

## CHAPTER XLVIII.

## CHAPTER XLIX.

## CHAPTER L.

# NAVAL HISTORY

OF THE

# UNITED STATES.

---

## CHAPTER I.

### 1607.

NOTWITHSTANDING the insular position of its seat of authority, the naval ascendency of England is of comparatively recent date ; Spain, and even the diminutive communities of Portugal and Holland, manifesting as great a spirit of nautical enterprise, during the century and a half that succeeded the important discovery of the western hemisphere, and that of a passage by sea to India. While these three nations were colonising extensively, and laying the foundations of future states, the seamen of England expended their energies in predatory expeditions that were rapacious in their object and piratical in spirit. Familiar political causes, beyond a question, had an influence in bringing about these results ; for, while the accession of the House of Hapsbourg to the throne of Spain and the Indies, created a power able to cope with Europe, as it then existed, England, driven entirely from her continental possessions, had Scotland for a troublesome neighbour, and Ireland for a discontented and turbulent subject, to check her efforts abroad. It is probable, too, that the civil contests, in which England was so long engaged, had a serious effect on her naval advancement, and the struggle that succeeded the dethronement of the family of Stuart, could not fail to lessen exertions that were directed to interests without the territory more immediately in dispute. As a consequence of all these causes, or of that portion of them which was in existence at the commencement of the seventeenth century, when England seriously commenced the business of colonisation, Spain, France, and Portugal were already in possession of what were then considered the most favourable regions on the American continent. When, indeed, the experiment was finally and successfully made, individual enterprise, rather than that of the government, achieved the object; and for many years the power of the crown was exercised with no other aim than to afford an ill-regulated, and frequently an insufficient protection. It was Englishmen, and not England, that founded the country which is now known as the United States of America.

The vessels employed in the earliest communications between the colonies and the mother country, were small, varying from fifty to two hundred tons in burthen. The expedition to Plymouth was first attempted in the May Flower, a bark of one hundred and eighty tons, and the Speedwell, of sixty tons ; but the latter proving leaky, after twice returning to port to refit, was abandoned, and the voyage was made in the former vessel alone. The May Flower sailed from Plymouth, in England, on the 6th of September, and, after a stormy passage, made Cape Cod on the 9th of November.

The first conflict that took place between the colonists and any of their civilized neighbours, occurred in 1613, when an expedition from Virginia, under the orders of Captain Samuel Argal, arriving on the coast of Nova Scotia, made an attack on the new French post of St. Sauveur, which was reduced without difficulty. Argal had eleven vessels with him, most of which, however, were quite small, and his armaments amounted in the whole to fourteen light guns. The French were entirely without artillery. The avowed object of this enterprise was fishing, but the armament has induced a suspicion that the end actually effected was also kept in view. Whatever might have been the intention in fitting out the first force under Captain Argal, it is quite certain, that, on his return to Virginia, he was formally sent against the French in Acadie, with three vessels, better prepared, and that he laid waste the whole of their possessions. Both of these occurrences took place in a time of profound peace, and grew out of a claim of the English, to the possession of the whole coast, as far north as the 46th degree of latitude.

On his return to Virginia, Captain Argal entered the bay of New York, and demanded possession of that territory also, under the plea that it had been discovered by an Englishman. Hendrick Christaens, whom Argal styled " a pretended Dutch Governor," had no force to resist such a claim, and was compelled to submit. On the return to Virginia, one of the three vessels employed in this expedition was lost, and another having been driven as far east as the Azores, proceeded to England, while Captain Argal alone got into the Chesapeake. The prisoners taken on this occasion narrowly escaped being executed as pirates!

This was the first warlike maritime expedition attempted by the American colonists, if a few parties sent in boats against the savages be excepted. The Dutch were not dispossessed by the useless attempt on their settlement, which appears to have been viewed more as a protest than a conquest, for they continued to increase and to govern themselves for near half a century longer. The first decked vessel built within the old United States, of which we have any account, was constructed by Schipper Adrian Blok, on the banks of the Hudson, and probably within the present limits of New York, during the summer of 1614. This vessel De Laet terms a "yacht," and describes as having been of the dimensions of thirty-eight feet keel, forty-four and a half feet on deck, and eleven feet beam. In this "yacht" Blok passed through Hell Gate, into the Sound, and steering eastward, he discovered a small island, which he named after himself; going as far as Cape Cod, by the Vineyard passage.

According to the same authority, the Dutch at New Amsterdam, who had constructed a fort, and reinforced their colony, soon after built many more small vessels, sloops and periaguas, opening a trade with the savages, by means of the numerous bays, sounds, and rivers of their territory.

It was also in 1614 that the celebrated Capt. John Smith arrived from England, and sailed on a coasting voyage, with the double purpose of trade and discovery. He went himself in a boat, having a crew of only eight men, and the profits, as well as the discoveries, abundantly rewarded the risks.

As early as in 1629 the New England Company employed five ships of respectable size, in the trade with the colony. Most of these vessels were armed, and all took colonists in their outward passages. A small ship was built at or near Boston, in 1633, which was one of the first vessels, if not the first vessel of any size constructed in New England. But the progress of the colony of Massachusetts Bay was so rapid, that in 1639 laws were passed to encourage the fisheries, which may be considered as the elementary school of American nautical enterprise. The first engagement that probably ever occurred between inhabitants of the American colonies, and ene-

mies afloat, was a conflict between John Gallop, who was engaged in a trade with the Indians, in a sloop of twenty tons,
and some Narragansetts, who had seized upon a small vessel
belonging to a person of the name of Oldham, known to have
been similarly occupied.   As this, in a certain sense, may be
deemed the earliest sea-fight of the nation, it is worthy to be
related.

Some time in May, 1636, Gallop in his little sloop, manned
by two men and two boys, himself included, was standing
along the Sound, near Plum Island, when he was compelled
by stress of weather to bear up for the islands that form a chain
between Long Island and Connecticut.   On nearing the land,
he discovered a vessel very similar to his own, which was immediately recognised as the pinnace of Mr. Oldham, who had
sailed with a crew of two white boys and two Narragansett
Indians.   Gallop hailed on approaching the other craft, but
got no answer; and, running still nearer, no less than fourteen Indians were discovered lying on her deck.   A canoe,
conveying goods, and manned by Indians, had just started for
the shore.   Gallop now suspected that Oldham had been overpowered by the savages; a suspicion that was confirmed by
the Indians slipping their cable, and standing off before the
wind, in the direction of Narragansett Bay.   Satisfied that
a robbery had been committed, Gallop made sail in chase, and
running alongside the pinnace, he fired a volley of duck-shot
at the savages.   The latter had swords, spears, and some fire-
arms, and they attempted a resistance, but Gallop soon drove
them below to a man.   Afraid to board in the face of such
odds, Gallop now had recourse to a novel expedient to dislodge
his enemies.   As the pinnace was virtually adrift, she soon
fell to leeward, while the sloop hauled by the wind.   As soon
as the two vessels were far enough asunder, Gallop put his
helm up, and ran directly down on the weather quarter of the
pinnace, striking her with so much violence as to come near
forcing her over on her side.   The shock so much alarmed
the Indians, that six of them rushed frantically on deck, and
leaped into the sea.   The sloop again hauled off, when Gallop
lashed an anchor to her bows, and running down on the pinnace a second time, he forced the flukes through the sides of
the latter, which are represented as having been made of boards.
The two vessels were now fast to each other, and the crew of
the sloop began to fire through the sides of the pinnace, into
her hold.   Finding it impossible, however, to drive his ene-

mies up, Gallop loosened his fasts, and hauled up to windward a third time, when four or five more of the Indians jumped overboard. One Indian now appeared on deck and offered to submit. Gallop ran alongside, and received this man in the sloop; he was bound hands and feet, and put into the hold. Another soon followed this example, and he was also received on board the sloop and bound; but, fearful if two of his wily foes were permitted to commune together, that they would liberate themselves, the second prisoner was thrown into the sea. Only two Indians now remained in the pinnace. They had got into a small apartment below, and being armed, they showed a disposition to defend themselves, when Gallop removed all the goods that remained into his own sloop, stripped the pinnace of her sails, took her in tow, and hauled up for the islands again. But the wind increasing, the pinnace was cut adrift, and she disappeared in the direction of Narragansett Bay, where it is probable she was stranded in the course of a few hours.

On board the pinnace, Gallop found the body of Mr. Oldham. The head had been cleft, the hands and legs were much mangled, and the flesh was still warm. The corpse was thrown into the sea.

Thus terminated this extraordinary conflict, in which Gallop appears to have shown as much conduct as courage, and which in itself illustrates the vast superiority that belongs to professional skill on an element like the sea. As it was of the last importance to create a respect for the English name, the report of the conqueror on this occasion induced the government of Massachusetts to send an expedition against the offenders, under Mr. Endecott, one of the assistants, which did the Indians much injury in the destruction of their dwellings and crops, though the savages themselves took to flight. This expedition, however, was followed up by others that met with greater success.

The French in Acadie, also, gave rise to two or three unimportant armaments, which led to no results worthy of being recorded.

Notwithstanding the frequency of the Indian conflicts, and the repeated visits of the French, the first regular cruisers employed by the American colonists appear to have owed their existence to misunderstandings with the Dutch of the New Netherlands. The colony of New Haven had so far increased as to cause a vessel of one hundred and fifty tons to be

2 *

built in Rhode Island, as early as the year 1646, but the ship was lost at sea on her first passage. Shortly after, a small cruiser, carrying ten guns, and forty men, was employed by the united colonies of Hartford and New Haven, to cruise in Long Island Sound, with a view to prevent the encroachments of the Dutch, and to keep open the communication with the settlements they had made on the opposite shore. In 1654, orders were received from Parliament to treat the Dutch as enemies, but both communities were still too young and feeble to engage in a warfare that was not considered of paramount necessity. Nothing effective appears to have been done under these instructions.

At a later day, or in 1665–6, Connecticut kept another small vessel cruising off Watch Hill, in order to prevent the Narragansett Indians from crossing to attack the Montauk tribe, which had been taken under the protection of the colony.

In 1645, a ship of some size was built at Cambridge, Massachusetts, and receiving an armament of fourteen guns, and a crew of thirty men, she sailed for the Canary Isles. This vessel fell in with a rover, of twenty guns, and seventy men, supposed to belong to Barbary, when an action took place that continued the entire day. The rover receiving some serious injury in her rudder, the New England ship was enabled to escape. Although the conflict between Gallop and the Narragansetts is, in one sense, entitled to the precedency, this action may be set down as the first regular naval combat in which any American vessel is known to have been engaged.

An important change occurred, in 1664, in the situation of the American colonies, by the capture of New Netherlands from the Dutch. The vessels employed on this service were under the orders of Sir Robert Carr, while Colonel Richard Nicoll commanded the troops. No resistance was made. In consequence of this accession of territory, and the submission of the Swedish settlements on the Delaware, the English Colonies had entire possession of the coast, between the Bay of Fundy and the Floridas.

While the English were thus occupying the coast, the French were gradually extending themselves along the chain of Great Lakes in the interior, drawing a belt around the territories of their rivals. In the course of events of this nature, de la Salle launched a vessel of ten tons on Lake Ontario, in 1678, which was the first decked boat that ever sailed on those waters.

The following year, he caused a vessel of sixty tons to be launched on Lake Erie.

The buccaneers began to commit depredations in the American seas, about the year 1666; and piracies on a smaller scale, were not unfrequent at a much earlier day. These buccaneers originally were mere outlaws in the West India Islands. Compelled at length to unite, they assembled at the Tortugas, and began to plunder such vessels as approached the shore; most of their robberies being committed by means of open boats. The Spanish vessels, in particular, became the objects of their assaults; and encouraged by success, they began to cruise farther from the land. Their numbers rapidly increased, and ere long they ventured to make descents on the coasts, more especially on those of the Spanish settlements, in quest of plunder. It is a mark of the peculiar character of the age, that these freebooters often commenced their enterprises with prayer!—They spent their ill-gotten wealth as profligately as it had been obtained, and like more powerful bodies of men, were finally destroyed by the excesses engendered by their own prosperity.

In consequence of the great number of privateers that sailed out of Acadie, the general court of Massachusetts sent an expedition against Port Royal, in 1690. The forces were commanded by Sir William Phipps, and amounted to between 700 and 800 men, who were embarked in eight small vessels. This expedition sailed on the 28th of April, and returned on the 30th of May, having been successful. The good fortune that attended this enterprise, induced the government of Massachusetts to attempt another against a place as important as Quebec. Sir William Phipps again commanded, having between thirty and forty vessels, the largest of which was of 44 guns and 200 men, and the whole number of the troops and seamen employed was about 2000. These forces reached Quebec, October the 5th, 1690, and landed, October the 8th. The force disembarked was about 12 or 1300 men, but it was repulsed without much fighting. On their return to Boston, the ships were dispersed by a gale, and little credit was gained by the undertaking.

The Falkland, a fourth-rate, was launched in the Piscataqua, in 1690, and was the first ship-of-the-line ever built in America.

Much alarm existed along the coast, about this time, from an apprehension of the French, who were understood to be cruising in the American seas. We learn, indeed, from the whole history of that period, how nearly balanced were the naval powers of Europe; England, France, Spain, and Holland, standing in mutual awe of each other, on the high seas.

## CHAPTER II.

THE close of the seventeenth century was the period when the piracies had got to be the most serious, and when Kidd was guilty of those acts that have since given him a notoriety that would seem to be altogether disproportioned to his deeds. During the wars of that day, the seas had been much infested with a species of privateers, that often committed aggressions, and even piracies, on neutral vessels. Most of these rovers were English; and it is said that they sometimes plundered their own countrymen. New York was not entirely exempt from the suspicion of having equipped several vessels of this description, and very unpleasant surmises affected the characters of some distinguished men of the colony, the governor, Fletcher, among others. In appreciating such charges, it is necessary to remember the character of the age, there being no disgrace attached to adventures in private armed ships, and the transition from fighting for plunder, and plundering unlawfully, is very trifling, in remote seas, where testimony is not easily obtained, and the law is impotent. That which men can practise with impunity, they are apt to undertake, when tempted by cupidity; and that which is frequent, ceases to shock the sense of right. It is by no means probable that either Governor Fletcher, or any distinguished colonist, deliberately engaged in piratical adventures; but it is quite possible that such men may have been concerned in the equipment of private cruisers, that subsequently committed acts which the laws condemned. It is possible, that when such vessels have returned, a rigid inquiry into the origin of the plunder they brought with them, was not always made. Such, in some measure, was the case with Kidd, whose subsequent notoriety appears to have been as much owing to the *éclat* with which he sailed, sanctioned by government, and supported by men of character, and to some striking incidents that accompanied his return, as to any extraordinary excesses as a pirate. The facts of his case appear to have been as follows:

Much odium having been cast on the colony of New York, in consequence of the number of piracies that had been committed by rovers sailing from the port of that name, the government in England deemed it necessary to take serious measures to repress the evil. This duty was in particular confided to the Earl of Bellamont, who had been appointed the governor of several of the colonies. Mr. Robert Livingston happening to be in England when the subject was under discussion, and being a man of influence in the colony of New York, he was conferred with, as to the most advisable means of putting an end to the practice. Mr. Livingston advised that a cruiser of force should be sent out expressly to seize all lawless rovers, and he introduced to Lord Bellamont, Captain Wm. Kidd, whom he recommended as a seaman qualified to be put at the head of such an adventure. Captain Kidd was said to have a knowledge of the pirates, and of their places of resort; and at the same time, to be a man on whose integrity and services full reliance might be placed. The first proposition was to employ a king's ship of 30 guns and 150 men on this service; but the war requiring all the regular cruisers, it is a proof of the spirit of the times, that the matter was referred to private enterprise, although the sanction of government was not only promised, but obtained. Mr. Livingston took one-fifth of the shares, and became the usual security for the lawfulness of Kidd's proceedings. The Lord Chancellor, and several other distinguished noblemen, took shares in the adventure also, and the crown reserved to itself a tenth of the proceeds, as a proof that it approved of the enterprise. Kidd received his commission and his orders from the Earl of Bellamont, whom he followed to America for that purpose, sailing from Plymouth in England, April 1696, for New York. There is much reason for thinking that Captain Kidd was not guilty of any illegal act himself, until he found that his more legitimate enterprise was not likely to be successful. In the end, however, he went to the eastward of the Cape of Good Hope, where he certainly committed piracies, though to what extent is now questionable. He was accused of ravaging the sea between Madagascar and the coast, from Babelmandel to Malabar, and of committing the usual excesses, though it is probable that there was much exaggeration mixed up with the histories and rumours of the day.

Some accounts confine his piracies to a single ship, though it is more than probable that he had a disposition to the vocation, and that he was easily diverted from the object with which he had sailed, even if he did not contemplate piracy on quitting port.    After an absence of about three years, Kidd returned to the American coast, first appearing off the east end of Long Island.    About thirty miles to the westward of Montauk, protected from the ocean by the southern branch of the island just mentioned, is a capacious bay that obtains its name from another small island, which is so placed as to defend it against the northeast gales.    The latter island contains about three thousand acres of land, and ever since the country has been settled, or for two centuries, it has been the property of an honourable family of the name of Gardiner, which has given its name to both the island and the bay.    The latter has an anchorage that has long been known to seamen, and into Gardiner's Bay Kidd sailed on this occasion.    Anchoring near the island, he landed, and buried some treasure; entrusting Mr. Gardiner with the secret, and making the life of the latter the pledge of his fidelity.    This effected, the pirate again sailed, and made similar deposits on other parts of the coast.

After a short interval, Kidd paid and discharged his crew, and it is said burned his ship.    He appeared in Boston in 1699, and was immediately seized by the order of Governor Bellamont.    Among his papers was found a record, containing lists of his several deposits, which it is probable he held in reserve for his own share of the booty, when he should have made his peace with those in power with the remainder.    The authorities, however, were inflexible, and commissioners were immediately sent in quest of the buried booty.    When these persons presented themselves to Mr. Gardiner, and assured him that Kidd was in confinement, that gentleman led them to the spot where the box was concealed, and it was recovered.    The papers of the Gardiner family show that the contents of the box were bags of gold dust, bags of gold bars, the latter to a considerable amount, coined gold and silver, silver bars, precious stones, silver lamps, &c., &c., in all to the amount of near twenty thousand dollars.    Most, if not all, of the other deposits were also obtained.    Kidd was sent to England, tried and condemned.    The indictments were for both murder and piracy, but being found guilty of the first crime, he was never tried for the last.    He was not executed, until May the 9th, 1701.

The year that Kidd was sent to England, seven pirates were executed in Charleston, South Carolina, that coast having been much infested with these robbers.

From an early day the possession of Port Royal in Acadie, appears to have been a favourite object with the colonists, most probably from the great interest they felt in the fisheries. We have already seen that expeditions were sent against this place, in the earlier wars, while we now find no less than three undertaken, with the same object, in the war of 1702–12. The first of these expeditions was set on foot in 1707, being almost purely of colonial origin. It sailed in May, in twenty-three transports and whale-boats, under the convoy of the Deptford man-of-war, Captain Stuckley, accompanied by the Province, galley, Captain Southack. This expedition effected nothing. The second attempt was not made until the year 1709, when an enterprise on a larger scale was planned. According to Trumbull, the colonies east of Connecticut were ordered to raise 1200 men for this undertaking, and to provide transports, pilots, and provisions for three months, while Connecticut itself and the more southern provinces, were to send a force of 1500 men, by land, against Montreal. The maritime part of the expedition was abandoned, after waiting three months in the port of Boston for the British ships that were to convoy it, and to aid in subduing the place. The attack on Montreal was also given up, for want of the expected co-operation. The third attempt was made in 1710, when a Colonel Nicholson, of the English service, was entrusted with the command. On this occasion the preparations were made conjointly by the crown and the provinces, the latter furnishing the transports and several cruisers. The fleet consisted, in all, of 36 sail; viz. three fourth-rates, two fifth-rates, five frigates, a bomb ketch, the Province, galley, and twenty-four transports. In these vessels were embarked a regiment of marines, and five regiments of provincials. The expedition sailed from Boston on the 18th of September, arrived off Port Royal on the 24th, and on the 1st of October the place submitted. Its name was changed to Annapolis, by which appellation it is yet known. Stimulated by this success, a still more important attempt was made in 1711, against the French possessions on the banks of the St. Lawrence. England now appeared disposed to put forth her power in earnest, and a fleet of fifteen sail, twelve of which were sent directly from England, and three of which had been stationed on the coast, were put under the orders of Vice-admiral Sir Hovenden Walker, for that purpose. In this fleet were several ships of the line, and it was accompanied by forty transports and six store vessels. Five of the veteran regiments that had served under Marlborough, were sent out with the fleet, and two regiments raised in New England being added to them, the land forces amounted to between 6000 and 7000 men.

After considerable delay, the fleet sailed on the 30th of July, 1711, when the Governor of Massachusetts ordered a fast to be observed every Thursday, until the result should be known. On the 14th of August the ships entered the St. Lawrence, and on the 18th the admiral, in order to collect his transports, put into the bay of Gaspé. Here he remained until the 20th, when the fleet proceeded. On the 20th the ships were off soundings, out of sight of land, and enveloped in a fog, with a gale at E. S. E. The fleet now brought to with the ships' heads to the southward. Notwithstanding this precaution, it was soon discovered that the whole of them were in imminent jeopardy among the rocks, islands, and currents of the north-shore, which was, moreover, a lee shore. Some of the vessels saved themselves by anchoring, among which was the Edgar, 70, the admiral's own ship; but eight transports were lost, together with a thousand people; and the expedition was abandoned. The admiral now dismissed the provincial troops and vessels, and sailed for England with the remainder of the fleet. These signal disasters led to loud complaints and to bitter recriminations between the English and the American officers. To the latter was attributed a fatal loss of time, in raising their levies and making other preparations, which brought the expedition too late in the season; and they were also accused of furnishing incompetent pilots. It is probable that the first accusation was not without foundation, since it has been a known national failing to defer all military preparations to the latest possible moment, from the day the country has been peopled; though the last was no doubt unmerited, as there could be no motive for furnishing any other pilots than the best that the colonies possessed. On the part of the Americans, the admiral, and the English commanders in general, were said to be opinionated and indisposed to take advice; a charge quite as likely to be true, as it also accords with national character, and more especially with the superciliousness with which the English were known to regard the provincials. The admiral threw the responsibility of having hove-to the fleet on the pilots, who, in their turn, declared that it was done contrary to their advice. Some French pilots are said, by Charlevoix, to have also warned the admiral of his danger, but he equally disregarded their information. It is in favour of the provincials, that, one small victualler excepted, none of their own vessels were lost, and that the crew of this victualler was saved. Many of the pilots were sent to England to be examined before the Privy Council, but no investigation into the affair took place. The loss of the admiral's papers is thought to have put an end to the contemplated inquiry, the Edgar having been blown up, by accident, at Plymouth, shortly after her return, by which event 400 men lost their lives; thus terminating a most disastrous expedition by a dire calamity. It ought to be mentioned, that the colonies met the charge of delay, by showing that the orders to raise troops, and to make the other requisite preparations, were received only sixteen days before Sir Hovenden Walker arrived in port with his fleet.

The first negro slaves brought into the country, were landed from a Dutch man-of-war, at James Town, in 1620.* Where these poor Africans were obtained is not now known, but they were most probably the victims of perfidy. The increase among the blacks was very slow, however; for thirty years later the whites of Virginia were said to outnumber the negroes, in the proportion of fifty to one; and even when the colony had been settled seventy years, the slaves were not at all numerous.†

The first American vessel engaged in the slave-trade, of which we have any account, sailed from Boston, for the coast of Guinea, in 1645, having been fitted out by Thomas Keyser and James Smith.‡ The last of these worthies was a member of the church. To the credit of the people of Boston, their sense of right revolted at the act, the parties concerned were arraigned, and the slaves were ordered to be restored to their native country at the public expense.

We turn with satisfaction to the whale-fisheries. The commencement of this manly, lucrative, and hardy pursuit, dates from an early period in the history of the country. The whale frequenting the American seas at that time, the people of the coasts kept boats, organized themselves into gangs, and whenever a spout was seen, they would launch in pursuit. This irregular system prevailed many years, until sloops, and other small craft, began to be employed in the offing. These vessels would range the coast, as far south as the West Indies, and north to Davis's Straits. They occasionally crossed to the Azores, where a rich booty was sometimes obtained in the spermaceti.

The whale-fishery on a larger scale, dates from about the middle of the eighteenth century, when Massachusetts in particular, engaged extensively in the enterprise. This colony alone is said to have had no less than three hundred vessels employed in the northern and southern whale-fisheries, previously to the war of the Revolution. Her vessels led the way to the South Atlantic, to the African coast, and to the Pacific Ocean.

After the war which was terminated by the peace of Utrecht, most of the maritime colonies employed a species of guarda-costas, small armed vessels, that were maintained for the suppression of piracies, and for the general protection of the coasts. Some of these vessels were commanded by young officers, who afterwards rose to more or less distinction, either at home, or in the British service. Among others was Lieutenant Wooster, afterwards Captain Wooster, who commanded the armed vessel employed by Massachusetts. This gentleman was subsequently killed at Danbury, during the Revolution, holding the rank of a Brigadier-General in the militia of his native state.

England declared war, in 1739, against Spain, and the American Colonies became the seat of many of her preparations and levies. Natives of the country were much employed in the different expeditions, and it is well known that the estate which has since acquired so much celebrity on account of its having been the property of Washington, obtained the appellation of Mount Vernon from the circumstance that an elder brother, from whom that great man inherited it, had served in the celebrated attack against Carthagena, under the admiral of that name. In 1741, the colonies supplied many of the transports sent against Cuba.

The year 1744 became memorable in the history of the colonies, by another declaration of war against France. By this time the importance of all the American provinces, whether English, French, or Spanish, was certain to render them, more or less, the seat of the contests ; and the great European states interested, were now found seriously exhibiting their power in

the Western hemisphere.   The short duration of the war, probably, alone prevented America from being the scene of those
severe struggles that were deferred a few years by the peace
of Aix la Chapelle.   Short as was the contest, however, it afforded the colonists an opportunity of manifesting both their
spirit and their resources, by an expedition against Louisbourg.

The French had long been aware of the importance of a
port that commanded the entrance of the St. Lawrence, as
Gibraltar commands the approach to the Mediterranean, and
vast sums of money had been expended on the fortifications of
Louisbourg.   It is said that no less than $6,000,000 were ap-
propriated to this object, and a quarter of a century had been
consumed in the preparations.   The place was so formidable
as to have been termed a second Dunkirk.   So conscious had
Massachusetts become of her strength, however, that no sooner
was the declaration of war known, than Governor Shirley laid
propositions before the English ministry and the colonial legislature, for the reduction of this great naval and military station.   The General Court of Massachusetts, at first, was afraid
to embark in so serious an enterprise without assurances of
support from home, as England was then affectionately termed,
but the people of the colony getting a knowledge of the
Governor's wishes, seconded him so strongly with petitions,
that the measure was finally carried by a majority of one.
Connecticut, Rhode Island, and New Hampshire lent their aid,
and by the 25th of March, 1745, the expedition was ready to
sail.   Not a British soldier was employed, and when the fleet
left Boston, it was with very uncertain hopes of being supported
by any of the King's ships.

The land forces, all levies of New England, no other colony
joining in the enterprise, were led by Colonel William Pepperel, of Kittery, in Maine, and the fleet was commanded by
Captain Edward Tyng, of the Massachusetts colonial marine.
The naval part of these forces consisted principally of vessels
equipped, or hired, for this especial service.   There appear to
have been twelve in all, besides the transports, the largest carrying but 20 guns.   The land forces amounted to 4070 men.
From the various and contradictory accounts of this armament, we gather the following list of the colonial cruisers engaged in the expedition, viz : Ships, Massachusetts, 20, Commodore Tyng ; Cæsar, 20, Captain Snelling ; Snows, Shirley,
20, Captain Rouse ; Prince of Orange, 16, Captain Smethurst ;

Brig Boston Packet, 16, Captain Fletcher; and Sloops, ——,
12, Donahue; ——, 8, Saunders; ——, Bosch; a ship hired
by Rhode Island, 20, Captain Griffen, and two vessels of 16
guns each, belonging to Connecticut.

The fleet reached Canseau on the 4th of April, where it remained some weeks, to be joined by the levies of New Hampshire and Connecticut, as well as to allow time for the ice to
dissolve in the neighbourhood of Cape Breton.   For the first
time, probably, in the history of the colonies, large military
preparations had been made in season, and the result triumph-
antly showed the benefit of the unwonted alacrity.   Here
Com. Warren, of the British navy, joined the expedition, with a
part of the squadron from the West-Indies, in which seas, and on
the American coast, he had long commanded.   This excellent
and efficient officer, than whom there was not a braver in the
British marine, brought with him the Superb, 60, and three
ships of forty guns; his broad pennant flying in the former.
Of course, he assumed the command of the naval operations,
though great distrust appears to have existed between him and
Colonel Pepperel to the last.   After a conference with the
latter, he went off Louisbourg, which he blockaded.

Louisbourg was invested by land on the 30th of April, and
after a vigorous siege of forty-seven days, during which time
a severe cannonade was carried on, the place submitted.   The
French flags were kept flying for some time after the surrender,
by which *ruse* two East Indiamen and a South Sea ship, all
richly laden, were decoyed into the mouth of the harbour and
captured.   The value of these three vessels has been estimated
as high as $3,000,000.

While cruising off the port, Commodore Warren captured
the French man-of-war, Vigilant, 60, with troops and supplies
for the garrison.   This important event, no doubt, was of great
moment to the result of the siege.

Although the naval part of the colonial expedition could
have been of no great account after the arrival of Commodore
Warren, it took the sea with creditable vigour, as soon as
Louisbourg had submitted.   The Shirley, Galley, 20, Captain
Rouse, or as the vessel is sometimes called, the Snow, Shirley,
captured eight French vessels, and, in one instance, she brought
in two, taken after an obstinate and gallant resistance.   For
this exploit, that officer received the commission of a captain
in the King's service.

No less than 400 privateers are said to have been out from

the colonies in this war, but the number is so incredible as to give rise to the conjecture that the estimate includes letters of marque and boats on the coast.   Nothing worthy of much notice occurred in America, during this short war, besides the capture of Louisbourg, and this place was restored to the French at the peace.

---

## CHAPTER III.

THE peace of Aix la Chapelle found the navigation of the American colonies in a very flourishing condition.  More than a century had elapsed since the settlements had passed the ordeal of their infant struggles, and although distant from each other, and labouring under the disadvantages of a scattered population, they were fast rising to the dignity and power of states.   The necessity of maintaining all their more important communications by water, had a direct tendency to encourage a disposition to the sea, and, although without a regular war-like marine, their mercantile tonnage probably equalled that of the mother country, when considered in reference to popu-lation.   The number of souls in all the provinces, at that period, did not much exceed a million, if the Indians be excluded from the computation.   Of the tonnage it is not easy to speak with accuracy, though we possess sufficient authority by which to form some general estimates.   The year of the peace, 500 vessels are said to have cleared from the single port of Boston, and 430 to have entered; this was exclusively of coasters and fishing vessels.   At Portsmouth, New Hampshire, there were 121 clearances, and 73 entries, besides 200 coasting vessels in regular employment.   The trade of New York and Philadel-phia was less than that of Boston, but still respectable.   Thus in 1749, or the year succeeding that of the peace, the clear-ances at Philadelphia were 291, and the entries 303 ; while Boston, during the same period, had 504 clearances, and 489 entries.   In 1750, a year in which the navigation had sensibly diminished, the clearances of the former port were 286, and the entries 232.   Many ports, which have since lost most of their navigation, then enjoyed a respectable trade, among

3 *

which may be mentioned Newport, Rhode Island, and Perth
Amboy, New Jersey.

Up to this period, the common white oak of the forest was
the wood principally used in naval constructions, though the
chestnut was also found serviceable in particular parts of the
frames.    But a new era in ship-building was at hand, through
the introduction of a wood that greatly abounded in the more
southern maritime regions of British America.   In 1750, a
vessel called the Live Oak arrived in Charleston, South Carolina, having been built of the invaluable timber named, which
was now discovered to be one of the best materials for naval
architecture known.   The Live Oak is said to have been the
first vessel in which this wood was ever used.

The tranquillity established by the treaty of Aix la Chapelle,
like that produced by the peace of Utrecht, was of short continuance.   Disputes early commenced between the English and
French provinces, in relation to their boundaries; and an inland war actually broke out between them in 1754, though the
peace of Europe was not immediately disturbed by this remote
and local contest.   This singular state of things continued
throughout 1755, and the campaign of that year was one of
the most important that had then occurred on the American
continent.   Both nations reinforced their troops from Europe,
and strong squadrons were employed to protect the convoys;
but there being no technical hostilities, commissions were not
issued to letters of marque and privateers.   After many ineffectual attempts at an accommodation, however, the King of
Great Britain made a formal declaration of war on the 17th of
May, 1756.

Such was the commencement of the struggle that in America
is familiarly called "the old French war."   Although this
contest was of the last importance to the colonies, by driving
the French from their part of the continent, and by leaving the
savages without an ally, its events were more properly connected with the movements of armies, than with any naval
operations of magnitude, so far as the latter belong to the
subject of this work.   The beginning of the war was disastrous; but in the end, the celebrated Earl of Chatham succeeded in infusing a portion of his own energy into the councils
of the King, and from that moment the most brilliant success
rewarded his efforts.

Peace was signed on the 10th of February, 1763, and from
that day France ceased to claim any portion of the American

Continent north of Louisiana, with the exception of two insignificant fishing stations, near the outlet of the St. Lawrence. The conquests of this war were an incipient step towards the eventual independence of the colonies, since the latter found themselves without any enemy in their vicinity, to cause them to lean on England for succour, or to divert their policy from those domestic measures which were more immediately connected with their internal prosperity.

At the close of this great contest, the original American colonies, or those which have since constituted the United States, without including the Floridas and Louisiana, are supposed to have contained more than 1,200,000 souls, exclusively of Indians. Censuses were actually taken in one or two of the provinces. That of Massachusetts gave a return a little exceeding 245,000, including 5000 people of colour. That of Maryland, taken in 1755, gave a total of 107,208 whites, a number considerably exceeding the estimates after the peace.

Immediately after the peace of 1763, commenced that legislative usurpation on the part of the mother country, which twenty years later terminated in the independence of the colonies.

Among the offensive measures adopted by parliament was a duty on stamps, and another on tea. By the first, vessels could not regularly proceed to sea, unless furnished with the required stamps; yet so strong was the opposition, that ships actually ventured on the ocean without the necessary papers, nor is it known that any serious consequences resulted from so bold a step. In the end, the stamp-officers having resigned, and no one being willing to incur the odium of filling their places, the courts of justice themselves transacted business without regard to those forms that the acts of parliament had rendered necessary. This tax was finally abandoned, and substitutes were sought, that were believed to be more manageable.

Fresh attempts to enforce the navigation act, which had virtually become a dead letter, were made in 1768, and a sloop from Madeira, loaded with wine, was actually seized in Boston, and placed under the guns of the Romney man-of-war. A mob followed, and the public officers were compelled to seek protection in the castle.

One of the first overt acts of resistance that took place in this celebrated struggle, occurred in 1772, in the waters of Rhode Island. A vessel of war had been stationed on the coast to enforce the laws, and a small schooner, called the Gaspé, with a light armament and twenty-seven men, was employed as a tender, to run into the shallow waters of that coast. On the 17th of June, 1772, a Providence packet, that plied between New York and Rhode Island, named the Hannah, and commanded by a Captain Linzee, hove in sight of the man-of-war, on her passage up the bay. The Hannah was ordered to bring to, in order to be examined; but her master refused to comply; and being favoured by a fresh southerly breeze, that was fast sweeping him out of gunshot, the Gaspé was signalled to follow. The chase continued for five-and-twenty miles, under a press of sail, when the Hannah coming up with a bar, with which her master was familiar, and drawing less water than the schooner, Captain Linzee led the latter on a shoal, where she stuck. The tide falling, the Gaspé sewed, and was not in a condition to be removed for several hours.

The news of the chase was circulated on the arrival of the Hannah at Providence. A strong feeling was excited among the population, and towards evening the town drummer appeared in the streets, assembling the people. A crowd being collected, the drummer led his followers in front of a shed, when a man disguised as an Indian suddenly appeared on the roof, and proclaimed a secret expedition for that night, inviting all of " stout hearts " to assemble on the wharf, precisely at nine, disguised like himself. At the appointed hour, most of the men in the place collected at the spot designated, when sixty-four were selected for the undertaking that was in view.

This party embarked in eight of the launches of the different vessels lying at the wharves, and taking with them a quantity of round paving-stones, they pulled down the river in a body. The commander is supposed to have been a Captain Whipple, who afterwards held a commission in the service of Congress, but none of the names were publicly mentioned at the time. On nearing the Gaspé, about two in the morning, the boats were hailed by a sentinel on deck. This man was driven below by a volley of stones. The commander of the Gaspé now appeared, and ordering the boats off, he fired a pistol at them. This discharge was returned from a musket, and the officer was shot through the thigh. By this time, the crew of the Gaspé had assembled, and the party from Providence boarded. The conflict was short, the schooner's people being knocked down and secured. All on board were put into the boats, and the Gaspé was set on fire. Towards morning, she blew up.

This bold step naturally excited great indignation in the British officers, and all possible means were taken to discover the offenders.   The Government at home offered a reward of £1000 sterling for the leader, and £500 to any person who would discover the other parties, with the promise of a pardon should the informer be an accomplice.   But the feeling of the times was too high for the ordinary means of detection, no evidence having ever been obtained sufficient even to arraign a solitary individual, notwithstanding a Commission of Inquiry, under the Great Seal of England, sat with that object, from January to June, during the year 1773.

Although this affair led to no immediate results, it doubtless had its influence in widening the breach between the opposing parties, and it is worthy of remark, that in it was shed the first blood that flowed in the struggle for American Independence ; the whole transaction being as direct a resistance to oppression, as the subsequent, and better known fight at Lexington.

The year 1773 is memorable in American history, for the resistance made by the colonists to the duty on tea.   By means of some management on the part of the British ministry, in permitting the East India Company to export their teas free of charges, it was possible to sell the article at a lower rate in America, subject to the duty, than it could have been sold previously to the imposition of the tax.   Fancying that this circumstance would favour the views of all the parties in Europe, for the warehouses of the company were glutted in consequence of the system of non-importation adopted by the colonists, several cargoes were sent to different ports, including New York, Philadelphia, Charleston and Boston.   The inhabitants of the two former places compelled the ships to return to London, without unloading, while the people of Charleston caused their vessel to be discharged, and the tea to be stored in damp cellars, where it finally spoiled.

Three vessels loaded with the offensive article had been sent to Boston, and the inhabitants succeeded in persuading the shipmasters to consent to return to London, without discharging, but the consignees refused to release them from their charterparties, while the authorities denied the necessary clearances. The Governor even withheld the permit necessary to pass the fort.   This conduct produced great excitement, and preparations were made to destroy the tea, under an apprehension that it might be gradually and clandestinely landed.   Suddenly, in the dusk of the evening, a party disguised as Indians, and

which has been differently represented as composed of twenty
men up to eighty, appeared in the streets, marching swiftly in
the direction of the wharves.   It was followed by a mob, and
proceeded to one of the tea-ships, which it boarded, and of
which it took possession without resistance.   The hatches were
broken open, and the chests of tea were struck on deck, staved,
and their contents were thrown into the water.   The whole
proceedings were conducted in the most orderly manner, and
with little or no noise, the labourers seldom speaking.   So
much mystery attended this affair, that it is not easy, even at
this remote day, to ascertain all the particulars ; and, although
the names of the actors have been mentioned openly of late,
for a long period apprehensions are said to have been entertained, by some engaged—men of wealth—that they might yet
be made the subjects of a prosecution for damages, by the East
India Company.   Three hundred and forty-two chests of tea
were destroyed, which was probably the cargo of a single ship,
the two others quitting the port soon after.

This daring act was followed by the Boston Port Bill, a political measure that was equally high-handed, since it denied
the people of the town all direct participation in commerce.
This sudden check, at twenty days' notice, to the trade of a
place that, the previous year, had seen 411 clearances, and
587 entries, to and from foreign ports, produced much distress
in the town itself, and greater indignation throughout the country.   It had been the misfortune of England, never to understand the character of the people of the American colonies ;
for, accustomed to dependencies that had been humbled by
conquest, she had not yet learned to appreciate the spirit of
those who were rapidly shooting up into political manhood by
their own efforts, and who had only placed themselves in the
situation they occupied, because they had found the liberty of
England herself, insufficient for their opinions and wants.

The people now began seriously to prepare for an appeal to
force, and they profited by the liberty that was still left them,
to organise military corps, with a view to recover that which
they had lost.   A Congress of representatives from the different colonies convened, and a system of organisation and concert was adopted, that served to unite as many as possible in
the struggle that was fast approaching.

Towards the close of the year 1774, various steps were
taken in different parts of the country, that had a direct bearing on the civil war that was known to be at hand.  Laws had

been passed in England prohibiting the exportation of arms and military supplies to America ; and the cannon and powder of the Crown were seized at various points, either by the local governments, or by private individuals. Twenty-six guns, of different calibres, were found on Fort Island and carried to Providence, and the people of Rhode Island are said to have got possession, in the whole, of quite forty guns, by these bold measures. At Portsmouth, New Hampshire, a body of 400 men proceeded to the castle, at the harbour's mouth, kept the garrison in check, and breaking open the magazine, they carried off one hundred barrels of powder.

While means like these were used to obtain the necessary military equipments, provisions, as well as arms, were collected in different parts of the country, in readiness for a campaign. Among other dépôts of this nature, one had been made at Concord, a small town at the distance of eighteen miles from Boston, and General Gage, who commanded the British forces in America, deemed it essential that it should be destroyed. A strong detachment was sent on this service, and it fell in with a small body of American minute-men at Lexington. These militia were dispersed by a volley, in which a few men were killed. This affair has always been considered the commencement of the War of the Revolution ; and justly, as the hostilities which were then commenced did not cease, until the Independence of the Colonies was acknowledged by Treaty. The British proceeded to Concord, where they effected their object, though not without resistance. The people now began to collect in force, and as soon as the British resumed their march, on the return to Boston, they were assailed by the former from behind the walls and fences. So vigorously were the troops pressed on this occasion, that it is thought they must have surrendered, had they not been met by a strong reinforcement, commanded by Lord Percy, which enabled them to halt and recover their breath. As soon as the march was resumed, however, the provincials renewed the attack, and the British did not succeed in gaining a place of security, until they reached Charlestown neck. In this affair the loss of the Americans has been ascertained to have amounted to 50 killed, 34 wounded, and 4 missing ; that of the British to 73 killed, 174 wounded, and 26 prisoners.

The intelligence of this important event circulated like a raging fire throughout the country, and it was everywhere received as a call to battle. Reserve was thrown aside ; the population flew to arms, and the military stores of the Crown were seized wherever they could be found. An irregular body of 20,000 men appeared before Boston, with incredible rapidity, confining the royal army to the occupation of the town. With a view to reduce their enemies to still narrower limits, Breed's Hill, a height that commands the inner harbour of Boston, was seized, and a redoubt commenced. This step brought on the combat that has since been termed the Battle of Bunker's Hill, one of the most extraordinary conflicts of modern times, and which may be said to have given birth to American Independence. Washington was appointed Commander-in-Chief by the Congress of the United Colonies, and the war commenced under the usual laws of civilised nations, with the exception of the formality of a declaration.

## CHAPTER IV.

THE thirteen United Colonies possessed but scanty means to contend with a power like that of Britain. Their population was less than three millions, their pecuniary resources were of no great amount, and their military preparations insignificant. But the fire of true patriotism had been kindled, and that which in other nations is effected by means of laboured combinations and political management, the people of America were bent on doing of their own voluntary motion and united efforts. The colonies of New England, in particular, which possessed a population trained to liberty; hardy, simple, ingenious and brave; rose as it might be to a man; and as this was the part of the country in which the flame broke out, thither we must first direct our attention in order to find the earliest evidences of its intensity.

On the ocean, the preparations for the struggle were even smaller than those which had been made on the land. Congress had done nothing, and the provisions for naval defence which, from time to time, had existed among the different colonies, had never amounted to more than maintaining a few guarda-costas, or to the temporary exertions of an expedition. As soon as the struggle commenced in earnest, however, the habits of the people, their aptitude for sea service, and the advantages of both a public and a private nature, that were to be obtained from successful cruising, induced thousands to turn longing eyes to an element that promised so many flattering results. Nothing but the caution of Congress, which body was indisposed at first to act as if general warfare, instead of a redress of grievances, was its object, prevented a rushing towards the private cruisers, that would probably have given the commerce of England a heavier and more sudden blow, than it had ever yet received. But a different policy was pursued, and the orders to capture, first issued, were confined to vessels bringing stores and supplies to the British forces in America. It was as late as the 10th of Nov. 1775, before Massachusetts, the colony which was the seat of war, and which may be said to have taken the lead in the revolt, established courts of admiralty, and enacted laws for the encouragement of nautical enterprises. Washington followed this example by granting commissions to vessels to cruise in the vicinity of Boston, with the object already stated. But a due examination of the practical measures of that day, will render it necessary to separate the subject into three branches; viz. one that refers solely to the exertions of private, and frequently of unauthorized adventures; another that shall speak of the proceedings of the different colonies; and a third, which more properly comprises the theme of this work, that shall refer to the policy pursued by Congress, in behalf of the entire nation. In making these distinctions, we shall be compelled to use brevity, as but few authorities now exist, and because the sameness and unimportance of many of the details deprive the subject of any interest beyond that which is connected with a proper understanding of the true condition of the country.

The first nautical enterprise that succeeded the battle of Lexington, was one purely of private adventure. The intelligence of this conflict was brought to Machias in Maine, on Saturday, the 9th of May, 1775. An armed schooner in the service of the crown, called the Margaretta, was lying in port, with two sloops under her convoy, that were loading with lumber on behalf of the King's government. The bearers of the news were enjoined to be silent, a plan to capture the Margaretta having been immediately projected among some of the more spirited of the inhabitants. The next day being Sunday, it was hoped that the officers of the schooner might be seized while in church, but the scheme failed in consequence of the

4

precipitation of some engaged. Captain Moore, who commanded the Margaretta, saw the assailants, and, with his officers, escaped through the windows of the church to the shore,
where they were protected by the guns of their vessel. The
alarm was now taken, springs were got on the Margaretta's
cables, and a few harmless shot were fired over the town, by
way of intimidation. After a little delay, however, the schooner
dropped down below the town, to a distance exceeding a league.
Here she was followed, summoned to surrender, and fired on
from a high bank, which her own shot could not reach. The
Margaretta again weighed, and running into the bay, at the
confluence of the two rivers, anchored.

The following morning, which was Monday, the 11th of
May, four young men took possession of one of the lumber
sloops, and bringing her alongside of a wharf, they gave three
cheers as a signal for volunteers. On explaining that their
intentions were to make an attack on the Margaretta, a party
of about thirty-five athletic men was soon collected. Arming
themselves with fire-arms, pitchforks, and axes, and throwing
a small stock of provisions into the sloop, these spirited free-
men got under way, with a light breeze at northwest. When
the Margaretta observed the approach of the sloop she weighed
and crowded sail to avoid a conflict that was every way unde-
sirable, her commander not yet being apprised of all the facts
that had occurred near Boston. In jibing, the schooner carried away her main-boom, but continuing to stand on, she ran
into Holmes's Bay, and took a spar out of a vessel that was
lying there. While these repairs were making, the sloop hove
in sight again, and the Margaretta stood out to sea, in the hope
of avoiding her. The breeze freshened, and, with the wind
on the quarter, the sloop proved to be the better sailer. So
anxious was the Margaretta to avoid a collision, that Captain
Moore now cut away his boats; but finding this ineffectual,
and that his assailants were fast closing with him, he opened
a fire, the schooner having an armament of four light guns,
and fourteen swivels. A man was killed on board the sloop,
which immediately returned the fire with a wall piece. This
discharge killed the man at the Margaretta's helm, and cleared
her quarter-deck. The schooner broached to, when the sloop
gave a general discharge. Almost at the same instant the two
vessels came foul of each other. A short conflict now took
place with musketry, Captain Moore throwing hand-grenades,
with considerable effect, in person. This officer was shot

down, however, when the people of the sloop boarded and took possession of their prize.

The loss of life in this affair was not very great, though twenty men, on both sides, are said to have been killed and wounded. The force of the Margaretta, even in men, was much the most considerable, though the people of no regular cruiser can ever equal in spirit and energy a body of volunteers assembled on an occasion like this. There was originally no commander in the sloop, but previously to engaging the schooner, Jeremiah O'Brien was selected for that station. This affair was the Lexington of the seas, for, like that celebrated land conflict, it was a rising of the people against a regular force, was characterised by a long chase, a bloody struggle, and a triumph. It was also the first blow struck on the water, after the war of the American Revolution had actually commenced.

The armament of the Margaretta was transferred to a sloop, and Mr. O'Brien made an attack on two small English cruisers that were said to have been sent out from Halifax, expressly to capture him. By separating these vessels, he took them both, with little resistance, and the prisoners were all carried to Watertown, where the provincial legislature of Massachusetts was then assembled. The gallantry and good conduct of Mr. O'Brien were so generally admired, that he was immediately appointed a captain in the marine of the colony, and sent on the coast with his two last prizes, with orders to intercept vessels bringing supplies to the royal forces.

Many adventures or enterprises, more or less resembling these of Captain O'Brien, took place on different parts of the coast, though none of so brilliant and successful a character. By way of retaliation, and with a view to intimidate, the English commander-in-chief, Admiral Graves, sent a force under the orders of Captain Mowat, to destroy the town of Falmouth, and four hundred buildings were burned. An attempt to land, however, was repulsed, when the ships retired. This and similar steps produced the law of Massachusetts, already mentioned as having been passed in Nov. 1775, granting commissions and directing the seizure of British vessels under certain circumstances, and which consequently put an end to the expeditions we have classed among the unauthorised.

The colony of Massachusetts had recourse to energetic measures for annoying the enemy on the coast, and for procuring military supplies. Many small vessels were fitted out by that as well as by other colonies, and ships were sent in different directions with a view to purchase stores.

The want of powder, in particular, was so severely felt, that all practicable means were adopted to obtain it. Among others, General Washington borrowed two schooners of Massachusetts and sent them into the Gulf of St. Lawrence, under the orders of Captain Broughton, to intercept two brigs, that were known to be bound to Quebec with military supplies. The brigs were not seen, but ten other English vessels were captured by Captain Broughton, all of which were released as not coming within the hostilities meditated by Congress.

That body, however, was by no means blind to the importance of naval means of defence, without which no war can ever be conducted with credit and success by a country situated like America ; and we have now properly arrived at the period when it is necessary to advert to the acts and legislation of the General Government on this interesting subject.

Soon after he assumed the command of the troops before Boston, General Washington, who so deeply felt the want of munitions of war, issued several commissions to different small vessels, giving their commanders instructions to cruise in or near Massachusetts Bay, in order to intercept the British store ships.

The first vessel that got to sea under this arrangement, was the schooner Lee, Captain John Manly, which sailed from Marblehead near the close of November. On the 29th, Captain Manly fell in with and captured the English brig Nancy, having on board ordnance stores, several brass guns, a considerable stock of fire-arms, and various military supplies. Among other things of this nature, was a large mortar, which was justly deemed an important addition to the means of a besieging army ; for, up to this time, the Americans before Boston were particularly in want of artillery of every sort. On the 8th of December, Captain Manly captured three more store-ships, and succeeded in getting all his prizes safely into port.

Although it may not be strictly true to term the Lee, and the other small cruisers similarly employed, the first vessels that ever belonged to the General Government of this country, they may be deemed the first that ever actually sailed with authority to cruise in behalf of the entire republic. But, while we yield this precedency to Captain Manly and his associates, who acted under the orders of Washington, Congress itself had not been altogether idle, and it is probable that the Commander-in-Chief took the step just mentioned in accordance with the expressed views of that body.

The first legislation of Congress on the subject of a navy, preceded the law of Massachusetts, in point of time, though the act was worded with great reserve.  On the 13th of October, 1775, a law passed ordering one vessel of 10 guns, and another of 14 guns to be equipped as national property, and to be sent to the eastward on a cruise of three months, to intercept supplies for the royal troops.  On the 29th of the same month a resolution passed denying to private ships of war and merchant vessels the right to wear pennants in the presence of " continental ships, or vessels of war," without the permission of the commanding officers of the latter.  The next day another law passed, authorising the fitting out of two more cruisers, one to carry 20, and the other 36 guns.

A change in this cautious policy was produced by the depredations committed by the vessels under the command of Captain Mowat.  When the intelligence of that ruthless proceeding reached Philadelphia, it produced a general prize law, with authority to capture all British vessels that were in any manner connected with the pending struggle.  As the country still acknowledged its connexion with the crown, perhaps this reserve in conducting the war, was, in a measure, due to sound policy.  This law was followed by another, passed December 13th, ordering thirteen sail of cruisers, to be constructed.  Of the latter vessels, three were to be of 24 guns, five of 28, and five of 32.

These vessels appear to have been judiciously appointed in order to effect the object in view.  The resources of America did not admit of the construction of ships of a size fit to contend with the fleets of England; and even had the colonies been in a condition to make such an exhibition of their power, the time necessary to organise a proper marine, the want of navy yards, and the impossibility of procuring, in season, naval stores of the required quality, would have prevented them from attempting it.  The ships ordered were large enough to resist the small cruisers of the crown, and were well adapted to destroy convoys and to capture transports and store-ships.

Bad as was the condition of the colonies, as respects naval stores and the munitions of war, the country might be said to be even worse off for persons suited to form a navy list. There was no lack of competent navigators, or of brave sea-

4 *

men, but the high moral qualities which are indispensable to
the accomplished officer, were hardly to be expected among
those who had received all their training in the rude and imperfect schools of the merchant service.   Still, as a whole, the
merchant seamen of America were of a class superior to those
of most other nations; the very absence of a regular marine,
which induced young men of enterprise to incur the dangers of
the seas in this mode in preference to remaining on shore, and
the moral superiority of the level of the population, producing
such a result.   The Committee of Congress, to which the
duties of a Navy Department were assigned, was compelled,
in consequence of these difficulties, to select the new corps of
officers, principally, from such conspicuous persons among the
masters and mates of merchant ships as the country afforded ;
a few of those who had been trained in the English marine,
but who had left it previously to the struggle, excepted.   The
result was such as might have been anticipated.   While many
gallant and suitable men were chosen, some of the corps had
little to recommend them besides their practical knowledge of
seamanship.   These were valuable qualities, certainly; but the
habits of subordination, the high feelings of personal pride and
self-respect that create an *esprit de corps*, and the moral courage and lofty sentiments that come in time, to teach the
trained officer to believe any misfortune preferable to professional disgrace, were not always to be expected under such
circumstances.

It has become impossible to establish, in all cases, who did
and who did not actually serve in the marine of the United
States, officers so frequently passing from the privateers into
the public vessels, and from the public vessels to the privateers,
as to leave this important branch of our subject involved in
much obscurity.   Before we enter more fully into the details
on which reliance can be placed, it may be well, also, to ex-
plain that the officers in the navy of the Confederation derived
their authority from different sources, a circumstance that adds
to the difficulties just mentioned.   In a good many instances,
Congress made the appointments by direct resolutions of its
own, as will appear in the case of the officers first named.
Subsequently, the Marine Committee possessed this power ;
and, in the end, not only did the diplomatic agents of the Government abroad exercise this high trust, but even the commanders of squadrons and of ships were put in possession of
blank commissions to be filled at their particular discretion.

It will easily be understood how much this looseness in mana-
ging an interest of so much moment, increases the difficulty of
obtaining the truth.

That the brave men who acted under the authority of
Washington, at the commencement of the contest, were not in
the navy, is evident from the circumstance that several of them
obtained rank in the service, as the reward of their conduct
while cruising in the sort of semi-official vessels that have been
already mentioned.  It has been said, that the first regular
legislation of Congress, in reference to a marine, with a view
to resist the aggressions of the British Parliament, dates from
a resolution of that body passed the 13th of October, 1775.
This resolution directed a committee of three, Messrs. Deane,
Langdon and Gadsden, to fit out two swift-sailing vessels, the
one of ten, and the other of fourteen guns, to cruise to the eastward, to intercept the supplies and transports intended for the
British army at Boston.  Under this law it is believed that a
brig called the Lexington, and a sloop named the Providence,
were equipped ; though it does not appear that either went on
the particular duty named in the resolution.  On the 30th of
the same month, the committee was increased to seven ; and a
ship of 36 guns, and another of 20, were ordered to be provided.  Under this law, the Alfred and Columbus were purchased, though neither was of the force implied by the highest
rate named.  The first of these ships is said to have had a
main-deck battery of 20 nines, while her armament on the
quarter-deck and forecastle, varied in the course of her service, from ten guns to two.  At the end of her career, she
carried no guns above.  Less is known of the Columbus, but
she is believed to have had a gun-deck battery of 18 nines.
Both were clumsy and crank ships, and neither proved to be
a very good sailer.

On the 13th of December, of the same year, Congress directed the thirteen ships of war to be built, and the next day
the Marine Committee was so far increased as to contain one
member from each colony ; all the proceedings that have yet
been mentioned, having been directed rather to a redress of
grievances, than to independence.

On the 22d of December, 1775, Congress passed a resolution declaring Esek Hopkins Commander-in-Chief, and appointing officers for all the vessels then in service.

By this law it will be seen that Mr. Hopkins was not made
a captain, but the " Commander-in-Chief," a rank that was

intended to correspond in the navy, to that held by Washington in the army.   His official appellation, among seamen, appears to have been that of " Commodore," though he was frequently styled " Admiral," in the papers of the period.   The
captains were particularly named to the respective ships, and
the law was so construed, that the lieutenants were attached
to the different vessels in the order in which they were re-
spectively named.

By this resolution, or law, it would appear that two brigs,
the Andrea Doria, and the Cabot, had been purchased, most
probably by the Marine Committee, previously to its passage.
Of the precise force of the latter vessel no authentic account
can be found, but it is thought to have been 16 sixes.   It
appears by a letter of Paul Jones, however, that the armament
of the Doria was 14 fours, and the Cabot may have been of
the same force.

The equipment of all the vessels mentioned, as well as of
two or three more of less size, was going on in the autumn
of 1775, the appointment of their officers was made at the
close of the year, and the first ensign ever shown by a regular American man-of-war, was hoisted in the Delaware, on
board the Alfred, by the hands of Paul Jones, some time about
the last of December.   This event could not have occurred
previously to the vote appointing a commander-in-chief, as we
are expressly told that the flag was shown when that officer
first repaired on board his ship.   What that ensign was, is not
now certainly known, but it is thought to have been a device
representing a pine tree, with a rattlesnake about to strike,
coiled at its root, and bearing the motto " don't tread on me."

The first regular cruisers that ever got to sea under the new
government were the Hornet 10, and Wasp 8, a sloop and a
schooner that had been equipped at Baltimore by the Marine
Committee, and which sailed in November, to join the squad
ron under Commodore Hopkins, in the Delaware.   This passage, however, cannot properly be called a cruise.   For the
first of these we must probably refer to the Lexington 14, a
brig, the command of which had been given to John Barry, a
ship-master of Philadelphia, of credit and skill.   By other
statements, the squadron under the orders of Commodore Hopkins got out before the Lexington ; but we are disposed to
believe that this is an error ; not only because the sailing of
the Lexington appears to be asserted on the most probable authority, but because it is more reasonable to believe, that, as

between vessels fitted in the same place, and near the same time, a single cruiser could precede a squadron. It would seem that the Lexington was purchased earlier than the Alfred, and, in the nature of things, was more readily equipped. The honour has long been claimed for Captain Barry, and, on as close an examination of the facts, as our means will allow, we believe it to be his due. The Lexington must have left the Capes of the Delaware late in January, or early in February, 1776, with orders to cruise to the southward.

The plans of Congress had changed between the time when the vessels were ordered and that on which they were ready for service. Commodore Hopkins was accordingly directed also to proceed to the southward, with a view to act against the naval force, which was then ravaging the coast of Virginia, under Lord Dunmore. The squadron had got into the Bay, and rendezvoused under Cape Henlopen, early in February. It consisted of the Alfred 24, Columbus 20, Doria 14, Cabot 14, Providence 12, Hornet 10, Wasp 8, and Fly despatch vessel. With this force Commodore Hopkins got to sea on the 17th of February. On the night of the 19th, as the squadron was steering south with a fresh breeze, the Hornet and Fly parted company, and did not join again during the cruise. No vessel of any importance was met until the ships reached Abaco, in the Bahamas, where the squadron had been ordered to rendezvous. Here Commodore Hopkins determined to make a descent on New Providence, where it was understood a considerable amount of military stores was collected. For this purpose, a body of 300 men, marines and landsmen, under the command of Captain Nichols, the senior marine officer of the service, was put into two sloops, with the hope of surprising the place. As the squadron approached the town, however, an alarm was given, when the sloops were sent in, with the Providence 12, and Wasp 8, to cover the landing. This duty was handsomely performed, and Captain Nichols got complete possession of the forts, and entire command of the place, in the course of the afternoon and of the following morning, after a very insignificant resistance. Unfortunately, the governor, aware of the motive of the descent, found means to send away a considerable quantity of powder during the night. Near a hundred cannon, and a large quantity of other stores, however, fell into the hands of the Americans. On this occasion, the first that ever occurred in the regular American Navy, the marines under Captain Nichols, appear to have behaved with a spirit and steadiness that have distinguished the corps, from that hour down to the present moment.

After retaining possession a few days, Commodore Hopkins left New Providence on the 17th of March, bringing away with him the governor and one or two men of note, and shaping his course to the northward. Some of the smaller vessels appear to have left him, as he proceeded along the coast, but, with most of his force in company, he arrived off the east end of Long Island, early in April. On the 4th, he captured a tender of six guns, commanded by a son of Commodore Wallace, and on the 5th he fell in with and took the British Bomb Brig Bolton, 8, Lieutenant Snead.

About one o'clock in the morning of the 6th of April, the squadron being a little scattered, a large ship was discovered steering towards the Alfred. The wind was light, and the sea quite smooth; and about two, the stranger having gone about, the Cabot closed with him, and hailed. Soon after the latter fired a broadside. The first discharge of this little vessel appears to have been well directed, but her metal was altogether too light to contend with an enemy like the one she had assailed. In a few minutes she was compelled to haul aboard her tacks, to get from under the guns of her antagonist, having had her captain severely wounded, her master killed, and a good many of her people injured.

The Alfred now took the place of the Cabot, ranging handsomely alongside of the enemy and delivering her fire. Soon after, the Providence got under the stern of the English ship, and the Andrea Doria was enabled to come near enough to do some service. The Columbus was kept at a distance for want of wind. After a smart cannonade of near an hour, the block and wheel-rope of the Alfred were shot away, and the ship broached to; by which accident the enemy was enabled to rake her with effect. Being satisfied, however, that victory was impossible, the English commander profited by this accident, to put his helm up, and brought all the American vessels astern. Sailing better than any of the squadron, most of which were deep, as well as dull, in consequence of the cannon and stores they had taken on board, the enemy slowly but steadily gained on his pursuers, though a warm cannonade was kept up by both parties until past daylight. By six o'clock the ships had got so far to the eastward, that Commodore Hopkins felt apprehensive the firing would bring out the Newport squadron ; and seeing little chance of overtaking the chase, he made a signal for his vessels to haul by the wind.   Capturing a tender that was in company with the ship that had escaped, the squadron now went into New London, the port to which it was bound.

The vessel that engaged the American ships, on this occasion, was the Glasgow, 20, Captain Tyringham Howe, with a crew of about one hundred and fifty souls.   In every thing but the number of her men, the Glasgow was probably superior to any one ship in the American squadron ; but her close encounter with, and eventual escape from so many vessels, reflected great credit on her commander.   She was a good deal cut up, notwithstanding, and had four men killed and wounded.   On the other hand, both the Alfred and the Cabot suffered materially, the former from having been raked, and the latter from lying close alongside a vessel so much her superior in force. The Alfred and Cabot had twenty-three men killed and wounded, and one man on board the Columbus lost an arm while in chase.

The result of this first essay of the American navy, caused much exultation in the country.   The affair was represented as a sort of victory, in which three light vessels of war had been taken, and one of force compelled to run.   A short time, however, served to correct these errors, and public opinion probably went as far in the opposite extreme, where it would seem to have been permanently fixed, by subsequent historians.

Commodore Hopkins was left in command some time longer, it is true, and he carried the squadron to Rhode Island, a few weeks after his arrival, but he never made another cruise in the navy.   On the 16th of October, Congress passed a vote of censure on him, for not performing the duties on which he had been sent to the southward ; and on the 2d of January, 1777, by a vote of that body, he was formally dismissed from the service.   No commander-in-chief was subsequently appointed, though such a measure was recommended to the national legislature by a committee of its own body, August 24th, 1781.

As an offset to the escape of the Glasgow, the Lexington, Captain Barry, fell in with the Edward, an armed tender of the Liverpool, on the 17th of April, off the Capes of Virginia, and after a close and spirited action of near an hour, captured her.   The Lexington had four of her crew killed and wounded, while the Edward was cut nearly to pieces, and met with a very heavy comparative loss in men.

It may better connect the history of this little brig, if we add here, that she went to the West-Indies the following October, under the command of Captain Halleck, and on her return was captured near the spot where she had taken the Liverpool's tender, by the Pearl frigate. It was blowing fresh at the time, and, after taking out a few officers, and putting a crew on board his prize, the commander of the Pearl ordered her to follow his own ship. That night the Americans rose, and overpowering the prize-crew, they carried the brig into Baltimore. The Lexington was immediately recommissioned, under the orders of Captain Johnston, and in March she sailed for Europe, where there will soon be occasion to note her movements.

## CHAPTER V.

WHEN the American squadron had got into Newport, it became useless, from want of men. Many of the seamen had entered for the cruise only, and Congress having authorised the capture of all British vessels in March, so many persons were now induced to go on board the privateers, that crews were not easily obtained for the vessels of war. It is a singular feature of the times, too, that the sudden check to navigation, and the delay in authorising general captures, had driven a great many of the seamen into the army. It is also easy to imagine that the service was out of favour, after the affair with the Glasgow; for by events as trifling as this, are the opinions of ordinary men usually influenced.

It has been said that the vessels were carried to Providence, Rhode Island, and soldiers were borrowed from the army, in order to effect even this. At Providence, courts-martial, the usual attendants of military misfortunes, were assembled to judge the delinquents. Captain Whipple, of the Columbus, was tried for not aiding the Alfred in the action with the Glasgow, and seems to have been acquitted. Captain Hazard, of

BOMBARDMENT OF TRIPOLI.

the Providence, was cashiered, though it does not appear on what charge.

The day after the dismissal of her former commander, or May the 10th, 1776, Paul Jones was directed by Commodore Hopkins to take charge of the Providence, and to carry the borrowed soldiers to New York, there to enlist a regular crew, and return to the station. This duty having been successfully performed, the sloop was hove out, cleaned, refitted, armed, and manned for a cruise. On the 13th of June, Captain Jones sailed from Newport, with a convoy loaded with military stores, which he saw into Long Island Sound, a service attended with risk, on account of the numerous cruisers of the enemy. While thus employed, he covered the escape of a brig from St. Domingo, laden also with military stores, and bound to New York. This brig was soon after bought into the service, and became the Hampden 14. After performing this duty, the Providence was employed in cruising between Boston and the Delaware, and she even ran as far south as Bermuda. On the 1st of September, while on the latter service, this little sloop made five sail, one of which was mistaken for a large merchantman. On getting near the latter vessel, she proved to be a light English frigate, and a fast sailer. After a chase of four hours by the wind, and in a cross sea, the enemy had so far gained on the Providence as to be within musket-shot, on her lee-quarter. The stranger had early opened with his chase guns, and the Providence now returned the fire with her light four-pounders, showing her colours. Perceiving that capture, or some bold expedient, must soon determine his fate, Captain Jones kept edging away, until he had got rather on the lee-bow of the enemy, when the Providence suddenly went off dead before the wind, setting every thing that would draw. This unexpected manœuvre brought the two vessels within pistol-shot, but the English ship having been taken completely by surprise, before she could get her light sails set, the sloop was nearly out of reach of grape. The Providence sailed the best before the wind, and in less than an hour she had drawn quite beyond the reach of shot, and finally escaped. This affair has been represented as an engagement of several hours with the Solebay 28, but, as has been said, it was little more than a clever artifice, in which Captain Jones discovered much steadiness and address. Not a shot touched the Providence, though the Solebay fired a hundred.

Captain Jones now went to the eastward, where he made

5

several prizes. Here he was chased by the Milford 32, and finding he could easily outsail her, he kept just out of gunshot for several hours, the enemy, who measured his distance badly, firing most of the time. This affair has also been exaggerated into a running fight.

After this chase the Providence went upon the coast, off Canseau, and did much damage to the enemy's fishermen, taking no less than twelve sail. Having made sixteen prizes in all, some of which were valuable, Captain Jones returned to Newport.

Ere the return of the Providence, independence was declared, and Congress had set about a more regular organisation of the navy. October the 3d, it ordered another frigate and two cutters to be built; and November the 9th, a law was passed, authorising the construction of three seventy-fours, five more frigates, a sloop of war, and a packet. In January of the succeeding year, another frigate and another sloop of war were ordered. Eight of the prizes were also directed to be taken into the service, in the course of the years 1776 and 1777, while, as the war proceeded, divers small vessels were directed to be built, or purchased.

When the squadron, under Commodore Hopkins, broke up, all the ships did not remain idle, but the Columbus 20, made a cruise, under Captain Whipple, to the eastward, and took a few prizes. The Andrea Doria 14, Captain Biddle, went in the same direction, and was even more successful than the Providence in annoying the enemy. This vessel, a little brig, carrying 14 fours, actually took two armed transports filled with soldiers, and made prizes of so many merchantmen, that, it is affirmed on plausible authority, when she got back into the Delaware, but five of the common men who composed her original crew were in her; the rest having been put in the prizes, and their places supplied by volunteers from among the prisoners. Captain Biddle gained much credit for this cruise, and he was appointed to the command of the Randolph 32, then recently launched.

While the United States' cruisers were thus active in intercepting the British transports on the high seas, the colony cruisers and privateers were busy in the same way in-shore. Boston had been evacuated by the enemy on the 17th of March, of this year, but vessels continued to arrive from England until midsummer; the fact not being known in time to prevent their steering towards the wrong port. No less than

thirty sail fell into the hands of the Americans, in consequence of these mistakes.

The Connecticut colony brig Defence 14, Captain Harding,
left Plymouth, Massachusetts, early on the morning of the
17th of June, and, on working out into the bay, a desultory
firing was heard to the northward. The Defence crowded
sail in the direction of the cannonading, and about dusk she
fell in with four light American schooners, which had been engaged in a running fight with two British transports, that
proved too heavy for them. The transports, after beating off
the schooners, went into Nantasket Roads and anchored.
One of the schooners was the Lee 8, Captain Waters, in the
service of Massachusetts, the little cruiser that had so successfully begun the maritime warfare under Captain Manly. The
three others were privateers.

After laying his plans with the commanders of the schooners,
Captain Harding stood into the roads, and, about eleven
o'clock at night, he anchored between the transports, within
pistol-shot. The schooners followed, but did not approach
near enough to be of much service. Some hailing now passed,
and Captain Harding ordered the enemy to strike. A voice
from the largest English vessel answered, " Ay, ay—I'll
strike," and a broadside was immediately poured into the Defence. A sharp action, that lasted more than an hour, followed, when both the English vessels struck. These transports contained near two hundred soldiers of the same corps
as those shortly after taken by the Doria, and on board the
largest of them was Lieutenant Colonel Campbell, who commanded the regiment.

In this close and sharp conflict, the Defence was a good
deal cut up aloft, and she had nine men wounded. The
transports lost eighteen killed and a large number wounded.
Among the slain was Major Menzies, the officer who had
answered the hail in the manner stated.

The next morning the Defence, with the schooners in company, saw a sail in the bay, and gave chase. The stranger
proved to be another transport, with more than a hundred men
of the same regiment on board. Thus did about five hundred
men, of one of the best corps in the British army, fall into the
hands of the Americans, by means of these light cruisers. It
should be remembered that, in this stage of the war, every
capture of this nature was of double importance to the cause,
as it not only weakened the enemy, but checked his intention

of treating the American prisoners as rebels, by giving the colonists the means of retaliation, as well as of exchange. Colonel Campbell was subsequently imprisoned by Washington, to compel the English to extend better treatment to the Americans who had fallen into their hands.

To return to the vessels left at Rhode Island. When Captain Jones came in from his last cruise in the Providence, a project was formed to send a small squadron under his orders to the coast of Nova Scotia, with the double view of distressing the British trade, and of liberating about a hundred Americans who were said to be confined in the coal-pits of that region. For this purpose the Alfred 24, Hampden 14, and Providence 12, were put under the orders of Captain Jones; but not having men enough for all three, that officer selected the two first for his purpose. While clearing the port, the Hampden got on a ledge of rocks, and sustained material damage. The crew of the Hampden were now transferred to the Providence, and in the month of November Captain Jones got to sea, with both vessels rather short manned. A few days out, the Alfred made one or two small captures, and soon after she fell in with, and, after a short combat, took the armed ship Mellish, loaded with supplies for the army that was then assembling in Canada, to compose the expedition under General Burgoyne. On board this vessel, in addition to many other articles of the last importance, were ten thousand suits of uniform, in charge of a company of soldiers. It was said at the time, that the Mellish was the most valuable English ship that had then fallen into the hands of the Americans. Of so much importance did Captain Jones consider his prize, that he announced his intention to keep her in sight, and to sink her in preference to letting her fall into the enemy's hands again. This resolution, however, was changed by circumstances.

The Providence had parted company in the night, and having taken a letter of marque from Liverpool, the Alfred was making the best of her way to Boston, with a view to get the Mellish in, when, on the edge of George's Banks, she made the Milford 32, the frigate that had chased Captain Jones the previous cruise, while in command of the Providence. The enemy was to windward, but there was not time for him to close before dark. The Alfred and the letter of marque hauled up between the frigate and the other prizes, in order to cover them, and directions were given to the latter to stand on the same tack all night, regardless of signals. At midnight the Alfred and letter of marque tacked, and the latter showed a top-light until morning. This artifice succeeded, the Milford appearing in chase of the Alfred when the day dawned, while the Mellish and her consorts had disappeared in the southern board.

The Milford had run to leeward in the course of the night, and was now on the Alfred's lee quarter. Some manœuvring took place to ascertain the stranger's force, for it was not then known that the ship in sight was actually a frigate. In the course of the day, the Alfred was compelled to carry sail hard, but she escaped, though the letter of marque fell into the enemy's hands. After eluding her enemy, and covering all her prizes, the one just mentioned excepted, the Alfred went into Boston, where she found the rest of the vessels, and where she landed her prisoners. Another officer took charge of the ship, and Captain Jones, who had been flattered with the hope of having a still larger force put under his orders, was placed so low on the list by the new regulation of navy rank, as to be obliged to look round for a single ship, and that, too, of a force inferior to the one he had just commanded.

While this service was in the course of execution at the north, several small cruisers had been sent into the West Indies, to convoy, in quest of arms, or to communicate with the different public agents in that quarter. We have seen the manner in which the Lexington had been captured and retaken on her return passage from this station, and we have now to allude to a short cruise of the Reprisal, Captain Wickes, in the same quarter. This ship sailed early in the summer, for Martinique, capturing several prizes by the way. When near her port, the English sloop of war Shark 16, Captain Chapman, laid her close alongside, and commenced a brisk attack, the Reprisal being both lighter than the enemy, and short-handed. Captain Wickes made so gallant a defence, however, that the Shark was repulsed with loss, and the American got into the island with credit, hundreds having witnessed the affair from the shore. As this occurred early in the season, and before the Declaration of Independence, the Shark followed the Reprisal in, and her captain demanded that the governor should deliver up the American ship as a pirate. This demand was refused of course, and shortly after Captain Wickes returned home. With a view to connect the train of events, we will now follow this excellent officer to the European seas.

The Reprisal was the first American man-of-war that ever showed herself in the other hemisphere. She sailed from home not long after the Declaration of Independence, and appeared in France in the autumn of 1776, bringing in with her several prizes, and having Dr. Franklin on board as a passenger.  A few privateers had preceded her, and slight difficulties had occurred in relation to some of their prizes that had gone into Spain, but it is believed these were the first English captured ships that had entered France since the commencement of the American Revolution.  The English ambassador complained of this infraction of the treaty between the two countries, but means were found to dispose of the prizes without detection. The Reprisal having refitted, soon sailed towards the bay of Biscay, on another cruise.  Here she captured several more vessels, and among the rest a king's packet that plied between Falmouth and Lisbon.  When the cruise was up, Captain Wickes went into Nantes, taking his prizes with him.  The complaints of the English now became louder, and the American commissioners were secretly admonished of the necessity of using greater reserve.  The prizes were directed to quit France, though the Reprisal, being leaky, was suffered to remain in port, in order to refit.  The former were taken into the offing, and sold ; the state of the times rendering these informal proceedings necessary.  Enormous losses to the captors were the consequences, while it is not improbable that the gains of the purchasers had their influence in blinding the local authorities to the character of the transaction.  The business appears to have been managed with dexterity, and the proceeds of the sales, such as they were, proved of great service to the agents of government, by enabling them to purchase other vessels.

In April the Lexington 14, Captain Johnston, arrived in France, and the old difficulties were renewed.  But the commissioners at Paris, who had been authorised to equip vessels, appoint officers and do other matters to annoy the enemy, now planned a cruise that surpassed any thing of the sort that had yet been attempted in Europe under the American flag.  Captain Wickes was directed to proceed to sea, with his own vessel and the Lexington, and to go directly off Ireland, in order to intercept a convoy of linen ships that was expected to sail about that time.  A cutter of ten guns, called the Dolphin, that had been procured by the commissioners to carry despatches to America, was diverted from her original destination and placed under the orders of Captain Wickes.  The Dolphin was commanded by Lieutenant S. Nicholson, a brother of the senior captain, and a gentleman who subsequently died himself at the head of the service.

Captain Wickes, in command of this light squadron, sailed from Nantes about the commencement of June, going first into the Bay of Biscay, and afterwards entirely around Ireland, sweeping the sea before him of every thing that was not of a force to render an attack hopeless. The linen ships were missed, but many vessels were taken or destroyed. As the American cruisers approached the French coast, on their return, a line of battle ship gave chase, and followed them nearly into port. The Lexington and Dolphin appear to have escaped without much difficulty, by separating; but the Reprisal was so hard pressed, as to be obliged to saw her bulwarks, and even to cut away some of her timbers; expedients that were much in favour among the seamen of the day, though of questionable utility.

This was the first exploit of the kind in the war, and its boldness and success seem to have produced so much sensation in England, that the French government was driven to the necessity of entirely throwing aside the mask, or of taking some more decided step in relation to these cruisers. Not being yet prepared for war, it resorted to the latter expedient. The Reprisal and Lexington were ordered to be seized, and held until security was given that they would quit the European seas, while the prizes were commanded to leave France without delay. The latter were accordingly taken outside the port, and disposed of to French merchants, in the same in formal manner, and with the same loss, as in the previous cases, while the vessels of war prepared to return home.

In September the Lexington sailed from Morlaix, in which port she had taken refuge in the chase, and next day she fell in with the British man-of-war-cutter Alert, Lieutenant Bazely, a vessel of a force a trifle less than her own, when an engagement took place. The lightness of the vessels, and the roughness of the water, rendered the fire on both sides very ineffective; and after an action of two hours and a half, the Lexington had expended nearly all her powder, without subduing her gallant opponent. The Alert, however, had suffered so much aloft, as to enable the brig to leave her. Notwithstanding this advantage, so much activity was shown on board the English vessel, that, after a chase of four hours, she was enabled to get alongside of the Lexington again, while the latter was herself repairing damages. A one-sided battle now occurred, the

Lexington not having it in her power to keep up a fire of any moment, and after receiving that of his persevering antagonist for another hour, Captain Johnston was compelled to strike, to save the lives of his crew.

The fate of the Reprisal, a vessel that had even been more successful than her consort, was still harder. This ship also sailed for America, agreeably to the conditions made with the French government, and foundered on the banks of Newfoundland, all on board perishing with the exception of the cook. In Captain Wickes the country lost a gallant, prudent, and efficient officer, and one who promised to rise high in the profession had his life been spared.

To the untimely loss of the Reprisal, and the unfortunate capture of the Lexington, must be attributed the little éclat that attended the services of these two vessels in Europe. They not only preceded all the other national cruisers in the European seas, but they did great positive injury to the commerce of the enemy, besides exciting such a feeling of insecurity in the English merchants, as to derange their plans, and to produce other revolutions in the course of trade, that will be adverted to in the close of the chapter.

While the commissioners* were directing the movements of Captain Wickes, in the manner that has been mentioned, they were not idle in other quarters. A small frigate was building at Nantes, on public account, and there will be occasion hereafter to speak of her services and loss, under the name of the Queen of France. Some time in the spring of 1777, an agent was sent to Dover by the American commissioners, where he purchased a fine, fast-sailing English-built cutter, and had her carried across to Dunkirk. Here she was privately equipped as a cruiser, and named the Surprise. To the command of this vessel Captain Gustavus Conyngham was appointed, by filling up a blank commission from John Hancock, the President of Congress. This commission bore date March 1st, 1777, and it would seem, as fully entitled Mr. Conyngham to the rank of a captain in the navy, as any other that was ever issued by the same authority. Having obtained his officers and crew in Dunkirk, Captain Conyngham sailed on a cruise, about the 1st of May, and on the 4th he took a brig called the Joseph. On the 7th, when within a few leagues of the coast of Holland, the Surprise ran alongside of the Harwich packet,

---

* Dr. Franklin and Silas Deane.

the Prince of Orange, which she boarded and took with so little previous alarm, that Captain Conyngham, stepping upon the deck of his prize, walked coolly down into her cabin, where he found her master and his passengers at breakfast. The mail for the north of Europe being on board the Prince of Orange, Captain Conyngham believed his acquisition to be of sufficient importance to return to port, and accordingly reappeared at Dunkirk in a day or two.

By referring to the dates, it will be seen, though both the Reprisal and the Lexington, especially the first, had cruised in the European seas prior to the sailing of the Surprise, that the latter vessel performed the exploit just mentioned, shortly before Captain Wickes sailed on his cruise in the Irish and English Channels. Coming as it did so soon after the capture of the Lisbon packet, and occurring on one of the great thoroughfares between England and the continent, coupled with the fact that the cutter had been altogether equipped in a French port, the loss of the Prince of Orange appears to have attracted more attention than the transactions before described. The remonstrances of the English ambassador were so earnest, that Captain Conyngham and his crew were imprisoned, the cutter was seized, and the prizes were liberated. On this occasion the commission of Captain Conyngham was taken from him, and sent to Versailles, and it seems never to have been returned.

So completely was the English government deceived by this demonstration of an intention on the part of the French ministry to cause the treaty to be respected, that two sloops of war were actually sent to Dunkirk to carry Captain Conyngham and his people to England, that they might be tried as pirates. When the ships reached Dunkirk, as will be seen in the succeeding events, the birds had flown.

The commissioners had in view the capture of some of the transports with Hessian troops on board, and they were no sooner notified of the seizure of the Surprise, than Mr. Hodge, an agent who was of great service to the cause, was directed to procure another cutter. One was accordingly purchased at Dunkirk, and fitted, with all despatch, for a cruise. Means were found to liberate Captain Conyngham and his people, and this second vessel, which was called the Revenge, sailed from Dunkirk on the 18th of July, or about the time that Captain Wickes returned from his cruise with the three other vessels. A new commission had been obtained for Cap-

tain Conyngham, previously to putting to sea, which bore date
May 2d, 1777. As this second commission was dated ante-
rior to the seizure of the old one, there is no question that it
was also one of those in blank, which had been confided to
the commissioners to fill at their discretion.

The Revenge proved exceedingly successful, making prizes
daily, and generally destroying them. Some of the most valuable, however, were ordered into Spain, where many arrived;
their avails proving of great moment to the agents of the American government in Europe. It is even affirmed that the money advanced to Mr. Adams for travelling expenses, when he
landed in Spain from the French frigate La Sensible, a year
or two later, was derived from this source.

Having suffered from a gale, Captain Conyngham disguised
the Revenge, and took her into one of the small English ports,
where he actually refitted without detection. Shortly after, he
obtained supplies in Ireland, paying for them by bills on his
agents in Spain. In short, after a cruise of almost unprece-
dented success, so far as injury to the English merchants was
concerned, the Revenge went into Ferrol, refitted, and finally
sailed for the American seas, where it would derange the order of events to follow her at this moment.

The sensation created among the British merchants, by
the different cruises in the European seas, that have been
recorded in this chapter, is stated in the diplomatic correspondence of the day, to have been greater than that produced, in
the previous war, by the squadron of the celebrated Thurot.
Insurance rose to an enormous height, and, in speaking of the
cruise of Captain Wickes in particular, Mr. Deane observes
in one of his letters to Robert Morris, that it "effectually
alarmed England, prevented the great fair at Chester, occasioned insurance to rise, and even deterred the English merchants from shipping goods in English bottoms, at any rate,
so that in a few weeks, *forty sail of French ships* were loading in the Thames on freight; an instance never before
known." In the same letter, this commissioner adds,—" In a
word, Cunningham (Conyngham) by his first and second bold
expeditions, is become the terror of all the eastern coast of
England and Scotland, and is more dreaded than Thurot was,
in the late war."

Insurance, in some instances, rose as high as twenty-five
per cent., and it is even affirmed that there was a short period

when ten per cent. was asked between Dover and Calais, a
distance of only seven leagues.

With a view to increase the naval force of the country, the
commissioners had caused a frigate of extraordinary size, and
of peculiar armament and construction for that period, to be
laid down at Amsterdam.   This ship had the keel and sides
of a two-decker, though frigate-built, and her main deck armament was intended to consist of thirty-two pounders.   Her
name was the Indien.   In consequence of the apprehensions of the Dutch government, and the jealousy of that of
England, Congress was induced, about this time, to make an
offering of the Indien to Louis XVI., and she was equipped
and got ready for sea, as a French vessel of war.   In the end,
the manner in which this frigate was brought into the service
of one of the new American States, will be shown.

## CHAPTER VI.

It is now necessary to revert to events that will require the
time to be carried back more than a twelvemonth.

Soon after the British left Boston, a Captain Mugford obtained the use of a small armed vessel belonging to government, called the Franklin, and getting to sea, he succeeded in
capturing the Hope, a ship that had on board fifteen hundred
barrels of powder, and a large quantity of intrenching tools,
gun-carriages, and other stores.   This vessel was got into
Boston, in sight of the British squadron.   Attempting another
cruise immediately afterwards, Captain Mugford lost his life
in making a gallant and successful effort to repel some of the
enemy's boats, which had endeavoured to carry the Franklin
and a small privateer that was in company, by boarding.

On the 6th of July, or two days after the Declaration of
Independence, the Sachem 10, Captain Robinson, sailed from
the Delaware on a cruise.   The Sachem was sloop-rigged,
and one of the lightest cruisers in the service.   When a few
days out she fell in with an English letter of marque, a Jamaica-man, and captured her, after a sharp contest.   Both
vessels are said to have suffered severely in this affair, and to

have had an unusual number of their people killed and wounded. Captain Robinson was now compelled to return to refit, and arriving at Philadelphia with his prize, the Marine Committee rewarded him for his success by giving him the command of the Andrea Doria 14, then recently returned from her cruise to the eastward under Captain Biddle, which officer had been transferred to the Randolph 32.

The Doria sailed shortly after for St. Eustatia, to bring home some arms; and it is said that the first salute ever paid to the American flag, by a regular government, was fired in return for the salute of the Doria, when she went into that island. For this indiscretion the Dutch governor was subsequently displaced.

On her return passage, off the western end of Porto Rico, the Doria made an English vessel of war, bearing down upon her with a disposition to engage. On ranging up abeam, the enemy commenced the action by firing a broadside, which was immediately returned by the Doria. A very sharp contest of two hours followed, when the Englishman struck. The prize proved to be the Racehorse 12, Lieutenant Jones, who had been sent by his admiral to cruise expressly for the Doria. Lieutenant Jones was mortally wounded, and a very large proportion of the Racehorse's officers and crew were either killed or wounded. The Doria lost twelve men, including all the casualties. Captain Robinson and his prize got safely into Philadelphia, in due season. The Doria never went to sea again, being shortly after burned by the Americans to prevent her falling into the hands of the British fleet, when the evacuation of Fort Mifflin gave the enemy the command of the Delaware.

The galleys in the Delaware had a long and well-contested struggle with the Roebuck, 44, Captain Hammond, and the Liverpool, 20, Captain Bellew, about the first of May of this year. The cannonade was handsomely conducted, and it resulted in driving the enemy from the river. During this affair, the Wasp, 8, Captain Alexander, was active and conspicuous, cutting out a tender of the English ships from under their guns.

A spirited attack was also made on the Phœnix, 44, and Rose, 24, in the Hudson, on the third of August, by six American galleys. The firing was heavy and well maintained for two hours, both sides suffering materially. On the part of the galleys, eighteen men were killed and wounded, and several guns were dismounted by shot. The loss of the enemy is not known, though both vessels were repeatedly hulled.

By this time the whole coast was alive with adventures of such a nature, scarcely a week passing that did not give rise to some incident that would have interest for the reader, did the limits of our work permit us to enter into the details. Wherever an enemy's cruiser appeared, or attempted to land, skirmishes ensued; and in some of these little affairs as much personal gallantry and ingenuity were displayed as in many of the more important combats. The coast of New England generally, the Chesapeake, and the coast of the Carolinas, were the scenes of most of these minor exploits, which, like all the subordinate incidents of a great struggle, are gradually becoming lost in the more engrossing events of the war.

October 12th, of this year, an armed British brig, the name of which has been lost, fitted out by the government of the Island of Jamaica, made an attempt on a small convoy of American vessels, off Cape Nicola Mole, in the West-Indies, then in charge of the privateer Ranger, 18, Captain Hudson. Perceiving the aim of the enemy, Captain Hudson ran under her stern, and gave her a severe raking fire. The action thus commenced, lasted nearly two hours, when the Ranger boarded, and carried the brig, hand to hand. The English vessel, in this affair, reported thirteen men killed and wounded, by the raking broadside of the Ranger alone. In the whole, she had between thirty and forty of her people injured. On her return from this cruise, the Ranger was purchased for the navy.

In order to command the Lakes Champlain and George, across which lay the ancient and direct communication with the Canadas, flotillas had been constructed on both those waters, by the Americans. To resist this force, and with a view to co-operate with the movements of their troops, the British commenced the construction of vessels at St. John's. Several men-of-war were laid up, in the St. Lawrence, and their officers and crews were transferred to the shipping built on Lake Champlain.

October 11th, General Arnold, who commanded the American flotilla, was lying off Cumberland Head, when at eight in the morning, the enemy appeared in force, to the northward, turning to windward with a view to engage. On that day the American vessels present, consisted of the Royal Savage, 12,

Revenge, 10, Liberty, 10, Lee, cutter, 4, Congress, galley, 10, Washington, do., 10, Trumbull, do., 10, and eight gondolas. Besides the changes that had been made since August, two or three of the vessels that were on the lake were absent on other duty. The best accounts state the force of this flotilla, or of the vessels present, as follows, viz :

> Guns, 90,
> Metal, 647 lbs.
> Men, 600, including soldiers.

On this occasion, the British brought up nearly their whole force, although having the disadvantage of being to leeward, all their vessels could not get into close action. Captain Douglas, of the Isis, had commanded the naval movements that preceded the battles, and Lieutenant-General Sir Guy Carleton, was present, in person, on board the Maria. The first officer, in his official report of the events, mentions that the Inflexible was ready to sail, within twenty-eight days after her keel had been laid, and that he had caused to be equipped, between July and October, " thirty fighting vessels of different sorts and sizes, and all carrying cannon." Captain Pringle, of the Lord Howe, was the officer actually in charge of the British naval force on the lake, and he commanded in person in the different encounters.

The action of the 11th of October commenced at eleven in the forenoon, and by half-past twelve it was warm. On the part of the British, the battle for a long time was principally carried on by the gun-boats, which were enabled to sweep up to windward, and which, by their weight of metal, were very efficient in smooth water. The Carleton, 12, Lieutenant Dacres, was much distinguished on this day, being the only vessel of size that could get into close fight. After maintaining a hot fire for several hours, Captain Pringle judiciously called off the vessels that were engaged, anchoring just out of gun-shot, with an intention to renew the attack in the morning. In this affair the Americans, who had manifested great steadiness throughout the day, had about 60 killed and wounded, while the British acknowledged a loss of only 40. The Carleton, however, suffered considerably.

Satisfied that it would be impossible, successfully, to resist so great a superiority of force, General Arnold got under way, at two P. M., on the 12th, with the wind fresh ahead. The enemy made sail in chase, as soon as this departure was discovered, but neither flotilla could make much progress on ac-

count of the gondolas, which were unable to turn to windward.
In the evening the wind moderated, when the Americans gained
materially on their pursuers.   Another change occurred, however, and a singular variation in the currents of air, now favoured the enemy ; for while the Americans in the narrow
part of the lake, were contending with a fresh southerly breeze,
the English got the wind at northeast, which brought their
leading vessels within gunshot at 12, meridian, on the 13th.

On this occasion, Captain Pringle, in the Maria, led in person, closely supported by the Inflexible and Carleton.   The
Americans were much scattered, several of their gondolas
having been sunk and abandoned, on account of the impossibility of bringing them off.   General Arnold, in the Congress
galley, covered the rear of his retreating flotilla, having the
Washington galley, on board of which was Brigadier-General
Waterbury, in company.   The latter had been much shattered
in the fight of the 11th, and after receiving a few close broadsides, she was compelled to strike.   General Arnold now defended himself like a lion, in the Congress, occupying the three
vessels of the enemy so long a time, as to enable six of his
little fleet to escape.   When further resistance was out of the
question, he ran the Congress on shore, set fire to her, and she
blew up with her colours flying.

Although the result of this action was so disastrous, the
American arms gained much credit by the obstinacy of the resistance.   General Arnold, in particular, covered himself with
glory, and his example appears to have been nobly followed by
most of his officers and men.   Even the enemy did justice to
the resolution and skill with which the American flotilla was
managed, the disparity in the force rendering victory out of
the question from the first.   The manner in which the Congress was fought until she had covered the retreat of the galleys, and the stubborn resolution with which she was defended
until destroyed, converted the disasters of this part of the day,
into a species of triumph.

In these affairs, the Americans lost eleven vessels, principally gondolas ; while on the part of the British, two gondolas
were sunk, and one blown up.   The loss of men was supposed
to be about equal, no less than sixty of the enemy perishing in
the gondola that blew up.   This statement differs from the
published official accounts of the English ; but those reports,
besides being meagre and general, are contradicted by too
much testimony on the other side, to command our respect.

There has been occasion, already, to mention Mr. John
Manly, who, in command of the schooner Lee, made the first
captures that occurred in the war.   The activity and resolution of this officer, rendered his name conspicuous at the commencement of the struggle, and it followed as a natural consequence, that, when Congress regulated the rank of the captains,
in 1776, he appears as one of them, his appointment having
been made as early as April the 17th, of this year.   So highly,
indeed, were his services then appreciated, that the name of
Captain Manly stands second on the list, and he was appointed
to the command of the Hancock, 32.   When Captain Manly
was taken into the navy, the Lee was given to Captain Waters, and was present at the capture of the three transports off
Boston, as has been already stated.   This little schooner, the
name of which will ever remain associated with American history, in consequence of her all-important captures in 1775,
appears to have continued actively employed, as an in-shore
cruiser, throughout this year, if not later, in the pay of the
new state of Massachusetts.   Captain Waters, like his prede-
cessor, Captain Manly, was received into the navy on the
recommendation of Washington, a commission to that effect
having been granted by Congress, March 18th, 1777.

## CHAPTER VII.

THE year 1777 opened with better prospects for the American cause.   The hardy movements of Washington in New
Jersey had restored the drooping confidence of the nation, and
great efforts were made to follow up the advantage that had
been so gloriously obtained.   Most of the vessels authorised by
the laws of 1775, had been built and equipped during the year
1776; and America may now be said, for the first time, to
have had something like a regular navy, although the service
was still, and indeed continued to be throughout the war, deficient in organization, system, and unity.   After the first effort connected with its creation, the business of repairing losses,
of increasing the force, and of perfecting that which had
been so hastily commenced, was either totally neglected,

or carried on in a manner so desultory and inefficient, as soon to leave very little of method or order in the marine. As a consequence, officers were constantly compelled to seek employment in private armed ships, or to remain idle, and the discipline did not advance, as would otherwise have been the case during the heat of an active war. To the necessities of the nation, however, and not to a want of foresight and prudence, must be attributed this state of things, the means of raising and maintaining troops being obtained with difficulty, and the cost of many ships entirely exceeding its resources. It is probable, had not the public armed vessels been found useful in conveying, as well as in convoying the produce, by means of which the loans obtained in Europe were met, and perhaps indispensable to keeping up the diplomatic communications with that quarter of the world, that the navy would have been suffered to become extinct, beyond its employment in the bays and rivers of the country. This, however, is anticipating events, for at the precise moment in the incidents of the war at which we have now arrived, the exertions of the republic were perhaps at their height, as respects its naval armaments.

One of the first, if not the very first of the new vessels that got to sea, was the Randolph 32. It has been seen that Captain Biddle was appointed to this ship, on his return from his successful cruise in the Andrea Doria 14. The Randolph was launched at Philadelphia in the course of the season of 1776, and sailed on her first cruise early in 1777. Discovering a defect in his masts, as well as a disposition to mutiny in his people, too many of whom were volunteers from among the prisoners, Captain Biddle put into Charleston for repairs. As soon as the ship was refitted, he sailed again, and three days out, he fell in with and captured four Jamaica-men, one of which, the True Briton, had an armament of 20 guns. The Randolph returned to Charleston with her prizes, in safety. Here she appears to have been blockaded by a superior English force, during the remainder of the season. The state authorities of South Carolina were so much pleased with the zeal and deportment of Captain Biddle, that they now added four small cruisers of their own, the General Moultrie 18, the Polly 16, the Notre Dame 16, and the Fair American 14, to his command. With these vessels in company, and under his orders, Captain Biddle sailed early in 1778, in quest of the British ships, the Carrysfort 32, the Perseus 20, the Hinchinbrook 16, and a privateer, which had been cruising off Charleston for

6 *

some time.   The American squadron, however, had been detained so long by foul winds, that, when it got into the offing,
no traces of the enemy were to be discovered.   For the further
history of the Randolph, we are unhappily indebted to the
British accounts.

By a letter from Captain Vincent, of his Britannic Majesty's
ship Yarmouth 64, dated March 17th, 1778, we learn that,
on the 7th of that month, while cruising to the eastward of
Barbadoes, he made six sail to the southwest, standing on a
wind.   The Yarmouth bore down on the chases, which proved
to be two ships, three brigs and a schooner.   About nine
o'clock in the evening she succeeded in ranging up on the
weather quarter of the largest and leading vessel of the strangers ; the ship next in size being a little astern and to leeward.
Hoisting her own colours, the Yarmouth ordered the nearest
ship to show her ensign, when the American flag was run up,
and the enemy poured in a broadside.   A smart action now
commenced, and was maintained with vigour for twenty
minutes, when the stranger blew up.   The two ships were so
near each other at the time, that many fragments of the wreck
struck the Yarmouth, and among other things, an American
ensign, rolled up, was blown in upon her forecastle.   This flag
was not even singed.   The vessels in company now steered
different ways, and the Yarmouth gave chase to two, varying
her own course for that purpose.   But her sails had suffered
so much in the engagement, that the vessels chased soon run
her out of sight.   In this short action the Yarmouth, by the
report of her own commander, had five men killed and twelve
wounded.   On the 12th, while cruising near the same place, a
piece of wreck was discovered, with four men on it, who were
making signals for relief.   These men were saved, and when
they got on board the Yarmouth, they reported themselves as
having belonged to the United States ship Randolph 32, Captain Biddle, the vessel that had blown up in action with the
English ship on the night of the 7th of the same month.
They had been floating ever since on the piece of wreck, without any other sustenance than a little rain-water.   They stated
that they were a month out of Charleston.

We regard with admiration the steadiness and spirit with
which, according to the account of his enemy, Captain Biddle
commenced this action, against a force so vastly his superior ;
and, although victory was almost hopeless, even had all his
vessels behaved equally well with his own ship, we find it dif-

NAVAL HISTORY. **67**

ficult, under the circumstances, to suppose that this gallant seaman did not actually contemplate carrying his powerful antagonist, most probably by boarding.

In March, 1777, the United States brig Cabot, Captain Olney, was chased ashore, on the coast of Nova Scotia, by the British frigate Milford, which pressed the Cabot so hard that there was barely time to get the people out of her. Captain Olney and his crew retreated into the woods, and subsequently they made their escape by seizing a schooner, in which they safely arrived at home. The enemy, after a long trial, got the Cabot off, and she was taken into the British navy.

Shortly after this loss, or on the 19th of April, the Trumbull 28, Captain Saltonstall, fell in with, off New York, and captured after a smart action, two armed transports, with stores of value on board. In this affair the enemy suffered severely, and the Trumbull herself had 7 men killed and 8 wounded.

The following month the Hancock 32, Captain Manly, and Boston 24, Captain M'Neil, sailed on a cruise to the eastward. Towards the middle of May they made a sail to windward, and gave chase. The Hancock being the fastest sailer approached the stranger, a British frigate, first ; the two vessels crossing each other on opposite tacks, and exchanging broadsides in passing, at long shot. The American immediately tacked and continued to gain on the chase. As soon as she got within range of the stranger, the latter re-opened his fire, but Captain Manly sent his people to their breakfast, finding that little harm was done. In a short time the Hancock had got far enough ahead and to windward to open her fire, when the action commenced in earnest. After a close and warm engagement of an hour and thirty-five minutes, the enemy struck. At this time, or while the Hancock was lowering her boat to take possession, the Boston came down from a weatherly position she had gained, and, it is said, fired a broadside at the captured ship. Captain Manly rebuked his consort, and the cannonade ceased altogether. The prize proved to be the Fox 28, Captain Fotheringham. Her loss was heavy, having no less than 32 men killed. The Hancock had 8 killed and 13 wounded.

Manning her prize, the Hancock now proceeded off Halifax, the Boston in company. The vessels appeared before the port on the first day of June. This brought out the Rainbow 44, Captain Sir George Collier, with the Flora 32, and Victor

brig.  The Flora gave chase to the Fox, the Boston being
about a league to windward, while the Rainbow and Victor
pursued the Hancock.  The Fox was captured after a short
action, the Boston keeping aloof, and eventually escaping.
The wind fell, and Captain Manly was induced to lighten his
ship.  This destroyed her trim, and it is thought occasioned
her loss.  Shé was captured by the Rainbow and the Victor.
The enemy took the Hancock into their service, calling her
the Iris.  She proved to be one of the fastest vessels they had,
but was eventually taken by the French in the West-Indies.
Capt. M'Neil was dismissed the service for his bad conduct on
these two occasions.

The occupation of Philadelphia by the British army, this
year, wrought a material change in the naval arrangements
of the country.  Up to this time, the Delaware had been a
safe place of retreat for the different cruisers, and ships had
been constructed on its banks in security and to advantage.
Philadelphia offered unusual facilities for such objects, and
many public and private armed cruisers had been equipped at
her wharves, previously to the appearance of the British forces
under Sir William Howe.  That important event completely
altered the state of things, and the vessels that were in the
stream at the time, were compelled to move higher up the river,
or to get to sea in the best manner they could.  Unfortunately,
several of the ships constructed, or purchased, under the laws
of 1775 were not in a situation to adopt the latter expedient,
and they were carried to different places that were supposed
to offer the greatest security.

As a part of the American vessels and galleys were above,
and a part below the town, the very day after reaching the
capital, the English commenced the erection of batteries to intercept the communications between them.  Aware of the consequences, the Delaware 24, Captain Alexander, and the Andrea Doria 14, seconded by some other vessels, belonging to
the navy, and to the State of Pennsylvania, moved in front of
these works, and opened a cannonade, with a view to destroy
them.  The Delaware was so unfortunately placed, that when
the tide fell, she took the ground, and her guns became unmanageable.  Some field-pieces were brought to bear on her,
while in this helpless situation, and she necessarily struck.
The other vessels were compelled to retire.

As the command of the river was indispensable to the British, they now turned their attention at once to the destruction

of the American works below the town.  An unsuccessful
land attack was made by the Hessians, on Red Bank, and this
was soon followed by another on Fort Mifflin, which, as it
was entrusted to the shipping, comes more properly within our
observation.  With a view to effect the reduction or abandon-
ment of Fort Mifflin, the British assembled a squadron of ships
of a light draft of water, among which was the Augusta 64,
which had been partially stripped, and fitted in some measure
as a floating battery.  As soon as the troops advanced against
Red Bank, as stated, the ships began to move, but some che-
vaux de frise anchored in the river, had altered its channel,
and the Augusta, and the Merlin sloop of war, got fast, in unfavourable positions.  Some firing between the other vessels
and the American works and galleys now took place, but was
soon put a stop to by the approach of night.  The next day
the action was renewed with spirit, the Roebuck 44, Isis 32,
Pearl 32, and Liverpool 28, being present, in addition to the
Augusta and Merlin.  Fire-ships were ineffectually employed
by the Americans, but the cannonade became heavy.  In the
midst of the firing, it is said that some pressed hay, which
had been secured on the quarter of the Augusta, to render her
shot-proof, took fire, and the ship was soon in flames.  It now
became necessary to withdraw the other vessels, in order to
escape the effects of the explosion, and the attack was abandoned.  The Augusta blew up, and the Merlin having been
set on fire by the British shared the same fate.  A number of
the crew of the Augusta were lost in that ship, the conflagration being so rapid as to prevent their removal.  A second and
better-concerted attack, however, shortly after, compelled the
Americans to evacuate the works, when the enemy got command of the river from the capes to the town.  This state of
things induced the Americans to destroy the few sea vessels
that remained below Philadelphia, among which were the U.
S. brig Andrea Doria 14, and schooner Wasp 8, and it is believed the Hornet 10 ; though the galleys, by following the Jersey shore, were enabled to escape above.

 While these important movements were occurring in the
middle states, the Raleigh, a fine twelve-pounder frigate, that
had been constructed in New Hampshire, under the law of
1775, was enabled to get to sea for the first time.  She was
commanded by Captain Thompson, and sailed in company
with the Alfred 24, Captain Hinman.  These two ships went

to sea, short of men, bound to France, where military stores
were in waiting to be transported to America.

The Raleigh and Alfred had a good run off the coast, and
they made several prizes of little value during the first few
days of their passage. On the 2d of September they over-
took and captured a snow, called the Nancy, which had been
left by the outward-bound Windward Island fleet, the previous
day. Ascertaining from his prisoners the position of the West-
Indiamen, Captain Thompson made sail in chase. The fleet
was under the charge of the Camel, Druid, Weasel, and Grass-
hopper, the first of which is said to have had an armament of
twelve-pounders. The following day, or September 3d, 1777,
the Raleigh made the convoy from her mast-heads, and by
sunset was near enough to ascertain that there were sixty sail,
as well as the positions of the men-of-war. Captain Thompson had got the signals of the fleet from his prize, and he now
signalled the Alfred, as if belonging to the convoy. After
dark he spoke his consort, and directed her commander to
keep near him, it being his intention to run in among the enemy, and to lay the commodore aboard. At this time, the two
American ships were to windward, but nearly astern.

In the course of the night the wind shifted to the northward,
and the convoy hauled by the wind, bringing the American
ships to leeward. At daylight the wind had freshened, and it
became necessary to carry more sail than the Alfred (a ten-
der-sided ship) could bear. Here occurred one of those instances of the unfortunate consequences which must always
follow the employment of vessels of unequal qualities in the
same squadron, or the employment of officers not trained in
the same high school. The Alfred would not bear her canvass, and while the Raleigh fetched handsomely into the fleet,
under double-reefed topsails, the former fell to leeward more
than a league. Captain Thompson did not dare to shorten
sail, lest his character might be suspected, and despairing of
being supported by the Alfred, he stood boldly in among the
British ships alone, where he hove his ship to, in order to permit the merchantmen astern to draw more ahead of him.

When his plan was laid, Captain Thompson filled away,
and stood directly through the convoy, luffing up towards the
vessel of war that was most to windward. In doing this he
spoke several of the merchantmen, giving them orders how to
steer, as if belonging himself to the fleet, and repeating all the
commodore's signals. Up to this moment the Raleigh appears

to have escaped detection, nor had she had any signs of preparation about her, as her guns were housed, and her ports lowered.

Having obtained a weatherly position, the Raleigh now ran alongside of the vessel of war, and when within pistol-shot, she hauled up her courses, ran out her guns, set her ensign, and commanded the enemy to strike. So completely was this vessel taken by surprise, that the order threw her into great confusion, and even her sails got aback. The Raleigh seized this favourable moment to pour in a broadside, which was feebly returned. The enemy were soon driven from their guns, and the Raleigh fired twelve broadsides into the English ship in twenty minutes, scarcely receiving a shot in return. A heavy swell rendered the aim uncertain, but it was evident that the British vessel suffered severely, and this the more so, as she was of inferior force.

A squall had come on, and at first it shut in the two ships engaged. When it cleared away, the convoy was seen steering in all directions, in the utmost confusion; but the vessels of war, with several heavy well-armed West-Indiamen, tacked and hauled up for the Raleigh, leaving no doubt of their intentions to engage. The frigate lay by her adversary until the other vessels were so near, that it became absolutely necessary to quit her, and then she ran to leeward and joined the Alfred. Here she shortened sail, and waited for the enemy to come down, but it being dark, the British commodore tacked and hauled in among his convoy again. The Raleigh and Alfred kept near this fleet for several days; but no provocation could induce the vessels of war to come out of it, and it was finally abandoned.

The ship engaged by the Raleigh, proved to be the Druid 20, Captain Carteret. She was much cut up, and the official report of her commander, made her loss six killed, and twenty-six wounded. Of the latter, five died soon after the action, and among the wounded was her commander. The Druid was unable to pursue the voyage, and returned to England.

The Raleigh had three men killed and wounded in the engagement, and otherwise sustained but little injury.

On the 14th of June of this year, Congress first adopted the stars and stripes as the national flag.

## CHAPTER VIII.

THE year 1778 opened with still more cheerful prospects
for the great cause of American Independence; the capture
of Burgoyne, and the growing discontents in Europe, rendering a French alliance, and a European war, daily more probable. These events, in truth, soon after followed; and from
that moment, the entire policy of the United States, as related
to its marine, was changed. Previously to this great event,
Congress had often turned its attention towards the necessity
of building or purchasing vessels of force, in order to counteract
the absolute control which the enemy possessed, in the immediate waters of the country, and which even superseded the
necessity of ordinary blockades, as two or three heavy frigates
had been able, at any time since the commencement of the
struggle, to command the entrance of the different bays and
sounds.

The French fleet, soon after the commencement of hostilities between England and France, appeared in the American
seas, and, in a measure, relieved the country from a species
of warfare that was particularly oppressive to a nation that
was then so poor, and which was exposed on so great an extent of coast.

As the occupation of New York and Philadelphia prevented
several of the new frigates from getting to sea at all, or occasioned their early loss, Congress had endeavoured to repair
these deficiencies by causing other vessels to be built, or purchased, at points where they would be out of danger from any
similar misfortunes. Among these ships were the Alliance 32,
Confederacy 32, Deane 32, (afterwards called the Hague,)
and Queen of France 28, all frigate-built, and the Ranger,
Gates, and Saratoga sloops of war. To these were added a
few other vessels, that were either bought or borrowed in
Europe. The Alliance, which, as her name indicates, was
launched about the time the treaty was made with France, was
the favourite ship of the American navy, and it might be added,
of the American nation, during the war of the Revolution;
filling some such space in the public mind, as has since been
occupied by her more celebrated successor, the Constitution.

She was a beautiful and an exceedingly fast ship, but, as will be seen in the sequel, was rendered less efficient than she might otherwise have proved, by the mistake of placing her under the command of a French officer, with a view to pay a compliment to the new allies of the republic.   This unfortunate selection produced mutinies, much discontent among the officers, and, in the end, grave irregularities.   The Alliance was built at Salisbury, in Massachusetts, a place that figured as a building station, even in the seventeenth century.

The naval operations of the year open with a gallant little exploit, achieved by the United States sloop Providence, 12, Captain Rathburne.   This vessel carried only four-pounders, and, at the time, is said to have had a crew of but fifty men on board.   Notwithstanding this trifling force, Captain Rathburne made a descent on the Island of New Providence, at the head of twenty-five men.   He was joined by a few American prisoners, less than thirty, it is said, and, while a privateer of sixteen guns, with a crew of near fifty men, lay in the harbour, he seized the forts, got possession of the stores, and effectually obtained command of the place.   All the vessels in port, six in number, fell into his hands, and an attempt of the armed population to overpower him, was suppressed, by a menace to burn the town.   A British sloop of war appeared off the harbour, while the Americans were in possession, but, ascertaining that an enemy was occupying the works, she retired, after having been fired on.   The following day, the people assembled in such force, as seriously to threaten the safety of his party and vessel, and Captain Rathburne caused the guns of the fort to be spiked, removed all the ammunition and small-arms, burned two of his prizes, and sailed with the remainder, without leaving a man behind him.   In this daring little enterprise, the Americans held the place two entire days.

Captain John Barry, whose spirited action off the capes of Virginia, in the Lexington 14, has been mentioned, and whose capture of the Edward, on that occasion, is worthy of note, as having been the first of any vessel of war, that was ever made by a regular American cruiser in battle, was placed on the regulated list of October, 1776, as the seventh captain, and appointed to the command of the Effingham 28, then building at Philadelphia.   The Effingham was one of the vessels that had been taken up the Delaware, to escape from the British army; and this gallant officer, wearied with a life of inactivity, planned an expedition down the stream, in the hope of striking a blow at some of the enemy's vessels anchored off, or below the town. Manning four boats, he pulled down with the tide. Some alarm was given when opposite the town, but dashing ahead, the barges got past without injury. Off Port Penn lay an enemy's schooner of ten guns, and four transports, with freight for the British army. The schooner was boarded and carried, without loss, and the transports fell into the hands of the Americans also. Two cruisers appearing soon after in the river, however, Captain Barry destroyed his prizes, and escaped by land, without losing a man.

Following the order of time, we now return to the movements of the two ships under the command of Captain Thompson, the Raleigh and the Alfred. After taking in military stores in France, these vessels sailed for America, making a circuit to the southward, in order to avoid the enemy's vessels of force, and to pick up a few prizes by the way. They sailed from l'Orient in February, 1778, and on the 9th of March, were chased by the British ships Ariadne and Ceres, which succeeded in getting alongside of the Alfred, and engaging her, while the Raleigh was at a distance. Believing a contest fruitless, after exchanging a few broadsides, the Alfred struck; but the Raleigh, though hard pressed, in the chase that succeeded, made her escape. Captain Thompson was blamed in the journals of the day, for not aiding his consort on this occasion; and he appears to have been superseded in the command of his ship, to await the result of a trial.

Among the frigates ordered by the act of 1775, was one called the Virginia 28, which had been laid down in Maryland. To this vessel was assigned Captain James Nicholson, the senior captain on the list, an officer who had already manifested conduct and spirit in an affair with one of the enemy's tenders off Annapolis, while serving in the local marine of Maryland. The great embarrassment which attended most of the public measures of the day, and a vigilant blockade, prevented the Virginia from getting to sea, until the spring of this year, when having received her crew and equipments, she made the attempt on the 30th of March.

The frigate appears to have followed another vessel down the Chesapeake, under the impression that the best pilot of the bay was in charge of her. About three in the morning, however, she struck on the middle ground, over which she beat with the loss of her rudder. The ship was immediately anchored. Day discovered two English vessels of war at no great distance, when Captain Nicholson got ashore with his papers, and the ship was taken possession of by the enemy. An inquiry, instituted by Congress, acquitted Captain Nicholson of blame.

Leaving the ocean, we will again turn our attention to the proceedings of the enemy in the Delaware.    Early in May, an expedition left Philadelphia, under the command of Major Maitland, and ascended that river with a view to destroy the American shipping, which had been carried up it to escape the invading and successful army of the enemy.    The force consisted of the schooners Viper and Pembroke; the Hussar, Cornwallis, Ferret, and Philadelphia galleys; four gun-boats, and eighteen flat-boats, under the orders of Captain Henry of the navy.    The 2d battalion of the light-infantry, and two field-pieces composed the troops.    Ascending the stream to a point above Bristol, the troops landed, without opposition.    There does not appear to have been any force to oppose the British on this occasion, or, if any, one of so little moment, as to put a serious contest out of the question.    The Washington 32, and Effingham 28, both of which had been built at Philadelphia, but had never got to sea, were burned.    These ships had not yet received their armaments.

About this time the celebrated Paul Jones, whose conduct as a lieutenant in the Alfred, and in command of that ship, as well as in that of the Providence 12, had attracted much attention, appeared in the European seas in command of the Ranger 18.    So cautious had the American government become, in consequence of the British remonstrances, that orders were given to the Ranger to conceal her armament while in France.

After going into Brest to refit, Captain Jones sailed from port on the 10th of April, 1778, on a cruise in the Irish Channel.    As the Ranger passed along the coast, she made several prizes, and getting as high as Whitehaven, Captain Jones determined, on the 17th, to make an attempt to burn the colliers that were crowded in that narrow port.    The weather, however, prevented the execution of this project, and the ship proceeded as high as Glentine bay, on the coast of Scotland, where she chased a revenue vessel without success.

Quitting the Scottish coast, the Ranger next crossed to Ireland, and arrived off Carrickfergus, where she was boarded by some fishermen.    From these men Captain Jones ascertained that the Drake sloop of war, Captain Burden, a vessel of a force about equal to that of the Ranger, lay anchored in the roads, and he immediately conceived a plan to run in and take her. Preparations were accordingly made to attempt the enterprise as soon as it was dark.

It blew fresh in the night, but when the proper hour had arrived, the Ranger stood for the roads, having accurately obtained the bearings of her enemy. The orders of Captain Jones were to overlay the cable of the Drake, and to bring up on her bows, where he intended to secure his own ship, and abide the result. By some mistake, the anchor was not let go in season, and instead of fetching up in the desired position, the Ranger could not be checked until she had drifted on the quarter of the Drake, at the distance of half a cable's length. Perceiving that his object was defeated, Captain Jones ordered the cable to be cut, when the ship drifted astern, and, making sail, she hauled by the wind as soon as possible. The gale increasing, it was with great difficulty that the Ranger weathered the land, and regained the channel.

Captain Jones now stood over to the English coast, and believing the time more favourable, he attempted to execute his former design on the shipping of Whitehaven. Two parties landed in the night; the forts were seized and the guns were spiked; the few look-outs that were in the works being confined. In effecting this duty, Captain Jones was foremost in person, for, having once sailed out of the port, he was familiar with the place. An accident common to both the parties into which the expedition had been divided, came near defeating the enterprise in the outset. They had brought candles in lanterns, as lights and torches, and, now that they were wanted for the latter purpose, it was found that they were all consumed. As the day was appearing, the party under Mr. Wallingford, one of the lieutenants, took to its boat without effecting any thing, while Captain Jones sent to a detached building and obtained a candle. He boarded a large ship, kindled a fire in her steerage, and by placing a barrel of tar over the spot, soon had the vessel in flames. The tide being out, this ship lay in the midst of more than a hundred others, high and dry, and Captain Jones flattered himself with the hope of signally revenging the depredations that the enemy had so freely committed on the American coast. But, by this time, the alarm was effectually given, and the entire population appeared on the adjacent high ground, or were seen rushing in numbers towards the shipping. The latter were easily driven back by a show of force; and remaining a sufficient time, as he thought, to make sure of an extensive conflagration, Captain Jones took to his boats and pulled towards his ship.  Some guns were fired on the retiring boats without effect ; but the people of the place succeeded in extinguishing the flames before the mischief became very extensive.

The hardihood, as well as the nature of this attempt, produced a great alarm along the whole English coast ; and from that hour, even to this, the name of Jones, in the midst of the people of Whitehaven, is associated with audacity, destruction, and danger.

While cruising, with the utmost boldness, as it might be in the very heart of the British waters, with the coasts of the three kingdoms frequently in view at the same moment, Captain Jones, who was a native of the country, decided to make an attempt to seize the Earl of Selkirk, who had a seat on St. Mary's Isle, near the point where the Dee flows into the channel.  A party landed, and got possession of the house, but its master was absent.  The officer in command of the boats so far forgot himself as to bring away a quantity of the family plate, although no other injury was done, or any insult offered.  This plate, the value of which did not exceed a hundred pounds, was subsequently purchased of the crew by Captain Jones, and returned to Lady Selkirk, with a letter expressive of his regrets at the occurrence.

After the landing mentioned, the Ranger once more steered towards Ireland, Captain Jones still keeping in view his design on the Drake, and arrived off Carrickfergus again, on the 24th.  The commander of the latter ship sent out an officer, in one of his boats, to ascertain the character of the stranger.  By means of skilful handling, the Ranger was kept end-on to the boat, and as the officer in charge of the latter could merely see the ship's stern, although provided with a glass, he suffered himself to be decoyed alongside, and was taken.  From the prisoners, Captain Jones learned that intelligence of his descents on Whitehaven and St. Mary's Isle had reached Belfast, and that the people of the Drake had weighed the anchor he had lost in his attempt on that ship.

Under these circumstances, Captain Jones believed that the commander of the Drake would not long defer coming out in search of his boat ; an expectation that was shortly realised, by the appearance of the English ship under way.  The Ranger now filled and stood off the land, with a view to draw her enemy more into the channel, where she lay to, in waiting

7 *

for the latter to come on. Several small vessels accompanied the Drake, to witness the combat, and many volunteers had gone on board her, to assist in capturing the American privateer, as it was the fashion of the day to term the vessels of the young republic. The tide being unfavourable, the Drake worked out of the roads slowly, and night was approaching before she drew near the Ranger.

The Drake, when she got sufficiently nigh, hailed, and received the name of her antagonist, by way of challenge, with a request to come on. As the two ships were standing on, the Drake a little to leeward and astern, the Ranger put her helm up, a manœuvre that the enemy imitated, and the former gave the first broadside, firing as her guns bore. The wind admitted of but few changes, but the battle was fought running free, under easy canvass. It lasted an hour and four minutes, when the Drake called for quarter, her ensign being already down.

The English ship was much cut up, both in her hull and aloft, and Captain Jones computed her loss at about forty men. Her captain and lieutenant were both desperately wounded, and died shortly after the engagement. The Ranger suffered much less, having Lieutenant Wallingford and one man killed, and six wounded. The Drake was not only a heavier ship, but she had a much stronger crew than her antagonist. She had also two guns the most.

After securing her prize and repairing damages, the Ranger went round the north of Ireland, and shaped her course for Brest. She was chased repeatedly, but arrived safely at her port with the Drake, on the 8th of May.

Mr. Silas Talbot, of Rhode Island, who had been a seaman in his youth, had taken service in the army, and, October 10th, 1777, he had been raised to the rank of a Major, to reward him for a spirited attempt to set fire to one of the enemy's cruisers in the Hudson. In the autumn of the present year (1778), Major Talbot headed another expedition against the British schooner Pigot 8, then lying in the eastern passage between Rhode Island and the main land, in a small sloop that had two light guns, and which was manned by 60 volunteers. The Pigot had 45 men, and one heavy gun in her bows, besides the rest of her armament. Her commander showed great bravery, actually fighting alone on deck, in his shirt, when every man of his crew had run below. Major Talbot carried the schooner without loss, and for his conduct and gallantry was promoted to be a Lieutenant-Colonel. The following year this officer was transferred to the navy, Congress passing an especial resolution to that effect, with directions to the Marine Committee to give him a ship on the first occasion. It does not appear, however, that it was in the power of the committee, at that period of the war, to appoint Captain Talbot to a government vessel, and he is believed to have served, subsequently, in a private armed ship.

In consequence of the investigation connected with the loss of the Alfred, Captain Thompson was relieved from the command of the Raleigh 32, as has been said already, and that ship was given to Captain Barry. Under the orders of her new commander, the Raleigh sailed from Boston on the 25th of September, at six in the morning, having a brig and a sloop under convoy. The wind was fresh at N. W., and the frigate ran off N. E. At twelve, two strange sail were seen to leeward, distant fifteen or sixteen miles. Orders were given to the convoy to haul nearer to the wind, and to crowd all the sail it could carry, the strangers in chase. After dark the Raleigh lost sight of the enemy, and the wind became light and variable. The Raleigh now cleared for action, and kept her people at quarters all night, having tacked towards the land. In the morning it proved to be hazy, and the strangers were not to be seen. The Raleigh was still standing towards the land, which she shortly after made ahead, quite near. About noon, the haze clearing away, the enemy were seen in the southern board, and to windward, crowding sail in chase. The weather became thick again, and the Raleigh lost sight of her two pursuers, when she hauled off to the eastward. That night no more was seen of the enemy, and at daylight Captain Barry took in every thing, with a view to conceal the position of the ship, which was permitted to drift under bare poles. Finding nothing visible at 6, A. M., the Raleigh crowded sail once more, and stood S. E. by S. But at half past 9, the two ships were again discovered astern, and in chase. The Raleigh now hauled close upon a wind, heading N. W., with her larboard tacks aboard. The enemy also came to the wind, all three vessels carrying hard with a staggering breeze. The Raleigh now fairly outsailed the strangers, running 11 knots 2 fathoms, on a dragged bowline.

Unfortunately, at noon the wind moderated, when the leading vessel of the enemy overhauled the Raleigh quite fast, and even the ship astern held way with her. At 4, P. M., the

Raleigh tacked to the westward, with a view to discover the force of the leading vessel of the enemy; and about the same time she made several low islands, the names of which were not known. At 5, P. M., the leading vessel of the enemy having nearly closed, the Raleigh edged away and crossed her fore foot, brailing her mizzen, and taking in her staysails. The enemy showed a battery of 14 guns of a side, including both decks, and set St. George's ensign. In passing, the Raleigh delivered her broadside, which was returned, when the stranger came up under the lee quarter of the American ship, and the action became steady and general. At the second fire, the Raleigh unfortunately lost her fore-topmast and mizzen top-gallant-mast, which gave the enemy a vast advantage in manœuvring throughout the remainder of the affair. Finding the broadside of the Raleigh getting to be too hot for him, the enemy soon shot ahead, and, for a short time, while the people of the former ship were clearing the wreck, he engaged to windward, and at a distance. Ere long, however, the English vessel edged away and attempted to rake the Raleigh, when Captain Barry bore up, and bringing the ships alongside each other, he endeavoured to board, a step that the other, favoured by all his canvass, and his superiority of sailing in a light breeze, easily avoided. By this time, the second ship had got so near as to render it certain she would very soon close, and, escape by flight being out of the question in the crippled condition of his ship, Captain Barry called a council of his officers. It was determined to make an attempt to run the frigate ashore, the land being then within a few miles. The Raleigh accordingly wore round, and stood for the islands already mentioned, her antagonist following her in the most gallant manner, both ships maintaining the action with spirit. About midnight, however, the enemy hauled off, and left the Raleigh to pursue her course towards the land. The engagement had lasted seven hours, much of the time in close action, and both vessels had suffered materially, the Raleigh in particular, in her spars, rigging, and sails. The darkness, soon after, concealing his ship, Captain Barry had some hopes of getting off among the islands, and was in the act of bending new sails for that purpose, when the enemy's vessels again came in sight, closing fast. The Raleigh immediately opened a brisk fire from her stern guns, and every human effort was made to force the ship towards the land. The enemy, however, easily closed again, and opened a heavy fire, which was

CONSTITUTION AND GUERRIERE.

returned by the Raleigh until she grounded, when the largest
of the enemy's ships immediately hauled off, to avoid a
similar calamity, and, gaining a safe distance, both vessels
continued their fire, from positions they had taken on the
Raleigh's quarter.  Captain Barry, finding that the island
was rocky, and that it might be defended, determined to land,
and to burn his ship; a project that was rendered practicable
by the fact that the enemy had ceased firing, and anchored at
the distance of about a mile.  A large party of men got on
shore, and the boats were about to return for the remainder,
when it was discovered that, by the treachery of a petty officer,
the ship had surrendered.

The officers and men on the island escaped, but the vessel
was got off and placed in the British navy.  The two ships
that took the Raleigh were the Experiment 50, Captain Wallace, and the Unicorn 22.  The latter mounted 28 guns, and
was the ship that engaged the Raleigh so closely, so long, and
so obstinately.  She was much cut up, losing her masts after
the action, and had 10 men killed, besides many wounded.
The Americans had 25 men killed and wounded in the course
of the whole affair.

## CHAPTER IX.

The year 1779 opens with the departure of the Alliance,
32, for France.  It has already been stated that the command
of this ship had been given to a Captain Landais, who was
said to be a French officer of gallantry and merit.  Unfortunately the prejudices of the seamen did not answer to the com-
plaisance of the Marine Committee in this respect, and it was
found difficult to obtain a crew willing to enlist under a French
captain.  When General Lafayette reached Boston near the
close of 1778, in order to embark in the Alliance, it was found
that the frigate was not yet manned.  Desirous of rendering
themselves useful to their illustrious guest, the government of
Massachusetts offered to complete the ship's complement by
impressment, an expedient that had been adopted on more than
one occasion during the war; but the just-minded and benevo-

lent Lafayette would not consent to the measure. Anxious to
sail, however, for he was entrusted with important interests,
recourse was had to a plan to man the ship, which, if less objectionable on the score of principle, was scarcely less so in
every other point of view.

The Somerset 64, had been wrecked on the coast of New
England, and part of her crew had found their way to Boston.
By accepting the proffered services of these men, those of some
volunteers from among the prisoners, and those of a few
French seamen that were also found in Boston after the departure of their fleet, a motley number was raised in sufficient
time to enable the ship to sail on the 11th of January. With
this incomplete and mixed crew, Lafayette trusted himself on
the ocean, and the result was near justifying the worst fore-
bodings that so ill-advised a measure could have suggested.

After a tempestuous passage, the Alliance got within two
days' run of the English coast, when her officers and passengers, of the latter of whom there were many besides General
Lafayette and his suite, received the startling information that
a conspiracy existed among the English portion of the crew,
some seventy or eighty men in all, to kill the officers, seize the
vessel, and carry the frigate into England. With a view to
encourage such acts of mutiny, the British Parliament had
passed a law to reward all those crews that should run away
with American ships; and this temptation was too strong for
men whose service, however voluntary it might be in appearances, was probably reluctant, and which had been compelled
by circumstances, if not by direct coercion.

The plot, however, was betrayed, and by the spirited conduct of the officers and passengers, the ringleaders were ar-
rested.

On reaching Brest, the mutineers were placed in a French
gaol, and after some delay, were exchanged as prisoners of
war, without any other punishment; the noble-minded Lafayette, in particular, feeling averse to treating foreigners as it
would have been a duty to treat natives under similar circumstances.

On the 18th of April, the U. S. ships Warren 32, Captain
J. B. Hopkins, Queen of France 28, Captain Olney, and Ranger 18, Captain Simpson, sailed from Boston, in company, on
a cruise; Captain Hopkins being the senior officer. When a
few days from port, these vessels captured a British privateer
of 14 guns, from the people of which they ascertained that a

small fleet of armed transports and store-ships had just sailed from New York, bound to Georgia, with supplies for the enemy's forces in that quarter. The three cruisers crowded sail in chase, and off Cape Henry, late in the day, they had the good fortune to come up with nine sail, seven of which they captured, with a trifling resistance. Favoured by the darkness, the two others escaped. The vessels taken proved to be his Britannic Majesty's ship Jason, 20, with a crew of 150 men ; the Maria armed ship, of 16 guns, and 84 men ; and the privateer schooner Hibernia, 8, with a crew of 45 men. The Maria had a full cargo of flour. In addition to these vessels, the brigs Patriot, Prince Frederick, Bachelor John, and the schooner Chance, all laden with stores, fell into the hands of the Americans. Among the prisoners were twenty-four British officers, who were on their way to join their regiments at the south.

The command of the Queen of France was now given to Captain Rathburne, when that ship sailed on another cruise, in company with the Ranger, and the Providence 28, Captain Whipple ; the latter being the senior officer. In July, this squadron fell in with a large fleet of English merchantmen, that was convoyed by a ship of the line, and some smaller cruisers, and succeeded in cutting out several valuable prizes, of which eight arrived at Boston, their estimated value exceeding a million of dollars. In the way of pecuniary benefits, this was the most successful cruise made in the war.

Paul Jones had obtained so much celebrity for his services in the Ranger, that he remained in France, after the departure of his ship for America, in the hope of receiving a more important command, the inducement, indeed, which had originally brought him to Europe. Many different projects to this effect had been entertained and abandoned, during the years 1778 and 1779, by one of which a descent was to have been made on Liverpool, with a body of troops commanded by Lafayette. All of these plans, however, produced no results ; and after many vexatious repulses in his applications for service, an arrangement was finally made to give this celebrated officer employment that was as singular in its outlines, as it proved to be inconvenient, not to say impracticable, in execution.

By a letter from M. de Sartine, the minister of the marine, dated February 4th, 1779, it appears that the King of France had consented to purchase and put at the disposition of Captain Jones, the Duras, an old Indiaman of some size, then lying at

l'Orient. To this vessel were added three more that were procured by means of M. le Ray de Chaumont, a banker of emi-
nence connected with the court, and who acted on the occasion,
under the orders of the French ministry. Dr. Franklin, who,
as minister of the United States, was supposed, in a legal sense,
to direct the whole affair, added the Alliance 32, in virtue of
the authority that he held from Congress. The vessels that
were thus chosen, formed a little squadron, composed of the
Duras, Alliance, Pallas, Cerf, and Vengeance. The Pallas
was a merchantman bought for the occasion ; the Vengeance
a small brig that had also been purchased expressly for the
expedition ; the Cerf was a fine large cutter, and, with the exception of the Alliance, the only vessel of the squadron fitted
for war. All the ships but the Alliance were French-built,
and they were placed under the American flag, by the following arrangement.

The officers received appointments, which were to remain
valid for a limited period only, from Dr. Franklin, who had
held blank commissions to be filled up at his own discretion,
ever since his arrival in Europe, while the vessels were to
show the American ensign, and no other. In short, the French
ships were to be considered as American ships, during this
particular service, and when it was terminated, they were to
revert to their former owners. The laws and provisions of the
American navy were to govern, and command was to be exercised, and to descend, agreeably to its usages. Such officers
as already had rank in the American service, were to take
precedence of course, agreeably to the dates of their respective
commissions, while the new appointments were to be regulated
by the new dates. By an especial provision, Captain Jones
was to be commander-in-chief, a post he would have been
entitled to fill by his original commission ; Captain Landais
of the Alliance, the only other regular captain in the squadron, being his junior. The joint right of the American
minister and of the French government, to instruct the commodore, and to direct the movements of the squadron, was also
recognised.

From what source the money was actually obtained by
which this squadron was fitted out, is not actually known, nor
is it now probable that it will ever be accurately ascertained.
Although the name of the king was used, it is not impossible
that private adventure was at the bottom of the enterprise,
though it seems certain that the government was so far con-

cerned as to procure the vessels, and to a certain extent to lend the use of its stores. Dr. Franklin expressly states, that he made no advances for any of the ships employed.

As every thing connected with this remarkable enterprise has interest, we shall endeavour to give the reader a better idea of the materials, physical and moral, that composed the force of Commodore Jones, in this memorable cruise.

After many vexatious delays, the Duras, her name having been changed to that of the Bon Homme Richard, in compliment to Dr. Franklin, was eventually equipped and manned. Directions had been given to cast the proper number of eighteen-pounders for her; but, it being ascertained that there would not be time to complete this order, some old twelves were procured in their places. With this material change in the armament, the Richard, as she was familiarly called by the seamen, got ready for sea. She was, properly, a single-decked ship; or carried her armament on one gun-deck, with the usual additions on the quarter-deck and forecastle; but Commodore Jones, with a view to attacking some of the larger convoys of the enemy, caused twelve ports to be cut in the gun-room below, where six old eighteen-pounders were mounted, it being his intention to fight all the guns on one side, in smooth water. The height of the ship admitted of this arrangement, though it was foreseen that these guns could not be of much use, except in very moderate weather, or when engaging to leeward. On her main, or proper gun-deck, the ship had twenty-eight ports, the regular construction of an English 38, agreeably to the old mode of rating. Here the twelve-pounders were placed. On the quarter-deck and forecastle, were mounted eight nines, making in all a mixed and rather light armament of 42 guns. If the six eighteens were taken away, the force of the Bon Homme Richard, so far as her guns were concerned, would have been about equal to that of a 32 gun frigate. The vessel was clumsily constructed, having been built many years before, and had one of those high old-fashioned poops, that caused the sterns of the ships launched in the early part of the eighteenth century to resemble towers.

To manage a vessel of this singular armament and doubtful construction, Commodore Jones was compelled to receive on board a crew of a still more equivocal composition. A few Americans were found to fill the stations of sea-officers, on the quarter-deck and forward; but the remainder of the people were a mixture of English, Irish, Scotch, Portuguese, Norwegians,

8

Germans, Spaniards, Swedes, Italians and Malays, with occasionally a man from one of the islands.  To keep this motley
crew in order, one hundred and thirty-five soldiers were put on
board, under the command of some officers of inferior rank.
These soldiers, or marines, were recruited at random, and
were not much less singularly mixed, as to countries, than the
regular crew.

As the squadron was about to sail, M. Le Ray appeared at
l'Orient, and presented an agreement, or *concordat* as it was
termed, for the signature of all the commanders.  To this singular compact, which in some respects, reduced a naval expedition to the level of a partnership, Commodore Jones ascribed
much of the disobedience among his captains, of which he subsequently complained.

On the 19th of June, 1779, the ships sailed from the anchorage under the Isle of Groix, off l'Orient, bound to the southward, with a few transports and coasters under their convoy.
These vessels were seen into their several places of destination, in the Garonne, Loire, and other ports, but not without
the commencement of that course of disobedience of orders,
unseamanlike conduct, and neglect, which so signally marked
the whole career of this ill-assorted force.  While lying
to, off the coast, the Alliance, by palpable mismanagement,
got foul of the Richard, and lost her mizzen-mast; carrying
away, at the same time, the head, cut-water, and jib-boom of
the latter.  It now became necessary to return to port to
refit.

While steering northerly again, the Cerf cutter was sent in
chase of a strange sail, and parted company.  The next morning she engaged a small English cruiser of 14 guns, and after a
sharp conflict of more than an hour, obliged her to strike, but
was compelled to abandon her prize in consequence of the appearance of a vessel of superior force.  The Cerf, with a loss
of several men killed and wounded, made the best of her way
to l'Orient.

On the 22d, three enemy's vessels of war came in sight of
the squadron, and having the wind, they ran down in a line
abreast; when, most probably deceived by the height and general appearance of the Richard, they hauled up, and by carrying a press of sail, escaped.

On the 26th, the Alliance and Pallas parted company with
the Richard, leaving that ship with no other consort than the

Vengeance brig.   On reaching the Penmarks, the designated rendezvous, the missing vessels did not appear.   On the 29th, the Vengeance having made the best of her way for the roads of Groix by permission, the Richard fell in with two more of the enemy's cruisers, which, after some indications of an intention to come down, also ran, no doubt under the impression that the American frigate was a ship of two decks.   On this occasion Commodore Jones expressed himself satisfied with the spirit of his crew, the people manifesting a strong wish to engage.   On the last of the month, the Richard returned to the roads from which she had sailed, and anchored.   The Alliance and Pallas came in also.

Another delay occurred.   A court was convened to inquire into the conduct of Captain Landais of the Alliance, and of other officers, in running foul of the Richard, and both ships underwent repairs.   Luckily a cartel arrived from England, at this moment, bringing with her more than a hundred exchanged American seamen, most of whom joined the squadron. This proved to be a great and important accession to the composition of the crew of not only the Richard, but to that of the Alliance, the latter ship having been but little better off than the former in this particular.   Among those who came from the English prisons, was Mr. Richard Dale, who had been taken as a master's mate in the Lexington 14.   This young officer did not reach France in the cartel, however, but had previously escaped from Mill prison and joined the Richard. Commodore Jones had now become sensible of his merit, and in reorganizing his crew, he had him promoted, and rated him as his first lieutenant.   The Richard had now nearly a hundred Americans in her, and, with the exception of the commodore himself and one midshipman, all her quarter-deck sea-officers were of the number.   Many of the petty officers too, were Americans.   In a letter written August the 11th, Commodore Jones states that the crew of the Richard consisted of 380 souls, including 137 marines or soldiers.

On the 14th of August, 1779, the squadron sailed a second time from the roads of Groix, having the French privateers Monsieur and Granville in company, and under the orders of Commodore Jones.   On the 18th a valuable prize was taken, and some difficulties arising with the commander of the Monsieur in consequence, the latter parted company in the night of the 19th.   This was a serious loss in the way of force, that ship having mounted no less than forty guns.   A prize

was also taken on the 21st.   On the 23d, the ships were off
Cape Clear, and, while towing the Richard's head round in a
calm, the crew of a boat manned by Englishmen, cut the tow-
line, and escaped.   Mr. Cutting Lunt, the sailing-master of
the ship, manned another boat, and taking with him four soldiers, he pursued the fugitives.   A fog coming on, the latter
boat was not able to find the ships again, and her people fell
into the hands of the enemy.   Through this desertion and its
immediate consequences, the Richard lost twenty of her best
men.

The day after the escape of the boat, the Cerf was sent
close in to reconnoitre, and to look for the missing people, and
owing to some circumstance that has never been explained,
but which does not appear to have left any reproach upon her
commander, this vessel never rejoined the squadron.

A gale of wind followed, during which the Alliance and
Pallas separated, and the Granville parted company to convoy a
prize, according to orders.   The separation of the Pallas is
explained by the fact that she had broken her tiller; but that
of the Alliance can only be imputed to the unofficerlike, as
well as unseamanlike, conduct of her commander.   On the
morning of the 27th, the brig Vengeance was the only vessel
in company with the commodore.

On the morning of the 31st of August, the Bon Homme
Richard, being off Cape Wrath, captured a large letter of
marque bound from London to Quebec; a circumstance that
proves the expedients to which the English ship-masters were
then driven to avoid capture, this vessel having actually gone
north-about to escape the cruisers on the ordinary track.
While in chase of the letter of marque, the Alliance hove in
sight, having another London ship, a Jamaica-man, in company as a prize.   Captain Landais, of the Alliance, an officer,
who, as it has since been ascertained, had been obliged to quit
the French navy on account of a singularly unfortunate temper, now began to exhibit a disorganising and mutinous spirit,
pretending, as his ship was the only real American vessel in
the squadron, that he was superior to the orders of the commodore, and that he would do as he pleased with that frigate.

In the afternoon a strange sail was made, and the Richard
showed the Alliance's number, with an order to chase.   Instead of obeying this signal, Captain Landais wore and laid
the head of his ship in a direction opposite to that necessary
to execute the order.   Several other signals were disobeyed

in an equally contemptuous manner, and the control of Commodore Jones over the movements of this ship, which, on the whole, ought to have been the most efficient in the squadron, may be said to have ceased.

Commodore Jones now shaped his course for the second rendezvous he had appointed, in the hope of meeting the missing ships. On the 2d of September, the Pallas rejoined, having captured nothing. Between this date and the 13th of September, the squadron continued its course round Scotland, the ships separating and rejoining constantly, and Captain Landais assuming powers over the prizes, as well as over his own vessel, that were altogether opposed to discipline, and to the usages of every regular marine. On the last day named, the Cheviot Hills were visible.

Understanding that a twenty-gun ship with two or three man-of-war cutters were lying at anchor off Leith, in the Frith of Forth, Commodore Jones now planned a descent on that town. At this time the Alliance was absent, and the Pallas and Vengeance having chased to the southward, the necessity of communicating with those vessels produced a delay fatal to a project which had been admirably conceived, and which there is reason to think might have succeeded. After joining his two subordinates, and giving his orders, Commodore Jones beat into the Frith, and continued working up towards Leith, until the 17th, when, being just out of gun-shot of the town, the boats were got out and manned. The troops to be landed were commanded by M. de Chamilliard; while Mr. Dale, of the Richard, was put at the head of the seamen. The latter had received his orders, and was just about to go into his boat, when a squall struck the ships, and was near dismasting the commodore. Finding himself obliged to fill his sails, Commodore Jones endeavoured to keep the ground he had gained, but the weight of the wind finally compelled all the vessels to bear up, and a severe gale succeeding, they were driven into the North Sea, where one of the prizes foundered.

It is not easy to say what would have been the result of this dashing enterprise, had the weather permitted the attempt. The audacity of the measure might have insured a victory; and in the whole design we discover the decision, high moral courage, and deep enthusiasm of the officer who conceived it. It was the opinion of Mr. Dale, a man of singular modesty, great simplicity of character, and prudence, that success would have rewarded the effort.

8 *

Abandoning this bold project with reluctance, Commodore Jones appears to have meditated another still more daring; but his *colleagues*, as he bitterly styles his captains in one of his letters, refused to join in it.   It is worthy of remark, that when Commodore Jones laid this second scheme, which has never been explained, before the young sea-officers of his own ship, they announced their readiness as one man to second him, heart and hand.   The enterprise was dropped, however, in consequence principally of the objections of Captain Cottineau, of the Pallas, an officer for whose judgment the commodore appears to have entertained much respect.

The Pallas and Vengeance even left the Richard, probably with a view to prevent the attempt to execute this nameless scheme, and the commodore was compelled to follow his captains to the southward, or to lose them altogether.   Off Whitby the ships last named joined again, and on the 21st the Richard chased a collier ashore between Flamborough Head and the Spurn.   The next day the Richard appeared in the mouth of the Humber, with the Vengeance in company; and several vessels were taken or destroyed.   Pilots were enticed on board, and a knowledge of the state of things in-shore was obtained. It appeared that the whole coast was alarmed, and that many persons were actually burying their plate.   Some twelve or thirteen vessels in all had now been taken by the squadron, and quite as many more destroyed; and coupling these facts with the appearance of the ships on the coast and in the Frith, rumour had swelled the whole into one of its usual terrific tales.   Perhaps no vessels of war had ever before excited so much alarm on the coast of Great Britain.

Under the circumstances, Commodore Jones did not think it prudent to remain so close in with the land, and he stood out towards Flamborough Head.   Here two large sail were made, which next day proved to be the Alliance and the Pallas. This was on the 23d of September, and brings us down to the most memorable event in this extraordinary cruise.

The wind was light at the southward, the water smooth, and many vessels were in sight steering in different directions. About noon, his original squadron, with the exception of the Cerf and the two privateers, being all in company, Commodore Jones manned one of the pilot-boats he had detained, and sent her in chase of a brig that was lying-to, to windward.   On board this little vessel were put Mr. Lunt, the second lieutenant, and fifteen men, all of whom were out of the ship for

the rest of the day.  In consequence of the loss of the two
boats off Cape Clear, the absence of this party in the pilot-
boat, and the number of men that had been put in prizes, the
Richard was now left with only one sea-lieutenant, and with
little more than three hundred souls on board, exclusively of
the prisoners.  Of the latter, there were between one and two
hundred in the ship.

The pilot-boat had hardly left the Bon Homme Richard,
when the leading ships of a fleet of more than forty sail were
seen stretching out on a bowline, from behind Flamborough
Head, turning down towards the Straits of Dover.  From previous intelligence this fleet was immediately known to contain
the Baltic ships, under the convoy of the Serapis 44, Captain
Richard Pearson, and a hired ship that had been put into the
King's service, called the Countess of Scarborough.  The latter
was commanded by Captain Piercy, and mounted 22 guns.
As the interest of the succeeding details will chiefly centre in
the Serapis and the Richard, it may be well to give a more
minute account of the actual force of the former.

At the period of which we are now writing, forty-fours were
usually built on two decks.  Such, then, was the construction
of this ship, which was new, and had the reputation of being
a fast vessel.  On her lower gun-deck she mounted 20 eighteen-
pound guns ; on her upper gun-deck, 20 nine-pound guns ; and
on her quarter-deck and forecastle, 10 six-pound guns ;
making an armament of 50 guns in the whole.  She had a
regularly trained man-of-war's crew of 320 souls, 15 of whom,
however, were said to have been Lascars.

When the squadron made this convoy, the men-of-war were
in-shore, astern and to leeward, probably with a view to keep
the merchantmen together.  The bailiffs of Scarborough, perceiving the danger into which this little fleet was running, had
sent a boat off to the Serapis to apprise her of the presence of
a hostile force ; and Captain Pierson fired two guns, signalling
the leading vessels to come under his lee.  These orders were
disregarded, however, the headmost ships standing out until
they were about a league from the land.

Commodore Jones having ascertained the character of the
fleet in sight, showed a signal for a general chase, another to
recall the lieutenant in the pilot-boat, and crossed royal yards
on board the Richard.  These signs of hostility alarmed the
nearest English ships, which hurriedly tacked together, fired
alarm guns, let fly their top-gallant sheets, and made other

signals of the danger they were in, while they now gladly
availed themselves of the presence of the vessels of war, to run
to leeward, or sought shelter closer in with the land.   The
Serapis, on the contrary, signalled the Scarborough to follow,
and hauled boldly out to sea, until she had got far enough to
windward, when she tacked and stood in-shore again, to cover
her convoy.

The Alliance being much the fastest vessel of the American
squadron, took the lead in the chase, speaking the Pallas as
she passed.   It has been proved that Captain Landais told the
commander of the latter vessel on this occasion, that if the
stranger proved to be a fifty, they had nothing to do but to
endeavour to escape.   His subsequent conduct fully confirmed
this opinion, for no sooner had he run down near enough to the
two English vessels of war, to ascertain their force, than he
hauled up, and stood off from the land again.   All this was
not only contrary to the regular order of battle, but contrary
to the positive command of Commodore Jones, who had kept
the signal to form a line abroad, which should have brought
the Alliance astern of the Richard, and the Pallas in the van.
Just at this time, the Pallas spoke the Richard and inquired
what station she should take, and was also directed to form
the line.   But the extraordinary movements of Captain Landais appear to have produced some indecision in the commander of the Pallas, as he, too, soon after tacked and stood off from
the land.   Captain Cottineau, however, was a brave man, and
subsequently did his duty in the action; and this manœuvre
has been explained by the Richard's hauling up suddenly for
the land, which induced him to think that her crew had muti-
nied and were running away with the ship.   Such was the
want of confidence that prevailed in a force so singularly composed, and such were the disadvantages under which this celebrated combat was fought!

So far, however, from meditating retreat or mutiny, the people of the Bon Homme Richard had gone cheerfully to their
quarters, although every man on board was conscious of the
superiority of the force with which they were about to contend; and the high unconquerable spirit of the commander
appears to have communicated itself to the crew.

It was now quite dark, and Commodore Jones was compelled to follow the movements of the enemy by the aid of a night-
glass.   It is probable that the obscurity which prevailed added to the indecision of the commander of the Pallas, for from

this time until the moon rose, objects at a distance were distinguished with difficulty, and even after the moon appeared, with uncertainty. The Richard, however, stood steadily on, and about half-past seven, she came up with the Serapis, the Scarborough being a short distance to leeward. The American ship was to windward, and as she drew slowly near, Captain Pearson hailed. The answer was equivocal, and both ships delivered their entire broadsides nearly simultaneously. The water being quite smooth, Commodore Jones had relied materially on the eighteens that were in the gun-room; but at this discharge two of the six that were fired bursted, blowing up the deck above, and killing and wounding a large proportion of the people that were stationed below. This disaster caused all the heavy guns to be instantly deserted. It at once reduced the broadside of the Richard to about a third less than that of her opponent, not to include the disadvantage of the manner in which the force that remained was distributed among light guns. In short, the combat was now between a twelve-pounder and an eighteen-pounder frigate; a species of contest in which, it has been said, we know not with what truth, the former had never been known to prevail. Commodore Jones informs us himself, that all his hopes, after this accident, rested on the twelve-pounders that were under the command of his first lieutenant.

The Richard, having backed her topsails, exchanged several broadsides, when she filled again and shot ahead of the Serapis, which ship luffed across her stern and came up on the weather quarter of her antagonist, taking the wind out of her sails, and, in her turn, passing ahead. All this time, which consumed half an hour, the cannonading was close and furious. The Scarborough now drew near, but it is uncertain whether she fired or not. On the side of the Americans it is affirmed that she raked the Richard at least once; but, by the report of her own commander, it would appear that, on account of the obscurity and the smoke, he was afraid to discharge his guns. Unwilling to lie by, and to be exposed to useless injury, Captain Piercy edged away from the combatants, exchanging a broadside or two, at a great distance, with the Alliance, and shortly afterwards was engaged at close quarters by the Pallas, which ship compelled him to strike, after a creditable resistance of about an hour.

The Serapis kept her luff, sailing and working better than the Richard, and it was the intention of Captain Pearson to

pay broad off across the latter's fore-foot, as soon as he had
got far enough ahead; but making the attempt, and finding
he had not room, he put his helm hard down to keep clear of
his adversary, when the double movement brought the two
ships nearly in a line, the Serapis leading. By these uncertain evolutions, the English ship lost some of her way, while
the American, having kept her sails trimmed, not only closed,
but actually ran aboard of her antagonist, bows on, a little on
her weather quarter. The wind being light, much time was
consumed in these different manœuvres; and near an hour had
elapsed between the firing of the first guns, and the moment
when the vessels got foul of each other in the manner just described.

The English now thought it was the intention of the Americans to board, and a few minutes passed in the uncertainty
which such an expectation would create; but the positions of
the vessels were not favourable for either party to pass into
the opposing ship. There being at this moment a perfect cessation of the firing, Captain Pearson demanded, "Have you
struck your colours?" "I have not yet begun to fight," was
the answer.

The yards of the Richard were braced aback, and, the sails
of the Serapis being full, the ships separated. As soon as far
enough asunder, the Serapis put her helm hard down, laid all
aback forward, shivered her after-sails, and wore short round
on her heel, or was box-hauled, with a view, most probably,
of luffing up athwart the bow of her enemy, in order to again
rake her. Commodore Jones, by this time, was conscious of
the hopelessness of success against so much heavier metal,
and after having backed astern some distance, he filled on the
other tack, luffing up with the intention of meeting the enemy
as he came to the wind, and of laying him athwart hawse. In
the smoke one party or the other miscalculated the distance,
for the two vessels came foul again, the bowsprit of the English ship passing over the poop of the American. As neither
had much way, the collision did but little injury, and Commodore Jones, with his own hands, immediately lashed the enemy's head-gear to his mizzen-mast. The pressure on the after-
sails of the Serapis, which vessel was nearly before the wind
at the time, brought her hull round, and the two ships gradually fell close alongside of each other, head and stern, the jib-
boom of the Serapis giving way with the strain. A spare anchor of the English ship now hooked in the quarter of the

American, and additional lashings were got out on board the latter to secure her in this position.

Captain Pearson, who was as much aware of his advantage in a regular combat as his opponent could be of his own inferiority, no sooner perceived the vessels foul, than he dropped an anchor, in the hope that the Richard would drift clear of him. But such an expectation was perfectly futile, as the yards were interlocked, the hulls were pressed close against each other, there were lashings fore and aft, and even the ornamental work aided in holding the ships together. When the cables of the Serapis took the strain, the vessels slowly tended, with the bows of the Serapis and the stern of the Richard to the tide. At this instant the English made an attempt to board, but were repulsed with trifling loss.

All this time the battle raged. The lower ports of the Serapis having been closed to prevent boarding, as the vessel swung, they were now blown off, in order to allow the guns to be run out; and cases actually occurred in which the rammers had to be thrust into the ports of the opposite ship in order to be entered into the muzzles of their proper guns. It is evident that such a conflict must have been of short duration. In effect, the heavy metal of the Serapis, in one or two discharges, cleared all before it, and the main-deck guns of the Richard were in a great measure abandoned. Most of the people went on the upper-deck, and a great number collected on the forecastle, where they were safe from the fire of the enemy, continuing to fight by throwing grenades and using muskets.

In this stage of the combat, the Serapis was tearing her antagonist to pieces below, almost without resistance from her enemy's batteries; only two guns on the quarter-deck, and three or four of the twelves, being worked at all. To the former, by shifting a gun from the larboard side, Commodore Jones succeeded in adding a third, all of which were used with effect, under his immediate inspection, to the close of the action. He could not muster force enough to get over a second gun. But the combat would now have soon terminated, had it not been for the courage and activity of the people aloft. Strong parties had been placed in the tops, and, at the end of a short contest, the Americans had driven every man belonging to the enemy below; after which they kept up so animated a fire, on the quarter-deck of the Serapis in particular, as to drive nearly every man off it, that was not shot down.

Thus, while the English had the battle nearly to themselves

below, their enemies had the control above the upper-deck. Having cleared the tops of the Serapis, some American seamen lay out on the Richard's main-yard, and began to throw hand-grenades upon the two upper decks of the English ship; the men on the forecastle of their own vessel seconding these efforts, by casting the same combustibles through the ports of the Serapis. At length one man, in particular, became so hardy as to take his post on the extreme end of the yard, whence, provided with a bucket filled with combustibles, and a match, he dropped the grenades with so much precision, that one passed through the main hatch-way. The powder-boys of the Serapis had got more cartridges up than were wanted, and, in their hurry, they had carelessly laid a row of them on the main-deck, in a line with the guns. The grenade just mentioned set fire to some loose powder that was lying near, and the flash passed from cartridge to cartridge, beginning abreast of the main-mast, and running quite aft.

The effect of this explosion was awful. More than twenty men were instantly killed, many of them being left with nothing on them but the collars and wristbands of their shirts, and the waistbands of their duck trowsers; while the official returns of the ship, a week after the action, show that there were no less than thirty-eight wounded on board, still alive, who had been injured in this manner, and of whom thirty were then said to be in great danger. Captain Pearson described this explosion as having destroyed nearly all the men at the five or six aftermost guns. On the whole, near sixty of the enemy's people must have been instantly disabled by this sudden blow.

The advantage thus obtained, by the coolness and intrepidity of the topmen, in a great measure restored the chances of the combat, and, by lessening the fire of the enemy, enabled Commodore Jones to increase his. In the same degree that it encouraged the crew of the Richard, it diminished the hopes of the people of the Serapis. One of the guns under the immediate inspection of Commodore Jones had been pointed some time against the main-mast of his enemy, while the two others had seconded the fire of the tops, with grape and canister. Kept below decks by this double attack, where a scene of frightful horror was present in the agonies of the wounded, and the effects of the explosion, the spirits of the English began to droop, and there was a moment when a trifle would have induced them to submit. From this despondency they were tem-

porarily raised, by one of those unlooked-for events that cha-
racterise the vicissitudes of battle.

After exchanging the ineffective and distant broadsides,
already mentioned, with the Scarborough, the Alliance had
kept standing off and on, to leeward of the two principal ships,
out of the direction of their shot, when, about half-past eight
she appeared crossing the stern of the Serapis and the bow of
the Richard, firing at such a distance as to render it impossible
to say which vessel would suffer the most.   As soon as she
had drawn out of the range of her own guns, her helm was
put up, and she ran down near a mile to leeward, hovering
about until the firing had ceased between the Pallas and the
Scarborough, when she came within hail and spoke both of
these vessels.   Captain Cottineau of the Pallas earnestly entreated Captain Landais to take possession of his prize, and
allow him to go to the assistance of the Richard, or to stretch
up to windward in the Alliance himself, and succour the Commodore.

After some delay, Captain Landais took the important duty
of assisting his consort, into his own hands, and making two
long stretches, under his topsails, he appeared, about the time
at which we have arrived in the narration of the combat, directly to windward of the two ships, with the head of the Alliance to the westward.   Here the latter ship once more opened
her fire, doing equal damage, at least, to friend and foe.   Keeping away a little, and still continuing her fire, the Alliance was
soon on the larboard quarter of the Richard, and, it is even
affirmed, that her guns were discharged until she had got nearly
abeam.

Fifty voices now hailed to tell the people of the Alliance that
they were firing into the wrong ship, and three lanterns were
shown, in a line, on the off side of the Richard, which was the
regular signal of recognition for a night action.   An officer
was directed to hail, and to command Captain Landais to lay
the enemy aboard ; and the question being put whether the
order was comprehended, an answer was given in the affirmative.

As the moon had been up some time, it was impossible not
to distinguish between the vessels, the Richard being all black,
while the Serapis had yellow sides ; and the impression seems
to have been general in the former vessel, that she had been
attacked intentionally.   At the discharge of the first guns of
the Alliance, the people left one or two of the twelves on board

9

the Richard, which they had begun to fight again, saying that
the Englishmen in the Alliance had got possession of the ship,
and were helping the enemy.   It appears that this discharge
dismounted a gun or two, extinguished several lanterns on the
main deck, and did a great deal of damage aloft.

The Alliance hauled off to some distance, keeping always
on the off-side of the Richard, and soon after she reappeared
edging down on the larboard beam of her consort, hauling up
athwart the bows of that ship and the stern of her antagonist.
On this occasion, it is affirmed that her fire recommenced,
when, by possibility, the shot could only reach the Serapis
through the Richard.   Ten or twelve men appear to have
been killed and wounded on the forecastle of the latter ship,
which was crowded at the time, and among them was an officer of the name of Caswell, who, with his dying breath, maintained that he had received his wound by the fire of the
Richard's consort.

After crossing the bows of the Richard, and the stern of
the Serapis, delivering grape as she passed, the Alliance ran
off to leeward, again standing off and on, doing nothing, for
the remainder of the combat.

The fire of the Alliance added greatly to the leaks of the
Richard, which ship, by this time, had received so much water
through the shot-holes, as to begin to settle.   It is even affirmed
by many witnesses, that the most dangerous shot-holes on
board the Richard, were under her larboard bow, and larboard
counter, in places where they could not have been received
from the fire of the Serapis.   This evidence, however, is not
unanswerable, as it has been seen that the Serapis luffed up on
the larboard-quarter of the Richard in the commencement of
the action, and, forging ahead, was subsequently on her larboard bow, endeavouring to cross her fore-foot.   It is certainly
possible that shot may have struck the Richard in the places
mentioned, on these occasions, and that, as the ship settled in
the water, from other leaks, the holes then made may have
suddenly increased the danger.   On the other hand, if the Alliance did actually fire while on the bow and quarter of the
Richard, as would appear by a mass of uncontradicted testimony, the dangerous shot-holes may very well have come
from that ship.

Let the injuries have been received from what quarter they
might, soon after the Alliance had run to leeward, an alarm
was spread in the Richard that the ship was sinking.   Both

vessels had been on fire several times, and some difficulty had been experienced in extinguishing the flames; but here was a new enemy to contend with, and, as the information came from the carpenter, whose duty it was to sound the pump-wells, it produced a good deal of consternation. The Richard had more than a hundred English prisoners on board, and the master-at-arms, in the hurry of the moment, let them all up from below, in order to save their lives. In the confusion, the master of the letter of marque, that had been taken off the north of Scotland, passed through a port of the Richard into one of the Serapis, when he informed Captain Pearson, that a few minutes would probably decide the battle in his favour, or carry his enemy down, he himself having been liberated in order to save his life. Just at this instant the gunner, who had little to attend to at his quarters, came on deck, and not perceiving Commodore Jones, or Mr. Dale, both of whom were occupied with the liberated prisoners, and believing the master, the only other superior he had in the ship, to be dead, he ran up on the poop to haul down the colours. Fortunately the flag-staff had been shot away, and, the ensign already hanging in the water, he had no other means of letting his intention be known, than by calling out for quarter. Captain Pearson now hailed to inquire if the Richard demanded quarter, and was answered by Commodore Jones himself, in the negative. It is probable that the reply was not heard, or, if heard, supposed to come from an unauthorised source; for, encouraged by what he had learned from the escaped prisoner, by the cry, and by the confusion that prevailed in the Richard, the English captain directed his boarders to be called away, and, as soon as mustered, they were ordered to take possession of the prize. Some of the men actually got on the gunwale of the latter ship, but finding boarders ready to repel boarders, they made a precipitate retreat. All this time, the top-men were not idle, and the enemy were soon driven below again with loss.

In the mean while, Mr. Dale, who no longer had a gun that could be fought, mustered the prisoners at the pumps, turning their consternation to account, and probably keeping the Richard afloat by the very blunder that had come so near losing her. The ships were now on fire again, and both parties, with the exception of a few guns on each side, ceased fighting, in order to subdue this common enemy. In the course of the combat, the Serapis is said to have been set on

fire no less than twelve times, while, towards its close, as will
be seen in the sequel, the Richard was burning all the while.

As soon as order was once more restored in the Richard,
her chances of success began greatly to increase, while the
English, driven under cover, almost to a man, appear to
have lost, in a great degree, the hope of victory. Their fire
materially slackened, while the Richard again brought a few
more guns to bear; the main-mast of the Serapis began to
totter, and her resistance, in general, to lessen. About an
hour after the explosion, or between three hours and three
hours and a half after the first gun was fired, and between two
hours and two hours and a half after the ships were lashed together, Captain Pearson hauled down the colours of the Serapis with his own hands, the men refusing to expose themselves
to the fire of the Richard's tops.

When it was known that the colours of the English had
been lowered, Mr. Dale got upon the gunwale of the Richard,
and laying hold of the main-brace-pendant, he swung himself
on board the Serapis. On the quarter-deck of the latter he
found Captain Pearson, almost alone, that gallant officer having
maintained his post, throughout the whole of this close and
murderous conflict. Just as Mr. Dale addressed the English
captain, the first lieutenant of the Serapis came up from below
to inquire if the Richard had struck, her fire having entirely
ceased. Mr. Dale now gave the English officer to understand
that he was mistaken in the position of things, the Serapis
having struck to the Richard, and not the Richard to the Serapis. Captain Pearson confirming this account, his subordinate acquiesced, offering to go below and silence the guns that
were still playing upon the American ship. To this Mr. Dale
would not consent, but both the English officers were immediately passed on board the Richard. The firing was then
stopped below. Mr. Dale had been closely followed to the
quarter-deck of the Serapis, by Mr. Mayrant, a midshipman,
and a party of boarders, and as the former struck the quarter-
deck of the prize, he was run through the thigh, by a boarding-
pike, in the hands of a man in the waist, who was ignorant of
the surrender. Thus did the close of this remarkable combat
resemble its other features in singularity, blood being shed and
shot fired, while the boarding officer was in amicable discourse
with his prisoners!

As soon as Captain Pearson was on board the Richard, and
Mr. Dale had received a proper number of hands in the prize,

Commodore Jones ordered the lashings to be cut, and the vessels to be separated, hailing the Serapis, as the Richard drifted from alongside of her, and ordering her to follow his own ship. Mr. Dale, now had the head sails of the Serapis braced sharp aback, and the wheel put down, but the vessel refused to answer her helm or her canvass. Surprised and excited at this circumstance, the gallant lieutenant sprang from the binnacle on which he had seated himself, and fell his length on the deck. He had been severely wounded in the leg by a splinter, and until this moment was ignorant of the injury! He was replaced on the binnacle, when the master of the Serapis came up and acquainted him with the fact that the ship was anchored.

By this time, Mr. Lunt, the second lieutenant, who had been absent in the pilot boat, had got alongside, and was on board the prize. To this officer Mr. Dale now consigned the charge of the Serapis, the cable was cut, and the ship followed the Richard, as ordered.

Although this protracted and bloody combat had now ended, neither the danger nor the labours of the victors were over. The Richard was both sinking and on fire. The flames had got within the ceiling, and extended so far that they menaced the magazine, while all the pumps, in constant use, could barely keep the water at the same level. Had it depended on the exhausted people of the two combatants, the ship must have soon sunk, but the other vessels of the squadron sent hands on board the Richard, to assist at the pumps. So imminent did the danger from the fire become, that all the powder was got on deck, to prevent an explosion. In this manner did the night of the battle pass, with one gang always at the pumps, and another contending with the flames, until about ten o'clock in the forenoon of the 24th, when the latter were got under. After the action, eight or ten Englishmen in the Richard, stole a boat from the Serapis, and ran away with it, landing at Scarborough. Several of the men were so alarmed with the condition of their ship, as to jump overboard and swim to the other vessels.

When the day dawned, an examination was made into the condition of the Richard. Abaft, on a line with those guns of the Serapis that had not been disabled by the explosion, the timbers were found to be nearly all beaten in, or beaten out, for in this respect there was little difference between the two sides of the ship; and it was said that her poop and upper decks would have fallen into the gun-room, but for a few fut-

9 *

tocks that had been missed. Indeed, so large was the vacuum, that most of the shot fired from this part of the Serapis, at the close of the action, must have gone through the Richard without touching any thing. The rudder was cut from the stern-post, and the transoms were nearly driven out of her. All the after part of the ship, in particular, that was below the quarter-deck, was torn to pieces, and nothing had saved those stationed on the quarter-deck, but the impossibility of sufficiently elevating guns that almost touched their object.

The result of this examination was to convince every one of the impossibility of carrying the Richard into port, in the event of its coming on to blow. Commodore Jones was advised to remove his wounded while the weather continued moderate, and he reluctantly gave the order to commence. The following night and the morning of the succeeding day were employed in executing this imperious duty; and about nine o'clock, the officer of the Pallas, who was in charge of the ship, with a party at the pumps, finding that the water had reached the lower deck, reluctantly abandoned her. About ten, the Bon Homme Richard wallowed heavily, gave a roll, and settled slowly into the sea, bows foremost.

The Serapis suffered much less than the Richard, the guns of the latter having been so light, and so soon silenced; but no sooner were the ships separated, than her main-mast fell, bringing down with it the mizzen-top-mast. Though jury-masts were erected, the ship drove about, nearly helpless, in the North Sea, until the 6th of October, when the remains of the squadron, with the two prizes, got into the Texel, the port to which they had been ordered to repair.

In the combat between the Richard and the Serapis, an unusual number of lives was lost, though no regular authentic report appears to have been given by either side. Captain Pearson states the loss of the Richard at about 300 in killed and wounded; a total that would have included very nearly all hands, and which was certainly a great exaggeration, or at least a great mistake. According to a muster-roll of the officers and people of the Richard, excluding the marines, which is still in existence, 42 men were killed, or died of their wounds shortly after the battle, and 41 were wounded. This would make a total of 83, for this portion of the crew, which on the roll amounted to 227 souls. But many of the persons named on this list are known not to have been in the action at all; such as neither of the junior lieutenants, and some thirty men that were with them, besides those absent in prizes. As there were a few volunteers on board, however, who were not mustered, if we set down 200 as the number of the portion of the regular crew that was in the action, we shall probably not be far from the truth. By estimating the soldiers that remained on board at 120, and observing the same proportion for their casualties, we shall get 49 for the result, which will make a total of 132, as the entire loss of the Richard. It is known, however, that, in the commencement of the action, the soldiers, or marines, suffered out of proportion to the rest of the crew, and general report having made the gross loss of the Richard 150 men, we are disposed to believe that it was not far from the fact.

Captain Pearson reported a part of his loss at 117 men, admitting at the same time,.that there were many killed and wounded whose names he could not discover. It is probable that the loss of men, in the two ships, was about equal, and that nearly or quite half of all those who were engaged, were either killed or wounded. Commodore Jones, in a private letter, written some time after the occurrence, gives an opinion, however, that the loss of the Richard was less than that of the Serapis. That two vessels of so much force should lie lashed together more than two hours, making use of artillery, musketry, and all the other means of annoyance known to the warfare of the day, and not do even greater injury to the crews, strikes us with astonishment; but the fact must be ascribed to the peculiarities of the combat, which, by driving most of the English under cover, and by keeping the Americans above the line of fire, protected each party from the missiles of the other. As it was, it proved a murderous and sanguinary conflict, though its duration would probably have been much shorter, and its character still more bloody, but for these unusual circumstances.

## CHAPTER X.

The arrival of Paul Jones, in Holland, excited a great deal
of interest in the diplomatic world. The English demanded
that the prisoners should be released, and that Jones himself
should be given up as a pirate. The Dutch government,
though well disposed to favour the Americans, was not prepared for war, and it was induced to temporise. A long correspondence followed, which terminated in one of those political expedients that are so common, and in which the pains
and penalties of avowing the truth are avoided by means of
a mystification. The Serapis, which had been re-masted and
equipped, was transferred to France, as was the Scarborough,
while Commodore Jones took command of the Alliance, Captain Landais having been suspended, and was ordered to quit
the country.

The Alliance went to sea on the 27th of December, 1779,
and reached the roads of Groix again, in safety, on the 10th
of February, 1780. She passed down the Channel, was near
enough to the squadron in the Downs to examine its force, was
several times chased, and made a short cruise in the Bay of
Biscay, after having touched in Spain. Captain Conyngham,
who had been captured in a privateer and escaped, joined the
Alliance, and went round to l'Orient in the ship.

Although it will be anticipating the events of another year,
we shall finish the history of this vessel, so far as she was
connected with the officer who first commanded her, Captain
Landais. This gentleman had been sent for to Paris, to account for his conduct to the American minister, and subsequently his claim to command the Alliance was referred to
Mr. Arthur Lee, who was on the spot, and who had long been
in Europe, as a conspicuous agent of the government. The
decision of this commissioner restored the Alliance to Captain
Landais, on the ground that his command having been given
to him by the highest authority of the country, a vote of Congress, he could not legally be deprived of it by any subordinate
authority. In June, Captain Landais sailed in the ship for
America, where she was given to an officer better fitted to
show her excellent qualities, and who, in the end, succeeded in

redeeming her character. During the passage home, Captain Landais was deposed from the command, under the idea that he was insane, and soon after he was discharged from the navy. It is thought that the absence of Commodore Jones, alone, prevented his receiving severer punishment.

Commodore Jones, anxious to get back to America, took command of the Ariel 20, a little ship that the king of France lent to his allies, to aid in transporting military stores; and in this vessel, with a portion of the officers and men who had belonged to the Richard, he sailed from under Groix on the 7th of September. When a day or two out, the Ariel encountered a severe gale, in which she came near being lost. The ship was so pressed upon by the wind, that her lower yard-arms frequently dipped, and though an anchor was let go, she refused to tend to it. In order to keep her from foundering, the fore-mast was cut away, and the heel of the main-mast having worked out of the step, that spar followed, bringing down with it the mizzen-mast.

Returning to l'Orient to refit, the Ariel sailed a second time for America, on the 18th of December. During the passage, she fell in with an enemy of about her own size, in the night, and after much conversation, a short combat followed, when the English ship intimated that she had struck, but taking advantage of her position, she made sail and escaped. Some unaccountable mistake was made by, or an extraordinary hallucination appears to have come over Commodore Jones, in reference to this affair; for, in his journal, he speaks of his enemy as having been an English twenty-gun ship called the Triumph, and the result as a victory. The Triumph, if such was truly the name of the English ship, was probably a letter of marque, unable to resist a vessel of war of any force, and though not free from the imputation of treachery, she escaped by out-manœuvring the Ariel. On the 18th of February, 1781, after an absence of more than three years, Paul Jones reached Philadelphia in safety.

Before we return to the American seas, and to the more regular incidents of the year 1779, we will add that, after an inquiry into the conduct of Captain Jones, as it was connected with all his proceedings in Europe, Congress gave him a vote of thanks, and, by a formal resolution, bestowed on him the command of the America 74, the only one of the six ships of that class that was ever laid down under the law of 1776. The America never got to sea under the national colours, Congress presenting the ship to their ally, Louis XVI., to replace the Magnifique 74, which had been lost in the port of Boston.

To return to the more regular order of events.

During the summer of 1779, the Deane 32, Captain Samuel Nicholson, and the Boston 24, Captain Tucker, made a cruise in company. In August of that year, these two ships took many prizes, though no action of moment occurred. Among others were the Sandwich (a packet,) 16, two privateers, with the Glencairn 20, and the Thorn 18. The last of these vessels was a man-of-war.

In the spring of this year, the Providence 12, Captain Hacker, took a vessel of equal force, called the Diligent, after a sharp action. The particulars of this engagement are lost, though they are known to have been highly creditable to the American officer. The Diligent appears to have been taken into the service.

A bloody action also occurred, about the same time, between the Massachusetts state-cruiser Hazard 14, Captain John Foster Williams, and the Active 14, a vessel that Schomberg states to have belonged to the king. The combat lasted half an hour, and was determined in favour of the Hazard. The Active is said to have had 33 killed and wounded, and the Hazard 8. Shortly after this handsome affair, Captain Williams was appointed to the ship Protector 20, belonging to the same state, and in June he had a severe action with one of those heavy letters of marque it was so much the custom to send to sea, at the period of which we are writing, called the Duff; a ship said to have been quite equal in force to the Protector. After a sharp contest of more than an hour, the Duff blew up. The Protector succeeded in saving 55 of her crew, having had 6 of her own people killed and wounded in the battle.

The enemy having established a post on the Penobscot, and placed in it a strong garrison, the State of Massachusetts determined to drive them from its territory, without calling upon Congress for assistance. For this purpose, Massachusetts made a draft of 1500 of her own militia, and got an order for the U. S. ship Warren 32, Captain Saltonstall, the Diligent 14, Captain Brown, and the Providence 12, Captain Hacker, to join the expedition; these being the only regular cruisers employed on the occasion. Three vessels belonging to Massachusetts were also put under the orders of Captain Saltonstall, and a force consisting of thirteen privateers was added. In addition there were many transports and store-vessels.   General Lovel commanded the brigade.

This armament made its appearance off the Penobscot on the 25th of July.   While the militia were making their descent, the Warren, and another vessel of some force, engaged the enemy's works.   The cannonading was severe, and the Warren is said to have had 30 men killed and wounded, in the action with the batteries, and in landing the troops.   The latter duty, however, was successfully performed by General Lovel, with a loss of about one hundred men, including all arms. Finding it impossible to carry the place with his present force, the commanding officer now sent for reinforcements.   On the 13th of August, while waiting for a return of the messenger, information was received from the Tyrannicide, the look-out vessel, that Sir George Collier, in the Rainbow 44, accompanied by four other vessels of war, was entering the bay. The troops immediately re-embarked, and a general, hurried, and confused flight ensued.   The British squadron, consisting of five vessels of war, quickly appeared, and a pursuit up the river was commenced, and continued for a long distance.   The enemy soon got near enough to use their chase guns, and the fire was returned by the Americans.   It was undoubtedly the wish of Captain Saltonstall, to reach the shallow waters before he was overtaken ; but finding this impracticable, he ran his ship ashore, and set her on fire.   Others followed this example, and most of the vessels were destroyed, though three or four fell into the hands of the enemy.

Captain Saltonstall was much, and, in some respects, perhaps, justly censured, for this disaster, though it is to be feared that it arose more from that habit of publicity, which is common to all countries much influenced by popular feeling, than from any other cause.   Had a due regard been paid to secresy, time might have been gained in that remote region, to effect the object, before a sufficient force could be collected to go against the assailants.   In a military sense, the principal faults appear to have been a miscalculation of means, at the commencement, and a neglect to raise such batteries as might have protected the shipping against the heavy vessels of the enemy. It could not surely have been thought that privateers, armed with light guns, were able to resist two-deckers ; and the fact that the English had a fleet of such vessels on the coast was generally known.

The disastrous result of this expedition inflicted a severe blow on American nautical enterprises.   Many privateers and state vessels, that had been successful against the enemy's commerce, were either captured or destroyed.   Among the vessels blown up, was the Providence 12, one of the first cruisers ever sent to sea by the United States, and which had become noted for exploits greatly exceeding what might have been expected from her force,

## CHAPTER XI.

At the commencement of the year 1780, the French fleet under Comte d'Estaing retired to the West-Indies, leaving the entire American coast at the command of the British.   Sir Henry Clinton profited by the opportunity to sail against Charleston, with a strong force in ships and troops, which town he reduced after a short but vigorous siege.   Several American ships of war were in the harbour at the time, under the command of Captain Whipple, and finding escape impossible, this officer carried his squadron into the Cooper, sunk several vessels at its mouth, and landed all the guns and crews for the defence of the town, with the exception of those of one ship.   The Providence 28, Captain Whipple, the Queen of France 28, Captain Rathburne, the Boston 24, Captain Tucker, the Ranger 18, Captain Simpson, and several smaller vessels, fell into the hands of the enemy.

The English government, by this time, found the system of privateering so destructive to their navigation, that it had come to the determination of refusing to exchange any more of the seamen that fell into their power.   By acting on this policy, they collected a large body of prisoners, sending them to England in their return-ships, and sensibly affected the nautical enterprises of the Americans, who, of course, had but a limited number of officers and men fit to act on the ocean.

By the fall of Charleston, too, the force of the regular American marine, small as it had always been, was still more reduced.   Of the frigates, the Alliance 32, the Hague (late Deane) 32, Confederacy 32, Trumbull 28, and a ship or two bought or borrowed in Europe, appear to be all that were left, while the smaller cruisers, like the pitcher that is broken by going too often to the well, had not fared much better.

In consequence of all these losses, the advanced state of the war, and the French alliance, which had brought the fleets of France upon the American coast, Congress appears to have thought any great efforts for increasing the marine unnecessary at the moment. The privateers and state cruisers were out and active as usual, though much reduced in numbers, and consequently in general efficiency. In contrast to these diminished efforts we find the British Parliament authorizing the ministry to keep no less than 85,000 men employed in the English navy, including the marines.

The first action of moment that occured this year between any United States' vessel and the enemy, nevertheless, has the reputation of having been one of the most hotly and obstinately contested combats of the war. June 2d, 1780, the Trumbull 28, then under the command of Captain James Nicholson, the senior officer of the navy, while cruising in lat. 35° 54′, long. 66° W., made a strange sail to windward from the mast-heads. The Trumbull immediately furled all her canvass, in the hope of drawing the stranger down upon her before she should be seen. At eleven, the stranger was made out to be a large ship, steering for the Trumbull's quarter; but soon hauling more astern, sail was got on the American ship to close. After some manœuvring, in order to try the rate of sailing and to get a view of the stranger's broadside, the Trumbull took in her light sails, hauled up her courses, the chase all this time betraying no desire to avoid an action, but standing directly for her adversary. When near enough, the Trumbull filled, and outsailing the stranger, she easily fetched to windward of her. The chase now fired three guns, showed English colours, and edged away, under short sail, evidently with an intention to pursue her course. Captain Nicholson harangued his men, and then made sail to bring his ship up with the enemy. When about a hundred yards distant, the English ship fired a broadside, and the action began in good earnest. For two hours and a half the vessels lay nearly abeam of each other, giving and receiving broadsides without intermission. At no time were they half a cable's length asunder, and more than once the yards nearly interlocked. Twice was the Trumbull set on fire by the wads of her opponent, and once the enemy suffered in the same way.

10

At last the fire of the Englishman slackened sensibly, until it nearly ceased.

Captain Nicholson now felt satisfied that he should make a prize of his antagonist, and was encouraging his people with that hope, when a report was brought to him, that the main-mast was tottering, and that if it went while near the enemy, his ship would probably be the sacrifice. Anxious to secure the spar, sail was made, and the Trumbull shot ahead again, her superiority of sailing being very decided. She was soon clear of her adversary, who made no effort to molest her. The vessels, however, were scarcely musket-shot apart, when the main and mizzen top-masts of the Trumbull went over the side, and, in spite of every effort to secure them, spar after spar came down, until nothing was left but the fore-mast. Under such circumstances, the enemy, who manifested no desire to profit by her advantage, went off on her proper course. Before she was out of sight, her main top-mast also was seen to fall.

It was afterwards ascertained that the ship engaged by the Trumbull was a letter of marque called the Watt, Captain Coulthard, a vessel of size, that had been expressly equipped to fight her way. Her force is not mentioned in the English accounts, but her commander, in his narrative of the affair, in which he claims the victory, admits his loss to have been 92 men, in killed and wounded. Captain Nicholson estimates her force at 34 or 36 guns, mostly twelve-pounders; and he states that of the Trumbull to have been 24 twelve-pounders and 6 sixes, with 199 souls on board when the action commenced. The Trumbull lost 39, in killed and wounded, among the former of whom were two of her lieutenants.

In the way of a regular cannonade, this combat is generally thought to have been the severest that was fought in the war of the Revolution. There is no question of the superiority of the Watt in every thing but sailing, she having been essentially the largest and strongest ship, besides carrying more guns and men than her opponent. Owing to the difficulty of obtaining seamen, which has been so often mentioned, the Trumbull's crew was composed, in a great degree, of raw hands, and Captain Nicholson states particularly that many of his people were suffering under sea-sickness when they went to their guns.

This action was not followed by another, of any importance, in which a government cruiser was concerned, until the month

of October, when the U. S. sloop of war Saratoga 16, Captain
Young, fell in with, and captured a ship and two brigs, the
former, and one of the latter of which, were well armed. The
conflict with the ship, which was called the Charming Molly,
was conducted with a spirit and promptitude that are deserving of notice. Running alongside, Captain Young delivered
his fire, and threw fifty men on the enemy's decks, when a
fierce but short struggle ensued, that ended in the capture of
the British ship. Lieutenant Joshua Barney, afterwards so
distinguished in the service, led the boarders on this occasion ;
and the crew that he overcame is said to have been nearly
double in numbers to his own party.

After making these and one other capture, the Saratoga
made sail for the Capes of the Delaware, with the intention of
convoying her prizes into port. The following day, however,
the convoy was chased by the Intrepid 74, Captain Molloy,
which ship retook all the prizes, but was unable to get the
Saratoga under her guns. It is said, and we find no evidence
to contradict it, that the Saratoga never returned to port, the
vessel foundering, and her crew perishing at sea, unheard of.

The brevity of the regular naval annals of the three last
years of the war, compels us to compress their incidents into
a single chapter.

It has been stated already that Captain Landais was dismissed from the service soon after his return home, when the
command of the Alliance 32 was given to Captain John Barry,
the officer who had made so gallant a resistance in the Raleigh, not long previously. In February, 1781, Captain Barry
sailed from Boston for France, in command of this favourite
ship, with Colonel Laurens on board, which well-known and
much-regretted young officer was charged with an important
mission to the French court. On the outward passage, the
Alliance captured a small privateer called the Alert, but no
event of any moment occurred. After landing Mr. Laurens,
the frigate sailed from l'Orient on a cruise, with the Marquis
de la Fayette 40, bound to America with stores, in company.
Three days afterwards, or on the 2d of April, 1781, they fell
in with and captured two Guernsey privateers, one of which,
the Mars, is said to have been a heavy vessel of 26 guns and
112 men, and the other, the Minerva, to have had an armament of 10 guns, and a crew of 55 souls. Neither of these
cruisers appears to have made any resistance.

After this success, the Alliance parted company with her

consort and the prizes, and continued to cruise until the 28th of May, when she made two sail, that were standing directly for her.  It was late in the day, and the strangers, when near enough to remain in sight during the darkness hauled up on the same course with the Alliance, evidently with a view to defer the action until morning. At daylight on the succeeding day, it was nearly a dead calm, and when the mist cleared away, the two strangers were seen at no great distance, with English colours flying.  They were now distinctly made out to be a sloop of war apparently of 16 guns, and a brig of 14. The sea was perfectly smooth, and there being no wind, the two light cruisers were enabled to sweep up, and to select their positions, while the Alliance lay almost a log on the water, without steerage way.  Owing to these circumstances, it was noon before the vessels were near enough to hail, when the action commenced.  For more than an hour the Alliance fought to great disadvantage, the enemy having got on her quarters, where only a few of the aftermost guns would bear on them.  The advantage possessed by the English vessels, in consequence of the calm, at one time, indeed, gave their people the greatest hopes of success, for they had the fight principally to themselves.  While things were in this unfortunate state, Captain Barry received a grape-shot through his shoulder, and was carried below.  This additional and disheartening calamity added to the disadvantages of the Americans, who were suffering under the close fire of two spirited and persevering antagonists.  Indeed, so confident of success did the enemy now appear to be, that when the ensign of the Alliance was shot away, this fact, coupled with the necessary slackness of her fire, induced their people to quit their guns, and give three cheers for victory.  This occurred at a moment when a light breeze struck the Alliance's sails, and she came fairly under steerage way.  A single broadside from a manageable ship changed the entire state of the combat, and sent the enemy to their guns, again, with a conviction that their work yet remained to be done.  After a manly resistance, both the English vessels, in the end, were compelled to haul down their colours.

The prizes proved to be the Atalanta 16, Captain Edwards, with a crew of 130 men, and the Trepassy 14, Captain Smith, with a crew of 80 men.  Both vessels were much cut up, and they sustained a joint loss of 41 men in killed and wounded. The Alliance did not escape with impunity, having had 11 killed and 21 wounded, principally by the fire of her enemies, while they lay on her quarter and across her stern. Captain Barry made a cartel of the Trepassy, and sent her into an English port with the prisoners; but the Atalanta was retaken by the enemy's squadron that was cruising off Boston, while attempting to enter that harbour.

Fortune now became capricious, and we are compelled to present the other side of the picture. Among the ships built late in the war, was the Confederacy 32. This vessel had been launched in 1778, at or near Norwich, in Connecticut; and the command of her was given to Captain Seth Harding, the officer who was in the Defence 14, in the action in Nantasket Roads with the two transports captured in 1776. Captain Harding had been commissioned in the navy, in which his first command appears to have been this ship. The Confederacy sailed for Europe in 1779, with Mr. Jay, the minister to Spain, on board, and was suddenly dismasted, a little to the eastward of Bermuda. Spar followed spar, in this calamity, until the ship lay a log on the water, with even her bowsprit gone. This, like so many similar misfortunes that have succeeded it, must probably be attributed to the rigging's having slackened, when the ship got into a warm latitude, after having been set up in cold weather at home.

After several anxious weeks, the Confederacy got into Martinique, where Mr. Jay obtained a passage in the French frigate l'Aurore, and the American vessel remained to refit. From that time to the commencement of the present year, the Confederacy was employed, like most of the large vessels of the service in that stage of the war, in keeping open the communications between the country and the different ports where supplies were obtained, and in transporting stores. Early in 1781, she went to Cape François, and, on the 22d of June, while on her return, with clothing and other supplies on board, and with a convoy in charge, she was chased by a large ship, which succeeded in getting alongside of her. Captain Harding had gone to quarters, and was about to open his fire, when the enemy ran out a lower tier of guns, and a frigate being in company a short distance astern, the American struck. Several of the convoy were also taken.

Captain Nicholson continued in command of the Trumbull, after his severe conflict with the Watt, and we find him at sea again in that ship, in the summer of 1781. She left the Delaware on the 8th of August, with a crew short of 200 men, of

10 *

which near 50 were of the questionable materials to be found among the prisoners of war. She had a convoy of twenty-eight sail, and a heavy privateer was in company. Off the Capes, the Trumbull made three British cruisers astern. Two of the enemy, one of which was a frigate, stood for the Trumbull, which ship, by hauling up, was enabled to gain the wind of them. Night was near, and it blew heavily. The merchantmen began to diverge from the course, though, by carrying easy sail, the Trumbull was enabled to keep most of them ahead, and in their stations. While standing on in this manner, hoping every thing from the darkness, a squall carried away the Trumbull's fore-top-mast, which in falling brought down with it the main-top-gallant-mast. As the weather was thick and squally, the vessels in company of the Trumbull took advantage of the obscurity and scattered, each making the best of her way according to her particular rate of sailing. The Trumbull herself was compelled to bear up, in order to carry the canvass necessary to escape; but with the wreck over her bows, and a crew that was not only deficient in numbers, but which was raw, and in part disaffected, her situation became in the last degree embarrassing. Indeed, her condition has been described as being so peculiarly distressing, as to form a strong instance of the difficulties that sometimes accompany naval warfare.

About ten o'clock at night, the British frigate Iris 32, one of the vessels in chase, closed with the Trumbull, which ship, on account of the heaviness of the weather, had not yet been able to clear the wreck. In the midst of rain and squalls, in a tempestuous night, with most of the forward hamper of the ship over her bows, or lying on the forecastle, with one of the arms of the fore-topsail-yard run through her fore-sail, and the other jammed on deck, and with a disorganised crew, Captain Nicholson found himself compelled to go to quarters, or to strike without resistance. He preferred the first; but the English volunteers, instead of obeying the order, went below, extinguished the lights, and secreted themselves. Near half of the remainder of the people imitated this example, and Captain Nicholson could not muster fifty of even the diminished crew he had, at the guns. The battle that followed, might almost be said to have been fought by the officers. These brave men, sustained by a party of the petty officers and seamen, managed a few of the guns for more than an hour, when the General

Monk 18, coming up and joining in the fire of the Iris, the Trumbull submitted.

In this singular combat, it has even been asserted that at no time were forty of the Trumbull's people at quarters. It was probably owing to this circumstance, that her loss was so small, for the ship herself is said to have been extensively cut up. She had five men killed and eleven wounded. Among the latter were two of the lieutenants, and Mr. Alexander Murray, a gentleman of Maryland, who had been educated to the seas, and had been in the action with the Watt, but who was now serving as a volunteer, and who, after commanding several private cruisers, entered the navy, and subsequently died at the head of the service in 1821. Mr. Murray was particularly distinguished in this affair, and the conduct of Captain Nicholson met with much applause. The Iris suffered more than could have been expected under such circumstances, and reported seven men killed and wounded.

As affording some relief to the loss of the Trumbull, we now come to a handsome exploit that occurred soon after, which ought, perhaps, properly, to take its place among the deeds of the private cruisers, but which is of sufficient importance to be mentioned here, and this so much the more, as a portion of those engaged belonged to the regular service of the country. A private cruiser called the Congress had been fitted out in Philadelphia, in the course of the summer, and in September she was cruising on the coast of the Carolinas and Georgia. The Congress had an armament of 20 guns, according to the American accounts, and of 24 according to the English, and she was commanded by Captain Geddes. Few of her people were seamen, of which there was now a great scarcity in the country, but her complement was, in a great degree, made up of landsmen.

On the morning of the 6th of September, cruising to the eastward of Charleston, the Congress made a sail, to which she gave chase. The stranger was soon discovered to be a cruiser, and at first showed a disposition to engage, but after some manœuvring he stood off. At half-past ten the Congress began to fire her bow guns, and at eleven being close up on the enemy's quarter, she opened a heavy fire of musketry, which did a good deal of execution. Drawing ahead, the Congress now delivered her broadside, and it was returned with spirit. At first the enemy got a cross-fire upon the Congress, and the latter ship meeting with an accident, fell astern to refit. But soon closing again, the combat was renewed with fresh vigour, and the Congress having got her enemy fairly under her guns, in less than an hour she left her a nearly unmanageable wreck on the water.   Notwithstanding his condition, the Englishman showed no disposition to submit, and the Congress ran so close alongside, that the men were said to be reciprocally burned by the discharges of the guns.   The quarter-deck and forecastle of the enemy had scarcely a man left on it, and his fire began to slacken in consequence of several of his guns having been dismounted.   In this stage of the engagement, shot were even thrown by hand and did execution.   At length the mizzen-mast of the English ship fell, and the main-mast threatening to follow it, her boatswain appeared on the forecastle, with his hat in his hand, and called out that his commander had struck. The prize proved to be the British sloop of war Savage 16, Captain Sterling.

We have now reached the year 1782, which was virtually the last of the war of the Revolution, though some events will remain to be recorded in the early part of the year 1783.   In the commencent of this year, the Deane 32, made a successful cruise, in which she took several private armed vessels of the enemy.   On this occasion, the Deane was commanded by Captain Samuel Nicholson.

The favourite ship, the Alliance 32, Captain Barry, was much employed this year, her superior sailing making her a vessel in constant demand.   Among other services that she performed, this ship was sent to Havana for specie, whence she sailed, in company with the Luzerne, a ship loaded with supplies.   Shortly after quitting port, some enemy's vessels fell in with them, and gave chase.   While running from this force, a large sail was seen on the Alliance's weather bow, which was soon made out to be a French 50, on two decks. Exchanging signals, and supposing that the French frigate would sustain him, Captain Barry immediately wore round and brought the leading vessel of the enemy to action; the others manœuvring in a way to engage the attention of the fifty.   The latter, however, kept her wind; and after a sharp fight of more than half an hour, the English ship engaged with the Alliance, finding herself hard pushed, made signals to her consorts to join, when Captain Barry hauled off.   The Alliance now stood for the French ship, and speaking her, it was determined to bring the enemy to action again, in company.   On making sail in chase, however, it was soon found that the fifty was too dull a sailer to give the least hope of overtaking the enemy, and the attempt was abandoned.

In this action, the Alliance had 3 killed and 11 wounded ; while it is said that the loss of the enemy was very heavy. Some statements place the latter as high as 87 men ; but no accounts can be discovered, that give a very clear history of this affair. Even the name of the English ship appears to be lost. One of the enemy, by some of the accounts, was said to be a ship of the line, and the vessel engaged by the Alliance. a heavy sloop of war.*

The command of the Hague, one of the two frigates now left in the American marine, was given to Captain Manly, after her return from the cruise under Captain Nicholson ; and this officer who had virtuallly begun the maritime war, on the part of the United States, in a manner closed it, by an arduous and brilliant chase, in which he escaped from several of the enemy's ships in the West-Indies, after being for a considerable time under the guns of a vastly superior force. This occurrence may be said to have brought the regular naval warfare of the United States to an end, so far as the government cruisers were concerned, peace having been made early in 1783.

---

## CHAPTER XII.

In March, 1782, the Delaware was much infested by barges and small cruisers of the enemy, which not unfrequently made prizes of vessels belonging to the Americans, as well as molesting the people who dwelt near the water. With a view to keep the navigation open against these marauders, the State of Pennsylvania determined to fit out a few vessels at its own expense, and with such materials as could be hastily collected. With this object, a small ship called the Hyder Ally was purchased. So suddenly did the local government come to its

---

* James, very inaccurate authority in general, says that this vessel was the Sibyl, rating 20, and mounting 28 guns, Captain Vashon. It is quite probable he is right in this instance.

resolution, that the vessel just named, when bought, had actually dropped down the river, on an outward-bound voyage, loaded with flour.   She was brought back, her cargo was discharged, and an armament of 16 six-pounders was put upon her.   So little, however, was this ship ready for war, that she had to be pierced in order to receive her guns.   Indeed, so pressing was the emergency, that the merchants of Philadelphia anticipated the passage of the law to authorise the purchase and equipment of this ship, by advancing funds for that purpose ; and the act had not entirely gone through all its legal forms, until after the exploit we are about to record had been performed !   The commissioners entrusted with the duty of preparing the ship, selected Lieutenant Joshua Barney, of the United States navy, as her commander, a young officer of great decision of character and personal bravery, who had already distinguished himself in subordinate stations, on board of different cruisers of the general government, but who, like so many more of the profession, was obliged frequently to choose between idleness and a service less regular than that to which he properly belonged.

A crew of 110 men was put on board the Hyder Ally ; and within a fortnight after he was appointed to command her, Captain Barney sailed.   It was not the intention of the authorities of Pennsylvania, that this ship should go to sea, but merely that she should keep the navigation of the river and bay open, and drive off privateers, and other small cruisers.   On the 8th of April, the Hyder Ally got into the bay with a considerable convoy of outward-bound merchantmen.   The whole fleet had anchored in the roads off Cape May, in waiting for a wind to get to sea, when two ships and a brig, one of the former a frigate, were seen rounding the Cape, with a view to attack them.   Captain Barney immediately ran up a signal for the convoy to trip, and to stand up the bay again, the wind being to the southward.   This order was promptly obeyed, and in a few minutes, the merchant vessels, with one exception, were running off before the wind, with every thing set that would draw, the Hyder Ally covering their retreat, under easy sail. The vessel that remained, endeavoured to get to sea, by hauling close round the cape, but grounded and fell into the hands of the enemy.   Another vessel got on the shoals, and was taken by a boat from the nearest of the English cruisers.

An extensive shoal, called the " Over Falls," forms two channels, in the lower part of Delaware Bay, and while the

convoy passed up the easternmost of these channels, or that
which is known as the "Cape May Channel," the frigate stood
towards the western, which offered a better chance to head the
fugitives at the point where the two united, and which had the
most water. The remaining ship and the brig, stood on in the
direction of the Hyder Ally.

It was not long before the brig, which proved to be a British
privateer out of New York, called the Fair American, came
up with the Hyder Ally, when the latter offered her battle.
But firing a broadside, the privateer kept aloof, and continued
up the bay. Captain Barney declined to return this fire, holding himself in reserve for the ship astern, a large sloop of war,
which was fast coming up. When the latter got quite near,
the Hyder Ally, which had kept close to the shoal, luffed, threw
in her broadside, and immediately righting her helm, kept
away again. The enemy stood boldly on, and just as his forward guns were beginning to bear, the two vessels being within
pistol-shot, the Hyder Ally attempted to luff athwart his hawse,
when the jib-boom of the English ship ran into her fore-rigging,
and the two vessels got foul. It is said that Captain Barney
obtained this advantage by deceiving his enemy, having given
an order to port the helm, in a loud voice, when secret instructions had been given to the quarter-master at the wheel, to put
his helm hard a-starboard. The Hyder Ally now opened a
severe raking fire, and in less than half an hour from the commencement of the action, the stranger struck, the ships remaining foul of each other.

The frigate, which had not actually got into the western
channel, perceiving the state of things, changed her course,
with a view to get round to the combatants, and Captain Barney had no time to lose. Throwing his first lieutenant, with
a party, on board the prize, he ordered her to continue up the
bay, while he covered the retreat with his own ship. In the
mean while, the brig had run aground above, in chase of the
convoy. There is some reason to suppose that the commander
of the frigate did not know the result of the action, for he
made signals to the prize, and anchored about sunset, leaving
the Hyder Ally, which had been kept a long distance astern
of the other vessels, with a view to divert his attention, to proceed to Philadelphia without further molestation.

Up to this moment, Captain Barney did not know even the
name of his prize. He now made sail, however, and running
alongside of her, for the first time he learned that he had cap-

tured his Britannic Majesty's ship General Monk 18, Captain
Rogers. This vessel had formerly been the American privateer, General Washington, and having fallen into the power
of Admiral Arbuthnot, he had taken her into the king's service, given her a new name, and promoted a favourite officer
to her command. The Monk mounted twenty nines, and is
said to have had a crew of 136 men. Captain Rogers reported his loss at six killed, and twenty-nine wounded; but Captain Barney stated it at twenty killed, and thirty-six wounded.
It is probable that the latter account is nearest to the truth, as
the commander of a captured vessel has not always as good
an opportunity as his captor, to ascertain his own loss. The
Hyder Ally had four killed, and eleven wounded.

This action has been justly deemed one of the most brilliant that ever occurred under the American flag. It was
fought in the presence of a vastly superior force that was not
engaged; and the ship taken was, in every essential respect,
superior to her conqueror. The disproportion in metal, between a six-pounder and a nine-pounder, is one-half; and the
Monk, besides being a heavier and a larger ship, had the most
men. Both vessels appeared before Philadelphia a few hours
after the action, bringing with them even their dead; and most
of the leading facts were known to the entire community of
that place.

The steadiness with which Captain Barney protected his
convoy, the gallantry and conduct with which he engaged,
and the perseverance with which he covered the retreat of his
prize, are all deserving of high praise. Throughout the whole
affair, this officer discovered the qualities of a great naval captain; failing in no essential of that distinguished character.

The Monk, her old name having been restored, was taken
into the service of the State of Pennsylvania, and was shortly
after sent on duty in behalf of the United States, to the West-
Indies. During this cruise, Captain Barney, who commanded
her, had a warm engagement with an English brig, supposed
to be a privateer, of equal force, but she escaped from him,
the meeting occurring in the night, and the enemy manœuvring
and sailing particularly well. The name of his antagonist is
not known. In this affair, the Washington received some
damage in her spars, but met with no serious loss.

Massachusetts and South Carolina were the two states that
most exerted themselves, in order to equip cruisers of their
own. As early as September, 1776, one of the vessels of the

former is said to have captured an English sloop of war, after a sharp action ; but we can discover no more than general and vague accounts of the affair.

Among the vessels of Massachusetts was one named after the State itself, and a brig called the Tyrannicide. The latter was a successful cruiser, and made many captures, but she was lost in the unfortunate affair in the Penobscot. It is believed that the Tyrannicide was built expressly for a cruiser. But the favourite officer of this service appears to have been Captain John Foster Williams, who commanded a brig called the Hazard, in 1779. In this vessel, in addition to the action already related with the Active, Captain Williams performed many handsome exploits, proving himself, on all occasions, an officer of merit.

After quitting the Hazard, Captain Williams was transferred to the Protector 20, equally a state ship. In this vessel he had the two actions mentioned in another chapter,—that with the Duff, and that with the Thames,—in both of which this gallant officer greatly distinguished himself. Soon after this brilliant cruise he resumed the command of the Hazard, which was also lost to the state in the unfortunate expedition against the British in the Penobscot. It would probably have been better for Massachusetts had it named this meritorious officer to the command of the naval armament on that occasion. This unhappy affair appears, in a great degree, to have put an end to the maritime efforts of Massachusetts, a state, however, that was active to the last, in aiding the general cause.

Of the vessels of Carolina mention has already been made. In the early part of the war several light cruisers were employed, but as the contest advanced, this State entertained a plan of obtaining a few vessels of force, with an intention of striking a heavier blow than common against the enemy. With this view Commodore Gillon, the officer who was at the head of its little marine, went to Europe, and large amounts of colonial produce were transmitted to him, in order to raise the necessary funds. In his correspondence, this officer complains of the difficulty of procuring the right sort of ships, and much time was lost in fruitless negotiations for that purpose, in both France and Holland. At length an arrangement was entered into, for one vessel, that is so singular as to require particular notice. This vessel was the Indien, which had been laid down by the American commissioners, at Amsterdam, and

11

subsequently presented to France.  She had the dimensions of a small 74, but was a frigate in construction, carrying, however, an armament that consisted of 28 Swedish thirty-sixes on her gun-deck, and of 12 Swedish twelves on her quarter-deck and forecastle, or 40 guns in the whole.  This ship, though strictly the property of France, had been lent by Louis XVI. to the Duke of Luxembourg, who hired her to the State of South Carolina for three years, on condition that the State would insure her, sail her at its own expense, and render to her owner one-fourth of the proceeds of her prizes.  Under this singular compact, the ship, which was named the South Carolina for the occasion, got out in 1781, and made a successful cruise in the narrow seas, sending her prizes into Spain.  Afterwards she proceeded to America, capturing ten sail, with which she went into the Havana.  Here Commodore Gillon, with a view to distress the enemy, accepted the command of the nautical part of an expedition against the Bahamas, that had been set on foot by the Spaniards, and in which other American cruisers joined.  The expedition was successful, and the ship proceeded to Philadelphia.  Commodore Gillon now left her, and after some delay, the South Carolina went to sea in December, 1782, under the orders of Captain Joyner, an officer who had previously served on board her as second in command.  It is probable that the movements of so important a vessel were watched, for she had scarcely cleared the capes, when, after a short running fight, she fell into the hands of the British ship Diomede 44, having the Astrea 32, and the Quebec 32, in company.

The South Carolina was much the heaviest ship that ever sailed under the American flag, until the new frigates were constructed during the war of 1812, and she is described as having been a particularly fast vessel; but her service appears to have been greatly disproportioned to her means.  She cost the state a large sum of money, and is believed to have returned literally nothing to its treasury.  Her loss excited much comment.

Admiral Arbuthnot reports among the " rebel ships of war" taken or sunk at the capture of Charleston, " the Bricole, pierced for 60, mounting 44 guns, twenty-four and eighteen-pounders," &c.  As there never was a vessel of this name in the navy of the United States, it is probable that this ship was another heavy frigate obtained by the State of South Carolina, in Europe.  Although this state had the pecuniary means to equip a better marine than common, it had neither vessels, building-yards, nor seamen.  Most of its vessels were purchased, and its mariners were principally obtained from places out of its limits, Commodore Gillon and Captain Joyner being both natives of Holland.

Thus terminated the first war in which America was engaged as a separate nation, after a struggle that had endured seven years and ten months.  Orders of recall were immediately given to the different cruisers, and the commissions of all privateers and letters of marque were revoked.  The proclamation announcing a cessation of hostilities was made on the 11th of April, when the war finally terminated at all points.

It remains only to say that the navy of the Revolution, like its army, was disbanded at the termination of the struggle, literally leaving nothing behind it, but the recollections of its services and sufferings.

## CHAPTER XIII.

The country was too much exhausted by the war of the revolution to incur the expense of a marine during a time of peace.  But the growing commerce of the country, as well as its unprotected state, excited the cupidity of the Dey of Algiers, who captured the schooner Maine, of Boston, on the 25th of July, 1785.  This unprovoked outrage was succeeded by others, until the government of the United States, after negotiating in the best manner it could for the release of the vessels and captives, found itself under the necessity of arming.  This decided measure was not taken, however, until after the organisation of the government under the new constitution, and during the Presidency of Washington.  The construction of six frigates was authorised by law, and the keels of the following vessels were laid, viz: the Constitution 44, United States 44, President 44, Chesapeake 38, Constellation 38, and Congress 38.

This was the commencement of the actual and permanent marine of the country.  Three of the ships just named are now in use, and two are on foreign stations. In consequence of an arrangement of the difficulties with Algiers, neither of these vessels was launched for some years, the work on them being suspended by an order of government. A navy was so far created, notwithstanding, that the gentlemen appointed to command the frigates, continued in service, as did some of the inferior officers. Their duties were chiefly limited to taking care of the ships that were still on the stocks, and the stores that had been collected. The time was drawing near, however, when a more active and serviceable marine was established.

The President, in his annual speech to Congress, December, 1796, strongly recommended laws for the gradual increase of the navy. It is worthy of remark, as appears by documents published at the time, that, the peace obtained from the Dey of Algiers cost the government of the United States near a million of dollars, a sum quite sufficient to have kept the barbarian's port hermetically blockaded until he should have humbly sued for permission to send a craft to sea.

While these events were gradually leading to the formation of a navy, the maritime powers of Europe became involved in what was nearly a general war, and their measures of hostility against each other had a direct tendency to trespass on the privileges of neutrals. It would exceed the limits of this work to enter into the history of that system of gradual encroachments on the rights of the American people, which distinguished the measures of both the two great belligerents, in the war that succeeded the French Revolution; or the height of audacity to which the cruisers of France, in particular, carried their depredations, most probably mistaking the amount of the influence of their own country, over the great body of the American nation. Not only did they capture British ships within our waters, but they actually took the same liberties with Americans also. All attempts to obtain redress from the French government failed, and unable to submit any longer to such injustice, the president, in April, 1798, recommended to Congress a plan of armament and defence, that it was hoped would have the effect to check these aggressions, and avert an open conflict. Down to this period, the whole military organization of the country, was entrusted to one department, that of war; and a letter from the secretary of this branch of the government, to the chairman of a committee to devise means of protection and defence, was the form in which this high interest was brought before the nation, through its representatives. Twenty small vessels were advised to be built, and, in the event of an open rupture, it was recommended to Congress to authorise the President to cause six ships of the line to be constructed. This force was in addition to the six frigates authorised by the law of 1794.

The United States 44, Constitution 44, and Constellation 38, had been got afloat the year previous.

The United States was the first vessel that was got into the water, under the present organisation of the navy. She was launched at Philadelphia, on the 10th of July, 1797, and the Constellation followed her on the 7th of September.

Congress acted so far on the recommendation of the secretary of war, as to authorise the President to cause to be built, purchased, or hired, twelve vessels, none of which were to exceed twenty-two guns, and to see that they were duly equipped and manned. To effect these objects $950,000 were appropriated. This law passed on the 27th of April, 1798, and on the 30th, a regular navy department was formally created. Benjamin Stoddart, of Georgetown, in the District of Columbia, was the first secretary put at the head of this important branch of the government, entering on his duties in June of the same year.

Down to this moment, the old treaty of alliance, formed between France and the United States during the war of the Revolution, and some subsequent conventions, were legally in existence; but Congress by law solemnly abrogated them all, on the 7th of July, 1798, on the plea that they had been repeatedly disregarded by France, and that the latter country continued, in the face of the most solemn remonstrances, to practise a system of predatory warfare on the commerce of the country.

On the 11th of July, 1798, a new marine corps was established by law, the old one having been disbanded with the navy of the Revolution, to which it had properly belonged. On the 16th of the same month, a law was passed to construct three more frigates. This act was expressed in such terms as to enable the government immediately to complete the ships commenced under the law of 1794, and which had been suspended under that of 1796. The whole force authorised by law, on the 16th of July, consequently, consisted of twelve frigates; twelve ships of a force between 20 and 24 guns, inclusive; and six smaller sloops, besides galleys and revenue cutters; making a total of thirty active cruisers.

11 *

## CHAPTER XIV.

ALTHOUGH three of the frigates were launched in 1797, neither was quite ready for service when the necessities of the country required that vessels should be sent to sea. The want of suitable spars and guns, and other naval stores, had retarded the labour on the frigates, while vessels had been readily bought for the sloops of war, which, though deficient in many of the qualities and conveniences of regular cruisers, were made to answer the exigencies of the times. Among others that had been thus provided, was an Indiaman, called the Ganges. Retaining her name, this vessel was brought into the service, armed and equipped as a 24, and put under the command of Captain Richard Dale, who was ordered to sail on a cruise on the 22d of May. This ship, then, was the first man-of-war that ever got to sea since the present organisation of the navy, or since the United States have existed under the constitution. Captain Dale was instructed to do no more than pertains generally to the authority of a vessel of war, that is cruising on the coast of the country to which she belongs, in a time of peace; the law that empowered seizures not passing until a few days after he had sailed. His cruising ground extended from the east end of Long Island to the capes of Virginia, with a view to cover, as much as possible, the three important ports of Baltimore, Philadelphia, and New York; and, in anticipation of the act of the 28th of May, Captain Dale was directed to appear off the capes of the Delaware on the 12th of June, to receive new orders. On that day, instructions were accordingly sent to him to capture all French cruisers that were hovering on the coast with hostile views on the American commerce, and to recapture any of their prizes he might happen to fall in with.

The Constellation 38, Captain Truxtun, and the Delaware 20, Captain Decatur, went to sea, early in June, under the last of the foregoing orders, and with directions to cruise to the southward of Cape Henry, as far as the coast of Florida. When a few days out, the Delaware fell in with the French privateer schooner Le Croyable 14, with a crew of 70 men. Being satisfied that this vessel had already made several prizes, and that she was actually cruising on soundings, in search of more, Captain Decatur took her, and sent her into the Delaware. As the law directing the capture of all armed French vessels passed soon after her arrival, Le Croyable was condemned, and bought into the navy. She was called the Retaliation, and the command of her was given to Lieutenant Bainbridge.

Le Croyable was, consequently, not only the first capture made, in what it is usual to term the war of 1798, but she was the first vessel ever taken by the present navy, or under the present form of government.

The activity employed by the administration, as well as by the navy, now astonished those who had so long been accustomed to believe the American people disposed to submit to any insult, in preference to encountering the losses of a war. The United States 44, Captain Barry, went to sea early in July, and proceeded to cruise to the eastward. This ship carried out with her many young gentlemen, who have since risen to high rank and distinction in the service. But the law of the 9th of that month, occurring immediately afterwards, the government altered its policy entirely, and determined to send, at once, a strong force among the West-India islands, where the enemy abounded, and where the commerce of the country was most exposed to his depredations. On the 11th, instructions were sent to Captain Barry, who now hoisted a broad pennant, to go off Cape Cod, with the Delaware 20, Captain Decatur, where he would find the Herald 18, Captain Sevier, that officer preferring active service in a small vessel, to waiting for the frigate to which he had been appointed, and then to proceed directly to the West-Indies, keeping to windward.

That well-known frigate, the Constitution 44, had been launched at Boston, September 20th 1797 ; and she first got under way, July 20th of this year, under Captain Samuel Nicholson, who, in August, with four revenue vessels in company, was directed to cruise on the coast, to the southward of Cape Henry.

Early in August, the Constellation 38, Captain Truxtun, and the Baltimore 20, Captain Phillips, went to the Havana, and brought a convoy of sixty sail in safety to the United States ; several French cruisers then lying in the port, ready to follow the merchantmen, but for this force, the presence of which prevented them from appearing outside the castle. By the close of the year, a force consisting of three frigates eleven sloops and brigs, and nine smaller vessels, was at sea; most of the vessels being either in the West Indies, or employed in convoying between the islands and the United States.

Besides the vessels named, many more were already laid down; and so great was the zeal of the commercial towns, in particular, that no less than two frigates, and five large sloops were building by subscription, in the different principal ports. In addition to this force, must be enumerated eight large galleys, that were kept on the southern coast, to defend their inlets.

It has been stated that the privateer Le Croyable 14, captured by the Delaware 20, had been taken into the service, under the name of the Retaliation. In November, 1798, the Montezuma 20, Captain Murray, Norfolk 18, Captain Williams, and the Retaliation 12, Lieutenant-Commandant Bainbridge, were cruising in company off Guadaloupe, when three sails were made to the eastward, and soon after two more to the westward. Captain Murray, who was the senior officer, was led to suppose, from circumstances, that the vessels in the eastern board were British; and speaking the Retaliation, he ordered Lieutenant Bainbridge to reconnoitre them, while with the Norfolk in company, he gave chase, himself, in the Montezuma, to the two vessels to the westward. The Retaliation, in obedience to these orders, immediately hauled up towards the three strangers, and getting near enough for signals, she showed her own number, with a view to ascertain if they were Americans. Finding that he was not understood, Lieutenant Bainbridge mistook the strangers for English cruisers, knowing that several were on the station, and unluckily permitted them to approach so near, that when their real characters were ascertained, it was too late to escape. The leading ship, a French frigate, was an uncommonly fast sailer, and she was soon near enough to open her fire. It was not long before another frigate came up, when the Retaliation was compelled to lower her flag. Thus did this unlucky vessel become the first cruiser taken by both parties, in this war. The frigates by which the Retaliation was captured, proved to be the Volontaire 36, and the Insurgente 32, the former carrying 44, and the latter 40 guns. Mr. Bainbridge was put on board the Volontaire, while the Insurgente, perceiving that the schooner was safe, continued to carry sail in chase of the

Montezuma and Norfolk. As soon as a prize crew could be thrown into the Retaliation, the Volontaire crowded sail after her consort. The chase now became exceedingly interesting, the two American vessels being fully aware, by the capture of the schooner, that they had to deal with an enemy. The Insurgente was one of the fastest ships in the world, and her commander an officer of great skill and resolution. The two American vessels were small for their rates, and, indeed, were over-rated, the Montezuma being a little ship of only 347 tons, and the Norfolk a brig of 200. Their armaments were merely nines and sixes ; shot that would be scarcely regarded in a conflict with frigates. The officers of the Volontaire collected on the forecastle of their ship to witness the chase ; and the Insurgente being, by this time, a long way ahead, Captain St. Laurent, the commander of the Volontaire, asked Mr. Bainbridge, who was standing near him, what might be the force of the two American vessels. With great presence of mind, Mr. Bainbridge answered, that the ship carried 28 twelves, and the brig 20 nines. As this account quite doubled the real force of the Americans, Captain St. Laurent, who was senior to the commander of the Insurgente, immediately threw out a signal to the latter to relinquish the chase. This was an unmilitary order, even admitting the fact to have been as stated, for the Insurgente would have been fully able to employ two such vessels until the Volontaire could come up ; but the recent successes of the English had rendered the French cruisers wary, and the Americans and English, as seamen, were probably identified in the minds of the enemy. The signal caused as much surprise to Captain Murray, in the Montezuma, as to Captain Barreault, of the Insurgente; for the latter, an excellent and spirited officer, had got so near his chases as to have made out their force, and to feel certain of capturing both. The signal was obeyed, however, and the Montezuma and Norfolk escaped.

When the two French vessels rejoined each other, Captain Barreault naturally expressed his surprise at having been recalled under such circumstances. An explanation followed, when the *ruse* that had been practised by Mr. Bainbridge, was discovered. It is to the credit of the French officers, that, while they were much vexed at the results of this artifice, they never visited the offender with their displeasure.

The United States 44, and Delaware 20, captured the privateers Sans Pareil 16, and Jaloux 14, in the course of the autumn, and sent them in.

Thus terminated the year 1798, leaving the United States with a hastily collected, an imperfectly organised, and un-equally disciplined squadron of ships, it is true; but a service that contained the germ of all that is requisite to make an ac-tive, an efficient, and a glorious marine.

## CHAPTER XV.

THE year 1799 opened with no departure from the policy laid down by the government, and the building and equipping of the different ships in various parts of the country, were pressed with as much diligence as the public resources would then allow.   In the course of this season, many vessels were launched, and most of them got to sea within the year.   Inclu-ding all, those that were employed in 1798, those that were put in commission early in the ensuing year, and those that were enabled to quit port nearer to its close, the entire active naval force of the United States, in 1799, would seem to have been composed of the following vessels, viz:

| United States | 44, | Delaware | 20, |
|---|---|---|---|
| Constitution | 44, | Baltimore | 20, |
| Congress | 38, | Patapsco | 20, |
| Constellation | 38, | Maryland | 20, |
| Essex | 32, | Herald | 18, |
| General Greene | 28, | Norfolk | 18, |
| Boston | 28, | Richmond | 18, |
| Adams | 28, | Pinckney | 18, |
| John Adams | 28, | Warren | 18, |
| Portsmouth | 24, | Eagle, | 18, |
| Connecticut | 24, | Pickering | 14, |
| Ganges | 24, | Augusta | 14, |
| Geo. Washington, | 24, | Scammel | 14, |
| Merrimack | 24, | Enterprise | 12. |

To these must be added a few revenue vessels, though most of this description of cruisers appear to have been kept on the coast throughout this year.   As yet, the greatest confusion and irregularity prevailed in the rating, no uniform system appearing to have been adopted.   The vessels built by the different cities, and presented to the public, in particular, were rated too high, from a natural desire to make the offering as respectable as possible ; and it does not appear to have been thought expedient, on the part of the government, prematurely to correct the mistakes.

On the 9th of February, the Constellation 38, Commodore Truxtun, was cruising on her prescribed ground, Nevis bearing W. S. W., distant five leagues, when she made a large ship in the southern board.   The Constellation being to windward at the moment, Commodore Truxtun ran down towards the stranger, who now set American colours, when the private signals were shown.   As the chase was unable to answer, he seemed to think further disguise unnecessary, for he hoisted the French ensign, and fired a gun to windward, by way of a challenge, keeping under easy sail, to invite the contest.   This was the first opportunity that had occurred since the close of the Revolution, for an American vessel of war to get alongside of an enemy, of a force likely to render a combat certain, and the officers and men of the Constellation displayed the greatest eagerness to engage.   On the other hand, the stranger betrayed no desire to disappoint his enemy, waiting gallantly for her to come down.   When the Constellation had got abeam of the French frigate, and so near as to have been several times hailed, she opened her fire, which was returned promptly and with spirit.   The Constellation drew gradually ahead, both ships maintaining a fierce cannonade.   The former suffered most in her sails and rigging, and while under the heaviest of the fire of her antagonist, the fore-topmast was badly wounded, quite near the lower cap.   The fore-top was commanded by Mr. David Porter, a midshipman of great promise, and finding that his hails to communicate this important circumstance were disregarded, in the heat of the combat, this young officer took on himself the responsibility of cutting the stoppers and of lowering the yard.   By thus relieving the spar of the pressure of the sail, he prevented the fall of the topmast and all its hamper.   In the mean time the weight and effect of the fire were altogether in favour of the Constellation, and notwithstanding the injury she received in her fore-topmast, that ship was soon able to throw in two or three raking broadsides, which decided the combat.   After maintaining a close contest of about an hour, the Constellation shot out of the smoke, wore round, and hauling athwart her antagonist's stern, was ready again with every gun to rake her, when the enemy struck.

The prize proved to be the French frigate l'Insurgente, Captain Barreault, the vessel that has already been mentioned, as having captured the Retaliation, and chasing the Montezuma and Norfolk, and one of the fastest ships in the world.   She was much cut up, and had sustained a loss of 70 men, in killed and wounded ;  29 of the former, and 41 of the latter. The Constellation, besides the loss of the fore-topmast, which had to be shifted, was much damaged aloft, suffering no material injury in her hull, however, and had only 3 men wounded. Among the latter, was Mr. James M'Donough, a midshipman, who had a foot shot off.   Early in the combat, one of the men flinched from his gun, and he was killed by the third lieutenant, to whose division he belonged.

The Insurgente's armament consisted of 40 guns, French twelves, on her main-deck battery, and her complement of men was 409.   She was a ship a little heavier than a regular 32, which would probably have been her rate in the English marine, although a French twelve-pound shot weighs nearly thirteen English pounds.   On this occasion, the Constellation is said to have carried but 38 guns, twelve less than have been put upon her since the introduction of carronades, and she had a crew of 309 men.   But the main-deck battery of the Constellation was composed of twenty-fours, a gun altogether too heavy for her size and strength, and from which she was relieved at the termination of this cruise, by exchanging her armament for eighteens.

The Insurgente struck about half past three in the afternoon, and Mr. Rodgers,* the first lieutenant of the Constellation, together with Mr. Porter,† and eleven men, were thrown on board her, to take possession, and to superintend the removal of the prisoners.   It began to blow, and when the darkness rendered it necessary to defer the duty, 173 of the prize's crew were still in her.   The wind continued to rise, and, notwithstanding every effort, the ships separated in the darkness.

The situation of Mr. Rodgers was now exceedingly critical. The vessel was still covered with the wreck, while the wound-

* Late Commodore Rodgers.          † Commodore Porter.

ed, and even the dead were lying scattered about her decks, and the prisoners early discovered a disposition to rise. The gratings had been thrown overboard by the people of the Insurgente after she struck, and no handcuffs could be found. Fortunately, Mr. Rodgers was a man of great personal resolution, and of herculean strength, while Mr. Porter, though young and comparatively slight, was as good a second, in such trying circumstances, as any one could desire. As soon as it was ascertained that the prisoners could not be got out of the ship that night, they were all sent into the lower hold, the fire-arms were secured, and a sentinel was placed at each hatchway, armed to the teeth, with positive orders to shoot every man who should attempt to appear on deck, without permission. In this awkward situation, Mr. Rodgers and his party continued three days, unable to sleep, compelled to manage a frigate, and to watch their prisoners with the utmost vigilance, as the latter were constantly on the look-out for an opportunity to retake the ship. At the end of that time, they carried the Insurgente, in triumph, into St. Kitts, where they found that the Constellation had already arrived.

One of the effects of the victory of the Constellation was to render the navy still more popular, and the most respectable families of the nation discovered greater anxiety than ever to get their sons enrolled on its lists. The new ships were put into the water as fast as possible, and, as soon as manned and equipped, were sent on the different cruising grounds. L'Insurgente was taken into the service as a thirty-six, the command of her was given to Captain Murray, late of the Montezuma 20, and she was permitted to cruise with a roving commission.

In the mean time, the care of the government appeared to extend itself, and it began to cast its eyes beyond the hazards of the American seas.

At the close of the year, the Congress 38, Captain Sever, and Essex 32, Captain Preble, sailed with orders to convoy vessels as far as Batavia. The former of these vessels met with an accident to which all new ships are liable on quitting America in the winter. Her rigging having been set up in cold weather, it became slack when she got into the gulf stream, where she also encountered a strong southerly gale, and she lost not only all her masts, but her bowsprit. The main-mast went while Mr. Bosworth, the fourth lieutenant, was aloft, endeavouring to lower the main-topmast, by which acci-

12

dent that officer was lost. The crew of the top were all happily saved.

The Congress returned to port, for repairs, but Captain Preble proceeded on his cruise, carrying the pennant, for the first time in a regular cruiser, to the eastward of the Cape of Good Hope.

The active measures resorted to by the American government having better disposed that of France to negotiate, and pledges having been given that new ministers would be received with more respect than had been shown to those last sent, who had met with insults and neglect, the United States 44, Commodore Barry, sailed from Newport, Rhode Island, on the 3d of November, having on board envoys to the French Directory. Notwithstanding these measures to obtain peace, Congress proceeded in the legislation necessary to establish a marine. Many of the laws for the government of the navy were amended, and new regulations were introduced as substitutes for such of the old ones as were found defective. The appropriation for the support of the navy, during the year 1800, the marine corps included, amounted to $2,482,953 90.

The new year consequently opened with increased efforts to continue the singular war that had now existed eighteen months. Many acquisitions were made to the navy, and the following is a list of the vessels that appear to have been employed in the course of the season, principally in the West-Indies, viz:

| | | | |
|---|---|---|---|
| United States | 44, | Portsmouth | 24, |
| Constitution | 44, | Merrimack | 24, |
| President | 44, | Delaware | 20, |
| Constellation | 38, | Baltimore | 20, |
| Congress | 38, | Maryland | 20, |
| Chesapeake | 38, | Patapsco | 20, |
| Philadelphia | 38, | Herald | 18, |
| New York | 36, | Norfolk | 18, |
| Insurgente | 36, | Richmond | 18, |
| Essex | 32, | Pinckney | 18, |
| General Greene | 28, | Warren | 18, |
| Adams | 28, | Eagle | 14, |
| John Adams | 28, | Pickering | 14, |
| Boston | 28, | Augusta | 14, |
| Geo. Washington | 24, | Scammel | 14, |
| Connecticut | 24, | Enterprise | 12, |
| Ganges | 24, | Experiment | 12. |
| Trumbull | 24, | | |

By this time, the revenue vessels, with the exception of one or two, appear to have been retained at home, and in the foregoing list, no mention is made of galleys. Laws had been previously passed for the construction of six seventy-fours, and contracts were already made for the collection of the necessary materials.

The cruising portion of the vessels were distributed in two principal squadrons, the one on the St. Domingo station under the orders of Commodore Talbot, whose broad pennant was flying in the Constitution 44, and the other on the Guadaloupe station, under the orders, first of Commodore Truxtun, in the Constellation 38, and next under the orders of Commodore Decatur, in the Philadelphia 38. The force of the former varied from seven to twelve vessels, while that of the latter, in April, consisted of thirteen sail.

Notwithstanding this exhibition of a respectable and active force, the great facilities offered by the islands, and the strong temptations that were to be found in the American West-India trade, then one of the most considerable of the country, induced the enemy to be constantly on the alert, and the seas were still swarming with French cruisers, principally privateers. Guadaloupe, in particular, was distinguished for the number of captures made by its vessels; and it was for this reason that we now find the heaviest American squadron cruising in that vicinity.

On the 1st of February, 1800, the Constellation 38, Commodore Truxtun, was again off the island of Guadaloupe, alone, Basseterre bearing east five leagues, when a sail was seen to the southeast, steering westward. Commodore Truxtun at first supposed the ship in sight to be a large English merchantman, from Martinico, of which he had some knowledge, and, unwilling to be drawn to leeward of his cruising ground, he hoisted English colours, by way of inducing her to run down and speak him. This invitation being disregarded, sail was made in chase, the Constellation gaining fast on the stranger. As the former drew nearer, the ship to leeward was discovered to be a French vessel of war, when the English colours were hauled down, and the Constellation cleared for action. The chase was now distinctly made out to be a heavy frigate mounting 52 guns. As her metal was in all probability equal to her rate, the only circumstance to equalise this disparity against the Constellation, was the fact that the stranger

was very deep, which was accounted for by a practice of sending valuable articles to France, at that time, in the ships of
war, as the safest means of transmission.   Commodore Truxtun was not discouraged by his discovery, but continued to
carry every stitch of canvass that would draw.   Towards
noon, however, the wind became light, and the enemy had the
advantage in sailing.   In this manner, with variable breezes,
and a smooth sea, the chase continued until noon on the 2d,
when the wind freshened, and the Constellation again drew
ahead.   By the middle of the afternoon, the wind had every
appearance of standing, and the chase was rising fast.   It was
eight in the evening, nevertheless, before the two ships were
within speaking distance of each other, the stranger having
come up to the wind a little, and the Constellation doubling on
her weather quarter.   Commodore Truxtun was about to speak
to the enemy, when the latter opened a fire from his stern and
quarter guns.   In a few moments the Constellation, having
drawn still more on the weather quarter of the chase, poured in
a broadside, and the action began in earnest.   It was a little
past eight when the firing commenced, and it was maintained
with vigour until near one in the morning, the two ships, most
of the time, running free, side by side, when the stranger
hauled up, and drew out of the combat.   Orders were given
on board the Constellation to brace up in chase; but at this
moment, a report was brought to Commodore Truxtun that the
main-mast was supported almost solely by the wood, every
shroud having been shot away, and many of them so repeatedly
cut as to render the use of stoppers impossible.   At that time,
as has been said already, masts were usually, in the American
navy, of single sticks, and the spars, when they gave way,
went altogether.   Aware of this danger, Commodore Truxtun
ordered the men from the guns, to secure this all-important
mast, with the hope of getting alongside of his enemy again,
and, judging by the feebleness of her resistance for the last
hour, with the certainty of taking her, could this object be
effected.   But no exertion could obviate the calamity, the
mast coming by the board within a few minutes after the enemy had sheered off.   All the topmen, including Mr. Jarvis,
the midshipman in command aloft, went over the side with the
spars, and, that gallant young officer, who had refused to
abandon his post, with all but one man, was lost.
    The Constellation was no longer in a situation to resume

the action, and her enemy was in a far worse condition, with the exception that she still retained spars enough to enable her to escape. Finding it impossible to reach any friendly port to windward, as soon as the wreck was clear of his ship, Commodore Truxtun bore up for Jamaica, where he arrived in safety.

In this close and hard-fought action, the Constellation had 14 men killed and 25 wounded, 11 of the latter dying of their injuries. Her antagonist afterwards got into Curaçoa, dismasted, and in a sinking condition, reporting herself to have had 50 of her people killed, and 110 wounded, in an engagement with the Constellation, that had lasted five hours within pistol-shot. This statement is now known to be essentially true, and it enables us to form a comparative estimate of the merits of the action. The French vessel proved to be la Vengeance, Captain Pitot.

The armament of the Constellation had been changed since her action with the Insurgente, and her main-deck battery now consisted of 28 eighteens, and she had 10 twenty-four-pound carronades on her quarter-deck, which were among the first, if not the very first guns of this description ever introduced into the American navy. Her crew was composed of 310 souls.

The force of la Vengeance has been ascertained to have been 28 eighteens, 16 twelves, and 8 forty-two-pound carronades. Her crew has been variously stated as having been between 400 and 500 men. The metal was all according to the French mode of weighing, which adds one pound to every twelve.

There is no question that the Constellation engaged a materially superior force, or any doubt that she would have brought la Vengeance into port, but for the loss of the mast. It is even said that la Vengeance did strike her colours three times, during the action, but finding that the Constellation continued her fire, they were re-hoisted. If such an event occurred, it must have arisen from the fact that it was not perceived in the obscurity of the night. Commodore Truxtun gained a great name by this action, and on his return to America for repairs, he was appointed to the President 44, then fitting for sea. Congress gave him a gold medal for his good conduct, and the gallantry of Mr. Jarvis was approved in a solemn resolution. The Constellation was now given to Captain Murray, who had just returned from a short cruise in the

12 *

Insurgente, and that officer went in her to the West-Indies, where she joined the squadron under Commodore Talbot.

The latter officer had been cruising for some months on the St. Domingo station, and about this time he planned an expedition that was quite in character with his own personal enterprises during the war of the Revolution.

It was ascertained that a valuable French letter of marque, was lying in Port Platte, a small harbour on the Spanish side of the Island of St. Domingo, and as she was a dangerous ship on account of her sailing, Commodore Talbot determined to attempt cutting her out. This vessel had been the British packet the Sandwich, and she only waited to complete a cargo of coffee, to make a run for France. The legality of the enterprise was more than questionable, but the French picaroons received so much favour in the Spanish colonies, that the American officers were less scrupulous than they might otherwise have been.

As soon as it was determined to make the effort, Mr. Hull, the first lieutenant of the Constitution went in, at night, with one of the frigate's cutters, and reconnoitred. Commodore Talbot was compelled to defer the expedition, for want of a craft proper to avoid suspicion, when fortunately one was found by accident. An American sloop called the Sally had been employed on the coast of the island, under circumstances that rendered her liable to detention, and she was brought out of one of the small French ports, by a boat of the frigate. This sloop had recently left Port Platte, with an intention of soon returning there, and she, at once, afforded all the facilities that could be desired.

Commodore Talbot, accordingly, threw a party of seamen and marines into the Sally, and giving the command to Mr. Hull, that officer was directed to proceed on the duty without further delay. The sloop was manned at sea, to escape detection, and she sailed at an hour that would enable her to reach Port Platte, about noon of the succeeding day. In the course of the night, while running down for her port, under easy sail, a shot suddenly flew over the Sally, and, soon after, an English frigate ranged up alongside. Mr. Hull hove-to, and when the boarding lieutenant got on the sloop's deck, where he found so large a party of men and officers in naval uniforms, he was both startled and surprised. He was told the object of the expedition, however, and expressed his disappointment, as his own ship was only waiting to let the Sandwich complete her cargo, in order to cut her out herself!

The Sally's movements were so well timed, as to permit her to arrive off the harbour's mouth at the proper hour. The Sandwich was lying with her broadside bearing on the approach, and there was a battery at no great distance to protect her. As soon as near enough to be seen, Mr. Hull sent most of his people below, and getting an anchor ready over the stern, to bring the sloop up with, he stood directly for the enemy's bows. So admirably was every thing arranged, that no suspicion was excited, the Sally ran the Sandwich aboard, and the Constitution's people went into her, and carried her without the loss of a man. At the same moment, Captain Carmick landed with the marines, entered the battery, and spiked the guns.

Notwithstanding a great commotion on shore, the Americans now went to work to secure their prize. The Sandwich was stripped to a girtline, and every thing was below. Before sunset she had royal yards across, her guns were scaled, her new crew was quartered, and soon after she weighed, beat out of the harbour, and joined the frigate.

No enterprise of the sort was ever executed with greater steadiness, or discipline. Mr. Hull gained great credit by the neatness with which he fulfilled his orders, and it was not possible for an officer to have been better sustained; the absence of loss, in all cases of surprise, in which the assailed have the means of resistance, being one of the strongest proofs not only of the gallantry and spirit, but of the coolness of the assailants.

In the end, however, this capture, which was clearly illegal, cost the Constitution dear. Not only was the Sandwich given up, but all the prize money of the cruise went to pay damages.

Early in May, the Chesapeake 38, went to sea, under the command of Captain S. Barron. Her first duty was to convey a quantity of specie from Charleston to Philadelphia, after which she proceeded to cruise between the coast and the West-India islands.

The Insurgente 36 had been given to Captain Fletcher, when Captain Murray was transferred to the Constellation, and in July she sailed on a cruise, with instructions to keep between longitudes 66° and 68°, and to run as far south as 30° N. L. After this ship left the capes of Virginia, no authentic accounts, with the exception of a few private letters sent in by vessels spoken at sea, were ever received of her. She had been ordered to cruise a short time in the latitude and longitude mentioned, after which her commander was left at liberty to pursue his own discretion, provided he returned to Annapolis within eight weeks. Thirty-nine years have elapsed and no further tidings of any belonging to this ill-fated ship have ever reached their friends.

The Pickering 14, Captain Hillar, also sailed in August, for the Guadaloupe station, and never returned. As in the case of the Insurgente, all on board perished, no information that could be relied on ever having been obtained of the manner in which these vessels were lost. Vague rumours were set afloat at the time, and it was even affirmed that they had run foul of each other in a gale, a tale that was substantiated by no testimony, and which was probably untrue, as the Pickering was sent to a station, which the Insurgente, under discretionary orders, would be little apt to seek, since it was known to be already filled with American cruisers. These two ships swelled the list of vessels of war that had been lost in this manner to three, viz : the Saratoga 16, the Insurgente 36, and the Pickering 14 ; to which may be added the Reprisal 16, though the cook of the latter sloop was saved.

The nature of the warfare, which was now confined principally to chases and conflicts with small fast-sailing privateers, and a species of corsair that went by the local name of picaroons, or with barges that ventured no great distance at sea, soon satisfied the government that, to carry on the service to advantage, it required a species of vessel different from the heavy, short, sloop of twenty, or twenty-four guns, of which so many were used in the beginning of the contest. Two schooners had been built with this view, and each of them fully proved their superiority over the old clumsy cruiser, that had been inherited, as it might be, from the Revolution. One of these vessels was called the Experiment, and the other the Enterprise, and they were rated at twelve guns. The modern improvements, however, did not extend to the armaments of even these schooners, the old-fashioned six-pounder being still used, where an 18lb. carronade would now be introduced. The Enterprise, Lieutenant Commandant Shaw, was very active this year, capturing la Citoyenne, privateer, of 6 guns and 47 men ; la Seine 6, and 57 men ; l'Aigle 10, and 78 men ; la Pauline 6, and 40 men ; and la Guadaloupéenne 7, and 45 men. Most of these vessels resisted, though neither was of a force to afford much hope of success. La Citoyenne had 4 killed and 11 wounded before she struck; la Seine made an obstinate resistance, holding out until she had 24 of her crew killed and wounded, which was near half her complement; and l'Aigle lost 12 men, among whom was her first lieutenant, in an action of fifteen minutes. In the last affair the Enterprise had three men killed and wounded.

Near the close of her cruise, the Enterprise made a strange sail a long distance to windward, late in the day, and hauled up for her. Night coming on, the chase was lost sight of in the darkness, when the schooner hove-to, to keep her station. When the day dawned the stranger, a brig, was seen to windward as before, and nearly in the position in which she had last been observed. Both vessels now discovered a disposition to close. At noon the Enterprise made the American signal, which was not answered, the brig showing English colours. The signals that had been established between the English and the American commanders were next shown, but the stranger could not reply. Believing the brig to be an enemy of a force at least equal to his own, Lieutenant Commandant Shaw now set his ensign as a challenge to come down, but, instead of complying, the chase immediately hauled his wind. The Enterprise began turning to windward on short tacks, and sailing uncommonly fast, it was soon apparent that the enemy would be overhauled.

As soon as the French were satisfied that escape was impossible, they cleared for action, and waiting until the Enterprise was within half a mile to leeward, they began to fire. Instead of returning a gun, Lieutenant Commandant Shaw kept the schooner under all her canvass, and, about half an hour after the brig had opened on him, he tacked in her wake, and ranged up handsomely under her lee, within pistol-shot. As her guns bore, the Enterprise now poured in a close and destructive fire, which lasted for a little more than an hour, when the brig's fore-topmast being shot away, and the vessel otherwise seriously injured, she struck.

The prize was the Flambeau privateer. She mounted 14 guns, and had more than 100 men. Her loss was very heavy, about half her crew having been killed and wounded. The Enterprise had 3 men killed and 7 wounded. This little affair was considered one of the warmest combats of the war, and it is seldom that so sharp a conflict occurs between vessels of so small a force.

Lieutenant Shaw was justly applauded for his activity while in command of this schooner, recapturing eleven American vessels, besides taking those just mentioned, in a cruise of only eight months. It was a proof of the greater efficiency of this description of vessel than any other, in a warfare of such a nature, that the Enterprise, a schooner of only 165 tons, carrying an armament of 12 light guns, and with a crew that varied from 60 to 75 men, destroyed more of the enemy's privateers, and afforded as much protection to the trade of the country, as any frigate employed in the war.

In March, the Boston 28, Captain Little, being near the Point of St. Marks, having a merchant brig in tow, on her way to Port-au-Prince, nine barges were discovered pulling towards the vessels, coming from the small island of Gonaives, with every appearance of hostile intentions. The barges were large, as usual, pulled 20 oars, and contained from 30 to 40 men each. As soon as their characters were properly made out, the guns of the Boston were housed, and the ship was otherwise disguised. This stratagem succeeded so far as to draw the barges within gun-shot; but discovering their mistake before they got as near as could be wished, they turned and began to retreat. The Boston now cast off her tow, made sail in chase, ran out her guns, and opened her fire. For two hours she was enabled to keep some of the barges within reach of her shot, and three of them, with all their crews, were sunk. The remainder did not escape without receiving more or less injury.

After this punishment of the picaroons, which were often guilty of the grossest excesses, the Boston, having been home to refit, was directed to cruise a short time, previously to going on the Guadaloupe station again, between the American coast and the West-India islands. While in the discharge of this duty, November, 1800, in lat. 22° 50' N., and long. 51° W., she made a French cruiser, which, instead of avoiding her, evidently sought an encounter. Both parties being willing, the ships were soon in close action, when, after a plain, hard-fought combat of two hours, the enemy struck. The prize proved to be the French corvette le Berceau, Captain Senes, mounting 24 guns, and with a crew a little exceeding 200 men. The Berceau was much cut up, and shortly after the action her fore and main-masts went. Her loss in killed and wounded was never ascertained, but from the number of the latter found in her, it was probably between 30 and 40 men. Among the former were her first lieutenant, master, boatswain, and gunner. The Boston mounted eight more light guns than the Berceau, and had about an equal number of men. She had 4 killed and 11 wounded. Among the latter was her purser, Mr. Young, who died of his injuries. The Berceau was a singularly fine vessel of her class, and had the reputation of being one of the fastest ships in the French marine. Like the combat between the Constellation and l'Insurgente, the superiority of force was certainly in favour of the American ship, on this occasion, but the execution was every way in proportion to the difference.

The year 1800 was actively employed on both sides in the West-Indies, for while the force of the French in vessels of war seemed to decrease, as those of England and America increased, the privateers still abounded. A great many American merchantmen were captured, and the recaptures also amounted to a number that it is now difficult to ascertain, but which is known to have been large. Most of the privateers were small schooners, filled with men, sufficient to subdue a letter of marque by boarding; but, as they offered no resistance to any of the cruisers except the smallest, a brief catalogue of the prizes taken by the different large vessels, will at once give an idea of the nature of the service that was performed by the West-India squadrons during this year. The Baltimore 20, Captain Cowper, took la Brilliante Jeunesse 12, with a crew of 62 men, and a vessel whose name is not known; the Merrimack 24, Captain Brown, the Phenix 14, with 128 men; the Connecticut 24, Captain Tryon, le Piège 2, with 50 men, l'Unité 1, with 50 men, and le Chou Chou; the Boston 28, Captain Little, la Fortune, l'Heureux, and an open boat; Pickering 14, Captain Hillar, la Voltigeuse 10, with 60 men, the Fly, and l'Active 12, with 60 men; Boston 32, in company with different vessels, the Flying Fish, la Gourde, le Pelican, and l'Espoir; Herald 18 and Augusta 14, la Mutine 6, with 60 men; John Adams 28, Captain Cross, le Jason, with 50 men, la Decade; the Trumbull 24, Captain Jewett, la Peggie, la Vengeance 10, and la Tullie; Enterprise 12, Lieutenant Commandant Sterrett, l'Amour de la Patrie 6, with 72 men; the Patapsco 18, Captain Geddes, la Dorade 6, with 46 men; the Adams 28, Captain Morris, l'Heureuse Rencontre 4, with 50 men, le Gambeau, 4 swivels and 16 men, la Renommée, the Dove, and le Massena 6, with 49 men. Several of the frigates also made prizes of different small priva-

teers, barges, and boats; and many vessels were chased on
shore, and either destroyed by boats or were bilged in striking.
The privateers taken and brought into port, during the years
1798, 1799, and 1800, amounted in all to rather more than
fifty sail.   To these must be added several letters of marque.
But few merchant ships were taken, the French venturing but
little on the ocean, except in fast-sailing armed vessels.   Still,
some valuable prizes of this nature were made, and several
ships of this class were driven ashore among the islands.

The constant changes that occurred among the commanders
of the different vessels, render it difficult to give clear accounts
of the movements of both.   These changes were owing to the
rapidity and irregularities of the promotions in an infant service, officers who went out at the commencement of the season lieutenants, in many instances, returning home captains,
at its close.   In short, the officers, like the crews, were constantly passing from vessel to vessel, several serving in two or
three ships in as many years.

The Experiment 12, made her first cruise under the command of Lieutenant Commandant Maley, and was much employed in convoying through the narrow passages, where the
vessels were exposed to attacks from large barges manned
from the shores.   About the close of the year 1799, or at the
commencement of 1800, this schooner was becalmed in the
Bight of Leogane, with several sail of American merchantmen
in company and under convoy.   While the little fleet lay in
this helpless condition, a good deal scattered, ten of the barges
mentioned, filled with negroes and mulattoes, came out against
it.   The barges contained from 30 to 40 men each, who were
armed with muskets, cutlasses, and pikes, and in some of the
boats were light guns and swivels.   As the Experiment was
partially disguised, the enemy came within reach of her grape
before the assault was made, when Lieutenant Commandant
Maley ran out his guns and opened his fire.   This was the
commencement of a long conflict, in which the barges were
beaten off.   It was not in the power of the Experiment, however, to prevent the enemy from seizing two of her convoy,
which had drifted to such a distance as to be beyond protection.   A third vessel was also boarded, but from her the brig-
ands were driven by grape, though not until they had murder-
ed her master and plundered the cabin.

The barges went twice to the shore, landed their killed and
wounded, and took on board reinforcements of men.   The

second attack they made was directed especially at the Experiment, there being no less than three divisions of the enemy, each of which contained three heavy barges. But, after a protracted engagement, which, with the intermissions, lasted seven hours, the enemy abandoned further designs on this convoy, and retreated in disorder. The Experiment endeavoured to follow, by means of her sweeps, but finding that some of the more distant of the barges threatened two of her convoy that had drifted out of gun-shot, she was obliged to give up the chase.

In this arduous and protracted engagement the Experiment was fought with spirit, and handled with skill. The total absence of wind gave the enemy every advantage; but notwithstanding their vast superiority in numbers, they did not dare to close. Two of the barges were sunk, and their loss in killed and wounded was known to have been heavy, while the Experiment had but two wounded, one of whom was Lieutenant David Porter.

Shortly after this affair, the command of the Experiment was given to Lieutenant Charles Stewart, late of the United States 44. Not long after he had got upon his station, this officer fell in with, and took, after a slight resistance, the French privateer les Deux Amis, of 8 guns, and between 40 and 50 men. The Deux Amis was sent in.

About a month after this occurrence, while cruising on her station, the Experiment made two sail, which had the appearance of enemy's cruisers. The Frenchmen were a brig of 18 guns, and a three-masted schooner of 14, and they gave chase to the American. Lieutenant-Commandant Stewart, having soon satisfied himself of the superior sailing of his own vessel, manœuvred in a way to separate the enemy, and to keep them at a distance until after dark. At length, finding that the Frenchmen had given up the chase, and that the brig was about a league ahead of the schooner, he cleared for action, closed with the latter, by running up on her weather quarter, and gave her a broadside. The attack was so vigorous and close, that the enemy struck in a few minutes. Throwing his first lieutenant, Mr. David Porter, into the prize, Lieutenant-Commandant Stewart immediately made sail after the brig; but she had gained so much ahead, during the time lost with the schooner, that she was soon abandoned, and the Experiment returned to her prize, which she carried into St. Kitts.

Mr. Stewart probably owed his success to the boldness of his manœuvres, as the brig was of a force sufficient to capture him in a few minutes.

The vessel taken by the Experiment proved to be the French man-of-war schooner la Diane, Lieutenant Perradeau, of 14 guns, and about 60 men. She was bound to France, with General Rigaud on board ; and in addition to her regular crew, 30 invalid soldiers had been put in her, having served their time in the islands. Her commander had been the first lieutenant of l'Insurgente, and the prize-officer of the Retaliation.

Returning to her station, the Experiment had next a combat that was of a less agreeable nature. A suspicious sail had been made in the course of the day, and chase was given until dark. Calculating the courses and distances, Lieutenant-Commandant Stewart ordered the Experiment to be kept in the required direction until midnight, when, if he did not close with the stranger, he intended to give up the chase. At that hour, the schooner was hauled by the wind, accordingly ; but, in a few minutes, a sail was seen quite near, and to windward. The Experiment went to quarters, ran up under the stranger's lee, and hailed. Finding the other vessel indisposed to give an answer, Lieutenant-Commandant Stewart ordered a gun fired into him, which was returned by a broadside. A sharp action now commenced, but, it blowing heavily, and the schooner lying over, it was found impossible to depress the guns sufficiently to hull the enemy. Planks were cut and placed beneath the trucks of the gun-carriages, when the shot of the Experiment told with so much effect, that her antagonist struck. Mr. Porter, the first lieutenant of the Experiment, was directed to take possession of the prize, but, on getting alongside, he was refused permission to board. As soon as this was known in the schooner, the boat was directed to pull out of the line of fire, with a view to re-commence the action, when the stranger hailed to say he submitted.

This vessel proved to be a privateer called the Louisa Bridger, out of Bermuda, with an armament of 8 nine-pounders, and a crew of between 40 and 50 men. She was much cut up, and had four feet water in her hold when she surrendered. Her captain was among the wounded.

As soon as the nature of this unfortunate mistake was known, every aid was afforded the privateer, the Experiment lying by her all next day, to assist in repairing her damages.

The Experiment received a good deal of injury in her rigging, and had one man killed, and a boy wounded.

Active negotiations had commenced, and in the autumn of 1800 the hopes of peace became so strong, that the efforts to increase the navy were sensibly relaxed, and the sailing of many ships, that had been intended for distant stations, was suspended.

Negotiations for peace with France had been going on at Paris, and a treaty to that effect was ratified by the Senate, on the 3d of February, 1801. All the necessary forms having been complied with on both sides, the Herald 18, Captain Russel, was sent to the West-Indies, with orders of recall for the whole force.

Thus ended the short and irregular struggle with France, in which the present marine of the United States was founded, most of the senior officers now in service having commenced their careers as midshipmen during its existence.

The commencement of the year 1801, was distinguished by a change of administration, for the first time since the adoption of the constitution ; Mr. Jefferson and his political friends, who were usually known by the name of the republican party, expelling the federalists from power. A president of the United States, however, is little more than an executive officer while confined to the circle of his constitutional duties ; and the Congress that terminated on the 4th of March, 1801, the day the change occurred, had passed a law, in some measure regulating a peace establishment for the navy. This law gave great discretionary authority to the president, it is true ; for it empowered him, whenever he should deem it expedient, to sell any, or all of the vessels of the navy, with the exception of thirteen of the frigates, which were named in the act, if, in his opinion the good of the country might require it. To this part of the law no great objections could be taken, even by the friends of an enlarged and liberal policy, as most of the vessels not excepted had been bought into, and were unsuited to the service, more especially at a period, when new improvements in naval architecture, that had been borrowed from the French, were fast superseding the old mode of construction.

The law also directed the guns and stores of the vessels sold to be preserved ; a provision that proved singularly unprofitable in the end, as the carronade now began to supersede the small long gun, and two of the sloops would probably have

furnished all the nines and sixes that have been used in the navy
for the last five-and-thirty years.    The great error of this law
was in the limitation it set to the number of the different ranks
of officers.    The whole of the sea-officers, sailing-masters excepted, were confined to nine captains, thirty-six lieutenants,
and one hundred and fifty midshipmen ; the rank of master
commandant being abolished, should the president see fit to discharge those then in commission.    The phraseology, as well
as the provisions of this law, betrayed that ignorance of the
details of the service, which has been so common in the legislation of the country, omitting many directions that were indispensable in practice, and laying stress on others that were of
little or no moment.

The administration of 1801 exercised its authority under the
statute, which, it will be remembered, was enacted previously
to its accession to office, with a reasonable discretion ; and
though it may have made a few of those mistakes that are in-
cidental to the discharge of all such trusts, it conformed to the
spirit of the law, with a due regard to liberality.    The selection of the officers to be retained was one of great delicacy and
importance, as the future character of the navy depended more
on the proper discharge of this duty than on that of any other.
The great defect of the law, indeed, was the narrow limits to
which the list of the superior sea-officers was confined, it being
at all times easier to build ships, than to form professional men
fit to command them.    This part of his delegated duties the
president discharged in perfect good faith, apparently altogether
disregarding party considerations.

Although some meritorious officers were necessarily dismissed, on this occasion, there is no question that the navy
was greatly benefited by the reduction ; the hurried manner
in which the appointments were originally made, having been
the means of introducing many persons into the service who
were unfitted for its duties.

The law of Congress directed that thirteen vessels, named
in the act, should not be disposed of, leaving it discretionary
with the president to sell the remainder or not.    The following
ships were retained, viz :

Constitution .................... 44,
United States .................... 44,
President ....................... 44,

Congress ........................ 38,
Constellation .................... 38,
Chesapeake ...................... 38,
Philadelphia ..................... 38,
New York ....................... 36,
Essex ........................... 32,
General Greene .................. 28,
Boston .......................... 28,
Adams .......................... 28,
John Adams...................... 28,
Enterprise ...................... 12.

The reduction of the navy was greatly exaggerated at the time, so far as the vessels alone were concerned.   At the peace with France, the cruising vessels in the service were thirty-four in number, and of these, fourteen of the best were retained. No frigate, unless the George Washington could be considered one, was sold, and this ship had been purchased into the service, and not built for the public.   As regards force, materially more than one-half, perhaps four-fifths, was preserved, the eight largest frigates retained being more than strong enough to contend with all the vessels sold.

13*

## CHAPTER XVI.

WE have now reached the period when the American marine assumed a fixed and permanent character. No more reductions were anticipated by those who understood the necessities of the country, nor have any ever been seriously attempted.

As early as in 1800, the Bashaw of Tripoli, Jussuf Caramalli, who had deposed his brother Hamet, and now sat on the throne of this dependency of the Porte, manifested a disposition to war. He had learned the concessions made to Algiers, the manner in which the Dey of that regency had been bribed to do justice, and, by a course of reasoning that was certainly plausible, if not true, he inferred that the government which had been induced to pay tribute to one pirate, might be induced to pay tribute to another. The complaints on which this semblance of royalty grounded his justification for war, are such as ought to be generally known. He accused the American government of having bribed the subordinates of Tunis at a higher price than it had bribed him; he added, that Algiers had received a frigate, while he had received none; and even in a letter to the president he said significantly, in reply to some of the usual diplomatic professions of friendship, " we could wish that these your expressions were followed by deeds, and not by empty words. You will therefore endeavour to satisfy us by a good manner of proceeding"—" But if only flattering words are meant, without performance, every one will act as he finds convenient. We beg a speedy answer, without neglect of time, as a delay on your part cannot but be prejudicial to your interests."

Shortly after, the Bashaw informed the American consul at Tripoli, that he would wait six months for a present in money, and if it did not arrive within that time, he would formally declare war against the United States. Jussuf Caramalli was as good as his word. No tidings of the money having reached Tripoli, the flag-staff of the American consulate was cut down on the 14th of May, 1801, and war was proclaimed in the act.

While Tripoli went so directly to work, difficulties existed with the other states of Barbary. Algiers complained that the tribute was in arrears, and Tunis found fault with the quality of various articles that had been sent to her, by way of bribing her not to seize American vessels. Certain planks and oars were too short, and guns of a particular description were much wanted. Morocco was also distrusted, although the prince of that country had not yet deigned to intimate his wishes.

Timid as was the policy of the United States, and disgraceful as was that of all christendom, at that period, in reference to the Barbary powers, the former was too much flushed with its recent successes against France, and too proud of its infant marine, to submit to all these exactions without resistance. Before it was known that Tripoli had actually declared war, a squadron was ordered to be fitted for the Mediterranean, with a view to awe the different sovereigns of Barbary, by its presence. The vessels selected for this purpose consisted of the President 44, Captain J. Barron; Philadelphia 38, Captain S. Barron; Essex 32, Captain Bainbridge, and Enterprise 12, Lieutenant Commandant Sterrett. At the head of this force was Captain Dale, an officer whose career we have had frequent occasion to notice, and who now hoisted his broad pennant in the President 44.

The ships rendezvoused in Hampton Roads, and sailed for their place of destination. On the 1st of July they anchored at Gibraltar, where they found the Tripolitan admiral, a renegado of the name of Lisle, in a ship of 26 guns, with a brig of 16, in company. There is no question that the timely appearance of the American squadron prevented these two vessels from getting into the Atlantic, where they might have struck a severe blow at the commerce of the country. The admiral, however, protested there was no war, though the information derived from other sources, induced Commodore Dale to distrust his sincerity. The Essex was sent along the north shore to collect the American trade, and to give it convoy; the Philadelphia was ordered to cruise in the straits to watch the two Tripolitans, while the President and Enterprise shaped their course towards Algiers, as ordered. The latter, however, soon parted company from the President on duty.

The appearance of a ship of the President's force at Algiers and Tunis, had an extremely quieting effect on the resentments of their two princes; and Mr. O'Brien, the consul at the former regency, gave it as his opinion, that the arrival of the squadron in the Mediterranean, had more weight in preserving the peace,

than if the George Washington, which vessel was soon expected, had come in with the tribute.

On the 1st of August, while running for Malta, the Enterprise 12, Lieutenant Commandant Sterrett, fell in with and
spoke a polacre-rigged ship of 14 guns and 80 men, belonging
to Tripoli, that was known to be out on a cruise against the
American commerce.   Running close alongside, an action was
commenced within pistol-shot, and it continued with little intermission for three hours, when the Turk submitted.   During
the combat, however, the Tripolitan struck three several times,
twice re-hoisting his colours, and opening his fire again, when
he thought an advantage might be obtained by attacking the
Americans unprepared.   Irritated by this treachery, on the
last occasion the Enterprise resumed her fire, with an intention
to sink her opponent, but after some further though fruitless
resistance, the Turkish captain appeared in the waist of his
ship, and threw his ensign into the sea, bending his body and
supplicating for quarter by signs, when the fire of the schooner
was stopped.

The name of the captured ship was the Tripoli, and that of
her rais, or commander, Mahomet Sous.   Although the Turks
showed courage — desperation would be a better term — this
first trial of skill with their trans-atlantic enemies was far from
creditable to them.   The Enterprise raked her enemy repeatedly, and the consequences were dreadfully apparent in the
result, 50 of the corsair's people having been killed and
wounded in the battle.   The ship herself was a wreck, and
her mizzen-mast was shot away.   On the other hand, the
Enterprise sustained but little injury even aloft, and had not a
man hurt.   Neither did she suffer materially in her hull.

The instructions of Lieutenant Sterrett did not permit him
to carry the Tripoli in, and Lieutenant David Porter took possession, and proceeded to dismantle her.   Her armament was
thrown overboard, and she was stripped of every thing but one
old sail, and a single spar, that were left to enable her to reach
port.   After attending to the wounded, the prize was abandoned, and it is understood a long time elapsed before she
got in.   When her unfortunate rais appeared in Tripoli, even
his wounds did not avail him.   He was placed on a jackass,
paraded through the streets, and received the bastinado.   The
effect of this punishment appears to have been different from
what was expected, for it is said the panic among the sailors
became so great, in consequence, that it was found difficult to

obtain men for the corsairs that were then fitting for sea. One thing is certain, that, though this war lasted three years, and in the end became both spirited and active, very few Tripolitan cruisers ventured from port during its continuance; or if they quitted port, they were cautious to an extreme about venturing from the land.

The President appeared off Tripoli on the 24th of August, when an ineffectual attempt was made to establish a truce. Remaining eighteen days in the vicinity of the town, and discovering no movement in or about the port, Commodore Dale ran down the coast some distance, when he crossed over to Malta, in order to water his ship. As soon as this necessary duty was performed, the President returned to Tripoli, and on the 30th of August, she overhauled a Greek ship bound in, with a cargo of merchandise and provisions. On board this vessel was an officer and twenty Tripolitan soldiers besides twenty other subjects of the regency. All these persons were taken on board the frigate, and an attempt was made, by means of this lucky capture, to establish a system of exchange. The negotiations were carried on through Mr. Nissen, the Danish consul, a gentleman whose name, by means of his benevolence, philanthropy, and probity, has become indissolubly connected with the history of the American marine.

It was soon discovered that the Bashaw cared very little about his subjects, as he declared that he would not exchange one American for all the soldiers. There was a little of the art of the negotiator in this, however, as he agreed in the end to give three Americans for all the soldiers, the officer included, and three more for eight of the merchants, disclaiming the remaining six merchants as his subjects. Commodore Dale appears to have become disgusted with this unworthy mode of bargaining, for he sent his prisoners on board the Greek again, and allowed the ship to go into Tripoli, relinquishing his claim on the merchants altogether as non-combatants, and consenting to take the three Americans for the soldiers.

Finding it necessary to go down to Gibraltar, the commodore now left Tripoli, and proceeded direct to the former place. He was soon succeeded by the Essex, which also appeared off the different Barbary ports.

In the mean time, the two Tripolitan cruisers at Gibraltar, on its being ascertained that it was impossible for them to get out while they were so closely watched, were dismantled, and their crews were privately sent across to Tetuan in boats, to find their way home by land; men enough being left to take care of the ships, and to navigate them, should an opportunity occur to get to sea. The Bashaw complained loudly of the blockade, as an innovation on the received mode of warfare; and the governments of Algiers and Tunis, which appeared to distrust the precedent, manifested a disposition to join in the protest. The Dey of Algiers even went so far as to ask passports for the crews of the two vessels at Gibraltar, with a view to aid his neighbour; but the request was denied.

The return of Commodore Dale's squadron was ordered to take place on the 1st of December, at the latest; but discretionary powers appear to have been subsequently given to him, as he left the Philadelphia and Essex behind him, and proceeded home with his own ship and the Enterprise. The practice of entering men for only a twelvemonth still prevailed, and it was often imperative on vessels to quit stations at the most unfortunate moments. The Philadelphia was left to watch the Tripolitans, making Syracuse in Sicily her port of resort; while the Essex was kept at the straits, to blockade the two vessels at Gibraltar, and guard the passage into the Atlantic. Both ships gave convoys when required.

Thus ended the first year of the war with Tripoli. Although little had been effected towards bringing the enemy to terms, much was done in raising the tone and discipline of the service. At Gibraltar, Malta, and other ports, the finest cruisers of Great Britain were constantly met; and the American ships proving to be entirely their equals, in construction, sailing, and manœuvring, a strong desire was soon excited to render them, in all other respects, as good as those that were then deemed the model-ships of the world. A similar opportunity had occurred while cruising in the West-Indies; but then a large proportion of the vessels employed were of inferior qualities, and some of the officers were unfit to hold commissions in any service. All the purchased ships had now been sold, and the reduction law had cleared the lists of those who would be likely to lessen the ambition, or alarm the pride of an aspiring and sensitive marine. Each day added to the knowledge, tone, esprit de corps, and seamanship of the younger officers; and as these opportunities continued to increase throughout the whole of the Mediterranean service, the navy rapidly went on improving, until the commander of an American ship was as ready to meet comparisons, as the commander of any vessel of war that floated.

## CHAPTER XVII.

EARLY in the year 1802, Congress enacted laws that obviated some constitutional scruples of the executive, and which fully authorised the capture and condemnation of any Tripolitan vessels that might be found. It is worthy of remark, that this law itself did not contain a formal declaration of war, while it provided for all the contingencies of such a state of things, even to empowering the president to issue commissions to privateers and letters of marque; and it may be inferred from this fact, that it was supposed the act of the enemy was sufficient to render the country technically a belligerent. One of the sections of this law, however, was of great service to the navy, by enabling crews to be shipped for two years.

As the President and Enterprise had returned home, and the time of service of the people of the two ships that were left in the Mediterranean was nearly up, preparations were now made to send out a relief squadron. For this service the following ships were commissioned, viz. the Chesapeake 38, Lieutenant Chauncey, acting captain; Constellation 38, Captain Murray; New York 36, Captain James Barron; John Adams 28, Captain Rodgers; Adams 28, Captain Campbell; and Enterprise 12, Lieutenant Commandant Sterrett. Commodore Truxtun was selected to command this squadron, and he had proceeded to Norfolk for that purpose, when a question arising about allowing him a captain in the flag-ship, he was induced to resign. Commodore Morris was appointed to succeed Commodore Truxtun, and shortly after he hoisted his broad pennant in the Chesapeake.

The vessels fitting for the Mediterranean being in different states of forwardness, and there existing a necessity for the immediate appearance of some of them in that sea, they did not sail in a squadron, but as each was ready. The Enterprise was the first that left home, sailing in February; and she was followed, in March, by the Constellation. The Chesapeake did not get out until April, and the Adams followed her in June. The two other ships were detained until September. There was, however, one other vessel at sea, all this time, to which it will be necessary to make a brief allusion.

Shortly after his accession to office, in 1801, Mr. Jefferson appointed Mr. Robert R. Livingston minister to France, and the Boston 28, Captain M'Niell, was directed to carry the new envoy to his place of destination. This duty performed, the ship had been ordered to join the squadron in the Mediterranean, for service in that sea. The departure of the Boston was so timed as to bring her on the station under both commands, that of Commodore Dale, and that of Commodore Morris. This cruise has become memorable in the service, on account of the eccentricities of the officer in command of the ship. After encountering a heavy gale of wind in the Bay of Biscay, in which he showed perfect seamanship, and the utmost coolness, under circumstances particularly trying, Captain M'Niell landed his passengers, and proceeded to the Mediterranean. Here he cruised for some time, avoiding his senior officers, whenever he could, passing from port to port, appearing off Tripoli, and occasionally affording a convoy. After a time, the Boston returned home, and was put out of commission, her commander quitting the service under the reduction law. The Essex and Philadelphia also returned home, as soon as relieved.

We have now reached the summer of 1802, and must confine the narrative of events to the movements of the different vessels that composed the squadron under the orders of Commodore Morris. In some respects, this was the best appointed force that had ever sailed from America. The ships were well officered and manned, and the crews had been entered for two years, or double the usual period. The powers given to the commanding officer, appear to have been more ample than common; and so strong was the expectation of the government that his force was sufficient to bring the enemy to terms, that Commodore Morris was associated with Mr. Cathcart, the late consul at Tripoli, in a commission to negotiate a peace. He was also empowered to obtain gun-boats, in order to protect the American trade in the Straits of Gibraltar.

As there were no means of bringing the Bashaw of Tripoli to terms but blockade and bombardment, two material errors seem to have been made in the composition of the force employed, which it is necessary to mention. There was no frigate in this squadron that carried a long gun heavier than an eighteen-pounder, nor was there any mortar vessel. Heavy carronades had come into use, it is true, and most ships carried more or less of them; but these are guns unsuited to battering under any circumstances, and were particularly unfitted for an assault on works that it is difficult to approach very near, on account of reefs of rocks. There was also a singular deficiency in small vessels, without which a close blockade of a port like Tripoli, was extremely difficult, if not impossible. It will be remembered, that the schooner Enterprise was the only vessel left in the navy by the reduction law, that was not frigate-built, and none had yet been launched to supply the defect. The government, however, had become aware of the great importance of light cruisers, and several were laid down in the summer of this year, under authority granted for that purpose.

As has been seen, the Enterprise 12, Lieutenant Commandant Sterrett, was the first vessel of the new squadron that reached the Mediterranean. She was soon followed by the Constellation 38, Captain Murray, which ship arrived off Tripoli early in May, where she found the Boston 28, Captain M'Niell, blockading the port. The latter ship, in a few days, quitted the station, and never re-appeared on it. A Swedish cruiser was also off the port, assisting to blockade.*

After being off the port some time, the Constellation was lying three or four leagues from the town, when the look-out aloft reported several small vessels to the westward, stealing along shore. The wind was quite light, and the Swedish frigate, at the moment, was a long distance outside. Sail was got on the Constellation, and towards noon the strangers were made out to be seventeen Tripolitan gun-boats, which, as it was afterwards ascertained, had gone out at night, with the intention of convoying into port, an American prize that was expected from Tunis, but which had failed to appear. Fortunately the wind freshened as the Constellation drew in with the land, and about one o'clock hopes were entertained of cutting off all, or a portion of the enemy. The latter were divided into two divisions, however, and that which led, by pulling directly to windward, effected its escape. The division in the rear, consisting of ten boats, was less fortunate, the Constellation being enabled to get it, for a short time, under her fire.

The wind blew nearly from the direction of the town, and the Tripolitans still endeavoured to cross the bows of the ship,

---

* Sweden was at war with Tripoli, at this time, also; but peace was made in the course of the summer.

as she was standing in; but Captain Murray, having run into ten fathoms, opened upon the enemy, time enough to cut off all but one boat of the rear division. This boat, notwithstanding a hot discharge of grape, succeeded in getting to windward, and was abandoned to attend to the remainder. The enemy now opened a fire in return, but the Constellation having, by this time, got the nearest boats fairly under her broadside, soon compelled the whole nine to bear up, and to pull towards the shore. Here they got into nooks behind the rocks, or in the best places of refuge that offered, while a large body of cavalry appeared on the sand-hills above them, to prevent a landing. Deeming it imprudent to send in the boats of a single frigate against so formidable a force, Captain Murray wore and stood off shore, soon after speaking the Swede, who had not been able to close in time to engage.

This little affair was the first that occurred off the port of Tripoli, in this war; and it had the effect of rendering the enemy very cautious in his movements. The gun-boats were a good deal cut up, though their loss was never ascertained. The cavalry, also, suffered materially, and it was said that an officer of high rank, nearly allied to the Bey, was killed. The Constellation sustained some trifling damage aloft, but the gun-boats were too hard pressed to render their fire very serious. The batteries opened upon the ship, also, on this occasion, but all their shot fell short.

After waiting in vain for the re-appearance of the Boston, Captain Murray was compelled to quit the station for want of water, when Tripoli was again left without any force before it.

The Chesapeake 38, Acting Captain Chauncey, wearing the broad pennant of Commodore Morris, reached Gibraltar May 25th, 1802, where she found the Essex 32, Captain Bainbridge, still blockading the Tripolitan cruisers. The latter vessel was sent home, and the Chesapeake, which had need of repairs, having sprung her mainmast, continued in the straits for the purpose of refitting, and of watching the enemy. Commodore Morris also deemed it prudent to observe the movements of the government of Morocco, which had manifested a hostile disposition. The arrival of the Adams 28, Captain Campbell, late in July, finally placed the flag-ship at liberty, and she sailed with a convoy to various ports on the north shore, having the Enterprise in company. This long delay below, of itself, almost defeated the possibility of acting effi-

ciently against the town of Tripoli that summer, since, further
time being indispensable to collect the different vessels and to
make the necessary preparations, it would bring the ships before that place too late in the season.   The fault, however, if
fault there was, rested more with those who directed the preparations at home, than with the commanding officer, as the
delay at Gibraltar would seem to have been called for by circumstances.   The Chesapeake, following the north shore, and
touching at many ports, anchored in the roads of Leghorn, on
the 12th of October. · At Leghorn the Constellation was met,
which ship shortly after returned home, in consequence of a
discretionary power that had been left with the Commodore.
Orders were now sent to the different vessels of the squadron
to rendezvous at Malta, whither the Commodore proceeded
with his own ship.   Here, in the course of the month of January, 1803, were assembled the Chesapeake 38, Acting Captain Chauncey; New York 36, Captain J. Barron; John
Adams 28, Captain Rodgers, and Enterprise 12, Lieutenant
Commandant Sterrett.   Of the remaining vessels that had been
put under the orders of Commodore Morris, the Constellation
38, Captain Murray, had gone into a Spanish port to repair
some damages received in a gale of wind, and she shortly
after sailed for home; the Boston 28, Captain M'Niell, had
not joined, and the Adams 28, Captain Campbell, was cruising
off Gibraltar.   On the 30th of January, 1803, the ships first
named left Malta with an intention to go off Tripoli, but a severe gale coming on, which lasted eleven days, the Commodore was induced to bear up, and to run down to Tunis, where
it was understood the presence of the squadron would be useful.   On the 11th of March he left Tunis, touched at Algiers,
and anchored again at Gibraltar on the 23d of the month.

The reason assigned for carrying the ships below, when it
had been the original design to appear off the enemy's port,
was the want of provisions, as well as to make the transfers and
arrangements dependent on shifting the pennant of the commanding officer, from the Chesapeake to the New York, the
former ship having been ordered home by the navy department.   The squadron was now reduced to the New York 36,
the Adams 28, the John Adams 28, and the Enterprise 12.
Acting Captain Chauncey accompanied the Commodore to the
first of these vessels, and Captain Barron was transferred to
the Chesapeake.   The Adams was despatched with a convoy,

with orders to go off Tripoli, as soon as the first duty was performed.

The ships appear to have been detained some time at Malta by the repairs that were rendered necessary in consequence of an accident that had occurred to the New York. On the 3d of May, however, the John Adams was sent off Tripoli, alone, with orders to blockade that port. Shortly after this ship reached her station, she made a sail in the offing, which she intercepted. This vessel proved to be the Meshouda, one of the cruisers that had been so long blockaded at Gibraltar, and which was now endeavouring to get home under an assumed character. She had been sold by the Bashaw to the Emperor of Morocco, who had sent her to Tunis, where she had taken in supplies, and was now standing boldly for the harbour of Tripoli. The reality of the transfer was doubted, and as she was attempting to evade a legal blockade, the Meshouda was detained.

About the close of the month, Commodore Morris hove in sight, in the New York, with the Adams and Enterprise in company. As the flag-ship neared the coast, several small vessels, convoyed by a number of gun-boats, were discovered close in with the land, making the best of their way towards the port. Chase was immediately given, and finding themselves cut off from the harbour, the merchant vessels, eleven in all, took refuge in old Tripoli, while the gun-boats, by means of their sweeps, were enabled to pull under the batteries of the town itself. No sooner did the vessels, small latine-rigged coasters loaded with wheat, get into Old Tripoli, than preparations were made to defend them. A large stone building stood on a bank some twelve or fifteen feet from the shore, and it was occupied by a considerable body of soldiers. In the course of the night, breast-works were erected on each side of this building, by means of the sacks of wheat which composed the cargoes of the feluccas. The latter were hauled upon the beach, high and dry, immediately beneath the building, and a large force was brought from Tripoli, to man the breast-works.

Mr. Porter, the first lieutenant of the flag-ship, volunteered to go in that night, with the boats of the squadron, and destroy the enemy's craft; but, unwilling to expose his people under so much uncertainty, the commodore decided to wait for daylight, in order that the ships might co-operate, and in the hope of intimidating the Tripolitans by a show of all his force.

WASP AND FROLIC.

Mr. Porter, however, went in alone and reconnoitred in the dark, receiving a heavy fire from the musketry of the troops when discovered.

Next morning, the offer of Mr. Porter was accepted, and sustained by Lieutenant James Lawrence of the Enterprise, and a strong party of officers and men from the other ships, he went boldly in, in open day. As the boats pulled up within reach of musketry, the enemy opened a heavy fire, which there was very little opportunity of returning. Notwithstanding the great superiority of the Turks in numbers, the party landed, set fire to the feluccas, and regaining their boats opened to the right and left, to allow the shot of the ships to complete the work. The enemy now appeared desperately bent on preserving their vessels, and, regardless of the fire of the ships, they rushed on board the feluccas, succeeded in extinguishing the flames, and, in the end, preserved them.

This attack was made in the most gallant manner, and reflected high credit on all engaged. The parties were so near each other, that the Turks actually threw stones at the Americans, and their fire was sharp, heavy, and close. The loss of the enemy could never be ascertained, but a good many were seen to fall. Of the Americans, 12 or 15 were killed and wounded; and among the latter, was Mr. Porter, who received a slight wound in the right, and a musket-ball through the left thigh, while advancing to the attack, though he continued to command to the last. Mr. Lawrence was particularly distinguished, as was Mr. John Downes, one of the midshipmen of the New York.

Commodore Morris determined to follow up this attack on the wheat vessels, by making another on the gun-boats of the enemy.

These gun-boats were stationed well out, near the rocks and the mole, in a manner to admit of their giving and receiving a fire; and on the afternoon of the 28th of May, the preparations having been previously made, a signal was shown from the New York, for the John Adams to bear down upon the enemy and commence an attack. Captain Rodgers obeyed the order with promptitude, taking a position within reach of grape; but owing to the lightness of the wind, the two other ships were unable to second him, as was intended. In consequence of these unforeseen circumstances, the attack proved a failure, in one sense, though the boats soon withdrew behind the rocks,

14 *

and night brought the affair to an end. It is believed that neither party suffered much on this occasion.

The next day Commodore Morris made an attempt to negotiate a peace, through the agency of M. Nissen, the Danish consul, a gentleman who, on all occasions, appears to have been the friend of the unfortunate, and active in doing good. To this proposal the Bey listened, and one of his ministers was empowered to meet the American commander on the subject. Having received proper pledges for his safe return, Commodore Morris landed in person, and each party presented its outlines of a treaty. The result was an abrupt ending of the negotiation.

This occurred on the 8th of June; and on the 10th, the New York and Enterprise left the station for Malta. At the latter place, Commodore Morris received intelligence concerning the movements of the Algerine and Tunisian corsairs, that induced him to despatch the Enterprise, with orders to Captain Rodgers to raise the blockade of Tripoli, and to join him, as soon as circumstances would permit, at Malta.

After the departure of the flag-ship, the John Adams 28, Captain Rodgers, and the Adams 28, Captain Campbell, composed the force left before the enemy's port. The speedy return of the Enterprise 12, which was then commanded by Lieutenant Commandant Hull, who had succeeded Lieutenant Commandant Sterrett, added that light vessel to the squadron. Some movements in the harbour, on the evening of the 21st of June, induced Captain Rodgers, the senior officer present, to suspect that it was intended to get a cruiser to sea that night, or to cover the return of one to port. With a view to defeat either of these plans, the Adams was sent to the westward, the Enterprise to the eastward, while the John Adams remained in the offing.

On the following morning, about 7 o'clock, the Enterprise was seen to the southward and eastward with a signal for an enemy flying. At that moment the John Adams was a few leagues out at sea, and it was 8 o'clock before the two vessels could speak each other. Captain Rodgers now found that a large ship belonging to the Bashaw, had run into a deep narrow bay, about seven leagues to the eastward of Tripoli, where she had taken a very favourable position for defence, and anchored with springs on her cable. At the same time it was ascertained that nine gun-boats were sweeping along the shore, to aid in defending her, while, as usual, a large body of cavalry was hovering about the coast to resist any attack by means of boats. The ship was known to be the largest of the Bey's remaining corsairs, mounting 22 guns; and she was very full of men.

Captain Rodgers owed the opportunity that now offered to attack his enemy, to the steadiness and gallantry of Lieutenant Commandant Hull, who, on making his adversary at daylight, had cut him off from the town, with a spirit that did infinite credit to that officer. The Tripolitan was treble the force of the Enterprise, and had he chosen to engage the schooner, Mr. Hull would, probably, have been obliged to sacrifice his little vessel, in order to prevent his enemy from getting into port.

The dispositions of Captain Rodgers were soon made. He stood in, with the Enterprise in company, until the John Adams was within point-blank shot of the enemy, when she opened her fire. A smart cannonade was maintained on both sides, for forty-five minutes, when the people of the corsair abandoned their guns, with so much precipitation, that great numbers leaped overboard, and swam to the shore. The John Adams was now in quarter-less-five, by the lead, and she wore with her head off shore. At the same time, the Enterprise was ordered to occupy the attention of the enemy on the beach, while boats could be got out to take possession of the abandoned ship. But a boat returning to the corsair, the John Adams tacked and renewed her fire. In a few minutes the colours of the corsair were hauled down, and all her guns were discharged; those which were pointed towards the Americans, and those which were pointed towards the land. At the next moment she blew up.

The explosion was very heavy, and it tore the hull of the Tripolitan entirely to pieces. The two after-masts were forced into the air to twice their usual height, with all the yards, rigging, and hamper attached. The cause of this explosion is unknown, though it might have been thought intentional, were it not for the fact that the people of the boat that had returned to her, were blown up in the ship, none having left her after their arrival. As the shot of the John Adams was seen to hull the enemy repeatedly, the corsair is also supposed to have sustained a severe loss before her people first abandoned her.

The John Adams and Enterprise attempted to cut off the division of gun-boats, but found the water shoal too far to seaward of them to render the fire of their guns effective. Knowing the whole coast intimately, the latter were enabled to escape.

The ships before Tripoli, in obedience to the orders of Commodore Morris, now sailed for Malta to join this officer, when the whole squadron proceeded to different ports in Italy, together. From Leghorn, the John Adams was sent down to the straits with a convoy; the Adams to Tunis and Gibraltar, and the Enterprise back to Malta, in quest of despatches. Soon after, the New York herself went below, touching at Malaga, where Commodore Morris found letters of recall. The command was left temporarily with Captain Rodgers, who hoisted a broad pennant in the New York, while Commodore Morris took charge of the Adams, to proceed to America. Captain Campbell, late of the Adams, was transferred to the John Adams.

Commodore Morris reached home on the 21st of November, 1803; and the government, which professed great dissatisfaction at the manner in which he had employed the force entrusted to his discretion, demanded the usual explanations. These explanations not proving satisfactory, a Court of Inquiry was convened, by order of the department, dated March 10, 1804, and the result was an opinion that this officer had not exercised due diligence and activity in annoying the enemy, on various occasions, between the 8th of January, 1803, and the period of the expiration of his command. In consequence of the finding of the Court of Inquiry, the president dismissed Commodore Morris from the navy. This step has generally been considered high-handed and unjust.

The death of Commodore Barry, the resignations of Commodore Dale and Commodore Truxtun, with the dismissals of Commodore Morris and Captain M'Niell, reduced the list of captains to nine, the number named in the reduction law; for that act does not appear to have been rigidly regarded from the moment of its passage. After the death of Commodore Barry, Commodore S. Nicholson became the senior officer of the service, making the second member of the same family who had filled that honourable station.

## CHAPTER XVIII.

THE government soon became aware of the necessity of possessing some light cruisers, which, to a marine, are what the eyes and nerves are to man. Without vessels of this character, a commander could never conduct a vigorous blockade, like that required before Tripoli, in particular ; and a law passed February, 1803, authorising the construction of two brigs and two schooners. In the course of the spring of that year, these vessels were built, and the navy received an addition to its list, of the Argus 16, Siren 16, Nautilus 12, and Vixen 12. The two former were beautiful and very efficient brigs, mounting 16 twenty-four pound carronades, and 2 long twelves ; and the two latter were schooners, carrying 12 eighteen-pound carronades, and 2 light long guns, each. They were all finely modelled and serviceable vessels of their size, and are now intimately associated with the early traditions of the navy. There was a singular conformity in their fates, also, the whole four, in the end, falling into the hands of their enemies.

When Commodore Morris was recalled, the necessity of sending out a new squadron was foreseen, the time of the crews belonging to the ships left under the orders of Commodore Rodgers being so nearly expired. Indeed the latter officer, when he hoisted his broad pennant, was notified that a successor must soon arrive. The new squadron was so differently organised from the two which had preceded it, as to leave little doubt that the administration had discovered the error which had been made in sending so many light frigates on this service ; vessels that were nearly useless in a bombardment, while they could not command the shores, and that had no other quality particularly suited to the warfare in which they were engaged, than a fitness to convoy. Even for the latter employment, the same force distributed in twice the number of vessels, would have been much more efficient and safe.

The ships now selected to carry on the war against Tripoli, were of an entirely different description. They consisted of the Constitution 44, Philadelphia 38, Argus 16, Siren 16,

Nautilus 12, Vixen 12, and Enterprise 12. The latter was already on the station, and it was intended to keep her there, by sending out men to supply the places of those who declined to enter anew. As usual, these vessels sailed as they were ready; the Nautilus 12, Lieutenant Commandant Somers, being the first that got to sea. This schooner reached Gibraltar on the 27th of July, 1803. She was soon followed by the Philadelphia 38, Captain Bainbridge, which arrived at the same place, August 24th. The Constitution 44, bearing the broad pennant of Commodore Preble, who had been chosen to command the squadron, arrived September 12th; the Vixen 12, Lieutenant Commandant Smith, September 14th; the Siren 16, Lieutenant Commandant Stewart, October 1st; and the Argus 16, Lieutenant Commandant Decatur, November 1st. When the last fell in with the Enterprise, Mr. Decatur took command of that schooner, giving up the brig, by arrangement, to Mr. Hull, who was his senior officer.

The Philadelphia barely touched at Gibraltar, but hearing that two Tripolitans were cruising off Cape de Gatt, Captain Bainbridge proceeded, without delay, in quest of them. On the night of the 26th of August, blowing fresh, two sails were made from the Philadelphia, under Cape de Gatt; the largest of which, a ship, was carrying nothing but a fore-course. On running alongside this vessel, and hailing, with a good deal of difficulty, Captain Bainbridge learned that the stranger was a Barbary cruiser. Further examination showed that this vessel belonged to the Emperor of Morocco, and that she was the Meshboha 22, commanded by Ibrahim Lubarez, and had a crew of one hundred and twenty men.

The Moors were made to believe that the Philadelphia was an English frigate, and they admitted that the brig in company was an American. The suspicions of Captain Bainbridge were now awakened, for he could not well account for the brig's being under so little sail, and he sent his first lieutenant on board the Moor, to ascertain if there were any prisoners in his ship. When the boat reached the Meshboha, the Moors refused to let the officer come over the side. Captain Bainbridge now directed an armed force to go into the boat, when the officer succeeded in executing his orders.

Below deck, were found the master and crew of the brig in company, which was ascertained to be the Celia of Boston, a prize to the Meshboha. The brig had been captured near Malaga, nine days before; and there was no doubt that the Moors were waiting for other vessels, Cape de Gatt being a headland commonly made by every thing that keeps the north shore of the Mediterranean aboard.

Captain Bainbridge, on receiving this intelligence, did not hesitate about taking possession of the Meshboha.  Her people could not all be removed until near daylight; and during the time that was occupied in transferring them to the frigate, the brig had disappeared.  On the afternoon of the 27th, however, she was seen doubling the cape, coming from the eastward, and hugging the land, while she steered in the direction of Almeria, probably with the hope of getting to the westward of the ships, in order to run to Tangiers.  Owing to light winds, it was midnight before she could be re-taken.

It was now all-important to discover on what authority this capture had been made.  The Moorish commander, at first, stated that he had taken the Celia, in anticipation of a war; a serious misunderstanding existing between the Emperor and the American consul, when he left port.  This story seemed so improbable that it was not believed, and Captain Bainbridge could only get at the truth by threatening to execute his prisoner as a pirate, unless he showed his commission.  This menace prevailed, and Ibrahim Lubarez presented an order from the Governor of Tangiers, to capture all Americans that he might fall in with.

The Philadelphia returned to Gibraltar with her prizes, and leaving the latter, she went off Cape St. Vincent, in quest of a Moorish frigate that was said to be cruising there.  Not succeeding in finding the Moor, Captain Bainbridge ran through the straits again, and went aloft.  While at Gibraltar, Mr. David Porter joined him as first lieutenant.

Shortly after the Philadelphia had gone to her station off Tripoli, the New York 36, Commodore Rodgers, and the John Adams 28, Captain Campbell, reached Gibraltar, in the expectation of meeting the new flag-ship.  In a day or two the Constitution came in, as did the Nautilus, which had been giving convoy up the Mediterranean.  As soon as Commodore Preble was apprised of the facts connected with the capture of the Meshboha, he saw the necessity of disposing of the question with Morocco, before he left the entrance of the Mediterranean again open, by going off Tripoli.  Commodore Rodgers was the senior officer, and his authority in those seas had properly ceased, but, in the handsomest manner, he consented to accompany Commodore Preble to Tangiers, leaving the latter his power to act, as negotiator and commander-in-chief. Accordingly the Constitution 44, New York 36, John Adams 28, and Nautilus 12, went into the Bay of Tangiers, October the 6th, 1803. Commodore Preble, on this occasion, discovered that promptitude, spirit and discretion, which were afterwards so conspicuous in his character; and after a short negotiation, the relations of the two countries were placed on their former amicable footing. The commodore had an interview with the Emperor, which terminated in the happiest results. On the part of Morocco, the act of the Governor of Tangiers was disavowed; an American vessel that had been detained at Mogadore, was released; and the Emperor affixed his seal anew to the treaty of 1786. The commodore then gave up the Meshboha, and it was also agreed to return the Meshouda, the ship taken by the John Adams. Congress, in the end, however, appropriated an equivalent to the captors of these two vessels, in lieu of prize-money.

As soon as the difficulties with Morocco were settled, Commodore Rodgers sailed for America; and Commodore Preble devoted himself with energy and prudence in making his preparations to bring Tripoli to terms. The latter had an arduous task before him; and its difficulties were increased by the circumstance that he was personally known to scarcely an officer under his command. During the war with France, the ships had been principally officered from the states in which they had been built; and Captain Preble, a citizen of New Hampshire, had hitherto commanded vessels under these circumstances. He had sailed for the East Indies in 1800, in the Essex 32, and had been much removed from the rest of the navy, in the course of his service. By one of those accidents that so often influence the affairs of life, all the commanders placed under the orders of Commodore Preble, with the exception of Mr. Hull, came from the middle or the southern states; and it is believed that most of them had never even seen their present commander, until they went in person to report themselves and their vessels. This was not only true of the commanders, but a large portion of the subordinate officers, also, were in the same situation; even most of those in the Constitution herself, having been personally strangers to the commander of the squadron. The period was now approaching when the force about to be employed before Tripoli was to assemble, and a service was in perspective that promised to let the whole squadron into the secret of its com-

mander's true character.   Previously to relating the events
that then occurred, however, it will be necessary to return to
the movements of the Philadelphia 38, Captain Bainbridge.

---⟨⟩---

## CHAPTER XIX.

It has been seen that the Philadelphia captured the Meshboha, on the night of the 26th of August, 1803.   The return
to Gibraltar, the run off Cape Vincent, and the passage up the
Mediterranean, brought it late in the season, before that ship
could reach her station.   Here the Vixen 12, Lieutenant Commandant Smith, which schooner had arrived at Gibraltar about
the middle of September, appeared also, and the blockade was
resumed by these two vessels, the Enterprise having gone
below.   Unfortunately, soon after his arrival, Captain Bainbridge sent the schooner in quest of a Tripolitan cruiser, that
he learned from the master of a neutral had got to sea a short
time previously.   This left the frigate alone, to perform a very
delicate service, the blockading vessels being constantly compelled to chase in-shore.

Towards the last of the month of October, the wind, which
had been strong from the westward for some time previously,
drove the Philadelphia a considerable distance to the eastward
of the town, and on Monday, October the 31st, as she was
running down to her station again, with a fair breeze, about
nine in the morning, a vessel was seen in-shore, and to windward, standing for Tripoli.   Sail was made to cut her off.
Believing himself to be within long gun-shot a little before
eleven, and seeing no other chance of overtaking the stranger
in the short distance that remained, Captain Bainbridge opened
a fire, in the hope of cutting something away.   For near an
hour longer, the chase and the fire were continued ; the lead,
which was constantly kept going, giving from seven to ten
fathoms, and the ship hauling up and keeping away, as the
water shoaled or deepened.   At half-past eleven, Tripoli then
being in plain sight, distant a little more than a league, satisfied
that he could neither overtake the chase, nor force her ashore,
Captain Bainbridge ordered the helm a-port, to haul directly

15

off the land into deep water. The next cast of the lead, when this order was executed, gave but eight fathoms, and this was immediately followed by casts that gave seven, and six and a half. At this moment, the wind was nearly abeam, and the ship had eight knots way on her. When the cry of " half-six" was heard, the helm was put hard down, and the yards were ordered to be braced sharp up. While the ship was coming up fast to the wind, and before she had lost any of her way, she struck a reef forwards, and shot up on it, until she lifted between five and six feet.

This was an appalling accident to occur on the coast of such an enemy, at that season of the year, and with no other cruiser near! It was first attempted to force the vessel ahead, under the impression that the best water was to sea-ward; but on sounding around the ship, it was found that she had run up with such force, as to lie nearly cradled on the rocks; there being only 14 feet of water under the fore-chains, while the ship drew, before striking, $18\frac{1}{2}$ feet forward. Astern there were not 18 feet of water, instead of $20\frac{1}{2}$, which the frigate needed. Such an accident could only have occurred by the vessel's hitting the reef at a spot where it sloped gradually, and where, most probably the constant washing of the element had rendered the surface smooth; and by her going up, on the top of one of those long, heavy, but nearly imperceptible swells, that are always agitating the bosom of the ocean.

The vessel of which the Philadelphia had been in chase was a large xebeck, and her commander, acquainted with the coast, stood on, inside of the reef, doubled the edge of the shoal, and reached Tripoli in safety. The firing, however, had brought out nine gun-boats, which now appeared, turning to windward. Not a moment was to be lost, as it would shortly be in the power of these vessels to assail the frigate almost with impunity. Finding, on further examination, deep water in shore, the yards were next braced aback, and the guns were run aft, in the equally vain hope of forcing the ship astern, or to make her slide off the sloping rocks on which she had run so hard. It was some time before this project was abandoned, as it was the most practicable means of getting afloat.

On a consultation with his officers, Captain Bainbridge next gave orders to throw overboard the guns, reserving a few aft for defence; the anchors, with the exception of the larboard bower, were cut from the bows. Before this could be effected the enemy came within gun-shot, and opened his fire. Fortunately, the Tripolitans were ignorant of the desperate condition of the Philadelphia, and were kept at a respectful distance by the few guns that remained; else they might have destroyed most of the crew, it being certain that the colours would not be struck so long as there was any hope of getting the ship afloat. The cannonade, which was distant and inefficient, and the business of lightening the frigate, went on at the same time, and occupied several hours.

The enemy finally became so bold, that they crossed the stern of the frigate, where alone they were at all exposed to her fire, and took a position on her starboard, or weather quarter. Here it was impossible to touch them, the ship having heeled to port, in a way to render it impracticable to bring a single gun to bear, or, indeed, to use one at all, on that side.

Captain Bainbridge now called another council of his officers, and it was determined to make a last effort to get the vessel off. The water-casks, in the hold, were started, and the water was pumped out. All the heavy articles that could be got at, were thrown overboard, and finally the fore-mast was cut away, bringing down with it the main-top-gallant-mast. Notwithstanding all this, the vessel remained as immovable as the rocks on which she lay.

The gun-boats were growing bolder every minute, others were approaching, and night was at hand. Captain Bainbridge, after consulting again with his officers, felt it to be an imperious duty to haul down his flag, to save the lives of the people. Before this was done, however, the magazine was drowned, holes were bored in the ship's bottom, the pumps were choked, and every thing was performed that it was thought would make the final loss of the vessel sure. About five o'clock the colours were lowered.

It is a curious circumstance that this was the second instance in which an American vessel of war had been compelled to haul down her flag, since the formation of the new marine, and that in each case the same officer commanded. After the accounts given in this work, it is unnecessary to add that on both occasions an imperious necessity produced this singular coincidence.

The ship had no sooner struck than the gun-boats ran down alongside of her, and took possession. The barbarians rushed into the vessel, and began to plunder their captives. Not only were the clothes which the Americans had collected in their bags and in bundles, taken from them, but many officers and men were stripped half-naked. They were hurried into boats, and sent to Tripoli, and even on the passage the business of plundering went on. The officers were respected little more than the common men, and, while in the boat, Captain Bainbridge himself was robbed of his epaulets, gloves, watch, and money. His cravat was even torn from his neck. He wore a miniature of his wife, and of this the Tripolitans endeavoured to deprive him also, but, a youthful and attached husband, he resisted so seriously that the attempt was relinquished.

It was near 10 o'clock at night, when the boats reached the town. The prisoners were landed in a body, near the bashaw's palace, and they were conducted to his presence. The prince received his captives in an audience hall, seated in a chair of state, and surrounded by his ministers. Here Captain Bainbridge was formally presented to him, as his prisoner, when the bashaw himself directed all the officers to be seated. The minister of foreign affairs, Mohammed D'Ghies, spoke French, and through him the bashaw held a conversation of some length with Captain Bainbridge. The latter was asked many questions concerning the Philadelphia, the force of the Americans in the Mediterranean, and he was civilly consoled for his captivity, by being reminded that it was merely the fortune of war.

When the conversation had ended, the officers were conducted to another apartment, where a supper had been provided, and as soon as this meal had been taken by those who had a desire to eat, they were led back to the audience hall, and paid their parting compliments to the bashaw. Here the captives were informed that they were put under the special charge of Sidi Mohammed D'Ghies, who conducted them to the house that had lately been the American consulate. The building was spacious and commodious, but almost destitute of furniture. It was one o'clock in the morning, but at that late hour even, appeared Mr. Nissen, the Danish consul, bringing with him the consolations of sympathy and hope. This benevolent man was introduced to Captain Bainbridge, by Mohammed D'Ghies, as his personal friend, and as one on whose honour, humanity and good faith, full reliance might be placed. Mohammed D'Ghies, himself, was known by reputation to Captain Bainbridge, and he had shown delicacy and feeling in the exercise of his trust. His recommendation, which was pointedly significant, coupled with the manner of Mr. Nissen, excited a confidence that in the end proved to be most worthily bestowed. Every thing that could be devised at that unseason-able hour, was done by Mr. Nissen. This was but the commencement of a series of indefatigable and unwearying kindnesses, that endured to the last moment of the captivity of the Americans.

The misfortune that befel the Philadelphia, made a material difference in the state of the war. Until this moment, the bashaw had received but little to compensate him for the inconvenience to which he was put by the blockade, and for the loss of his different cruisers. His corsairs had captured but very few merchant vessels, and they ran the greatest risks, whenever they appeared out of their own ports. As yet, it is true, nothing had been attempted against his town, but he knew it was at any time liable to a bombardment. It was thought, therefore, that he was not indisposed to peace, when accident threw the crew of the Philadelphia so unexpectedly into his power.

The bashaw, however, had now a hold upon his enemy, that, agreeably to the usages of Barbary, enabled him to take much higher ground in proposing his terms. In his previous negotiations, he had asked a large sum as the price of the few captives he then held, but the demand had been rejected as unreasonable and exorbitant. On board the Philadelphia were three hundred and fifteen souls, and among them were no less than twenty-two quarter-deck officers,* gentlemen in whose fortunes the bashaw well knew there would be a lively interest felt, to say nothing of the concern that a government like that of America was expected to manifest for the fate of its seamen. Under these circumstances, therefore, the divan of Tripoli felt strongly encouraged to continue the war, in the hope of receiving a high ransom for the prisoners, and in the expectation of holding a check on the measures of its enemy, by its means of retaliation.

---

* William Bainbridge, captain; David Porter, first lieutenant; Jacob Jones, second do.; Theodore Hunt, third do.; Benjamin Smith, fourth do.; William Osborn, lieutenant of marines; John Ridgely, surgeon; J. Cowdery, do. mate; Nicholas Harwood, do. do.; Keith Spence, purser; and Bernard Henry, James Gibbon, Benjamin Franklin Reed, James Renshaw, Wallace Wormley, Robert Gamble, James Biddle, Richard R. Jones, Daniel T. Patterson, Simon Smith, and William Cutbush, midshipmen; William Anderson, captain's clerk. Of these gentlemen, Messrs. J. Jones, Renshaw, Biddle, and Patterson, are still in service, and have all worn broad pennants. Dr. Cowdery is the oldest surgeon now in the navy.

15 *

The Philadelphia ran on the reef on the 31st of October, and
her people were landed during the night of the same day.
The Tripolitans set about their arrangements to get the ship
off, next morning, and as they were near their own port, had
so many gun-boats and galleys at their disposal, and were
unmolested by any cruiser, it was announced to the bashaw
that there were hopes of saving the frigate.    In the course of
the 2d of November, it came on to blow fresh from the northwest, and the wind forcing the water up on the African coast,
while it bore on the larboard quarter of the ship, her stern was
driven round, and she floated, in part, though she continued to
thump as the seas left her.    Anchors were now carried out,
all the disposable force of the town was applied, and on the 5th,
the Philadelphia was got into deep water.    The same day, she
was brought within two miles of the city, where she was compelled to anchor, on account of the state of the weather.    Here
she was kept afloat by means of pumping, while men were employed in stopping the leaks.    The business of scuttling appears to have been but imperfectly performed, a few holes having been merely bored in the bottom of the ship, instead of
cutting through the planks, as had been ordered.    The weather
continuing remarkably pleasant, the Turks finally succeeded
in not only getting the frigate into port, but in weighing all her
guns and anchors which lay in shallow water on the reef, as
well as in getting up nearly every thing else that had been
thrown overboard.    The ship was partially repaired, her guns
were remounted, and she was moored off the town, about a
quarter of a mile from the bashaw's castle.

Commodore Preble, on his return from Tangiers to Gibraltar, on the 15th of October, went round to Cadiz ; soon after,
he re-appeared at the former place, made a formal announce-
ment of the blockade of Tripoli, on the 12th of November, on
which day the ship he believed to be in the active execution
of that duty, was in the possession of the enemy, and on the
13th, he sailed for Algiers.    After landing a consul at the latter place, he proceeded to Malta, off which port he arrived on
the 27th of November.    Here he was met by letters from Captain Bainbridge, and he obtained a confirmation of the loss of
the Philadelphia, a rumour of which event had reached him
lower down the coast.    The Constitution sailed immediately
for Syracuse, and got in next day.

On the 17th of December, 1803, Commodore Preble, after
making his preparations and disposing of his force in different

ways, sailed for Tripoli, with the Enterprise in company, off
which place he now appeared for the first time.   The 23d of
the month, the Enterprise 12, Lieutenant Commandant Decatur, fell in with and captured a ketch, with seventy souls on
board.   This ketch had been a French gun-vessel in Egypt,
that had been taken by the English and had passed into the
hands of the Tripolitans.   She was now bound to Constanti-
nople, with a present of female slaves for the Porte.   A few
days after this prize was taken, it came on to blow heavily
from the northeast, and finding the frigate in danger of being
lost on the coast, at that tempestuous season, Commodore Preble returned to Syracuse ; not, however, until he had reconnoitred his enemy, and formed his plan of operations for the
future.   Means had been found to communicate with Captain
Bainbridge, also ; and several letters were received from that
officer, pointing out different methods of annoying the enemy.

In a letter of the date of the 5th of December, 1803, Captain Bainbridge suggested the possibility of destroying the
Philadelphia, which ship was slowly fitting for sea, there being little doubt of her being sent out as a cruiser, as soon as
the mild season should return.   Commodore Preble listened
to the suggestion, and being much in the society of the commander of the vessel that was most in company with the Constitution, Lieutenant Stephen Decatur, he mentioned the project
to that spirited officer.   The expedition was just suited to the
ardour and temperament of Mr. Decatur, and the possession
of the prize at once afforded the means of carrying it into effect.
The ketch was accordingly appraised, named the Intrepid, and
taken into the service, as a tender.   About this time, Lieutenant Commandant Stewart, of the Siren, the officer who was
then second in command in the Mediterranean, and who had
just arrived from below, offered to cut out the Philadelphia
with his own brig ; but Commodore Preble was pledged to Mr.
Decatur, who, at first, had proposed to run in with the Enterprise
and carry the ship.   The more experienced Preble rejected the
propositions of both these ardent young men, substituting a
plan of his own.

Although Commodore Preble declined the proposal of Mr.
Decatur to carry in the Enterprise, the projected service was
assigned to the commander and crew of that schooner.   It
being necessary, however, to leave some of her own officers
and people in her, a selection of a few gentlemen to join
in the expedition, was made from the flag-ship, and orders to

that effect were issued accordingly. These orders were dated February the 3d, 1804, and they directed the different gentlemen named to report themselves to Lieutenant Commandant Decatur, of the Enterprise. As it was intended that the crew of the schooner should furnish the entire crew of the ketch, it was not thought proper to add any men to this draft. In short, the duty was strictly assigned to the Enterprise, so far as her complement could furnish the officers required. On the afternoon of the 3d, according to the orders they had just received, Messrs. Izard, Morris, Laws, Davis, and Rowe, midshipmen of the Constitution, went on board the schooner, and reported themselves for duty to her commander. All hands were now called in the Enterprise, when Lieutenant Commandant Decatur acquainted his people with the destination of the ketch, and asked for volunteers. Every man and boy in the schooner presented himself, as ready, and willing to go. Sixty-two of the most active men were selected, and the remainder, with a few officers, were left to take care of the vessel. As the orders to destroy the frigate, and not to attempt to bring her out, were peremptory, the combustibles, which had been prepared for this purpose, were immediately sent on board the Intrepid, her crew followed, and that evening the ketch sailed, under the convoy of the Siren 16, Lieutenant Commandant Stewart, who was properly the senior officer of the expedition, though, owing to the peculiar nature of the service, Mr. Decatur was permitted to conduct the more active part of the duty, at his own discretion.

The party in the ketch consisted of Lieutenant Commandant Decatur; Lieutenants Lawrence, Bainbridge, and Thorn; Mr. Thomas M'Donough,* midshipman, and Dr. Heerman, surgeon; all of the Enterprise;—Messrs. Izard, Morris, Laws, Davis, and Rowe, midshipmen of the Constitution; and Salvador Catalano the pilot, with sixty-two petty officers and common men, making a total of seventy-four souls.

It is scarcely necessary to say that the accommodations were none of the best, with so many persons cooped up in a vessel of between forty and fifty tons; and to make the matter worse, it was soon found that the salted meat put on board was spoiled, and that there was little besides bread and water left to subsist on. The weather, however, was pleasant, and the

---

* Mr. Thomas M'Donough, afterwards so distinguished, had belonged to the Philadelphia, but escaped captivity by being left at Gibraltar in the prize Meshboha.

wind favourable, and the two vessels got in sight of Tripoli on
the afternoon of the 9th.   To prevent suspicions, the Intrepid
now went ahead of the Siren ; and a little after dark, she had
stretched in quite near to the coast, with a breeze at southwest,
anchoring about a mile to the windward of the town.   Shortly
after, the Siren, disguised, brought-to a little to seaward of her..
The night came on dark and threatening, but it was in some
respects so favourable to the enterprise, that Mr. Decatur was
reluctant to let it pass without making the attempt.   The pilot,
however, pronounced it extremely hazardous to venture in
among the rocks at that moment, as he thought the sea must
be breaking across the entrance, by which it was proposed to
pass.   Under the circumstances, Mr. Decatur, who displayed
as much conduct and prudence as daring gallantry throughout
this whole affair, sent Mr. Morris and the pilot, in a boat with
muffled oars, to reconnoitre.   This young officer pulled close
up to the western passage, and ascertained that the sea was so
high that it was, in fact, breaking entirely across the entrance ;
when he returned, and reported that it would be hazardous to
go in, and that to come out would be impossible.

The report was scarcely needed, for, by this time, the wind
had risen so high, and so much sea had got up, that in hoisting
in the boat, it was stove, and when the anchor was weighed, for
it was necessary to get off the land as soon as possible, it was
found to be broken.   The Siren had anchored a little without
the ketch, and had hoisted out and armed her boats, which
were to cover the retreat, but she, too, was compelled to get
under way, by the increasing violence of the wind.   Several
hours were employed in a vain attempt to get her anchor, the
brig rolling gunwales-to, and a good many of her people,
together with Lieutenant Commandant Stewart, were hurt by
the capstan's running away with the bars.   In the end, the
weather came on so bad, and the danger of being seen as the
day dawned was so much increased, that the anchor and cable
were left, the latter having been cut without the hawse-hole.

So sudden and violent was the gale, that there had been no
communication between the two vessels, the Siren having no
other intimation of the departure of the ketch, than by seeing
her light as she stretched out to sea.   Luckily, the wind was
well to the westward, and both vessels got an offing before
they were seen from Tripoli.   Here they lay-to, with their
heads off shore, certain of being far enough to leeward, to be

out of sight in the morning. The wind began to haul to the
northward, and the gale lasted six days, during which time
great fears were entertained of the ketch's foundering at sea,
or of her being, at least, driven on the coast, the change in the
wind having brought the vessels on a lee shore. Before the
wind abated, they were driven up into the Gulf of Sydra, where
they were fairly embayed.

On the 15th the weather moderated, and the brig and ketch,
which had kept in company, notwithstanding the gale, endeavoured to fetch in with the land, and in the course of the night
they got so near, as to reconnoitre and ascertain their position.
Finding themselves too far to the eastward to effect any thing
that night, they hauled off again, in order to escape detection.
The next day, about noon, calculating that they were abreast
of the town, and the wind and weather being, in all respects,
favourable, both vessels kept away, the ketch leading some
distance, in order that the enemy might not suppose her a
consort of the Siren's, although the latter was so much disguised, as to render it impossible to recognise her. The wind
was fair, but light, and every thing looking favourable, Mr.
Decatur now seriously made his dispositions for the attack.
Apprehensive that they might have been seen, and that the
enemy had possibly strengthened the party on board the
frigate, Lieutenant Commandant Stewart sent a boat and eight
men from the Siren, to the ketch, under the orders of Mr. Anderson, one of his midshipmen ; which reinforcement increased
the number of the intended assailants to eighty-two, all told.

The orders of Lieutenant Commandant Decatur were clear
and simple. The spar-deck was first to be carried, then the
gun-deck ; after which the following distribution of the party
was made, in order to set fire to the ship. Mr. Decatur, with
Messrs. Izard and Rowe, and fifteen men, was to keep possession of the upper deck. Mr. Lawrence, with Messrs. Laws
and M'Donough and ten men, was to repair to the berth-deck
and forward store-rooms. Mr. Bainbridge, with Mr. Davis and
ten men, was to go into the ward-room and steerage ; Mr.
Morris, with eight men, was to go into the cockpit and after
store-rooms ; Mr. Thorn, with the gunner and surgeon, and
thirteen men, was to look after the ketch ; to Mr. Izard was
assigned the command of the launch should she be needed ; and
Mr. Anderson, with the Siren's cutter, was to secure all boats
alongside of the ship, and to prevent the people from swim-

ming ashore, with directions, however, to board as soon as the
first duty was performed.

Fire-arms were to be used only in the last extremity, and
the first object of every one was to clear the upper-deck and
gun-deck of the enemy.   The watch-word was " Philadelphia."
These arrangements were plain and judicious.

As the ketch drew in with the land, the ship became visible.
She lay not quite a mile within the entrance, riding to the
wind, and abreast of the town.   Her fore-mast, which had
been cut away while she was on the reef, had not yet been
replaced, her main and mizzen-top-masts were housed, and
her lower yards were on the gunwales.   Her lower standing
rigging, however, was in its place, and, as was shortly afterwards ascertained, her guns were loaded and shotted.   Just
within her, lay two corsairs, with a few gun-boats, and a galley or two.

It was a mild evening for the season, and the sea and bay
were smooth as in summer; as unlike as possible to the same
place a few days previously, when the two vessels had been
driven from the enterprise by a tempest.   Perceiving that he
was likely to get in too soon, when about five miles from the
rocks, Mr. Decatur ordered buckets and other drags to be towed
astern, in order to lessen the way of the ketch, without shortening sail, as the latter expedient would have been seen from
the port, and must have awakened suspicion.   In the mean
time the wind gradually fell, until it became so light as to leave
the ketch but about two knots' way on her, when the drags
were removed.

About 10 o'clock the Intrepid reached the eastern entrance
of the bay, or the passage between the rocks and the shoal.
The wind was nearly east, and, as she steered directly for the
frigate, it was well abaft the beam.   There was a young moon,
and as these bold adventurers were slowly advancing into the
hostile port, all around them was tranquil and apparently without distrust.   For near an hour they were stealing slowly
along, the air gradually failing, until their motion became
scarcely perceptible.

Most of the officers and men of the ketch had been ordered
to lie on the deck, where they were concealed by low bulwarks,
or weather-boards, and by the different objects that belong to
a vessel.   As it is the practice of those seas, to carry many
men even in the smallest craft, the appearance of ten or twelve
would excite no alarm, and this number was visible.   The

commanding officer, himself, stood near the pilo., M.. Catalano,* who was to act as interpreter.   The quarter-master at the
helm, was ordered to stand directly for the frigate's bows, it
being the intention to lay the ship aboard in that place, as the
mode of attack which would least expose the assailants to her
fire.

The Intrepid was still at a considerable distance from the
Philadelphia, when the latter hailed.   The pilot answered that
the ketch belonged to Malta, and was on a trading voyage ;
that she had been nearly wrecked, and had lost her anchors
in the late gale, and that her commander wished to ride by the
frigate during the night.   This conversation lasted some time,
Mr. Decatur instructing the pilot to tell the frigate's people
with what he was laden, in order to amuse them, and the Intrepid gradually drew nearer, until there was every prospect
of her running foul of the Philadelphia, in a minute or two,
and at the very spot contemplated.   But the wind suddenly
shifted, and took the ketch aback.   The instant the southerly
puff struck her, her head fell off, and she got a stern-board;
the ship, at the same moment, tending to the new current of
air.   The effect of this unexpected change was to bring the
ketch directly under the frigate's broadside, at the distance of
about forty yards, where she lay perfectly becalmed, or, if
any thing, drifting slowly astern, exposed to nearly every one
of the Philadelphia's larboard guns.

Not the smallest suspicion appears to have been yet excited
on board the frigate, though several of her people were looking over the rails, and notwithstanding the moonlight.   So
completely were the Turks deceived, that they lowered a boat,
and sent it with a fast.   Some of the ketch's men, in the mean
time, had got into her boat, and had run a line to the frigate's
fore-chains.   As they returned, they met the frigate's boat,
took the fast it brought, which came from the after part of the
ship, and passed it into their own vessel.   These fasts were
put into the hands of the men, as they lay on the ketch's
deck, and they began cautiously to breast the Intrepid alongside of the Philadelphia, without rising.   As soon as the latter
got near enough to the ship, the Turks discovered her anchors,
and they sternly ordered the ketch to keep off, as she had deceived them; preparing, at the same time, to cut the fasts.
All this passed in a moment, when the cry of " Amerikanos"

* Now a sailing-master in the navy.

was heard in the ship. The people of the Intrepid, by a strong pull, brought their vessel alongside of the frigate, where she was secured, quick as thought. Up to this moment, not a whisper had betrayed the presence of the men concealed. The instructions had been positive to keep quiet until commanded to show themselves; and no precipitation, even in that trying moment, deranged the plan.

Lieutenant Commandant Decatur was standing ready for a spring, with Messrs. Laws and Morris quite near him. As soon as close enough, he jumped at the frigate's chain-plates, and while clinging to the ship himself, he gave the order to board. The two midshipmen were at his side, and all the officers and men of the Intrepid arose and followed. The three gentlemen named were in the chains together, and Lieutenant Commandant Decatur and Mr. Morris sprang at the rail above them, while Mr. Laws dashed at a port. To the latter would have belonged the honour of having been first in this gallant assault, but wearing a boarding-belt, his pistols were caught between the gun and the side of the port. Mr. Decatur's foot slipped in springing, and Mr. Charles Morris first stood upon the quarter-deck of the Philadelphia. In an instant, Lieutenant Commandant Decatur and Mr. Laws were at his side, while heads and bodies appeared coming over the rail, and through the ports in all directions.

The surprise appears to have been as perfect, as the assault was rapid and earnest. Most of the Turks on deck crowded forward, and all ran over to the starboard-side, as their enemies poured in on the larboard. A few were aft, but as soon as charged, they leaped into the sea. Indeed, the constant plunges into the water, gave the assailants the assurance that their enemies were fast lessening in numbers by flight. It took but a minute or two to clear the spar-deck, though there was more of a struggle below. Still, so admirably managed was the attack, and so complete the surprise, that the resistance was trifling. In less than ten minutes Mr. Decatur was on the quarter-deck again, in undisturbed possession of his prize.

There can be no doubt that this gallant officer now felt bitter regrets that it was not in his power to bring away the ship he had so nobly recovered. Not only were his orders on this point peremptory, however, but the frigate had not a sail bent, nor a yard crossed, and she wanted her foremast. It was

16

next to impossible, therefore, to remove her, and the command was given to pass up the combustibles from the ketch.

The duty of setting fire to the prize, appears to have been executed with as much promptitude and order, as every other part of the service. The officers distributed themselves, agreeably to the previous instructions, and the men soon appeared with the necessary means. Each party acted by itself, and as it got ready. So rapid were they all in their movements, that the men with combustibles had scarcely time to get as low as the cock-pit and after-store-rooms, before the fires were lighted over their heads. When the officer entrusted with the duty last mentioned had got through, he found the after-hatches filled with smoke, from the fire in the ward-room and steerage, and he was obliged to make his escape by the forward ladders.

The Americans were in the ship from twenty to twenty-five minutes, and they were literally driven out of her by the flames. The vessel had got to be so dry in that low latitude, that she burnt like pine; and the combustibles had been as judiciously prepared, as they were steadily used. The last party up, were the people who had been in the store-rooms, and when they reached the deck, they found most of their companions already in the Intrepid. Joining them, and ascertaining that all was ready, the order was given to cast off. Notwithstanding the daring character of the enterprise in general, Mr. Decatur and his party now ran the greatest risk they had incurred that night. So fierce had the conflagration already become, that the flames began to pour out of the ports, and the head-fast having been cast off, the ketch fell astern, with her jigger flapping against the quarter-gallery, and her boom foul. The fire showed itself in the window at this critical moment; and beneath, was all the ammunition of the party, covered with a tarpaulin. To increase the risk, the stern-fast was jammed. By using swords, however, for there was not time to look for an axe, the hawser was cut, and the Intrepid was extricated from the most imminent danger, by a vigorous shove. As she swung clear of the frigate, the flames reached the rigging, up which they went hissing, like a rocket, the tar having oozed from the ropes, which had been saturated with that inflammable matter. Matches could not have kindled with greater quickness.

The sweeps were now manned. Up to this moment, every thing had been done earnestly, though without noise, but as soon as they felt that they had got command of their ketch again, and by two or three vigorous strokes had sent her away from the frigate, the people of the Intrepid ceased rowing, and as one man, they gave three cheers for victory. This appeared to arouse the Turks from their stupor; for the cry had hardly ended, when the batteries, the two corsairs, and the galley, poured in their fire. The men laid hold of the sweeps again, of which the Intrepid had eight of a side, and favoured by a light air, they went rapidly down the harbour.

The spectacle that followed, is described as having been both beautiful and sublime. The entire bay was illuminated by the conflagration, the roar of cannon was constant, and Tripoli was in a clamour. The appearance of the ship was, in the highest degree, magnificent; and, to add to the effect, as her guns heated, they began to go off. Owing to the shift of wind, and the position into which she had tended, she, in some measure, returned the enemy's fire, as one of her broadsides was discharged in the direction of the town, and the other towards Fort English. The most singular effect of this conflagration was on board the ship, where the flames having run up the rigging and masts, collected under the tops, and fell over, giving the whole the appearance of glowing columns and fiery capitals.

Under ordinary circumstances, the situation of the ketch would still have been thought sufficiently perilous, but after the exploit they had just performed, her people, elated with success, regarded all that was now passing as a triumphal spectacle. The shot constantly cast the spray around them, or were whistling over their heads; but the only sensation they produced, was by calling attention to the brilliant *jets d'eau* that they occasioned as they bounded along the water. But one struck the Intrepid, although she was within half a mile of many of the heaviest guns for some time, and that passed through her top-gallant-sail.

With sixteen sweeps, and eighty men elated with success, Mr. Decatur was enabled to drive the little Intrepid ahead with a velocity that rendered towing useless. Near the harbour's mouth, he met the Siren's boats, sent to cover his retreat, but their services were scarcely necessary. As soon as the ketch was out of danger, he got into one, and pulled aboard the brig, to report to Lieutenant Commandant Stewart, the result of his undertaking.

The Siren had got into the offing some time after the Intre-

pid, agreeably to arrangement, and anchored about three miles
from the rocks.  Here she hoisted out the launch and a cutter,
manned and armed them, and sent them in, under Mr. Caldwell, her first lieutenant.   Soon after the brig weighed, and
the wind having entirely failed outside, she swept into eight
fathoms water, and anchored again, to cover the retreat, should
the enemy attempt to board the Intrepid, with his gun-boats.
It will readily be supposed that it was an anxious moment, and
as the moon rose, all eyes were on the frigate.   After waiting
in intense expectation near an hour, a rocket went up from the
Philadelphia.   It was the signal of possession, and Mr. Stewart ran below to get another for the answer.   He was gone
only a moment, but when he returned, the fire was seen
shining through the frigate's ports, and in a few more minutes,
the flames were rushing up her rigging, as if a train had been
touched.    Then followed the cannonade, and the dashing of
sweeps, with the approach of the ketch.    Presently a boat was
seen coming alongside, and a man, in a sailor's jacket, sprang
over the gangway of the brig.   It was Decatur, to announce
his victory !

The ketch and brig lay near each other, for about an hour,
when a strong and favourable wind arose, and they made sail
for Syracuse, which port they reached on the 19th.   Here the
party was received with salutes and congratulations, by the
Sicilians, who were also at war with Tripoli, as well as by
their own countrymen.

The success of this gallant exploit laid the foundation of the
name which Mr. Decatur subsequently acquired in the navy.
The country generally applauded the feat ; and the commanding officer was raised from the station of a lieutenant to that
of a captain.    Most of the midshipmen engaged, were also promoted, and Lieutenant Commandant Decatur received a sword.

The Philadelphia was a frigate of the class that the English
termed a thirty-eight, previously to the war of 1812.   Her
armament consisted of 28 eighteens, on her gun deck, and of
16 carronades and chase guns, above ; or of 44 guns in the
whole.   No correct estimate has probably ever been made of
the number of men in her, when she was recaptured.   Twenty
were reported to have been killed, and one boat loaded with
Turks is said to have escaped ; many also swam ashore, or to
the nearest cruisers.   Some, no doubt, secreted themselves below, of whom the greater part must have perished in the ship,
as the party that set fire to the after-store-rooms had difficulty

in escaping from the flames. But one prisoner was made, a wounded Turk, who took refuge in the ketch. On the part of the Americans but a single man was hurt.

In whatever light we regard this exploit, it extorts our admiration and praise; the boldness in the conception of the enterprise, being even surpassed by the perfect manner in which all its parts were executed. Nothing appears to have been wanting, in a military point of view; nothing was deranged; nothing defeated. The hour was well chosen, and no doubt it was a chief reason why the corsairs, gun-boats, and batteries, were, in the first place, so slow in commencing their fire, and so uncertain in their aim when they did open on the Americans. In appreciating the daring of the attempt, we have only to consider what might have been the consequences had the assault on the frigate been repulsed. Directly under her guns, with a harbour filled with light cruisers, gun-boats, and galleys, and surrounded by forts and batteries, the inevitable destruction of all in the Intrepid must have followed. These were dangers that cool steadiness and entire self-possession, aided by perfect discipline, could alone avert. In the service, the enterprise has ever been regarded as one of its most brilliant achievements; and to this day, it is deemed a high honour to have been one among the Intrepid's crew. The effect on the squadron then abroad can scarcely be appreciated; as its seamen began to consider themselves invincible, if not invulnerable, and were ready for any service in which men could be employed.

## CHAPTER XX.

THUS opened the year 1804. The great distance, however, that lay between the seat of war and the country, as well as the infrequency of direct communications, prevented the government at home, from getting early information of what was passing in the Mediterranean. As a consequence, at the very moment when Commodore Preble was beginning to show that energy for which he was so remarkable, the department was making preparations for superseding him in the command; not

16 *

from dissatisfaction, but, as was then believed, from necessity. There were but three captains in the navy junior to Preble, and one of these was a captive in Tripoli. The loss of the Philadelphia had rendered it indispensable to send out another frigate, at least ; and the administration had now begun to take so serious a view of the state of the relations of the country with all the Barbary powers, as to see the importance of exhibiting a force that should look down any further attempts on a trade, which, in consequence of the general war that prevailed in Europe, was beginning to whiten the seas of the old world with American canvass. The Emperor of Morocco, who was said to be a relative of the Bashaw of Tripoli, was distrusted in particular, and many little occurrences had served to prove the interest that the former felt in the affairs of the latter.

The ships that it was now decided to send into the Mediterranean, were the President 44, Congress 38, Constellation 38, and Essex 32. They were put in commission early in the season, and as soon as the choice was made, Commodore Preble was apprised of it, and of the necessity that existed of sending out two officers who were his seniors in rank. About the same time, Mr. Decatur was made a captain, for the destruction of the Philadelphia, and the service received an important impulse in the revival of the rank of masters and commanders, which had been dropped altogether, under the reduction law of 1801.

The Siren and Intrepid returned to Syracuse, after the successful attempt on the Philadelphia, on the 19th of February of this year. On the 2d of March, Commodore Preble, who had so divided his force as to keep some of the small vessels off Tripoli blockading, proceeded to Malta, and on his return, he sailed again, on the 21st, for the station off the enemy's port. The Siren 16, Lieutenant Commandant Stewart, and Nautilus 12, Lieutenant Commandant Somers, were the blockading vessels at this time, and, early one morning, while coming from the eastward to recover lost ground, a vessel with the appearance of a brig of war, was seen lying-to in the offing. As soon as he made the Americans, the stranger endeavoured to beat back into the harbour again, out of which he had lately come, but, the Nautilus being sent close in to employ the gun-boats, should they attempt to come out, the Siren cut him off from the port, and soon got alongside. This vessel proved to be the Transfer, a privateer out of Malta, with a British commission, and she had an armament of 16 carronades, and a crew of 80

men.  When the Siren ran alongside, the Transfer's people
were at quarters ; but, no resistance being attempted, she was
captured for a violation of the blockade.   Subsequent information induced Commodore Preble to believe that she belonged, in
fact, to the Bashaw of Tripoli, and that the commission under
which she sailed was obtained by means of the Tripolitan consul in Malta, who was a native of that island, and for whose
appearance on board the brig was actually waiting when taken.

As the Transfer had been an English gun-brig, and was
equipped for war, Commodore Preble sent her to Syracuse,
where she was appraised, manned, and taken into the service
for the time being.   She was called the Scourge, and the command of her was given to Lieutenant Commandant Dent, the
acting captain of the Constitution.

Remaining off Tripoli a few days, Commodore Preble was
next actively employed in running from port to port, in order
to look into the affairs of the different regencies, to communicate with the captives in Tripoli, and to make his arrangements
for pursuing a warfare better suited to bringing the bashaw to
terms.   The king of the Two Sicilies being at war with Tripoli, also, in furtherance of the latter duty, the Constitution
went to Naples, in order to obtain some assistance in executing
these projects.   Here an order for two bomb-vessels and six
gun-boats was obtained, with the necessary equipments ; and
Commodore Preble sailed for Messina, where the different craft
lay.   From this time until the middle of July, he was as actively engaged as ever, in providing for the wants of the captives, in settling a serious difficulty with Tunis, and in preparing
for an attack on Tripoli ; and we shall quit him, for a moment,
to return to the movements before that place.

In April, the Siren, Lieutenant Commandant Stewart ; Argus, Lieutenant Commandant Hull ; Enterprise, Lieutenant
Commandant Decatur ; Vixen, Lieutenant Commandant Smith,
and Scourge, Lieutenant Commandant Dent, composed the
blockading force, when a felucca was seen stealing along
shore, coming from the westward, with a view to enter the harbour in a fog.   A general chase ensued, and the felucca took
refuge behind a reef of rocks, about ten miles to the westward
of Tripoli, where she was run upon a beach of sand.   The Siren now made a signal for the boats to go in, in order to destroy the enemy.   Mr. Caldwell, the first lieutenant of the Siren,
being nearest in, went ahead with the launch and cutter of that
brig, while the others followed as the vessels came up.   As he

approached the shore, the boat of Mr. Caldwell got on a sunken
rock, and the enemy, who had begun to collect in force, particularly in cavalry, opened a sharp fire of musketry.   Several
of the Americans were killed and wounded, and perceiving that
the enemy were both too strong and too well posted to be attacked by so feeble a force, Mr. Caldwell returned, directing
the different boats, as he met them, to retire also.

The Argus and schooners now obtained positions where they
could throw their shot into the felucca, which was soon rendered unseaworthy.   While this was doing, the Siren ran
down, opened a ravine in which the Turks were posted, and
dislodged them by a smart discharge of grape.   Afterwards, a
broadside or two were thrown in among a strong body of cavalry, which had the effect of rendering them cautious in their
operations on the coast.   This little affair illustrates the nature
of the ordinary warfare that was then carried on, the Tripolitans sending out bodies of soldiers to cover any vessel that was
expected with supplies.   On this occasion, the felucca was said
to be loaded with salt, an article that then bore an enormous
price in Tripoli.

It was July the 21st, 1804, when Commodore Preble was
able to sail from Malta, with all the force he had collected, to
join the vessels cruising off Tripoli.   The blockade had been
kept up with vigour for some months, and the Commodore felt
that the season had now arrived for more active operations.
He had with him the Constitution, Enterprise, Nautilus, the
two bomb-vessels, and the six gun-boats.   The bomb-vessels
were of only thirty tons measurement, and carried a thirteen-
inch mortar each.   In scarcely any respect were they suited
for the duty that was expected of them.   The gun-boats were
little better, being shallow, unseaworthy craft, of about twenty-
five tons burthen, in which long iron twenty-fours had been
mounted.   Each boat had one gun, and thirty-five men ; the
latter, with the exception of a few Neapolitans, being taken
from the different vessels of the squadron.   The Tripolitan
gun-boats, which have already been described, were altogether superior, and the duty should have been exactly reversed,
in order to suit the qualities of the respective craft ; the boats
of Tripoli having been built to go on the coast, while those
possessed by the Americans were intended solely for harbour
defence.   In addition to their other bad qualities, these Neapo-
litan boats were found neither to sail nor to row even tolerably
well.   It was necessary to tow them, by larger vessels, the

moment they got into rough water; and when it blew heavily, there was always danger of dragging them under. In addition to this force, Commodore Preble had obtained six long twenty-six pounders for the upper-deck of the Constitution, which were mounted in the waist.

When the American commander assembled his whole force before Tripoli, on the 25th of July, 1804, it consisted of the Constitution 44, Commodore Preble; Siren 16, Lieutenant Commandant Stewart; Argus 16, Lieutenant Commandant Hull; Scourge 14, Lieutenant Commandant Dent; Vixen 12, Lieutenant Commandant Smith; Nautilus 12, Lieutenant Commandant Somers; Enterprise 12, Lieutenant Commandant Decatur; the two bomb-vessels, and six gun-boats. In some respects this was a well-appointed force for the duty required, while in others it was lamentably deficient. Another heavy ship, in particular, was wanted, and the means for bombarding had all the defects that may be anticipated. The two heaviest brigs had armaments of twenty-four-pound carronades; the other brig, and two of the schooners, armaments of eighteen-pound carronades; while the Enterprise retained her original equipment of long sixes, in consequence of her ports being unsuited to the new guns. As the Constitution had a gun-deck battery of thirty long twenty-fours, with six long twenty-sixes, and some lighter long guns above, it follows that the Americans could bring twenty-two twenty-fours and six twenty-sixes to bear on the stone walls of the town, in addition to a few light chase-guns in the small vessels, and the twelve-pounders of the frigate's quarter-deck and forecastle. On the whole, there appears to have been in the squadron, twenty-eight heavy long guns, with about twenty lighter, that might be brought to play on the batteries simultaneously. Opposed to these means of offence, the bashaw had one hundred and fifteen guns in battery, most of them quite heavy, and nineteen gun-boats that, of themselves, so far as metal was concerned, were nearly equal to the frigate. Moored in the harbour were also two large galleys, two schooners, and a brig, all of which were armed and strongly manned. The American squadron was manned by one thousand and sixty persons, all told, while the bashaw had assembled a force that has been estimated as high as twenty-five thousand, Arabs and Turks included. The only advantage possessed by the assailants, in the warfare that was so soon to follow, were those which are dependent on spirit, discipline, and system.

The vessels could not anchor until the 28th, when they ran in, with the wind at E. S. E., and came-to, by signal, about a league from the town.　This was hardly done, however, before the wind came suddenly round to N. N. W., thence to N. N. E., and it began to blow strong, with a heavy sea setting directly on shore.　At 6 P. M., a signal was made for the vessels to weigh, and to gain an offing.　Fortunately, the wind continued to haul to the eastward, or there would have been great danger of towing the gun-boats under, while carrying sail to claw off the land.　The gale continued to increase until the 31st, when it blew tremendously.　The courses of the Constitution were blown away, though reefed, and it would have been impossible to save the bomb-vessels and gun-boats, had not the wind hauled so far to the southward as to give them the advantage of a weather shore, and of comparatively smooth water.　Fortunately, the gale ceased the next day.

On the third of August, 1804, the squadron ran in again and got within a league of the town, with a pleasant breeze at the eastward.　The enemy's gun-boats and galleys had come outside of the rocks, and were lying there in two divisions; one near the eastern, and the other near the western entrance, or about half a mile apart.　At the same time, it was seen that all the batteries were manned, as if an attack was not only expected, but invited.

At half-past 12, the Constitution wore with her head off shore, and showed a signal for all vessels to come within hail. As he came up, each commander was ordered to prepare to attack the shipping and batteries.　The bomb-vessels and gunboats were immediately manned, and such was the high state of discipline in the squadron, that in one hour, every thing was ready for the contemplated service.

On this occasion, Commodore Preble made the following distribution of that part of his force, which was manned from the other vessels of his squadron.

One bomb-ketch was commanded by Lieutenant Commandant Dent, of the Scourge.

The other bomb-ketch was commanded by Mr. Robinson, first lieutenant of the Constitution.

### First Division of gun-boats.

No. 1. Lieut. Com. Somers, of the Nautilus.
" 2. Lieut. James Decatur, of the Nautilus.
" 3. Lieut. Blake, of the Argus.

*Second division of gun-boats.*

No. 4. Lieut. Com. Decatur, of the Enterprise.
"    5. Lieut. Bainbridge, of the Enterprise.
"    6. Lieut. Trippe, of the Vixen.

At half-past one, the Constitution wore again, and stood towards the town. At two, the gun-boats were cast off, and formed in advance, covered by the brigs and schooners, and half an hour later, the signal was shown to engage. The attack was commenced by the two bombards, which began to throw shells into the town. It was followed by the batteries, which were instantly in a blaze, and then the shipping on both sides opened their fire, within reach of grape.

The eastern, or most weatherly division of the enemy's gun-boats, nine in number, as being least supported, was the aim of the American gun-boats. But the bad qualities of the latter craft were quickly apparent, for, as soon as Mr. Decatur steered towards the enemy, with an intention to come to close quarters, the division of Mr. Somers, which was a little to leeward, found it difficult to sustain him. Every effort was made by the latter officer, to get far enough to windward to join in the attack ; but finding it impracticable, he bore up, and ran down alone on five of the enemy to leeward, and engaged them all within pistol-shot, throwing showers of grape, canister, and musket-balls, among them. In order to do this, as soon as near enough, the sweeps were got out, and the boat was backed astern to prevent her from drifting in among the enemy. No. 3 was closing fast, but a signal of recall* being shown from the Constitution, she hauled out of the line to obey, and losing ground, she kept more aloof, firing at the boats and shipping in the harbour; while No. 2, Mr. James Decatur, was enabled to join the division to windward. No. 5, Mr. Bainbridge, lost her latine-yard, while still in tow of the Siren, but, though unable to close, she continued advancing, keeping up a heavy fire, and finally touched on the rocks.

By these changes, Lieutenant Commandant Decatur† had three boats that dashed forward with him, though one belonged to the division of Mr. Somers, viz. No. 4, No. 6, and No. 2,

---

* The signal was bent on by mistake, and was abroad a moment only, but the fact that it was shown, was established before a Court of Inquiry, which exonerated Mr. Blake from censure.

† He was Captain Decatur at the time, but the fact was not yet known in the squadron.

The officers in command of these three boats, went steadily on until within the smoke of the enemy. Here they delivered their fire, throwing in a terrible discharge of grape and musket-balls, and the order was given to board. Up to this moment, the odds had been as three to one against the assailants; and it was now, if possible, increased. The brigs and schooners could no longer assist. The Turkish boats were not only the heaviest and the best in every sense, but they were much the strongest manned. The combat now assumed a character of chivalrous prowess and of desperate personal efforts, that belongs to the middle ages, rather than to struggles of our own times. Its details, indeed, savour more of the glow of romance, than of the sober severity that we are accustomed to associate with reality.

Lieutenant Commandant Decatur took the lead. He had no sooner discharged his shower of musket-balls, than No. 4 was laid alongside the opposing boat of the enemy, and he went into her, followed by Lieutenant Thorn, Mr. M'Donough, and all the Americans of his crew. The Tripolitan boat was divided nearly in two parts, by a long open hatchway, and as the people of No. 4 came in on one side, the Turks retreated to the other, making a sort of ditch of the open space. This caused an instant of delay, and, perhaps, fortunately, for it permitted the assailants to act together. As soon as ready, Mr. Decatur charged round each end of the hatchway, and after a short struggle, a portion of the Turks were piked and bayoneted, while the rest submitted, or leaped into the water.*

No sooner had Mr. Decatur got possession of the boat first assailed, than he took her in tow, and bore down on the one next to leeward. Running the enemy aboard, as before, he went into him, with most of his officers and men. The captain of the Tripolitan vessel was a large powerful man, and Mr. Decatur personally charged him with a pike. The weapon, however, was seized by the Turk, wrested from the hands of the assailant, and turned against its owner. The latter parried a thrust, and made a blow with his sword at the pike, with a view to cut off its head. The sword hit the iron, and broke at the hilt, and the next instant the Turk made another thrust.

---

* It is probable that the crew of this boat was in a measure staggered by the close fire of the gun, as No. 4 approached, her captain having received no fewer than fourteen musket-balls in his body, by that one discharge.

HORNET SINKING THE PEACOCK

Nothing was left to the gallant Decatur, but his arm, with which he so far averted the blow, as to receive the pike through the flesh of one breast. Pushing the iron from the wound, by tearing the flesh, he sprang within the weapon, and grappled his antagonist. The pike fell between the two, and a short trial of strength succeeded, in which the Turk prevailed. As the combatants fell, however, Mr. Decatur so far released himself as to lie side by side with his foe on the deck. The Tripolitan now endeavoured to reach his poniard, while his hand was firmly held by that of his enemy. At this critical instant, when life or death depended on a moment well employed, or a moment lost, Mr. Decatur drew a small pistol from the pocket of his vest, passed the arm that was free round the body of the Turk, pointed the muzzle in, and fired. The ball passed entirely through the body of the Mussulman, and lodged in the clothes of his foe. At the same instant, Mr. Decatur felt the grasp that had almost smothered him relax, and he was liberated. He sprang up, and the Tripolitan lay dead at his feet.

In such a *mêlée* it cannot be supposed that the struggle of the two leaders would go unnoticed. An enemy raised his sabre to cleave the skull of Mr. Decatur, while he was occupied by his enemy, and a young man of the Enterprise's crew interposed an arm to save him. The blow was intercepted, but the limb was severed to a bit of skin. A fresh rush was now made upon the enemy, who was overcome without much further resistance.

An idea of the desperate nature of the fighting that distinguished this remarkable assault, may be gained from the amount of the loss. The two boats captured by Lieutenant Commandant Decatur, had about eighty men in them, of whom fifty-two are known to have been killed and wounded ; most of the latter very badly. As only eight prisoners were made who were not wounded, and many jumped overboard and swam to the rocks, it is not improbable that the Turks suffered still more severely. Lieutenant Commandant Decatur himself being wounded, he secured his second prize, and hauled off to rejoin the squadron ; all the rest of the enemy's division that were not taken, having by this time, run into the harbour, by passing through the openings between the rocks.

While Lieutenant Commandant Decatur was thus employed to windward, his brother, Mr. James Decatur, the first lieutenant of the Nautilus, was nobly emulating his example in No. 2. Reserving his fire, like No. 4, this young officer dashed into the smoke, and was on the point of boarding, when he received a musket-ball in his forehead.    The boats met and rebounded ; and in the confusion of the death of the commanding officer of No. 2, the Turk was enabled to escape, under a heavy fire from the Americans.    It was said, at the time, that the enemy had struck before Mr. Decatur fell, though the fact must remain in doubt.    It is, however, believed that he sustained a very severe loss.

In the mean time, Mr. Trippe, in No. 6, the last of the three boats that was able to reach the weather division, was not idle. Reserving his fire, like the others, he delivered it with deadly effect, when closing, and went aboard of his enemy in the smoke.    In this instance, the boats also separated by the shock of the collision, leaving Mr. Trippe, with Mr. J. D. Henley, and nine men only, on board the Tripolitan.    Here, too, the commanders singled each other out, and a severe personal combat occurred, while the work of death was going on around them.    The Turk was young, and of a large athletic form, and he soon compelled his slighter but more active foe to fight with caution.    Advancing on Mr. Trippe, he would strike a blow and receive a thrust in return.    In this manner, he gave the American commander no less than eight sabre wounds in the head, and two in the breast ; when, making a sudden rush, he struck a ninth blow on the head, which brought Mr. Trippe upon a knee.    Rallying all his force in a desperate effort, the latter, who still retained the short pike with which he fought, made a thrust that passed the weapon through his gigantic adversary, and tumbled him on his back.    As soon as the Tripolitan officer fell, the remainder of his people submitted.

The boat taken by Mr. Trippe, was one of the largest belonging to the bashaw.    The number of her men is not positively known, but, living and dead, thirty-six were found in her, of whom twenty-one were either killed or wounded. When it is remembered that but eleven Americans boarded her, the achievement must pass for one of the most gallant on record.*

---

* While Mr. Trippe was so hard pressed by his antagonist, a Turk aimed a blow at him, from behind ; but just before the latter struck, Sergeant Meredith, of the marines, passed a bayonet through his body. While the prizes were hauling off, no one had thought, in the confusion of such a scene, of lowering the flag of the Tripolitan boat, and she was seen advancing with the enemy's ensign set.    The Vixen gave her a broadside, which brought down colours, mast, latine-yard, and all.    Fortunately, no one was hurt.

All this time the cannonade and bombardment continued without ceasing. Lieutenant Commandant Somers, in No. 1, sustained by the brigs and schooners, had forced the remaining boats to retreat, and this resolute officer pressed them so hard as to be compelled to ware within a short distance of a battery of twelve guns, quite near the mole. Her destruction seemed inevitable, as the boat came slowly round, when a shell fell into the battery, most opportunely blew up the platform, and drove the enemy out, to a man. Before the guns could be again used, the boat had got in tow of one of the small vessels.

There was a division of five boats and two galleys of the enemy, that had been held in reserve within the rocks, and these rallied their retreating countrymen, and made two efforts to come out and intercept the Americans and their prizes, but they were kept in check by the fire of the frigate and small vessels. The Constitution maintained a very heavy fire, and silenced several of the batteries, though they re-opened as soon as she had passed. The bombards were covered with the spray of shot, but continued to throw shells to the last.

At half-past four, the wind coming round to the northward, a signal was made for the gun-boats and bomb-ketches to rejoin the small vessels, and another to take them and the prizes in tow. The last order was handsomely executed by the brigs and schooners, under cover of a blaze of fire from the frigate. A quarter of an hour later, the Constitution herself hauled off, and ran out of gun-shot.

Thus terminated the first serious attack that was made on the town and batteries of Tripoli. Its effect on the enemy, was of the most salutary kind; the manner in which their gun-boats had been taken, by boarding, having made a lasting and deep impression. The superiority of the Christians in gunnery, was generally admitted before; but here was an instance in which the Turks had been overcome by inferior numbers, hand to hand, a species of conflict in which they had been thought particularly to excel. Perhaps no instance of more desperate fighting of the sort, without defensive armour, is to be found in the pages of history. Three gun-boats were sunk in the harbour, in addition to the three that were taken; and the loss of the Tripolitans by shot, must have been very heavy. About fifty shells were thrown into the town, but little damage appears to have been done in this way, very few of the bombs, on account of the imperfect materials that had been furnished, exploding. The batteries were a good deal damaged, but the town suffered no essential injury.

On the part of the Americans, only 14 were killed and wounded in the affair; and all of these, with the exception of one man, belonged to the gun-boats. The Constitution, though under fire two hours, escaped much better than could have been expected. She received one heavy shot through her main-mast, had a quarter-deck gun injured,* and was a good deal cut up aloft. The enemy had calculated his range for a more distant cannonade, and generally overshot the ships. By this mistake the Constitution had her main-royal-yard shot away.

On the occasion of the battle of the 3d of August, the officers who had opportunities of particularly distinguishing themselves, were Lieutenants Commandant Decatur and Somers; Lieutenants Trippe, Decatur, Bainbridge, and Thorn, and Messrs. M'Donough, Henley, Ridgely, and Miller. But the whole squadron behaved well; and the Constitution was handled, under the fire of the batteries, with the steadiness of a ship working into a roadstead.

---

## CHAPTER XXI.

THE vessels hauled off and anchored about two leagues from Tripoli, to repair their damages. On the morning of the 5th, the Argus brought-to a small French privateer that had just got out of the harbour, and Commodore Preble induced her commander to return and carry in all the badly wounded among his prisoners.† From the captain of this vessel, he learned that the enemy had suffered even more than

---

* A shot came in aft, hit the gun, and broke in several pieces. Commodore Preble was directly in its range, but he escaped by the shot's breaking. One of the fragments took off the tip of a marine's elbow, quite near him.

† Mr. Morris of the Argus was rowing guard, close in, when he found himself unexpectedly alongside of a strange sail. Without hesitating, he boarded and carried her by surprise, when she proved to be the privateer in question.

had been supposed in the attack of the 3d, particularly in and about the port.   On the 7th, the privateer came out, bringing a letter from the French consul, stating that the Bashaw was much more disposed to treat than previously to the late affair, and advising the commodore to send in a flag of truce, with a view to negotiate.   As the castle made no signal to support this proposition, it was not regarded.

Between the 3d and the 7th, the squadron was occupied in altering the rig of the three captured gun-boats, and in putting them in a condition for service.   As soon as the latter were equipped, they were numbered 7, 8, and 9, and the command of them was given to Lieutenants Crane, Caldwell, and Thorn. At 9 A. M., on the 7th, the light vessels weighed, and the bombards proceeded to take a position in a small bay to the westward of the town, where they were not much exposed to shot. At half-past 2, the bombards, having gained their anchorage, commenced throwing shells, and the gun-boats opened a heavy fire on the batteries.   The effect on the latter was soon apparent, and many of their guns were rendered useless.   In the height of the cannonade, a strange vessel appeared in the offing, and the Argus was sent in chase.   The enemy now began to get his galleys and gun-boats in motion, and once or twice they advanced towards the opening between the rocks, and commenced a fire; but the Constitution, Nautilus, and Enterprise, being stationed to windward to cut them off, and the Siren and Vixen lying near the American gun-vessels to cover the latter, the enemy, after the lesson received on the 3d, were afraid to venture.

At half-past 3, or after the action had lasted about an hour, a hot shot passed through the magazine of No. 8, Lieutenant Caldwell, the boat taken by Mr. Trippe in the affair of the 3d, and she immediately blew up.   When the smoke cleared away, all the after part of the boat was under water, while Mr. Robert T. Spence, of the Siren, and 11 men were forward, loading the long twenty-six-pounder that formed her armament. This gun was loaded and fired, and its gallant crew gave three cheers as their vessel sunk beneath them.   Mr. Spence, who could not swim, saved himself on an oar, while the rest of the people got on board the different boats, where they continued to fight during the remainder of the action.

No. 8, when she blew up, had a crew of 28 persons in all, of whom 10 were killed and 6 wounded.   Among the former was Mr. Caldwell, her commander, the first lieutenant of the

17 *

Siren, and Mr. Dorsey, a midshipman of the same vessel.
These two officers were greatly regretted, as both bade fair to
be ornaments to their profession.*

At half-past 5, or after the cannonade had lasted nearly
three hours, the Constitution made a signal for the brigs and
schooners to take the bombards and gun-boats in tow, and the
squadron hauled off for its anchorage again.   Just at this time,
the Argus made a signal that the sail in sight was a friend.

The gun-boats, in this attack, suffered considerably.   In
consequence of the wind's being on-shore, Commodore Preble
had kept the frigate out of the action, and the enemy's batteries
had no interruption from the heavy fire of that ship.   Several
of the American boats had been hulled, and all suffered materially in their sails and rigging.   No. 6, Lieutenant Wadsworth, had her latine-yard shot away.   The killed and wounded
amounted to 18 men.

At 8 o'clock in the evening, the John Adams 28, Captain
Chauncey, from America, came within hail of the Constitution,
and reported herself.   By this ship, Commodore Preble received despatches informing him of the equipment of the vessels
that were to come out under Commodore Barron, and of the
necessity, which was thought to exist, of superseding him in
the command.   Captain Chauncey also stated the probability
of the speedy arrival of the expected ships, which were to sail
shortly after his own departure.   As the John Adams had
brought stores for the squadron, and had put most of her gun-
carriages in the other frigates to enable her to do so, she could
be of no immediate use; and the rest of the vessels being so
soon expected, Commodore Preble was induced to delay the
other attacks he had meditated, on the ground of prudence.

By the John Adams, intelligence reached the squadron of
the re-establishment of the rank of masters and commanders,

---

* Mr. Edmund P. Kennedy, one of the gunner's crew belonging to the
Siren, was the captain of the gun, on board No. 8, when she blew up.
Mr. Kennedy was a young gentleman of Maryland, who had quitted
school in quest of adventure, and, having been impressed into the British
navy, on obtaining his discharge in the Mediterranean, he entered under
the flag of his country.   In consequence of his good conduct on this occasion, and from a desire to place him in a station better suited to his
pretensions, Commodore Preble made Mr. Kennedy an acting midshipman.   The appointment was confirmed at home, and the gentleman in
question has since worn a broad pennant.   It is believed that this officer
and one other, are the only two in the navy who can boast of having gone
through all the gradations of the service, from forward, aft.

and the new commissions were brought out to the officers before Tripoli, who had been promoted.  In consequence of these changes, Lieutenant Commandant Decatur was raised to the rank of captain, and became the second in command then present; while Lieutenants Commandant Stewart, Hull, Chauncey, Smith, and Somers, became masters commandant, in the order in which they are named.  Several of the young gentlemen were also promoted, including most of those who had a share in the destruction of the Philadelphia.

The bashaw now became more disposed than ever to treat, the warfare promising much annoyance, with no corresponding benefits.  The cannonading did his batteries and vessels great injuries, though the town probably suffered less than might have been expected, being in a measure protected by its walls.  The shells, too, that had been procured at Messina, turned out to be very bad, few exploding when they fell.*  The case was different with the shot, which did their work effectually on the different batteries.  Some idea may be formed of the spirit of the last attack, from the report of Commodore Preble, who stated that nine guns, one of which was used but a short time, threw 500 heavy shot, in the course of little more than two hours.

Although the delay caused by the expected arrival of the reinforcement, was improved to open a negotiation, it was without effect.  The bashaw had lowered his demands quite half, but he still insisted on a ransom of $500 a man for his prisoners, though he waived the usual claim for tribute in future.  These propositions were not received, it being expected that, after the arrival of the reinforcement, the treaty might be made on the usual terms of civilised nations.

On the 9th of August, the Argus, Captain Hull, had a narrow escape.  That brig having stood in towards the town, to reconnoitre, with Commodore Preble on board, one of the heaviest of the shot from the batteries, raked her bottom for some distance, and cut the planks half through.  An inch or two of variation in the direction of this shot, would infallibly have sunk the brig, and that probably in a very few minutes.

---

* According to the private journal of Captain Bainbridge, then a prisoner in the town, out of forty-eight shells thrown by the two bombards in the attack of the 7th, but one exploded.  Agreeably to the records made by this officer at the time, the bombs on no occasion did much injury, and the town generally suffered less by shot even than was commonly supposed.

No intelligence arriving from the expected vessels, Commodore Preble, about the 16th, began to make his preparations for another attack, sending the Enterprise, Lieutenant Commandant Robinson, to Malta, with orders for the agent to forward transports with water, the vessels being on a short allowance of that great essential.   On the night of the 17th, Captains Decatur and Chauncey went close in, in boats, and reconnoitred the situation of the enemy.   These officers, on their return, reported that the vessels of the Tripolitan flotilla were moored abreast of each other, in a line extending from the mole to the castle, with their heads to the eastward, which was making a defence directly across the inner harbour or galley-mole.

A gale, however, compelled the American squadron to stand off shore on the morning of the 18th, which caused another delay in the contemplated movements.   While lying-to, in the offing, the vessels met the transports from Malta, and the Enterprise returned, bringing no intelligence from the expected reinforcement.

On the 24th, the squadron stood in towards the town again, with a light breeze from the eastward.   At 8 P. M., the Constitution anchored just out of gun-shot of the batteries, but it fell calm, and the boats of the different vessels were sent to tow the bombards to a position favourable for throwing shells. This was thought to have been effected by 2 A. M., when the two vessels began to heave their bombs, covered by the gunboats.   At daylight, they all retired, without having received a shot in return.   Commodore Preble appears to have distrusted the result of this bombardment, the first attempted at night, and there is reason to think it produced but little effect.*

The weather proving very fine and the wind favourable, on the 28th, Commodore Preble determined to make a more vigorous assault on the town and batteries, than any which had preceded it, and his dispositions were taken accordingly.   The gun-boats and bombards requiring so many men to manage them, the Constitution and the small vessels had been compelled to go into action short of hands, in the previous affairs. To obviate this difficulty, the John Adams had been kept before the town, and a portion of her officers and crew, and nearly all her boats, were put in requisition, on the present

---

* Captain Bainbridge, in his private journal, says that all the shells thrown on this occasion fell short.

occasion. Captain Chauncey, himself, with about seventy of his people, went on board the flag-ship, and all the boats of the squadron were hoisted out and manned. The bomb vessels were crippled and could not be brought into service, a circumstance that probably was of no great consequence, on account of the badness of the materials they were compelled to use.\* These two vessels, with the Scourge, transports, and John Adams, were anchored well off at sea, not being available in the contemplated cannonading.

Every thing being prepared, a little after midnight the following gun-boats proceeded to their stations, viz : No. 1, Captain Somers ; No. 2, Lieutenant Gordon ; No. 3, Mr. Brooks, master of the Argus; No. 4, Captain Decatur ; No. 5, Lieutenant Lawrence ; No. 6, Lieutenant Wadsworth ; No. 7, Lieutenant Crane ; and No. 9, Lieutenant Thorn. They were divided into two divisions, as before, Captain Decatur having become the superior officer, however, by his recent promotion. About 3 A. M. the gun-boats advanced close to the rocks at the entrance of the harbour, covered by the Siren, Captain Stewart, Argus, Captain Hull, Vixen, Captain Smith, Nautilus, Lieutenant Reed, and Enterprise, Lieutenant Commandant Robinson, and accompanied by all the boats of the squadron. Here they anchored, with springs on their cables, and commenced a cannonade on the enemy's shipping, castle, and town. As soon as the day dawned, the Constitution weighed and stood in towards the rocks, under a heavy fire from the batteries, Fort English, and the castle. At this time, the enemy's gun-boats and galleys, thirteen in number, were closely and warmly engaged with the eight American boats ; and the Constitution, ordering the latter to retire by signal, as their ammunition was mostly consumed, delivered a heavy fire of round and grape on the former as she came up. One of the enemy's boats was soon sunk, two were run ashore to prevent them from meeting a similar fate, and the rest retreated.

The Constitution now continued to stand on, until she had run in within musket-shot of the mole, when she brought-to, and opened upon the town, batteries, and castle. Here she lay three-quarters of an hour, pouring in a fierce fire, with

---

\* It is stated that Commodore Preble subsequently discovered lead in the fuse-holes of many of the bombs. It was supposed that this had been done by treachery, by means of French agents in Sicily, the shells having been charged to resist the French invasion.

great effect, until finding that all the small vessels were out of gun-shot, she hauled off. About 700 heavy shot were thrown at the enemy, in this attack, besides a good many from the chase-guns of the small vessels. The enemy sustained much damage, and lost many men. The American brigs and schooners were a good deal injured aloft, as was the Constitution. Although the latter ship was so long within reach of grape, many of which shot struck her, she had not a man hurt! Several of her shrouds, back-stays, trusses, spring-stays, chains, lifts, and a great deal of running rigging were shot away, and yet her hull escaped with very trifling injuries. A boat belonging to the John Adams, under the orders of Mr. John Orde Creighton, one of that ship's master's mates, was sunk by a double-headed shot, which killed three men, and badly wounded a fourth, but the officer and the rest of the boat's crew were saved.

In this attack a heavy shot from the American gun-boats struck the castle, passed through a wall, and rebounding from the opposite side of the room, fell within six inches of Captain Bainbridge, who was in bed at the moment, and covered him with stones and mortar; from under which he was taken, considerably hurt, by his own officers. More injury was done the town in this attack, than in either of the others, the shot appearing to have told on many of the houses.

From this time to the close of the month, preparations were making to use the bombards again, and for renewing the cannonading, another transport having arrived from Malta, without bringing any intelligence of the vessels under the orders of Commodore Barron. On the 3d of September, every thing being ready, at half-past two the signal was made for the small vessels to advance. The enemy had improved the time as well as the Americans, and they had raised three of their own gun-boats that had been sunk in the affairs of the 3d and of the 28th of August. These craft were now added to the rest of their flotilla.

The Tripolitans had also changed their mode of fighting. Hitherto, with the exception of the affair of the 3d, their galleys and gun-boats had lain either behind the rocks, in positions to fire over them, or at the openings between them, and they consequently found themselves to leeward of the frigate and small American cruisers, the latter invariably choosing easterly winds to advance with, as they would permit crippled vessels to retire. On the 3d of August, the case excepted, the Turks had been so roughly treated by being brought hand to hand, when they evidently expected nothing more than a cannonade, that they were not disposed to venture again outside of the harbour. On the 3d of September, however, the day at which we have now arrived, their plan of defence was judiciously altered. No sooner was it perceived that the American squadron was in motion, with a fresh design to annoy them, than their gun-boats and galleys got under way, and worked up to windward, until they had gained a station on the weather side of the harbour, directly under the fire of Fort English, as well as of a new battery that had been erected a little to the westward of the latter.

This disposition of the enemy's force, required a corresponding change on the part of the Americans. The bombards were directed to take stations and to commence throwing their shells; while the gun-boats, in two divisions, commanded as usual by Captains Decatur and Somers, and covered by the brigs and schooners, assailed the enemy's flotilla. This arrangement separated the battle into two distinct parts, leaving the bomb vessels very much exposed to the fire of the castle, the mole, crown, and other batteries.

The Tripolitan gun-boats and galleys stood the fire of the American flotilla until the latter had got within reach of musketry, when they retreated. The assailants now separated, some of the gun-boats following the enemy, and pouring in their fire, while the others, with the brigs and schooners, cannonaded Fort English.

In the mean while, perceiving that the bombards were suffering severely from the undisturbed fire of the guns to which they were exposed, Commodore Preble ran down in the Constitution, quite near the rocks, and within the bomb vessels, and brought to. Here the frigate opened as warm a fire as probably ever came out of the broadside of a single-decked ship, and in a position where seventy heavy guns could bear upon her. The whole harbour in the vicinity of the town, was glittering with the spray of her shot, and each battery, as usual, was silenced as soon as it drew her attention. After throwing more than three hundred round shot, besides grape and canister, the frigate hauled off, having previously ordered the other vessels to retire from action, by signal.

The gun-boats, in this affair, were an hour and fifteen minutes engaged, in which time they threw four hundred round shot, besides grape and canister. Lieutenant Trippe, who

had so much distinguished himself, and who had received sc
many wounds that day month, resumed the command of No.
6, for this occasion.   Lieutenant Morris, of the Argus, was in
charge of No. 3.   All the small vessels suffered, as usual,
aloft, and the Argus sustained some damage in her hull.

The Constitution was so much exposed in the attack just
related, that her escape can only be attributed to the weight of
her own fire.   It had been found, in the previous affairs, that
so long as this ship could play upon a battery, the Turks could
not be kept at its guns ; and it was chiefly while she was veer-
ing, or tacking, that she suffered.   But, after making every
allowance for the effect of her own cannonade, and for the imperfect gunnery of the enemy, it creates wonder that a single
frigate could lie opposed to more than double her own number
of available guns, and these too, principally, of heavier metal,
while they were protected by stone walls.   On this occasion,
the frigate was not supported by the gun-boats at all, and she
became the sole object of the enemy's aim after the bombards
had withdrawn.

As might have been expected, the Constitution suffered more
in the attack just recorded, than in any of the previous affairs,
though she received nothing larger than grape in her hull.
She had three shells through her canvass, one of which rendered the main-top-sail momentarily useless.   Her sails, standing and running rigging were also much cut with shot.   Captain Chauncey, of the John Adams, and a party of his officers
and crew, served in the Constitution again on this day, and
were of essential use.   Indeed, in all the service which succeeded her arrival, the commander, officers, and crew of the
John Adams were actively employed, though the ship herself
could not be brought before the enemy, for the want of gun-
carriages.

The bombards, having been much exposed, suffered accordingly.   No. 1, was so much crippled, as to be unable to move,
without being towed, and was near sinking when she was got
to the anchorage.   Every shroud she had was shot away.
Commodore Preble expressed himself satisfied with the good
conduct of every man in the squadron.   All the vessels appear
to have been well conducted, and efficient in their several stations.   Of the effect of the shells, there is no account to be relied on, though it is probable that, as usual, many did not explode.   There is no doubt, however, that the bombs were well
directed, and that they fell into the town.

While Commodore Preble was thus actively employed in carrying on the war against the enemy, the attack just related having been the fifth made on the town within a month, he was meditating another species of annoyance, that was now ready to be put in execution.

---

## CHAPTER XXII.

THE ketch Intrepid, which had been employed by Mr. Decatur in burning the Philadelphia, was still in the squadron, having been used of late as a transport between Tripoli and Malta. This vessel had been converted into an "infernal," or, to use more intelligible terms, she had been fitted as a floating mine, with the intention of sending her into the harbour of Tripoli, to explode among the enemy's cruisers. As every thing connected with the history of this little vessel, as well as with the enterprise in which she was about to be employed, will have interest with the public, we shall be more particular than common in giving the details of this affair, as they have reached us through public documents, and oral testimony that is deemed worthy of entire credit.

A small room or magazine had been planked up in the hold of the ketch, just forward of her principal mast. Communicating with this magazine was a trunk or tube, that led aft, to another room filled with combustibles. In the planked room, or magazine, were placed one hundred barrels of gunpowder in bulk, and on the deck immediately above the powder, were laid fifty thirteen and a half inch shells, and one hundred nine inch shells, with a large quantity of shot, pieces of kentledge, and fragments of iron of different sorts. A train was laid in the trunk, or tube, and fuses were attached in the proper manner. In addition to this arrangement, the other small room mentioned was filled with splinters and light wood, which, besides firing the train, were to keep the enemy from boarding, as the flames would be apt to induce them to apprehend an immediate explosion.

The plan was well laid. It was the intention to profit by the first dark night that offered, to carry the ketch as far as

18

possible into the galley-mole, to light the fire in the splinter-room, and for the men employed, to make their retreat in boats.

The arrangements for carrying this project into effect appear to have been made with care and prudence. Still the duty, on every account, was deemed desperate. It was necessary, in the first place, to stand in by the western or little passage, in a dull-sailing vessel, and with a light wind, directly in the face of several batteries, the fire of which could only be escaped by the enemy's mistaking the ketch for a vessel endeavouring to force the blockade. It would also be required to pass quite near these batteries, and, as the ketch advanced, she would be running in among the gun-boats and galleys of the enemy. It is not necessary to point out the hazards of such an exploit, as a simple cannonade directed against a small vessel filled with powder, would of itself be, in the last degree, dangerous. After every thing had succeeded to the perfect hopes of the assailants, there existed the necessity of effecting a retreat, the service being one in which no quarter could be expected.

Such a duty could be confided to none but officers and men of known coolness and courage, of perfect self-possession, and of tried spirit. Captain Somers, who had commanded one division of the gun-boats in the different attacks on the town that have been related, in a manner to excite the respect of all who witnessed his conduct, volunteered to take charge of this enterprise ; and Lieutenant Wadsworth, of the Constitution, an officer of great merit, offered himself as the second in command. It being unnecessary to send in any more than these two gentlemen, with the few men needed to manage the ketch and row the boats, no other officer was permitted to go, though it is understood that several volunteered.

The night of the 4th of September, or that of the day which succeeded the attack last related, promising to be obscure, and there being a good leading wind from the eastward, it was selected for the purpose. Commodore Preble appears to have viewed the result of this expedition with great anxiety, and to have ordered all its preparations, with the utmost personal attention to the details. This feeling is believed to have been increased by his knowledge of the character of the officers who were to go in, and who, it was understood, had expressed a determination neither to be taken, nor to permit the ammunition in the ketch to fall into the enemy's hands. The latter point was one of great importance, it being understood that the

Tripolitans, like the Americans, were getting to be in want of powder.*   In short, it was the general understanding in the squadron, before the ketch proceeded, that her officers had determined not to be taken.   Two fast-rowing boats, one belonging to the Constitution, that pulled six oars, and one belonging to the Siren, that pulled four oars, were chosen to bring the party off, and their crews were volunteers from the Constitution and Nautilus.   At the last moment, Mr. Israel, an ardent young officer, whose application to go in had been rejected, found means to get on board the ketch, and, in consideration of his gallantry, he was permitted to join the party.

When all was ready, or about 8 o'clock in the evening of the day just mentioned, the Intrepid was under way, with the Argus, Vixen, and Nautilus in company.   Shortly after, the Siren also weighed, by a special order from the commodore, and stood in towards the western passage, or that by which the ketch was to enter, where she remained to look out for the boats.

The Nautilus, Captain Somers' own vessel, accompanied the ketch close in, but, on reaching a position where there was danger of her creating suspicions by being seen, she hauled off, to take her station, like the other small vessels, near the rocks, in order to pick up the retreating boats.   The last person of the squadron who had any communication with Captain Somers, was Mr. Washington Reed, the first lieutenant of his own schooner, the Nautilus, who left him about 9 o'clock.   At that time, all was calm, collected, and in order, on board the " infernal."   The general uneasiness was increased by the circumstance that three gun-boats lay near the entrance; and some of the last words of the experienced Decatur, before taking leave of his friend, were to caution him against these enemies.

The sea was covered with a dense haze, though the stars were visible, and the last that may be said to have been seen of the Intrepid, was the shadowy forms of her canvass, as she steered slowly, but steadily, into the obscurity, where the eyes

---

* A day or two before the ketch was ready, the commodore himself was trying a port-fire in the cabin of the Constitution, in the presence of Captain Somers, and of one or two other officers, and finding that one burned a particular time, by the watch, he remarked that he thought " it burned longer than was necessary, as the time might enable the enemy to approach and extinguish it before the train would be fired."   " I ask for no port-fire at all," was the quiet answer of Captain Somers.

of the many anxious spectators fancied they could still trace
her dim outline, most probably after it had totally disappeared.
This sinking into the gloom of night, was no bad image of the
impenetrable mystery that has veiled the subsequent proceedings of the gallant party on board her.

When the Intrepid was last seen by the naked eye, she was
not a musket-shot from the mole, standing directly for the harbour.   One officer on board the nearest vessel, the Nautilus,
is said, however, to have never lost sight of her with a night-
glass, but even he could distinguish no more than her dim pro-
portions.   There is a vague rumour that she touched on the
rocks, though it does not appear to rest on sufficient authority
to be entitled to much credit.   To the last moment, she appears to have been advancing.   About this time the batteries
began to fire.   Their shot are said to have been directed towards every point where an enemy might be expected, and it
is not improbable that some were aimed at the ketch.

The period between the time when the Intrepid was last
seen, and that when most of those who watched without the
rocks learned her fate, was not long.   This was an interval
of intense, almost of breathless expectation ; and it was inter-
rupted only by the flashes and the roar of the enemy's guns.
Various reports exist of what those who gazed into the gloom
beheld, or fancied they beheld ; but one melancholy fact alone
would seem to be beyond contradiction.   A fierce and sudden
light illuminated the panorama, a torrent of fire streamed up-
ward, and a concussion followed that made the cruisers in the
offing tremble from their trucks to their keels.   This sudden
blaze of light was followed by a darkness of two-fold intensity,
and the guns of the battery became mute, as if annihilated.
Numerous shells were seen in the air, and some of them descended on the rocks, where they were heard to fall.   The
fuses were burning, and a few exploded, but much the greater
part were extinguished in the water.   The mast, too, had risen
perpendicularly, with its rigging and canvass blazing, but the
descent veiled all in night.

So sudden and tremendous was the eruption, and so intense
the darkness which succeeded, that it was not possible to ascertain the precise position of the ketch at the moment.   In the
glaring, but fleeting light, no person could say that he had
noted more than the material circumstance, that the Intrepid
had not reached the point at which she aimed.   The shells had
not spread far, and those which fell on the rocks were so many

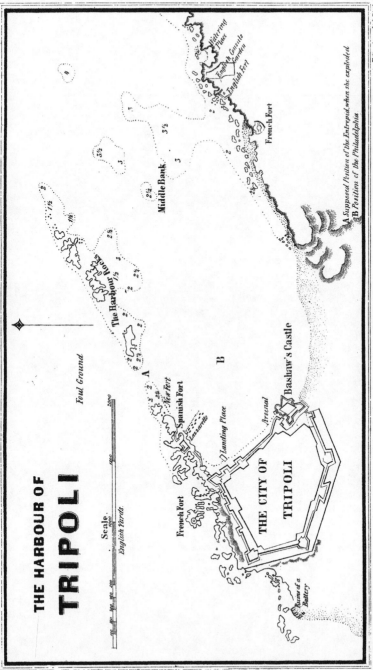

# THE HARBOUR OF
# TRIPOLI

Scale

1000    2000

English Yards

Foul Ground

T.Sinclairs Lith Phila

A Supposed Position of the Entrepid when she exploded
B Position of the Philadelphia

Watering Place

English Consuls Garden

English Fort

French Fort

Middle Bank

The Harbour Rock

New Fort

Spanish Fort

Lazaretto

Landing Place

French Fort

Arsenal

Bashaw's Castle

THE CITY OF
TRIPOLI

Ruins of a
Battery

A

B

proofs of this important truth.   There was no other fact to in-
dicate the precise spot where the ketch exploded.   A few cries
arose from the town, but the subsequent and deep silence that
followed was more eloquent than any clamour.   The whole
of Tripoli was like a city of tombs.

If every eye had been watchful previously to the explosion,
every eye now became doubly vigilant to discover the retreating boats.   Men got over the sides of the vessels, holding
lights, and placing their ears near the water, in the hope of
detecting the sounds of even muffled oars; and often was it
fancied that the gallant adventurers were near.   They never
re-appeared.   Hour after hour went by, until hope itself became exhausted.   Occasionally, a rocket gleamed in the darkness, or a sullen gun was heard from the frigate, as signals to
the boats; but the eyes that should have seen the first, were
sightless, and the last tolled on the ears of the dead.

The three vessels assigned to that service hovered around
the harbour until the sun rose ; but few traces of the Intrepid,
and nothing of her devoted crew, could be discovered.   The
wreck of the mast lay on the rocks near the western entrance,
and here and there a fragment was visible nigh it.   One of the
largest of the enemy's gun-boats was missing, and it was observed that two others, which appeared to be shattered, were
being hauled upon the shore.   The three that had lain across
the entrance had disappeared.   It was erroneously thought
that the castle had sustained some injury from the concussion,
though, on the whole, the Americans were left with the melancholy certainty of having met with a serious loss, without obtaining a commensurate advantage.

It is now known that the bottom of the ketch grounded on
the north side of the rocks, near the round battery at the end
of the mole ; and as the wind was at the eastward, this renders
it certain that the explosion took place in the western entrance
to the harbour, and fully a quarter of a mile from the spot that
it was intended the ketch should reach.   In the wreck were
found two mangled bodies, and four more were picked up on
the 6th, floating in the harbour, or lodged on the shore.   These
bodies were in the most shocking state of mutilation, and,
though Captain Bainbridge and one or two of his companions
were taken to see them, it was found impossible to distinguish
even the officers from the men.   It is understood that six more
bodies were found, the day after the explosion, on the shore to

18 *

the southward of the town, and that a six-oared boat, with one body in it, had drifted on the beach to the westward.*

These statements account for all those who went in the ketch, and furnish conjectural clues to facts that would otherwise be veiled in impenetrable mystery. The spot where the boat was found, was a proof that the ketch had not got very far into the passage, or the cutter could not have drifted clear of the natural mole to the westward. The reason that the boat and the ketch's bottom were not found near the same spot, was probably because the first was acted on more by the wind, and the last by the current; and the fact that a boat may have drifted through rocks, with which the shore is everywhere more or less lined, that would have brought up the wreck.

As there was but one body found in the boat, we are left to suppose it was that of the keeper. Of the four-oared boat, or that which belonged to the Siren, there does not appear to have been any tidings, and it was either destroyed by the explosion, sunk by the fall of fragments, or privately appropriated to himself by some Tripolitan.

From the fact of there being but a single man in the Constitution's cutter, there is reason to infer that most of the officers and men were on board the ketch, herself, when she blew up. No person is understood to say that any of the enemy's vessels were seen near the ketch, when she exploded, and, with these meagre premises, we are left to draw our inferences as to the causes of the disaster.

That Captain Somers was as capable of sacrificing himself, when there was an occasion for it, as any man who ever lived, is probably as true as it is certain that he would not destroy himself, and much less others, without sufficient reason. It has been supposed that the ketch was boarded by the enemy, and that her resolute commander fired the train in preference to being taken. The spirit created by the chivalrous exploits of Decatur, and the high-toned discipline and daring of Preble, had communicated to all under their orders as lofty sentiments of duty and zeal as probably were ever found among an equal body of generous and ardent young men; but it is not easy to discover a motive why the explosion should have been an intentional act of the Americans, and it is easy to discover many why it should not.

There would be but one sufficient justification for an offi-

---

* Captain Bainbridge's private journal.

cer's sacrificing himself or his people under such circumstances, and that was the impossibility of preventing the ketch
from falling into the hands of the enemy, by any other means.
Neither the evidence of eye-witnesses, so far as it is available,
nor the accounts of the Tripolitans themselves, would appear
to show, that when the Intrepid exploded, any enemy was near
enough to render so desperate a step necessary.  According
to the private journal of Captain Bainbridge, neither the town
nor the Turks suffered materially, and he was carried to the
beach to see the dead bodies, on the 8th, or two days after the
affair.  This alone would prove that the ketch did not reach
the mole.  If the object were merely to destroy the powder,
the men would have been previously ordered into the boats,
and, even under circumstances that rendered a resort to the
fuse inexpedient, the train would have been used.  That only
one man was in the largest boat, is known from the condition
in which she was found, and this could hardly have happened,
under any circumstances, had the magazine been fired intentionally, by means of the train.  Every contingency had doubtless been foreseen.  One man was as able as twenty to apply
the match, and we can see but one state of things, besides
being boarded by surprise, that would render it likely that the
match would have been used until the people were in their
boats, or that it would have been applied at any other spot, than
at the end of the train, or aft.  A surprise of the nature mentioned, would seem to have been impossible ; for, though the
night was misty, objects might still be seen at some little distance, and it is probable, also, that the party had glasses.

   From weighing these circumstances, it is the most rational
opinion that the Intrepid was not intentionally blown up.  She
was under fire at the time, and though it is improbable that the
enemy had any shot heated to repel an attack so unexpected,
a cold shot might easily have fired a magazine in the situation
of that of the Intrepid.  The deck of the ketch, moreover,
was covered with loaded shells, and one of these might have
been struck and broken.  Some other unforeseen accident may
have occurred.  On the other hand, it is necessary to state,
that Commodore Preble firmly believed that his officers blew
themselves up, in preference to being made prisoners ; an opinion in which it would not be difficult to coincide, were there
proof that they were in any immediate danger of such a calamity.  It was also the general conjecture in the squadron
then before Tripoli, that such had been the fate of these bold

adventurers; but it would seem to have been formed at the time, rather on an opinion of what the party that went in was capable of doing, than on any evidence of what it had actually done.

As it is the province of the historian to present all the leading facts of his subject, we shall add, on the other hand, that many little collateral circumstances appear to have occurred, which may be thought to give force to the truth of the common impression. One of the best authenticated of these, is connected with what was seen from a vessel that was watching the ketch, though it was not the schooner nearest in. On board this vessel a light was observed moving on a horizontal line, as if carried swiftly along a vessel's deck by some one in hurried motion, and then to drop suddenly, like a lantern sinking beneath a hatchway. Immediately afterwards the ketch exploded, and at that precise spot, which would seem to leave no doubt that this light was on board the Intrepid. But even this by no means establishes the fact that the explosion was intentional. The splinters, that were to keep the enemy aloof, had not been lighted, and this movement with the lantern may have been intended to fire them, and may have had some accidental connexion with the explosion.

In addition to this appearance of the light, which rests on testimony every way entitled to respect, there was a report brought off by the prisoners, then in Tripoli, when liberated, from which another supposition has been formed as to the fate of this devoted vessel, that is not without plausibility. It was said that most of the bodies found had received gun-shot wounds, especially from grape. One body, in particular, was described as having had the small remains of nankeen pantaloons on it, and it was also reported that the hair* was of a deep black. Through this person, according to the report, no less than three grape-shot had passed. This has been supposed to have been the body of Captain Somers himself, who was the only one of the party that wore nankeens, and whose hair was of a deep black. On the supposition that the proofs of the grape-shot wounds actually existed, it has been conjectured that, as the ketch advanced, she was fired into with grape, most of her people shot down, and that the magazine was touched off by the two whose bodies were found in the

* It is possible certainly that this mark may have been observed, but it is more probable that the hair would have been consumed. Still a hat may have saved it.

wreck, and who were probably below when the Intrepid exploded.

That a close fire was opened when the ketch appeared, is beyond doubt, and that she was quite near the mole and crown batteries when the explosion occurred, is known, not only by means of the glass, but by the parts of the wreck that fell on the rocks. Indeed, the situation of the latter would give reason to suppose there might be some truth in the rumour that she had grounded, in which case her destruction by means of shot would have been rendered certain.

The prevalent opinion that the Intrepid was boarded by one or more of the gun-boats that lay near the entrance, would seem to have been entertained without sufficient proof. These vessels lay some distance within the spot where the ketch blew up, and it was not probable that they would have advanced to meet a vessel entering the harbour; for did they suppose her a friend, there would have been no motive; and did they suppose her an enemy, they would have been much more likely to avoid her. So shy, indeed, had the Tripolitans become, after the burning of the Philadelphia, and the boarding of their boats, that it was found extremely difficult to get their small vessels within the range of musket-balls. Captain Somers was known to have felt no apprehensions of being boarded by these three boats; for, when cautioned by his friend Decatur on that head, his answer was, " they will be more likely to cut and run." In this opinion that cool and observant officer was probably right. Had there been any vessel near the Intrepid when she blew up, the light of the explosion would have permitted her also to be seen; some portions of her wreck would have been visible next day; and her masts and sails would probably have been flying in the air, as well as those of the ketch.

But the fact that only thirteen bodies are spoken of in the private journal of Captain Bainbridge, is almost conclusive on the subject that no Tripolitan vessel was blown up on this occasion. This entry was made at the time, and before the nature of the expedition, or the number of those who had been sent in the ketch, was known to the Americans in Tripoli. The thirteen bodies account exactly for all on board; and as they came ashore in a most mutilated state, without clothes, in some instances without legs, arms, or heads, it was impossible to say whether they were the mangled remains of friends or enemies. Had a Tripolitan blown up in company, there must have been many more bodies in the same state, instead of the precise number mentioned, and Captain Bainbridge would have been as likely to be taken to see a dead Turk, as to see a dead American.

The missing gun-boat, of which Commodore Preble speaks in his report, may have been sunk by a falling shell; she may have been shattered and hauled into the galley-mole, out of sight; or, she may have removed in the darkness, and been confounded next morning with others of the flotilla. Observations made, by means of glasses, in a crowded port, at a distance of two or three miles, are liable to many errors. In short, it would seem to be the better opinion, that, from some untoward circumstance, the Intrepid exploded at a point where she did little or no injury to the enemy.*

One of three things seems to be highly probable, concerning this long-disputed point. The ketch has either exploded by means of the enemy's shot, than which, nothing was easier in the situation where she lay; the men have accidentally fired the magazine, while preparing to light the splinters below; or it has been done intentionally, in consequence of the desperate condition to which the party was reduced, by the destruction caused by grape. Of the three, after weighing all the circumstances, it is natural to believe that the first was the most probable, as it was certainly easier to cause a vessel like the

---

* The entry in the private journal of Captain Bainbridge, is as follows: " Was informed that the explosion that we heard last night, proceeded from a vessel (which the Americans attempted to send into the harbour,) blowing up; which unfortunate scheme did no damage whatever to the Tripolitans; nor did it even appear to heave them into confusion." " On the 8th, by the bashaw's permission, with Lieutenant ——, went to the beach of the harbour, and there saw six persons in a most mangled and burnt condition, lying on the shore; whom we supposed to have been part of the unfortunate crew of the fire-vessel, the bottom of which grounded on the north side of the rocks near the round battery. Two of these distressed-looking objects were fished out of the wreck. From the whole of them being so much disfigured, it was impossible to recognise any known feature to us, or even to distinguish an officer from a seaman. Mr. Cowdery, who accompanied us, informed me that he saw six others yesterday, on the shore to the southward, which were supposed to have come from the same vessel. He also informed me that an American six-oared boat, with one man in her, was found drifted on the beach to the westward."

On the subject of Commodore Preble's impressions of the fate of the Intrepid, it may be well to say, that the Constitution left Tripoli soon after the ketch was blown up, and that his letter was dated at Malta, September 18th. Owing to this circumstance, he must necessarily have been ignorant of facts that were subsequently ascertained.

Intrepid, with a hundred barrels of loose powder in her magazine, to explode by means of shot, than to cause a vessel like No. 8, which is known to have been blown up, in this manner, in the action of the 7th of August.  As regards the grape-shot wounds, it will be seen that Captain Bainbridge is silent.

A sad and solemn mystery, after all our conjectures, must for ever veil the fate of those fearless officers and their hardy followers.  In whatever light we view the affair, they were the victims of that self-devotion which causes the seaman and soldier to hold his life in his hand, when the honour or interest of his country demands the sacrifice.  The name of Somers has passed into a battle-cry, in the American marine, while those of Wadsworth and Israel are associated with all that can ennoble intrepidity, coolness, and daring.

The war, in one sense, terminated with this scene of sublime destruction.  Commodore Preble had consumed so much of his powder, in the previous attacks, that it was no longer in his power to cannonade; and the season was fast getting to be dangerous to remain on that exposed coast.  The guns, mortars, shells, &c., were taken out of the small vessels, on account of the appearance of the weather, the day after the loss of the Intrepid; and on the 7th, the John Adams, Siren, Nautilus, Enterprise, and Scourge, were directed to take the bombards and gun-boats in tow, and to proceed to Syracuse; while the Constitution, with the Argus and Vixen in company, maintained the blockade.  It is not known that another shot was fired at Tripoli.

Three days later, or on the 10th of September, 1804, the President 44, wearing the broad pennant of Commodore Barron, hove in sight, with the Constellation 38, Captain Campbell, in company, when the command was regularly transferred to the former officer.  On the 12th, two sail were cut off, while attempting to enter Tripoli loaded with wheat.  On the 17th, the Constitution reached Malta, with the two prizes; and subsequently, Commodore Preble went to Syracuse in the Argus.  At a later day, he came home in the John Adams, where he arrived on the 26th of February, 1805.  In the mean time, Captain Decatur proceeded to Malta and took command of the Constitution, which was the first frigate this celebrated officer ever had under his orders.

The country fully appreciated the services of Commodore Preble.  He had united caution and daring in a way to denote the highest military qualities; and his success in general, had been in proportion. The attack of the Intrepid, the only material failure in any of his enterprises, was well arranged, and had it succeeded, it would probably have produced peace in twenty-four hours. As it was, the bashaw was well enough disposed to treat, though he seems to have entered into some calculations in the way of money, that induced him to hope the Americans would still reduce their policy to the level of his own, and prefer paying ransom to maintaining cruisers so far from home. Commodore Preble, and all the officers and men under his orders, received the thanks of Congress, and a gold medal was bestowed on the former. By the same resolution, Congress expressed the sympathy of the nation in behalf of the relatives of Captain Richard Somers, Lieutenants Henry Wadsworth, James Decatur, James R. Caldwell, and Joseph Israel, and Mr. John Sword Dorsey, midshipman; the officers killed off Tripoli.

---

## CHAPTER XXIII.

The squadron left in the Mediterranean, under the orders of Commodore Barron, after the departure of Commodore Preble, was much the strongest force that the country had then assembled in that sea. It consisted of the following vessels, viz. :

| | | |
|---|---|---|
| President | 44, | Capt. Cox; Com. Barron. |
| Constitution | 44, | "   Decatur. |
| Congress | 38, | "   Rodgers. |
| Constellation | 38, | "   Campbell. |
| Essex | 32, | "   J. Barron. |
| Siren | 16, | "   Stewart. |
| Argus | 16, | "   Hull. |
| Vixen | 12, | "   Smith. |
| Enterprise | 12, | Lieut. Com. Robinson. |
| Nautilus | 12, | "     "   Dent. |

The blockade of Tripoli was maintained by different vessels during the bad season of 1804–5 ; but no attack was attempted, although preparations were made to renew the war in the spring. One of the first measures of Commodore Preble, on reaching America, was to urge upon the government the necessity of building suitable bomb-ketches, and a few gun-boats

fitted to cannonade a place like Tripoli. His advice was followed, the vessels being immediately laid down; but it being
found impossible to have the ketches ready in time, the two
vessels before mentioned, were purchased, strengthened, and
equipped as bombards.

In November, Captain Rodgers, as the senior officer, was
put in command of the Constitution, while Captain Decatur
was transferred to the Congress. The winter and spring
passed in this manner, the blockade being maintained with
vigour, most of the time, though no event worthy of note occurred off the port. While matters remained in this state with
the ships, a movement by land was in the course of execution,
that must now be recorded, as it is intimately connected with
the history of the war.

It has been said already, that Jussuf Caramalli, the reigning
pacha, or bashaw of Tripoli, was a usurper, having deposed
his elder brother Hamet, in order to obtain the throne. The
latter had escaped from the regency, and, after passing a wan-
dering life, he had taken refuge among the Mamelukes of
Egypt. It had often been suggested to the American agents,
that the deposed prince might be made useful in carrying on
the war against the usurper; and at different times, several
projects had been entertained to that effect, though never with
any results. At length, Mr. Eaton, the consul at Tunis, who
had been a captain in the army, interested himself in the enterprise; and coming to America, he so far prevailed on the
government to lend itself to his views, as to obtain a species
of indirect support. Commodore Barron was directed to co-
operate with Mr. Eaton, as far as he might deem it discreet.

When the new squadron arrived out, it was accordingly ascertained where the ex-bashaw was to be found, and Mr. Eaton at once commenced his operations. Two or three days
after Commodore Barron had assumed the command before
Tripoli, he sent the Argus 16, Captain Hull, with that gentleman to Alexandria, where he arrived on the 26th of November. On the 29th, Mr. Eaton, accompanied by Lieutenant
O'Bannon, of the marines, and Messrs. Mann and Danielson,
two midshipmen of the squadron, proceeded to Rosetta, and
thence to Cairo. The viceroy of Egypt received them with
favour, and permission was obtained for the prince of Tripoli
to pass out of the country unmolested, though he had been
fighting against the government, with the discontented Mamelukes.

19

As soon as Hamet Caramalli received the proposals of Mr. Eaton, he separated himself from the Mamelukes, attended by about forty followers, and repaired to a point twelve leagues to the westward of the old port of Alexandria. Here he was soon joined by Mr. Eaton, at the head of a small troop of adventurers, whom he had obtained in Egypt. This party was composed of all nations, though Mr. Eaton expressed his belief, at the time, that had he possessed the means of subsistence, he might have marched a body of 30,000 men against Tripoli, the reigning bashaw having forced so many of his subjects into banishment. Soon after the junction agreed upon, Mr. Eaton, who now assumed the title of general, marched in the direction of Derne, taking the route across the Desert of Barca. This was early in 1805.

The Argus had returned to Malta for orders and stores, and on the 2d of April, she re-appeared off Bomba, with the Hornet 10, Lieutenant Commandant Evans, in company. Cruising on this coast a few days, without obtaining any intelligence of General Eaton and the bashaw, Captain Hull steered to the westward, and, a few leagues to the eastward of Derne, he fell in with the Nautilus, Lieutenant Commandant Dent. On communicating with this vessel, which was lying close in with the shore, Captain Hull ascertained that the expedition was on the coast, and that it waited only for the arms and supplies that had been brought, to attack Derne, from which town it was but a league distant. A field-piece was landed, together with some stores and muskets, and a few marines appear to have been put under the orders of Mr. O'Bannon, of the corps, when the vessels took their stations to aid in the attack.

It was 2, P. M., on the 27th of April, 1805, that this assault, so novel for Americans to be engaged in, in the other hemisphere, was commenced. The Hornet, Lieutenant Commandant Evans, having run close in, and anchored with springs on her cables, within pistol-shot of a battery of eight guns, opened her fire. The Nautilus lay at a little distance to the eastward, and the Argus still further in the same direction, the two latter firing on the town and battery. In about an hour, the enemy were driven from the work, when all the vessels directed their guns at the beach, to clear the way for the advance of the party on shore. The enemy made an irregular but spirited defence, keeping up a heavy fire of musketry, as the assailants advanced, from behind houses and walls. At half-past 3, however, Lieutenant O'Bannon and Mr. Mann stormed the principal work, hauling down the Tripolitan ensign, and, for the first time in the history of the country, hoisting that of the republic on a fortress of the old world. The enemy were driven out of this work with so much precipitation, that they left its guns loaded, and even primed. The cannon were immediately turned upon the town, and Hamet Caramalli having made a lodgment on the other side, so as to bring the enemy between two fires, the place submitted. At 4 o'clock, the boats of the vessels landed with ammunition for the guns and to bring off the wounded, Derne being completely in possession of the assailants.

In this affair, only 14 of the assailants were killed and wounded, General Eaton being among the latter. The attack was made by about 1200 men, while the place was supposed to be defended by three or four thousand. One or two attempts were made by the Tripolitans, to regain possession, but they were easily repulsed, and, on one occasion, with some loss. The deposed bashaw remained in possession of the town, and his authority was partially recognised in the province. General Eaton now earnestly pressed Commodore Barron for further supplies and reinforcements, with a view to march on Tripoli; but they were denied, on the ground that Hamet Caramalli was in possession of the second province of the regency, and if he had the influence that he pretended to possess, he ought to be able to effect his object by means of the ordinary co-operation of the squadron.

On the 22d of May Commodore Barron transferred the command, on account of ill health. The entire force under this new disposition, when the vessels known to be about to sail should arrive, would be as follows:

Constitution....44,........Com. Rodgers.  
President......44,........Capt. Cox.  
Constellation...38,........." Campbell.  
Congress......38,........." Decatur.  
Essex.........32,........." J. Barron.  
John Adams...28,........." Chauncey.  
Siren.........16,........." Stewart.  
Argus .........16,........." Hull.  
Vixen.........12,........." Smith.  
Nautilus.......12,........Lieut. Com. Dent.  
Enterprise.....12,........."   " Robinson.  
Hornet........12,........."   " Evans.

| Bombs | { | Vengeance.........Lieut. Com. Lewis. |
|-------|---|-------------------------------------|
|       | { | Spitfire................." M'Niell. |

| Gun-boats. | { | No. 2.......1 gun,......" Izard. |
|------------|---|----------------------------------|
|            |   | " 3.......2 ".........." Maxwell. |
|            |   | " 4.......2 ".........." J. D. Henley. |
|            |   | " 5.......2 ".........." Harrison. |
|            |   | " 6.......2 ".........." Lawrence. |
|            |   | " 8.......2 ".........." Harraden. |
|            |   | " 9.......2 ".........." Elbert. |
|            |   | " 10.......2 ".........." Carter. |
|            |   | " 11.......1 ".........." ——— |
|            |   | " 12.......1 ".........." ——— |

Shortly after assuming the command, Commodore Rodgers transferred Captain J. Barron from the Essex 32 to the President 44, giving the former ship to Captain Cox, who was only a master and commander.

Negotiations for peace now commenced in earnest, Mr. Lear having arrived off Tripoli, for that purpose, in the Essex, Captain Barron. After the usual intrigues, delays, and prevarications, a treaty was signed on the 3d of June, 1805. By this treaty, no tribute was to be paid in future, but $60,000 were given by America, for the ransom of the remaining prisoners, after exchanging the Tripolitans in her power, man for man.

Thus terminated the war with Tripoli, after an existence of four years. It is probable that the United States would have retained in service some officers, and would have kept up a small force, had not this contest occurred; but its influence on the fortunes and character of the navy is incalculable. It saved the first, in a degree at least, and it may be said to have formed the last.

## CHAPTER XXIV.

THE business at Tripoli was no sooner completed, than Commodore Rodgers sailed with thirteen vessels, gun-boats included, and anchored in Tunis Bay on the 1st of August. This movement was made in consequence of a dispute concerning a xebeck captured by the Constitution, for endeavouring to violate the recent blockade in company with her prizes. As soon as the consul had repaired on board and communicated the state of things in the regency, a council of war was called. The result was a letter to the Bey, demanding to know if a declaration made to the consul, in which he had said that the appearance of the American squadron off his port would be considered as the commencement of hostilities, was to be taken literally or not. In this letter the Bey was given to understand, in the plainest manner, that hostilities would commence on the part of the Americans, within thirty-six hours, should he decline answering, or neglect the application.

The Bey, accustomed to regard the Americans as tributaries, had been seeking a cause for war, when he was suddenly met by this high tone on the part of those whom he had hitherto found so much disposed to temporise. At first he appeared to place no faith in the demonstration, and the required answer was not sent. Commodore Rodgers, in consequence, directed Captain Decatur to land, to demand an audience of the Bey, and to obtain an unequivocal solution of the question of peace or war.

It is probable that the Bey regarded this mission as one of a doubtful nature, also; for he refused to receive Captain Decatur in the character in which he had been sent. That spirited officer, little accustomed to temporising, declined being admitted in any other. As soon as the intentions of both parties had been explained, Captain Decatur returned on board, when " the royal breast " of the Bey " appeared to be panic-struck." A letter was sent to the commodore, signed by the pacha himself, in which he expressed a desire to treat, and using the most pacific language. Shortly after he announced a wish to send a minister to Washington. This moderated tone put an end to the threatened hostilities, and after a negotiation that

19 *

lasted nearly a month, the affair was arranged with the regency, to the satisfaction of one of the parties at least. The xebeck was not given up. In September, a Tunisian ambassador embarked in the Congress 38, Captain Decatur, and in due time he was landed at Washington.

Commodore Rodgers remained in Tunis Bay more than a month, literally negotiating under the muzzles of his guns, and the result proved the wisdom of the course he had taken. The navy, the ablest of all negotiators in such matters, had completely reversed the ancient order of things; for, instead of an American agent's being compelled to solicit the restoration of prizes, illegally taken, in Africa, an African agent was now soliciting the restoration of prizes legally captured, in America. At a later day, the xebeck and her prizes were given up, as of no moment; but when the Tunisian minister added a demand for tribute, agreeably to former usage, he met with an explicit denial. After a short residence, he returned to his master with the latter answer, but the Bey did not see fit to take any steps in consequence. The impression made by the attacks on Tripoli, and by the appearance of the American squadron before his own town, would seem to have been lasting.

After the settlement of the dispute with Tunis, the vessels in the Mediterranean were gradually withdrawn, though it was still deemed necessary to keep a small squadron in that sea. The government also became better apprised of the nature of the force that was required, in carrying on a war with the Barbary states, and several new vessels were put into the water about this time, among which were two regularly constructed bombards, the Etna and the Vesuvius. Two sloops of war, of the most approved models, were also built, and became active cruisers on the peace establishment. These vessels were the Wasp 18, and the Hornet 18, the former being a ship and the latter a brig.

The condition of the navy may be said to have been negative at the period of which we are now writing; for, while all who reflected seriously on the subject, felt the necessity of greatly increasing this branch of the national defence, nothing efficient was attempted, or, apparently, contemplated. Ships of the line, without which it would be impossible to prevent any of even the secondary maritime states of Europe from blockading the ports of the country, were now scarcely mentioned, and the materials that had been collected for that object in 1800, were rapidly disappearing for the purposes of repairs and re-constructions. It is, indeed, difficult to imagine a policy as short-sighted and feeble, as that pursued by Congress at this particular juncture. With political relations that were never free from the appearances of hostilities, a trade that covered all the seas of the known world, and an experience that was replete with lessons on the necessity of repelling outrages by force, this great interest was treated with a neglect that approached fatuity. To add to this oversight, and to increase the despondency of the service, as well as of all those whose views extended to the future necessities of the country, the government appears to have adopted a policy, in connexion with the defence of the harbours, bays, and sounds of the coast, that was singularly adapted to breaking down the high tone that the navy had acquired in its recent experience. This " plan," which has been generally known as the " gun-boat policy," originated as far back as the year 1803, though it did not become of sufficient moment to be particularly noticed until the time at which we are now arrived, in the regular order of events.

The gun-boats, at first, were well received in the service, since they gave enterprising young officers commands; and the vessels originally constructed, were of an equipment, size and force, which in a measure removed the objections that young sea-officers would be apt to urge against serving in them. At the close of the year 1806, the President announced to Congress that the gun-boats already authorised by a law of April of the same year, 50 in number, were so far advanced as to put it in the power of the government to employ them all, the succeeding season; and the message contained a recommendation to extend the system.

An event soon occurred that not only stimulated this policy, but which induced the government to resort to new measures to protect the country, some of which were as questionable, as they were novel. A few ships had been kept in the Mediterranean, as stated; and it is worthy of being noted, that, with a commerce that, in 1807, employed 1,200,000 tons of shipping, this was the only foreign station on which an American cruiser was ever seen! Neither was there any proper home squadron, notwithstanding the constant complaints that were made of the wrongs inflicted by English and French cruisers, particularly the former, at the very mouths of the harbours of the country.

On the 25th of April, 1806, the British ship Leander **50,** Captain Whitby, in endeavouring to cut off a small coaster, that was running for Sandy Hook, fired a shot into her, which killed one of her people.    This outrage occurred quite near the shore, and it excited a strong feeling of indignation, in a portion of the country, at least.    But, unfortunately, party spirit had, at that period, taken the worst, most dangerous, and least creditable form, in which it can exist in any free country. By neglecting to place the republic in an attitude to command respect, the government had been compelled to appeal to arguments and principles, in those cases in which an appeal to force is the only preservative of national rights, and, in so doing, it opened the door to the admission of sophisms, counterarguments and discussions, that, in the end, effectually arrayed one-half of the community against the other, and this too, on matters in which foreign nations were the real parties on one side, and the common country on the other.    In a word, the great mistake was made of admitting of controversy concerning interests that all wise governments hold to be beyond dispute.

While the feelings, policy, and preparations of the United States were in the condition just mentioned, the Chesapeake 38, was put in commission, with a view of sending her to the Mediterranean, as the relief-ship, the time of the people of the Constitution 44, the only frigate left on that station, being nearly up.    Captain Charles Gordon, the youngest mastercommandant on the list, was attached to the Chesapeake as her captain, and Captain James Barron was selected to hoist a broad pennant in her, as commander of the squadron.

The ship remained at Washington, taking in her masts and stores, and receiving officers and men, until the close of the spring.    During this time the English minister informed the government that three deserters from his B. M. ship Melampus, had enlisted among the crew of the Chesapeake, and he requested that they might be given up.    Although the right to demand deserters is not recognised by the laws of nations, there is usually a disposition between friendly governments to aid each other in securing these delinquents, especially when it can be done under circumstances that produce no direct injury ; and the matter was referred by the navy department, to Commodore Barron, for investigation.    The inquiry appears to have been made in a proper temper, and with a sincere wish to dismiss the men, should they actually prove to be what was represented, though it might be questioned whether the Presi-

dent himself legally possessed any power to give them up to
their own officers.  Commodore Barron directed Captain Gordon to inquire into the matter with care, and to make his report.  It was ascertained that the three men were actually
deserters from the ship named, but they all claimed to be impressed Americans, who had availed themselves of the first
opportunity that offered on landing in their native country, to
make their escape from illegal and unjust detention.  One of
these men was said to be a native of the Eastern Shore, a part
of the country in which Captain Gordon was born ; and that
officer, after a careful examination, appears to have been satisfied with the truth of his account.  Another was a coloured
man, and there was hardly a doubt of the truth of his allega-
tions ; while the case of the third seaman, though in part established, was not entirely clear.  Under the circumstances,
however, a seaman found in the country, and demanding the
protection of its laws as a native, could not be given up to a
service that was known constantly to violate the rights of individuals, on the naked demand of that service, and in the
absence of all affirmative proof of its not having abused its
power.  The English minister received the report, and he appears to have been satisfied, as no more was said on the subject.

About the beginning of June, the Chesapeake sailed from
Washington to Norfolk.  At this time, there were but twelve
guns on board ; and, as it is customary for all vessels
of war to fire a salute in passing Mount Vernon, it was discovered, on that occasion, that some of the equipments were
imperfect.  Orders were issued by Captain Gordon in consequence, though the circumstance probably excited less attention than would otherwise have been the case, on account of
the unfinished state of the vessel.  The Chesapeake arrived in
Hampton Roads on the 4th of June ; and on the 6th, Commodore Barron paid her a short visit.

Between the 6th and the 19th of June, the remainder of the
guns and stores were received on board the Chesapeake, her
crew was completed to about 375 souls, and Captain Gordon
reported her to Commodore Barron as ready for sea.  Up to
the 6th of June, the people had not been quartered at all, and
between that day and the time of sailing, they had been at
quarters but three times ; on neither of which occasions were
the guns exercised.

About 8 A. M., June 22d, the Chesapeake got under way,
from Hampton Roads, bound to the Mediterranean.  At that

early day, the armament of the ship consisted of 28 eighteen-
pounders on her gun-deck, and of 12 carronades above, making a total of 40 guns.

A squadron of British ships of war, varying constantly in
numbers and vessels, had been watching some French frigates
that lay at Annapolis several months.   It was their practice to
lie in Lynnhaven, or occasionally to cruise in the offing.   On
the 21st of June, this squadron had consisted of three vessels
one of which was the Bellona 74, and another the Melampus
38, the ship from which the three seamen already mentioned,
had deserted.   On the evening of the same day, a fourth vessel, which was afterwards ascertained to be the Leopard 50,
Captain Humphreys, came in and anchored.   The Leopard was
a small two-decker, had a lower-deck battery of twenty-fours,
and is said to have mounted 56 guns.   When the Chesapeake
weighed, up at Hampton Roads, the Leopard lifted her anchor,
and preceded the American frigate to sea.   The wind was
light, at northwest; and as the Leopard got an offing, she disappeared behind Cape Henry.

A little after 12 o'clock, the Chesapeake was up with the
cape, when the wind shifted to the southward and eastward.
As she opened the offing, the Leopard was seen a few miles to
windward, heading to the eastward, with apparently very little
air.   She soon took the new wind, however, when both ships
made stretches to get off the land, there being a good working
breeze and perfectly smooth water.   The Leopard tacked with
the Chesapeake, though the latter ship appears to have closed
with her, the distance between the two vessels gradually lessening.   By some accounts, the English ship shortened sail in
order to allow this.   Up to this moment, however, it is the better opinion, that there was nothing unusual or suspicious in her
movements.   The British cruisers were in the habit of standing out in this manner, and the Leopard obtained the weather
gage altogether by the shift of wind.

About 3 o'clock, both vessels having an offing of some six
or eight miles, the Chesapeake tacked to the eastward again,
and the Leopard, then about a mile to windward, wore round,
and came down upon her weather quarter, when she hailed, informing Commodore Barron that she had despatches for him.
Commodore Barron answered that he would heave-to, and receive a boat.   Both vessels now came to, the Chesapeake by
laying her main-topsail to the mast, while the accounts appear
uncertain, whether the Leopard backed her forward or her after

sails.   At this time, it was observed by some of the officers on board the Chesapeake, that the English ship had her lower ports triced up, and the tompions out of her guns.   It does not appear that the latter fact, however, the only one of moment, was reported to either Captain Gordon or Commodore Barron.

In a few minutes, a boat from the Leopard came alongside of the Chesapeake, and her officer was shown into the cabin, where he was received by Commodore Barron.   Here the English lieutenant produced an order, signed by Vice-Admiral Berkley, dated Halifax, June 1st, and addressed to all the captains of the ships under his command, directing them, should they fall in with the Chesapeake out of the waters of the United States, and at sea, to show her commander this order ; to " require to search for deserters," and " to proceed and search for the same ;" offering at the same time, to allow of a similar search on board their own vessels.   Accompanying this order, was a note from the commander of the Leopard, addressed to the commander of the Chesapeake, referring to the order of the vice-admiral, and expressing a hope " that every circumstance respecting them (the deserters) may be adjusted in a manner that the harmony subsisting between the two countries may remain undisturbed."   To this note, Commodore Barron returned an answer, stating that he knew of no such deserters as described.   He added, that his recruiting officers had been particularly instructed by the government not to enter any deserters from the English ships, and that his orders would not allow him to suffer his people to be mustered by any officers but their own.

By referring to this correspondence, which has been often printed, it will be seen that neither the order of Vice-Admiral Berkley, the note of Captain Humphreys, nor the answer of Commodore Barron, was perfectly explicit on the important points, of whether force would be used, if the alleged deserters were not given up, or whether they would be refused, could it be shown, by any other means than that of being mustered by foreign officers, that the men required were among the Chesapeake's crew.   In a word, the order and note were vague and general ; and the answer, as far as it went, the most direct document of the three, appears to have been framed in a similar spirit.   The British officer was ordered to " require" of the captain of the Chesapeake, " to search his ship for deserters," &c., and " to proceed and search for the same,"

&c. Nothing is said of compelling a search; and though the term "require" was a strong one, the whole phraseology of the order was such as might very well raise doubts, under the peculiar circumstances, how far a party, who made professions of a desire to preserve the harmony of the two nations, might feel disposed to violate public law, in order to enforce its object. The note of Captain Humphreys was just as explicit, and just as vague as the order, being a mere echo of its spirit. Commodore Barron very clearly refused to permit a British officer to search for a deserter, while he did not touch the general principle, or what he might do, could it be shown by less objectionable means, that there was a British deserter, of the sort mentioned in the order, on board the Chesapeake, and the demand on the part of the English officers, to search in person, was abandoned. Had there even existed a clause in the treaty between England and America, rendering it obligatory on the two nations to deliver up each other's deserters, the requisition of Vice-Admiral Berkley, taken as an order to search in person, would have so far exceeded the probable construction of reason, as to justify an officer in supposing that nothing beyond a little well-managed intimidation was intended, since nations do not usually permit their treaties to be enforced by any but their own agents. While there was something very equivocal, beyond doubt, in the whole procedure of the British, it was so high-handed a measure to commence a demand for deserters, by insisting on a right to search a foreign vessel of war in person for them, that it would be very difficult to believe any design to enforce a demand so utterly out of the regular course of things, could be seriously entertained. It ought to be added, that the deserters alluded to in the order of Vice-Admiral Berkley, were not those from the Melampus, already spoken of, but men from other ships, who were supposed to have entered on board the Chesapeake at a much later day.

The English lieutenant was on board the Chesapeake some time; the accounts of the length of his visit varying from 15 to 45 minutes. It is probable he was fully half an hour in the cabin. His stay appears to have been long enough to excite uneasiness on board his own ship; for, while Commodore Barron was deliberating on the course he ought to pursue, information was sent below that a signal was flying on board the Leopard, which her officer immediately declared to be an order for the return of the boat. Soon after this signal was shown, the answer of Commodore Barron was delivered.

Commodore Barron now sent for Captain Gordon, and told him to get the gun-deck clear, a duty that had been commenced an hour or two before, without reference to the Leopard. He then went on deck. Soon after the English officer had passed out of the ship into his own boat, by the larboard, or lee-gang-way, Commodore Barron appeared in the starboard, or weather-gangway, to examine the Leopard. Here it would seem that the latter was forcibly struck with the appearance of preparation on board the English ship, and the idea that a resort might be had to force began to impress him seriously. He issued an order to Captain Gordon, to hasten the work on the gun-deck, and to go to quarters. In consequence of the latter order, a few taps were beaten on the drum, but that instrument was stopped by directions of Commodore Barron, and instructions were given to get the people to their quarters with as little noise and parade as possible, in order to gain time, if the Leopard really meditated hostilities.

It is not easy to imagine a vessel of war in a more unfortunate situation, than that of the Chesapeake at this particular moment. With a ship of superior force within pistol-shot, on her weather-quarter, her guns trained, matches burning, people drilled, and every thing ready to commence a heavy fire, while she herself was littered and lumbered, with a crew that had not yet exercised her guns, and which had been only three times even mustered at their quarters. The business of coiling away her cables, which had lain on the gun-deck until after two o'clock, was still going on, while the cabin bulk-head, cabin furniture, and some temporary pantries were all standing aft. A good deal of the baggage of the passengers in the ship was also on the gun-deck. It would seem, however, that some of the lieutenants had regarded the movements of the Leopard with distrust from the beginning; and the vessel being particularly well officered, these gentlemen soon made an active commencement towards getting the ship clear. The guns were all loaded and shotted, but on examination, it was found that there was a deficiency in rammers, wads, matches, gun-locks, and powder-horns. While things were in this awkward condition, Commodore Barron continued in the gangway examining the Leopard. The cutter of the latter was a few minutes in pulling back to that vessel, and as soon as the people were out of her, she was dropped astern, where most of the boats were towing, and the English ship hailed. Commodore Barron answered that he did not understand the hail, when the Leopard fired a

20

shot ahead of the Chesapeake. In a few seconds this shot was followed by an entire broadside. By this discharge, in addition to many injuries done the ship, Commodore Barron, who continued in the gangway, and his aid, Mr. Broom, were wounded. The Leopard was now hailed, and some answer was returned, but the noise and confusion rendered all attempts at a communication in this mode useless.

Every exertion was making all the while, to get the batteries ready, and with the exception of the forward gun below, the port of which was still down on account of the anchor, it appears that one broadside might have been fired, had not the means of discharging the guns been absolutely wanting. For some time, there was no priming powder, and when an insufficient quantity did finally arrive, there were no matches, locks, nor loggerheads. Some of the latter were brought from the galley, however, and they were applied to the priming, but were too cold to be of use. In the mean while, the Leopard, in an excellent position, and favoured by smooth water, was deliberately pouring in her whole fire upon an unresisting ship. This state of things lasted from twelve to eighteen minutes, when Commodore Barron, having repeatedly desired that one gun, at least, might be discharged, ordered the colours to be hauled down. Just as the ensign reached the taffrail, one gun was fired from the second division of the ship.*

The Chesapeake immediately sent a boat on board the Leopard, to say that the ship was at the disposal of the English captain, when the latter directed his officers to muster the American crew. The three men claimed to be deserters from the Melampus, and one that had run from the Halifax sloop of war, were carried away. Commodore Barron now sent another note to Captain Humphreys, to state his readiness to give up his ship; but the latter declining to take charge of her, a council of officers was called, and the Chesapeake returned to Hampton Roads the same evening.

In this affair, the Leopard, of course, did not suffer at all. Not so with the Chesapeake, although the injuries she sustained, were probably less than might have been expected. The accounts of the duration of the firing, vary from seven to twenty minutes, though the majority of opinions place it at

---

* This gun was discharged by means of a coal brought from the galley, which was applied by Lieutenant Allen, the officer of the division, with his fingers, after an unsuccessful attempt to make use of a loggerhead.

about twelve.   Three men were killed on the spot; eight were
badly, and ten were slightly wounded; making a total of
twenty-one casualties.   The Leopard appears to have thrown
the weight of her grape into the lower sails, the courses and
fore-topmast stay-sail having been riddled with that description
of shot.   Twenty-one round shot struck the hull.   All three
of the lower masts of the American frigate were injured,
and a good deal of rigging was cut; still the impression
left by the occurrence, went to convince the American service,
that English fire was not so formidable as tradition and rumour
had made it.

The attack on the Chesapeake, and its results, created a
strong and universal sensation in America.   At first, as ever
happens while natural feeling and national sentiment are unin-
fluenced by calculations of policy, there was but one voice of
indignation and resentment, though, in a short time, the fiend
of party lifted his head, and persons were not wanting who
presumed to justify the course taken by the English vice-admiral.   Notwithstanding these exceptions, the general effect
was certainly very adverse to the British cause in America;
and the injury was not fairly forgotten, until it had been ef-
faced from the public mind by many subsequent victories.

Courts-martial were held on Commodore Barron, Captain
Gordon, Captain Hall, of the marines, and the gunner of the
ship.   The first was distinctly acquitted of cowardice, but was
found guilty of " neglecting, on the probability of an engagement, to clear his ship for action."   The sentence was a suspension from pay and rank, for five years.   Captain Gordon
was found guilty of negligently performing some of his minor
duties, and was privately reprimanded.   Captain Hall received
the same sentence, a little mitigated; and the gunner was
cashiered.

## CHAPTER XXV.

CONGRESS was convened on the 26th of October; and, as soon as there had been time to deliberate on what had passed, the President, by his proclamation, interdicted all British vessels of war from entering the American waters. When the national legislature assembled, a proposition to increase the number of gun-boats was laid before it. Without a sufficient naval force to raise a blockade that should be sustained by three ships of the line; with all the experience of the war of the Revolution fresh in their recollections; and with the prospect of a speedy contest with a people that scarcely hesitated about closing the ports of the Union in a time of peace, the legislators of the day misdirected the resources of a great and growing country, by listening to this proposition, and creating a species of force that, in its nature, is merely auxiliary to more powerful means, and which is as entirely unfitted to the moral character of the people, as it is to the natural formation of the coast. On the 18th of December, a law was passed authorising the construction of 188 gun-boats, in addition to those already built, which would raise the total number of vessels of this description in the navy to 257. This was the development of the much-condemned " gun-boat system," which, for a short time, threatened destruction to the pride, discipline, tone, and even morals, of the service.

There can be no question, that, in certain circumstances, vessels of this sort may be particularly useful; but these circumstances are of rare occurrence, as they are almost always connected with attacks on towns and harbours. As the policy is now abandoned, it is unnecessary to point out the details by which it is rendered particularly unsuitable to this country, though there is one governing principle that may be mentioned, which, of itself, demonstrates its unfitness. The American coast has an extent of near two thousand miles, and to protect it by means of gun-boats, even admitting the practicability of the method, would involve an expenditure sufficient to create a movable force in ships, that would not only answer all the same purposes of defence, but which would possess the additional advantage of acting, at need, offensively. In other words, it was entailing on the country the cost of an efficient marine, without enjoying its advantages.

At the time when the laws of nations and the flag of the United States were outraged, in the manner related in the preceding chapter, the government was empowered to employ no more than 1425 seamen, ordinary seamen and boys, in all the vessels of the navy, whether in commission or in ordinary. The administration felt that this number was insufficient for the common wants of the service, and early in 1808, the secretary asked for authority to raise 1272 additional men, to be put on board the gun-boats that were now ready to receive them. The necessary law, however, was withheld.

The near approach of a war, that succeeded the attack of the Leopard, appears to have admonished the English government of the necessity of using some efficient means of settling the long-pending disputes between the two nations, and negotiations were carried on during the year 1808, in a temper that promised a pacific termination to the quarrel; and, in strict conformity with a practice, (it would be an abuse of terms to call it a policy,) that has long prevailed in the country, the time that should have been actively employed in preparations, was irreclaimably lost, in the idle expectation that they would not be needed. No act was passed, nor any appropriation made, either for the employment of more men, or for placing in commission any additional vessels, until the last ot January, 1809, when the President was directed to equip the United States 44, President 44, Essex 32, and John Adams 24; the latter vessel having been cut down to a sloop of war. By the same law, the navy was greatly increased in efficiency, as respects the officers and men, the President being authorised to appoint as many additional midshipmen as would make a total of 450, and to employ in all, 5025 seamen, ordinary seamen, and boys. By adding the remaining officers, and the marine corps, the whole service could not have contained a total of less than 7000 persons, when the act was carried into execution.

The equipment of the ships just mentioned, and the active employment of all the small vessels of the service, probably saved the navy of the United States from a total disorganisation. It was the means of withdrawing a large portion of the officers from the gun-boats, and of renewing that high tone and admirable discipline which had distinguished it at the close of the Tripolitan war. By this time, nearly all the midshipmen who had been before Tripoli, were lieutenants; and there

20 *

was already one instance in which an officer, who had entered the navy as a midshipman, commanded the frigate in which he had first served.*

In the course of the summer of 1808, too, it was thought prudent to make a commencement towards the employment of a force on the lakes; England already possessing ships on Ontario and Erie.

There being no especial law for such an object, advantage was taken of the discretionary powers granted to the President under the act for building gun-boats. A few officers were placed under the orders of Lieutenant M. T. Woolsey, and that gentleman was empowered to make contracts for the construction of three vessels, one of which was to be built on Lake Ontario, and the other two on Lake Champlain. The two vessels constructed on Lake Champlain were ordinary gun-boats, but that constructed on Lake Ontario was a regular brig of war. The latter was of about two hundred and forty tons measurement, was pierced for sixteen guns, and when delivered by the contractors, in the spring of 1809, to the sea-officers ordered to receive her, she mounted 16 twenty-four pound carronades. In consequence of an arrangement that was made, about this time, with England, but which was not ratified in Europe, this vessel, which was called the Oneida, was not equipped and sent upon the lake till the following year.

This was a period of vacillating policy in both nations, England, at times, appearing disposed to arrange amicably the many different points that had arisen with America, and the latter country acting, at moments, as if it believed war to be impossible, while at others, it seemed to be in earnest with its preparations. Thus passed the years 1808, 1809, and 1810, the embargo having been raised, followed by a non-intercourse law with Great Britain, and succeeded by an absence of all restrictions.

During this period of doubt, the vessels of the navy that were in commission, were principally employed on the coast, or they kept up the communications with the different diplomatic agents in Europe, by carrying despatches. There is no question that these were important years to the service; for, since the attack on the Chesapeake, the utmost vigilance prevailed, and every commander watched jealously for an oppor-

---

* Captain Decatur.

tunity to wipe out the disgrace, real or imaginary, of that unfortunate affair. No more vessels were sent to the Mediterranean, but the whole maritime force of the republic was kept
at home. The country had now in active service the following vessels, viz:

| | | | |
|---|---|---|---|
| President | 44, | Hornet | 18, |
| Constitution | 44, | Argus | 16, |
| United States | 44, | Siren | 16, |
| Essex | 32, | Nautilus | 12, |
| John Adams | 20, | Enterprise | 12, |
| Wasp | 18, | Vixen | 12. |

In addition to these cruisers, were a great number of gun-
boats, which were principally commanded by sailing-masters,
who had been selected from among the officers of merchant
vessels. The Nautilus and Vixen had both been rigged into
brigs; the Enterprise soon after was altered in the same manner; and an occasion to rebuild the Hornet occurring, she was
converted into a ship, and pierced for two more guns, making
twenty in all. Unhappily, the opportunity was lost of equipping a force that could prevent blockades.

The English increased their cruisers on the American coast,
in proportion to the Americans themselves, though their vessels no longer lay off the harbours, impressing men, and de-
taining ships. It was seldom that a British cruiser was now
seen near the land, the government probably cautioning its
commanders to avoid unnecessary exhibitions of this sort, with
a view to prevent collisions. Still they were numerous, cruised
at no great distance, and by keeping up constant communications between Bermuda and Halifax, may be said to have intercepted nearly every ship that passed from one hemisphere
to the other.

Such, in effect, was the state of things in the spring of the
year 1811, when information was received by the senior officer of the navy afloat, Commodore Rodgers, that a man had
been impressed from an American brig, at no great distance
from Sandy Hook, by an English frigate that was supposed to
be the Guerriere 38, Captain Dacres. The broad pennant of
Commodore Rodgers was flying on board the President 44,
Captain Ludlow, which ship was then anchored off Annapolis.
Repairing on board his vessel, he got under way, with an intention of proceeding off New York to inquire into the facts,
on the 10th of May; passing the capes shortly after.

On the 16th of May, at noon, a sail was made from the President, which ship was then about six leagues from the land, to the southward of New York.  It was soon perceived, by the squareness of his yards, and the symmetry of his sails, that the stranger was a vessel of war, and the American frigate stood for him, with an intention to get within hail.  At 2 the President set her broad pennant and ensign.  The stranger now made several signals; but finding they were not answered, he wore and stood to the southward.  Although the President gained upon the chase, the wind lessened, and night set in before she could get near enough to distinguish her force. It was past 7 o'clock in the evening when the stranger took in his studding-sails, hauled up his courses, and came by the wind on the starboard tack.  He now set an ensign at his gaff, but it was too dark to discover the nation.  As he came to the wind, he necessarily showed his broadside, and was taken for a small frigate.

The President continuing to stand down, the chase wore four several times, in order to prevent the American frigate from getting a position to windward.  It was consequently near half-past 8 before Commodore Rodgers could bring-to, as he had desired, on the weather-bow of the stranger, or a little forward of his beam; when, being within a hundred yards, he hailed, and demanded "what ship is that?"  No answer was given to this question; but it was repeated, word for word, from the stranger.  After a short pause the question was again put, when the stranger fired a gun, the shot from which cut away a breast-back-stay, and entered the main-mast.  Commodore Rodgers was on the point of ordering a shot to be returned, when a gun was discharged from the second division of the President.  The stranger now fired three guns in quick succession, and after a short pause, the remainder of his broadside and all his musketry.  The President, as a matter of course, delivered her broadside in return.  In a few minutes, however, it was perceived on board the American vessel, that they were engaged with an adversary so inferior as to render her resistance very feeble, and orders were sent to the different divisions to stop the fire.

The guns of the President were soon silent; when, to the surprise of all on board her, the stranger opened anew.  The fire of the American frigate recommenced, but it was again stopped in the course of a very few minutes, in consequence of the crippled condition of her antagonist, who lay nearly end on, and apparently unmanageable.  The American now hailed again, and got an answer that her adversary was a British ship of war, though the name was inaudible, on account of the wind, which had increased.  Satisfied that his late opponent was disabled, and having no desire to effect more than had already been accomplished, Commodore Rodgers gave the name of his own ship, wore round, and running a short distance to leeward, he hauled by the wind again, with a view to remain nigh the English vessel during the night.  The President kept lights displayed, in order to let her late antagonist know her position, and wore several times to remain near her.

When the day dawned, the English ship was discovered some distance to leeward, her drift in the night having been considerable.  The President bore up under easy canvass, and running down to her, lowered a boat, and Mr. Creighton, the first lieutenant, was sent on board, with an offer of services. The stranger proved to be his Britannic majesty's ship Little Belt 18, Captain Bingham.  The Little Belt was a vessel of twenty-two guns, but having a light spar-deck above, on which no guns were mounted, she had the external appearance of a small frigate.  She had suffered severely by the fire of the President, and thirty-one of her people had been killed and wounded.  As Captain Bingham declined receiving any assistance, the vessels parted, each making the best of her way to a port of her own nation.

This occurrence gave rise to much angry discussion in America, and widened the breach which already existed between the English and the American nations.  The account given by Captain Bingham differed essentially from that of Commodore Rodgers, and official investigations were made on both sides.  On that of the Americans a formal court of inquiry was held, and every sea-officer in the ship was examined, as well as a great many of the petty officers.  The testimony was very clear, and it was in a great measure free from the discrepancies that usually distinguish the accounts of battles, whether by sea or land.  The fact that the Little Belt fired the first gun was established by the oath of the officer who ordered the gun fired in return.  This gentleman distinctly testified that he gave the command, under a standing order of the ship, and in consequence of having seen the flash and heard the report of the Little Belt's gun.  He not only testified that he heard the report of the gun, but that he also heard the noise made by the shot which had entered the mast. Other officers and men corroborated this account, and in a way to render their evidence not only consistent with itself, but with probability. As the President was very fully officered, the number and respectability of the witnesses, put at rest all ca-villing about the facts.

It is believed that there was no proper court of inquiry held on the conduct of Captain Bingham, though affidavits of most of his officers were published. By that gentleman's official account, as it has been given to the world, as well as by the affidavits mentioned, it is affirmed that the President commenced the action by firing, not a single gun, but an entire broadside. He also intimated that the action lasted three quarters of an hour, and appeared desirous of leaving the impression that the President had sheered off.

As between the two governments, the question was reduced to one of veracity. If the account of the American officer was true, that of the English officer was untrue ; and if the account of the English officer was true, that of the American officer was un-true. Each government seeming disposed to believe its own officer, no political consequences followed this rencontre. The President sustained little injury, no round shot, besides the one in her main-mast, and another in her fore-mast, having struck her ; and, of her people, one boy alone was slightly wounded by a musket-ball. The Little Belt, on the other hand, having suffered even out of proportion to the disparity of force between the vessels, the American government was satisfied with the punishment already inflicted on the assailants ; while the En-glish government could not well insist on reparation, without demanding that the American functionaries would not believe their own officer. After some communications on the subject, and an exchange of the testimony that had been given, nothing further appears to have been done, or contemplated, by either government.

## CHAPTER XXVI.

It has been seen that no consequences, beyond an increased alienation between the two countries, followed the rencontre between the President and Little Belt.

Not long after the meeting between these two vessels, the United States 44, bearing the broad pennant of Commodore Decatur, fell in with the Eurydice and Atalanta, British ships, off New York, and, while the commanders were hailing, one of the seamen of the former vessel, in carelessly handling the lanyard of his lock, fired a gun. Happily both parties were cool and discreet, and proper explanations having been made, the English commander was entirely satisfied that no insult, or assault, was intended.

Between the reduction in 1801, and the commencement of 1812, a period of eleven eventful years, during which the nation was scarcely a day without suffering violation of its neutral rights, not a single frigate had been added to the navy! The ships of the line authorised in 1799 were entirely abandoned, and notwithstanding the critical relations of the country, the experience of the past, and so many years of commercial prosperity, the navy, in some respects, was in a worse situation than after the sale of the ships in 1801. Of the thirteen frigates retained at that time, the Philadelphia 38, had been taken and destroyed, and the New York 36, General Green 28, and Boston 28, had gone to decay, without repairs. Thus, in point of fact, though twelve ships of this class appear on the list of the day, but nine actually existed, for any practical purposes. The various vessels of inferior force, that have been already mentioned in this work, as constructed under different laws, had been added to the navy, while two or three temporarily taken into the service were already sold. A few small schooners had been purchased. Navy-yards had been established at Philadelphia, New York, Boston, Washington, Gosport, and Portsmouth, though they were still in their infancy, and very incomplete. One hundred and seventy gun-boats had also been built, and were distributed in the different ports of the country.

While the navy on the whole, the gun-boats excepted, had

rather lost than gained in physical force, since the reduction
of 1801, it had improved immeasurably in discipline, tone, and
in an *esprit de corps.*  The little that had been lost, in these
respects, through the service in gun-boats, was more than regained by the effect produced by the attack on the Chesapeake,
and the constant state of excitement that prevailed with regard
to English aggressions, during the few preceding years.  The
lists of captains, masters-commandant, and lieutenants were
small, but filled with men trained to obedience, and, consequently, qualified to command.  It is true, only one of the officers of the revolution remained, at the head of the service; and
he was nearly superannuated by years and infirmities; but
those to whom they had imparted their traditions and spirit
had succeeded them.  Commodore Samuel Nicholson, who
had been employed in the year 1776, even, as commander of
the Dolphin 10, died at the head of the service at the close of
the year 1811.  The celebrated Preble had preceded him to
the grave several years, and Commodore Murray alone remained of those officers who might be said to have belonged to
the old school.  Still, the new school was in no respect inferior; and in some particulars, it was greatly the superior of
that which had gone before it.  The vessels, generally, were
good ships of their respective classes, and the officers, as a
body, were every way worthy to take charge of them.  Several of those who had been retained as midshipmen, after the
war with France, were already commanders, and the vessels
beneath the rate of frigates, with one exception, were commanded by gentlemen of this description.  The exception was
in the case of the Wasp 18, on board which ship was Captain
Jones, who had been the youngest of the lieutenants retained
in 1801, and who was now nearly the oldest master-commandant.  He had joined the service, however, as a midshipman.

If the naval armaments made by the country, under the
prospect of a war with Great Britain, are to be regarded with
the eyes of prudence, little more can be said, than to express
astonishment at the political infatuation which permitted the
day of preparation to pass unheeded.  Still a little was done,
and that little it is our duty to record.

Early in 1809, the marine corps was augmented by an
addition of near 700 men, which probably put this important
branch of the navy, on a footing equal to the rest of the service, as it then existed; the entire corps containing about 1300
men when full.  On the 30th of March, 1812, or less than

CAPTURE OF THE ESSEX

three months previously to the war with England, Congress authorised the President to cause three additional frigates to be put in service, and the sum of $200,000 annually was appropriated for the purchase of timber to rebuild the three frigates that had been permitted to decay, and the one that had been captured.

When the amount of these appropriations is considered, the conclusion would seem inevitable, that the government did not at all anticipate hostilities, were it not for the more ample preparations that were making on land, and the large sums that had been expended on gun-boats. It is not improbable, therefore, that those to whom the direction of affairs was confided, believed the naval force of the country too insignificant, and that of Great Britain too overwhelming, to render any serious efforts to create a marine, at that late hour, expedient. A comparison of the naval forces of Great Britain and the United States, with their respective conditions, will render this idea plausible, although it may not fully justify it, as a measure of policy.

In 1812, the navy of Great Britain nominally contained a thousand and sixty sail, of which between seven and eight hundred were efficient cruising vessels. France had no fleets to occupy this great marine, Spain was detached from the alliance against England, the north of Europe no longer required a force to watch it, and Great Britain might direct towards the American coast, as many ships as the nature of the war could possibly demand.

As opposed to this unexampled naval power, America had on her list the following vessels, exclusively of gun-boats, viz:

| | | | |
|---|---|---|---|
| Constitution | 44, | John Adams | 28, |
| President | 44, | Wasp | 18, |
| United States | 44, | Hornet | 18, |
| Congress | 38, | Argus | 16, |
| Constellation | 38, | Siren | 16, |
| Chesapeake | 38, | Oneida | 16, |
| New York | 36, | Vixen | 14, |
| Essex | 32, | Nautilus | 14, |
| Adams | 28, | Enterprise | 14, |
| Boston | 28, | Viper | 12. |

Of these vessels, the New York 36, and Boston 28, were unseaworthy, and the Oneida 16, was on Lake Ontario. The remainder were efficient for their rates; though the Adams

21

required extensive repairs before she could be sent to sea. It follows that America was about to engage in a war with much the greatest maritime power that the world ever saw, possessing herself but seventeen cruising vessels on the ocean, of which nine were of a class less than that of frigates. At this time the merchant vessels of the United States were spread over the face of the entire globe. No other instance can be found of so great a stake in shipping with a protection so utterly inadequate.

There can be but one manner of- accounting for this extraordinary state of things; that already mentioned of the belief of the impossibility of keeping vessels at sea, in face of the overwhelming force of Great Britain. It is in corroboration of this opinion, that a project was entertained by the cabinet of laying up all the vessels in ordinary, with a view to prevent them from falling into the hands of the enemy. This step would have been a death-blow to the navy, since the people would have been perfectly justifiable in refusing to support a marine, that was intended solely for peace. It is now understood that this resolution was only prevented by the interference of two officers of the service, who happened to be at the seat of government when the subject was under discussion. These gentlemen* are said to have made a vigorous written remonstrance against the scheme, and by means of their representations to have induced the cabinet to change its policy.

Under ordinary circumstances the intention just stated, would have been indicative of great feebleness of action, and of a narrowness of views, that was entirely unsuited to the characters of statesmen. But the circumstances were extraordinary. Not only was the marine of Great Britain much the most powerful of any in the world, but it was more pow-

---

* Captains Bainbridge and Stewart. These two officers were shown orders to Commodore Rodgers not to quit New York, but to keep the vessels in port to form a part of its habour defence. They sought an interview with the Secretary, who was influenced by their representations, and who procured for them an audience of the President. Mr. Madison listened to the representations of the two captains, with attention, and observed that the experience of the Revolution confirmed their opinions. The Cabinet was convened, but it adhered to its former advice. Captains Bainbridge and Stewart then addressed a strong letter to the President, who took on himself to change the plan. It is said, that one or two of the cabinet acceded to this decision, on the ground that the ships would soon be taken, and that the country would thus be rid of the cost of maintaining them, and at more liberty to direct its energies to the army.

erful than those of all the rest of Christendom united.  In addition to its actual physical force, it had created for itself a
moral auxiliary that was scarcely less available in practice
than its guns and men.  The reputation of invincibility was
very generally attached to an English man-of-war, and perhaps no people gave England more ample credit for every
species of superiority, whether physical or moral, that she
claimed for herself, than those of the United States of America.
The success of the British navy was indisputable, and as few
Americans then read books, or journals, in foreign tongues,
while scarcely a newspaper appeared without its columns containing some tribute to British glory, it would not be easy to
portray the extent of the feeling, or the amount of the credulity
that generally existed on such subjects.

That the officers of the navy should, in a great degree, be
superior to this dependent feeling was natural.  They had enjoyed means of comparison that were denied the bulk of their
fellow-citizens, and the results had taught them more confidence in themselves.  They knew that their ships were at
least as good as those of England, that they sailed as fast,
were worked as well, and, in every essential on which a seaman prides himself, that England could justly claim no other
superiority than that which might be supposed to belong to her
greater experience in naval warfare.  Against this odds, they
were willing to contend.  Not so with the nation.  Notwithstanding the best dispositions on the part of a vast majority of
the American people, the conviction was general that an
American vessel of war would contend against an English vessel of war with very few chances of success.  After making
every allowance for equality in all the other essentials, the
great point of practice was against the former, and the confidence produced by a thousand victories, it was believed would
prove more available than zeal or courage.

It is not as easy to describe the feeling on the other side.
Among the young officers of the British navy it is pretty safe
to say that a notion of overwhelming superiority was very
generally prevalent ; but among the older men there were many
who had studied the American cruisers with observant eyes,
and a few who still recollected the war of the revolution, when
ill-equipped, uncoppered and half-manned ships, had rendered
victory dear, and, not unfrequently, defeat certain.  The journals of Great Britain indulged in that coarse and impolitic
abuse, which has probably done more towards raising a hostile

feeling throughout Christendom against their nation, than any political injustice, or political jealousies; and the few ships of the American navy did not escape their sneers and misrepresentations.   One of the very last of the vessels they attempted to hold up to the derision of Europe was the Constitution, a frigate that was termed " a bunch of pine boards," sailing " under a bit of striped bunting."   As indecorous as was this language, and as little worthy as it might be to excite feeling, or comment, America was too keenly alive to English opinion, to hear it with indifference, and the day was at hand when she exultingly threw back these terms of reproach, with taunts and ridicule almost as unbecoming as the gibes that had provoked them.

There is little doubt that even the friends of the navy looked forward to the conflict with distrust, while the English felt a confidence that, of itself, was one step towards victory.

---

## CHAPTER XXVII.

Owing to grievances, that had long been drawing to a head, Congress formally declared war against the King of Great Britain on the 18th of June, 1812.

At the moment when this important intelligence was made public, nearly all of the little American marine were in port, or were cruising in the immediate vicinity of the coast.   The Wasp 18, Captain Jones, was alone on foreign service; and she was on her return from Europe with despatches.

But the declaration of war did not find the little marine of America in a condition to act in a combined, intelligent, and military manner.   The vesels were scattered; some were undergoing repairs, others were at a distance; and with the exception of one small squadron, every thing was virtually committed to the activity, judgment, and enterprise of the different captains.   In the port of New York, were collected the President 44, Commodore Rodgers; Essex 32, Captain Porter; and Hornet 18, Captain Lawrence.   With the exception of the Essex, which ship was overhauling her rigging, and re-stowing her hold, these vessels were ready to sail at an hour's notice.   Com-

modore, Rodgers in anticipation of hostilities had dropped into
the bay, with the President and Hornet, where he was joined by
the United States 44, Commodore Decatur, Congress 38, Captain
Smith, and Argus 16, Lieutenant Commandant Sinclair, all of
which vessels arrived from the southward on the 21st of June.

Information had been received of the sailing of a large fleet
of Jamaica-men, under protection of a strong force; and as
these vessels would naturally be sweeping along the American
coast, in the gulf stream, it was determined to make a dash
at this convoy,—as judicious a plan, under the circumstances,
as could then have been adopted. Within an hour after he
had received official information of the declaration of war, together with his orders, Commodore Rodgers was under way.

The squadron passed Sandy Hook on the afternoon of the
21st of June, and ran off south-east. That night an American
was spoken that had seen the Jamaica ships, and sail was instantly crowded in pursuit. On the 23d, however, at 6 A. M.,
a vessel was seen to the northward and eastward, which was
soon made out to be an enemy's frigate, and a general chase
took place. The wind was fresh for the greater part of the
day, and, the enemy standing before it, the President, an uncommonly fast ship off the wind, soon gained, not only on the
stranger, but on the rest of the squadron. About 4 P. M., she
was within gun-shot of the chase, but the wind had unfortunately fallen, and the American ships being just out of port,
and deep, their greater comparative weight, under such circumstances, gave the enemy an advantage. Perceiving but
very faint hopes of getting alongside of the stranger, unless
he could be crippled, Commodore Rodgers determined to open
on him with his chase-guns. With this view, that officer went
forward, himself, to direct the cannonade, and about half-past
4, the forecastle gun was discharged. This was the first hostile shot fired afloat in the war of 1812, and the gun is understood to have been pointed by Commodore Rodgers in person.
The shot struck the chase in the rudder-coat, and drove through
the stern frame into the gun-room. The next gun was fired
from the first division below; it was pointed and discharged
by Mr. Gamble, the second lieutenant, who commanded the
battery. The shot struck the muzzle of one of the enemy's
stern chasers, which it damaged. Commodore Rodgers fired
the third shot, which struck the stern of the chase, killed two
men, badly wounded two more, and slightly injured a lieutenant and two others. Mr. Gamble again fired, when the gun

21 *

bursted. The shot flew broad off on the President's bow, and the explosion killed and wounded sixteen men. The forecastle deck was blown up, and Commodore Rodgers was thrown into the air, breaking a leg by the fall. This accident prevented the guns of that side from being used for some time. The pause enabled the enemy to open from four stern guns, otherwise he would have soon been driven from the after part of his ship. The fire of the chase was spirited and good, one of his shot plunging on the President's deck, killing a midshipman and one or two men. The President shortly after began to yaw, with a view to shoot away some of the chase's spars, and her fire soon compelled the latter to lighten. The enemy cut away his anchors, stove his boats and threw them overboard, and started fourteen tons of water. By these means he drew ahead, when about 7 o'clock the President hauled up, and as a last resort, fired three broadsides, most of the shot of which fell short.

Finding it impossible to get any nearer to the enemy, without rendering his own ships inefficient for a cruise, by lightening, Commodore Rodgers ordered the pursuit to be abandoned, about midnight. It was afterwards known that the vessel chased was the Belvidera 36, Captain Byron, who gained much credit for the active manner in which he saved his ship. The Belvidera got into Halifax a few days later, carrying with her the news of the declaration of war. The President had twenty-two men killed and wounded on this occasion, sixteen of whom suffered by the bursting of the gun. Among the former was the midshipman mentioned; and among the latter Mr. Gamble. The loss of the Belvidera was stated at seven killed and wounded by shot, and several others by accidents, Captain Byron included. She also suffered materially in her spars, sails, and rigging; while the injuries of this nature, received by the President, were not serious.

The squadron now hauled up to its course, in pursuit of the Jamaica-men; and, from time to time, intelligence was obtained from American vessels, of the course the fleet was steering. On the 1st of July, the pursuing ships fell in with large quantities of cocoa-nut shells, orange-peels, &c. &c., which gave an assurance that they had struck the wake of the Englishmen. This was a little to the eastward of the Banks of Newfoundland, and the strongest hopes were entertained of coming up with the fleet before it could reach the channel. On the 9th of July, an English letter of marque was captured by the

Hornet, Captain Lawrence, and her master reported that he had seen the Jamaica vessels the previous evening, under the convoy of a two-decked ship, a frigate, a sloop of war, and a brig. He had counted eighty-five sail. All possible means were now used to force the squadron ahead, but without success, no further information having been received of the fleet. The chase was continued until the 13th, when, being within a day's run of the chops of the channel, Commodore Rodgers stood to the southward, passing Madeira, and going into Boston by the way of the Western Islands and the Grand Banks.

This cruise was singularly unfortunate, for such a moment, although the ships were kept in the direct tracks of vessels in crossing the ocean, each time. Seven merchantmen were taken, however, and one American was recaptured. The squadron was absent on this service seventy days.

The report of the Belvidera induced the enemy to collect as many of his vessels in squadron as possible; and a force consisting of the Africa 64, Captain Bastard; Shannon 38, Captain Broke; Guerriere 38, Captain Dacres; Belvidera 36, Captain Byron; and Æolus 32, Captain Lord James Townsend, was soon united, in the hope of falling in with Commodore Rodgers. Of this squadron, Captain Broke, of the Shannon, was the senior officer. It appeared off New York early in July, where it made several captures. The Nautilus 14, Lieutenant Commandant Crane, arrived in the port of New York shortly after the squadron of Commodore Rodgers had sailed; and this little brig went out with an intention of cruising in the track of the English Indiamen, at the unfortunate moment when Commodore Broke appeared off the coast. The Nautilus got to sea quite early in July, and fell in with the British squadron the next day. A short, but vigorous chase succeeded, in which Mr. Crane threw overboard his lee-guns, and did all that a seaman could devise to escape; but the Nautilus buried, while the frigates of the enemy were enabled to carry every thing to advantage, and he struck to the Shannon. The Nautilus was the first vessel of war taken on either side, in this contest; and thus the service lost one of those cruisers, which had become endeared to it, and identified with its history, in connexion with the war before Tripoli. The enemy took out the officers and people of their prize, threw a crew into her, and continued to cruise in the hope of meeting the American ships.

On her return from a recent run to Europe, the Constitution

44, Captain Hull, had gone into the Chesapeake.  Here she
shipped a new crew, and on the 12th of July she sailed from
Annapolis, and stood to the northward.  So rapidly had her
equipment been effected, that her first lieutenant joined her
only a fortnight before she sailed, and a draft of a hundred
men was received on the evening of the 11th.  Friday, July
the 17th, the ship was out of sight of land, though at no great
distance from the coast, with a light breeze from the N. E.,
and under easy canvass.  At 1, she sounded in 22 fathoms;
and about an hour afterwards, four sail were made in the
northern board, heading to the westward.  At 3, the Constitution made sail, and tacked in 18½ fathoms.  At 4, she discovered a fifth sail to the northward and eastward, which had
the appearance of a vessel of war.  This ship subsequently
proved to be the Guerriere 38, Captain Dacres.  By this time,
the other four sail were made out to be three ships and a brig;
they bore N. N. W., and were all on the starboard tack, apparently in company.  The wind now became very light, and
the Constitution hauled up her main-sail.  The ship in the
eastern board, however, had so far altered her position by 6,
as to bear E. N. E., the wind having hitherto been fair for her
to close.  But at a quarter past 6, the wind came out light at
the southward, bringing the American ship to windward.  The
Constitution now wore round with her head to the eastward,
set her light studding-sails and stay-sails, and at half past 7,
beat to quarters, and cleared for action, with the intention of
speaking the nearest vessel.

The wind continued very light at the southward, and the
two vessels were slowly closing until 8.  At 10, the Constitution shortened sail, and immediately after she showed the private signal of the day.  After keeping the lights aloft near an
hour, and getting no answer from the Guerriere, the Constitution, at a quarter past 11, lowered the signal, and made sail
again, hauling aboard her starboard tacks.  During the whole
of the middle watch the wind was very light, from the southward and westward.  Just as the morning watch was called,
the Guerriere tacked, then wore entirely round, threw a rocket,
and fired two guns.  As the day opened, three sail were discovered on the starboard quarter of the Constitution, and three
more astern.  At 5 A. M., a fourth vessel was seen astern.

This was the squadron of Commodore Broke, which had
been gradually closing with the American frigate during the
night, and was now just out of gun-shot.  As the ships slowly

varied their positions, when the mists were entirely cleared away, the Constitution had two frigates on her lee quarter, and a ship of the line, two frigates, a brig and a schooner astern. The names of the enemy's ships have already been given; but the brig was the Nautilus, and the schooner another prize. All the strangers had English colours flying.

It now fell quite calm, and the Constitution hoisted out her boats, and sent them ahead to tow, with a view to keep the ship out of the reach of the enemy's shot. At the same time, she whipt up one of the gun-deck guns to the spar-deck, and run it out aft, as a stern-chaser, getting a long eighteen off the forecastle also for a similar purpose. Two more of the twenty-fours below were run out at the cabin windows, with the same object, though it was found necessary to cut away some of the wood-work of the stern frame, in order to make room.

By 6 o'clock the wind, which continued very light and baffling, came out from the northward of west, when the ship's head was got round to the southward, and all the light canvass that would draw was set. Soon after, the nearest frigate, the Shannon, opened with her bow guns, and continued firing for about ten minutes; but perceiving she could not reach the Constitution, she ceased. At half past 6, Captain Hull sounded in 26 fathoms, when finding that the enemy was likely to close, as he was enabled to put the boats of two ships on one, and was also favoured by a little more air than the Constitution, all the spare rope that could be found, and which was fit for the purpose, was payed down into the cutters, bent on, and a kedge was run out near half a mile ahead, and let go. At a signal given, the crew clapped on, and walked away with the ship, overrunning and tripping the kedge as she came up with the end of the line. While this was doing, fresh lines and another kedge were carried ahead, and, though out of sight of land, the frigate glided away from her pursuers, before they discovered the manner in which it was done. It was not long, however, before the enemy resorted to the same expedient. At half past 7, the Constitution had a little air, when she set her ensign, and fired a shot at the Shannon, the nearest ship astern. At 8, it fell calm again, and further recourse was had to the boats and the kedges, the enemy's vessels having a light air, and drawing ahead, towing, sweeping, and kedging. By 9, the nearest frigate, the Shannon, on which the English had put most of their boats, was closing fast, and there was every prospect, notwithstanding the steadiness and activity of the Constitution's people, that the frigate just mentioned would get near enough to cripple her, when her capture by the rest of the squadron would be inevitable. At this trying moment the best spirit prevailed in the ship. Every thing was stoppered, and Captain Hull was not without hopes, even should he be forced into action, of throwing the Shannon astern by his fire, and of maintaining his distance from the other vessels. It was known that the enemy could not tow very near, as it would have been easy to sink his boats with the stern guns of the Constitution, and not a man in the latter vessel showed a disposition to despondency. Officers and men relieved each other regularly at the duty, and while the former threw themselves down on deck to catch short naps, the people slept at their guns.

This was one of the most critical moments of the chase. The Shannon was fast closing, as has been just stated, while the Guerriere was almost as near on the larboard quarter. An hour promised to bring the struggle to an issue, when suddenly, at 9 minutes past 9, a light air from the southward struck the ship, bringing her to windward. The beautiful manner in which this advantage was improved, excited admiration even in the enemy. As the breeze was seen coming, the ship's sails were trimmed, and as soon as she was under command, she was brought close up to the wind, on the larboard tack; the boats were all dropped in alongside; those that belonged to the davits were run up, while the others were just lifted clear of the water, by purchases on the spare outboard spars, where they were in readiness to be used at a moment's notice. As the ship came by the wind, she brought the Guerriere nearly on her lee beam, when that frigate opened a fire from her broadside. While the shot of this vessel were just falling short of them, the people of the Constitution were hoisting up their boats with as much steadiness as if the duty was performing in a friendly port. In about an hour, however, it fell nearly calm again, when Captain Hull ordered a quantity of the water started, to lighten the ship. More than two thousand gallons were pumped out, and the boats were sent ahead again to tow. The enemy now put nearly all his boats on the Shannon, the nearest ship astern; and a few hours of prodigious exertion followed, the people of the Constitution being compelled to supply the place of numbers by their activity and zeal. The ships were close by the wind, and every thing that would draw was set, and the Shannon was slowly, but steadily, forging ahead. About noon of this day, there was a little relaxation from labour, owing to the occasional occurrence of cat's-paws, by watching which closely, the ship was urged through the water. But at quarter past 12, the boats were again sent ahead, and the toilsome work of towing and kedging was renewed.

At 1 o'clock a strange sail was discovered nearly to leeward. At this moment the four frigates of the enemy were about one point on the lee-quarter of the Constitution, at long gun-shot, the Africa and the two prizes being on the lee-beam. As the wind was constantly baffling, any moment might have brought a change, and placed the enemy to windward. At seven minutes before two, the Belvidera, then the nearest ship, began to fire with her bow guns, and the Constitution opened with her stern chasers. On board the latter ship, however, it was soon found to be dangerous to use the main-deck guns, the transoms having so much rake, the windows being so high, and the guns so short, that every explosion lifted the upper deck, and threatened to blow out the stern frame. Perceiving, moreover, that his shot did little or no execution, Captain Hull ordered the firing to cease at half-past 2.

For several hours, the enemy's frigates were now within gun-shot, sometimes towing and kedging, and at others endeavouring to close with the puffs of air that occasionally passed. At 7 in the evening, the boats of the Constitution were again ahead, the ship steering S. W. $\frac{1}{2}$ W., with an air so light as to be almost imperceptible. At half past 7, she sounded in 24 fathoms. For hours, the same toilsome duty was going on, until a little before 11, when a light air from the southward struck the ship, and the sails for the first time in many weary hours were asleep. The boats instantly dropped alongside, hooked on, and were all run up, with the exception of the first cutter. The topgallant studding-sails and stay-sails were set as soon as possible, and for about an hour, the people caught a little rest.

But at midnight it fell nearly calm again; though neither the pursuers nor the pursued had recourse to the boats, probably from an unwillingness to disturb their crews. At 2 A. M., it was observed on board the Constitution that the Guerriere had forged ahead, and was again off their lee-beam. At this time, the top-gallant studding-sails were taken in.

In this manner passed the night, and on the morning of the

next day, it was found that three of the enemy's frigates were within long gun-shot on the lee-quarter, and the other at about the same distance on the lee-beam. The Africa, and the prizes, were much farther to leeward.

A little after daylight, the Guerriere, having drawn ahead sufficiently to be forward of the Constitution's beam, tacked, when the latter ship did the same, in order to preserve her position to windward. An hour later the Æolus passed on the contrary tack, so near that it was thought by some who observed the movement, that she ought to have opened her fire; but, as that vessel was merely a twelve-pounder frigate, and she was still at a considerable distance, it is quite probable her commander acted judiciously. By this time, there was sufficient wind to induce Captain Hull to hoist in his first cutter.

The scene, on the morning of this day, was very beautiful, and of great interest to the lovers of nautical exhibitions. The weather was mild and lovely, the sea smooth as a pond, and there was quite wind enough to remove the necessity of any of the extraordinary means of getting ahead, that had been so freely used during the previous eight-and-forty hours. All the English vessels had got on the same tack with the Constitution again, and the five frigates were clouds of canvass, from their trucks to the water. Including the American ship, eleven sail were in sight, and shortly after a twelfth appeared to windward, that was soon ascertained to be an American merchantman. But the enemy were too intent on the Constitution to regard any thing else, and though it would have been easy to capture the ships to leeward, no attention appears to have been paid to them. With a view, however, to deceive the ship to windward they hoisted American colours, when the Constitution set an English ensign, by way of warning the stranger to keep aloof.

Until 10 o'clock the Constitution was making every preparation for carrying sail hard should it become necessary, and she sounded in 25 fathoms. At noon the wind fell again, though it was found that while the breeze lasted, she had gained on all of the enemy's ships; more, however, on some, than on others. The nearest vessel was the Belvidera, which was exactly in the wake of the Constitution, distant about two and a half miles, bearing W. N. W. The nearest frigate to leeward, bore N. by W. $\frac{1}{2}$ W. distant three or three and a half miles; the two other frigates were on the lee-quarter, distant about five miles ; and the Africa was hull down to leeward, on the opposite tack.

This was a vast improvement on the state of things that had existed the day previous, and it allowed the officers and men to catch a little rest, though no one left the decks. The latitude by observation this day, was 38° 47' N., and the longitude by dead reckoning 73° 57' W.

At meridian the wind began to blow a pleasant breeze, and the sound of the water rippling under the bows of the vessel was again heard. From this moment the noble old ship slowly drew ahead of all her pursuers, the sails being watched and tended in the best manner that consummate seamanship could dictate, until 4 P. M., when the Belvidera was more than four miles astern, and the other vessels were thrown behind in the same proportion, though the wind had again got to be very light.

In this manner both parties kept pressing ahead and to windward, as fast as circumstances would allow, profiting by every change, and resorting to all the means of forcing vessels through the water, that are known to seamen. At a little before 7, however, there was every appearance of a heavy squall, accompanied by rain ; when the Constitution prepared to meet it with the coolness and discretion she had displayed throughout the whole affair. The people were stationed, and every thing was kept fast to the last moment, when, just before the squall struck the ship, the order was given to clew up and clew down. All the light canvass was furled, a second reef was taken in the mizzen-topsail, and the ship was brought under short sail, in an incredibly little time. The English vessels, observing this, began to let go and haul down without waiting for the wind, and when they were shut in by the rain, they were steering in different directions to avoid the force of the expected squall. The Constitution, on the other hand, no sooner got its weight, than she sheeted home and hoisted her fore and main-top-gallant sails, and while the enemy most probably believed her to be borne down by the pressure of the wind, steering free, she was flying away from them, on an easy bowline, at the rate of eleven knots.

In a little less than an hour after the squall struck the ship, it had entirely passed to leeward, and a sight was again obtained of the enemy. The Belvidera, the nearest vessel, had altered her bearings in that short period two points more to leeward, and she was a long way astern. The next nearest

22

vessel was still farther to leeward, and more distant, while the
two remaining frigates were fairly hull down. The Africa was
barely visible in the horizon !

All apprehensions of the enemy now ceased, though sail was
carried to increase the distance, and to preserve the weather-
gage.   At half-past 10, the wind backed further to the southward, when the Constitution, which had been steering free for
some time, took in her lower studding-sails. At 11 the enemy
fired two guns, and the nearest ship could just be discerned.
As the wind baffled, and continued light, the enemy still perse-
vered in the chase, but at daylight the nearest vessel was hull
down astern and to leeward.   Under the circumstances it was
deemed prudent to use every exertion to lose sight of the
English frigates ; and the wind falling light, the Constitution's
sails were wet down from the skysails to the courses.   The
good effects of this care were soon visible, as at 6 A. M. the
topsails of the enemy's nearest vessels were beginning to dip.
At a quarter past 8, the English ships all hauled to the northward and eastward, fully satisfied, by a trial that had lasted
nearly three days, and as many nights, under all the circumstances that can attend naval manœuvres, from reefed topsails to kedging, that they had no hope of overtaking their
enemy.

Thus terminated a chase, that has become historical in the
American navy, for its length, closeness, and activity.   On
the part of the English, there were manifested much perseverance and seamanship, a ready imitation, and a strong desire
to get alongside of their enemy.   But the glory of the affair
was carried off by the officers and people of the Constitution.
Throughout all the trying circumstances of this arduous struggle, this noble frigate, which had so lately been the subject of
the sneers of the English critics, maintained the high character
of a man-of-war.   Even when pressed upon the hardest, nothing was hurried, confused, or slovenly ; but the utmost steadiness, order, and discipline reigned in the ship.   A cool, discreet, and gallant commander, was nobly sustained by his
officers ; and there cannot be a doubt that had the enemy succeeded in getting any one of their frigates fairly under the fire
of the American ship, that she would have been very roughly
treated.   The escape itself, is not so much a matter of admiration, as the manner in which it was effected.   A little water
was pumped out, it is true, and perhaps this was necessary, in
order to put a vessel fresh from port on a level, in light winds

and calms, with ships that had been cruising some time ; but not an anchor was cut away, not a boat stove, nor a gun lost. The steady and man-of-war like style in which the Constitution took in all her boats, as occasions offered ; the order and rapidity with which she kedged, and the vigilant seamanship with which she was braced up and eased off, extorted admiration among the more liberal of her pursuers.  In this affair, the ship, no less than those who worked her, gained a high reputation, if not with the world generally, at least with those who, perhaps, as seldom err in their nautical criticisms as any people living.

The English relinquished the pursuit at 8 A. M., and at half-past 8 the Constitution, discovering a vessel on her starboard bow, made sail in chase.  At three-quarters past 9 brought to, and spoke an American brig.  At 10 made sail again in chase of another vessel on the lee bow, which also proved to be an American, bound in.  At meridian, hoisted in the boat used in boarding, took a second reef in the topsails, and stood to the eastward, the ship going into Boston near the middle of the same month.

A few days after the chase of the Constitution, the English squadron separated, the Africa returning to port with the prisoners and prizes, and the frigates shaping their courses in different directions, in the hope that the ship which had avoided them so carefully when in company, might be less averse to meeting either singly.

The Essex 32, Captain Porter, got to sea from New York, not long after the departure of Commodore Rogers, and went first to the southward.  She made several prizes early, destroying most of them, and receiving the prisoners on board.  The weather now compelled the Essex to run to the northward. When a few weeks from port, a small fleet was approached at night, which was immediately understood to be enemies.  Out of this fleet the Essex succeeded in getting a ship.  On taking possession of her prize, it was found filled with soldiers, and so much time was necessarily consumed in securing the latter, that the day dawned, and it became inexpedient to renew the attempt on the convoy.  The frigate was said to be the Minerva 36, and the troops in the convoy amounted to near 1000 men.  About 150 were taken in the prize.

A few days after this success, the Essex made a strange sail to windward.  At the moment, the frigate was disguised as a merchantman, having her gun-deck ports in, top-gallant masts housed, and sails trimmed in a slovenly manner. Deceived by these appearances, the stranger came running down free, when the American ship showed her ensign and kept away, under short sail. This emboldened the stranger, who followed, and having got on the weather quarter of his chase, he began his fire, setting English colours. The Essex now knocked out her ports, and opened upon the enemy, who appears to have been so much taken by surprise, that after receiving one or two discharges, his people deserted their quarters, and ran below. In eight minutes after the Essex had begun to fire, the English ship struck. On sending Lieutenant Finch* on board to take possession, the prize proved to be his Britannic Majesty's ship Alert, Captain Laugharne, mounting 20 eighteen-pound carronades, and with a full crew. Mr. Finch found seven feet of water in the Alert, and was obliged to ware round, to keep her from sinking.

The Alert was the first vessel of war taken from the English in this contest, and her resistance was so feeble as to excite surprise. It was not to be expected, certainly, that a ship carrying eighteen-pound carronades, could successfully resist a ship carrying thirty-two-pound carronades, and double her number of guns and men; but so exaggerated had become the opinion of the British prowess on the ocean, that impossibilities were sometimes looked for. As it is understood that only a part of the Essex's guns bore on the Alert, the manner in which the latter was taken, must be attributed to a sudden panic among her people, some of whom were censured after their exchange. One or two of the officers even, did not escape, the first lieutenant having been dismissed the service, by a court-martial. The Alert had but three men wounded, and the Essex sustained no injury at all.

Captain Porter, with the addition made by the crew of the Alert, had many prisoners, and he felt the necessity of getting rid of them. He accordingly entered into an arrangement with Captain Laugharne, to convert the Alert into a cartel, and to send her into St. John's. This project, so favourable to the American interests, was successfully accomplished; and it is due to his character to say, that the officer in command at Newfoundland, Admiral Sir J. T. Duckworth, while he protested against the course, as unusual and injurious to a nation like England, which had so many cruisers at sea, by

---

* Now Captain Bolton.

depriving her of the chances of recapture, honourably complied
with the conditions entered into by his subordinate.

The Essex continued to cruise to the southward of the
Grand Banks. On two occasions, she fell in with enemy's
frigates, and at one time was so hard pressed, as to be reduced
to the necessity of making every preparation to carry one by
boarding in the night, since, another English vessel of war
being in company, an engagement in the usual manner would
have been indiscreet. The arrangments made on board the
Essex, on this occasion, are still spoken of with admiration,
by those who were in the ship ; and there is great reason to
think they would have succeeded, had the vessels met. By
some accident, that has never been explained, the ships passed
each other in the darkness, and shortly after, the Essex came
into the Delaware to replenish her water and stores.

In the meanwhile, the Constitution was not idle. Remaining
at Boston a short time after his celebrated chase, Captain Hull
sailed again on the 2d of August, standing along the land to
the eastward, in the hope of falling in with some of the enemy's
cruisers, that were thought to be hovering on the coast. The
ship ran down, near the land, as far as the Bay of Fundy,
without seeing any thing, when she went off Halifax and Cape
Sable, with the same want of success. Captain Hull now determined to go farther east, and he went near the Isle of
Sables, and thence to the mouth of the Gulf of St. Lawrence,
to intercept vessels bound to Halifax or Quebec. Here two
prizes, of little value, were taken and burned. On the morning
of the 15th, five sail were made, one of which was a sloop of
war. The Constitution gave chase, and the enemy soon set
one of his vessels, a prize brig, on fire. The chases now separated, and the sloop of war being to windward, the Constitution
followed a ship, which turned out to be an Englishman, already a prize to an American privateer. This vessel had been
spoken by the sloop of war, but the appearance of the Constitution prevented her recapture. A brig was next chased to
leeward, and proved to be an American, with a prize crew on
board. She was retaken, and sent in. The remainder of the
vessels escaped.

The Constitution next stood to the southward, and on the
19th, at 2 P. M., in lat. 41° 41', long. 55° 48', a sail was
made from the mast-heads, bearing E. S. E., and to leeward,
though the distance prevented her character from being discovered. The Constitution immediately made sail in chase,

22 *

and at 3, the stranger was ascertained to be a ship on the starboard tack, under easy canvass, and close hauled.  Half an
hour later, she was distinctly made out to be a frigate, and no
doubt was entertained of her being an enemy.  The American
ship kept running free until she was within a league of the
frigate to leeward, when she began to shorten sail.  By this
time, the enemy had laid his main-topsail aback, in waiting for
the Constitution to come down, with every thing ready to engage.  Perceiving that the Englishman sought a combat, Captain Hull made his own preparations with the greater deliberation.  The Constitution, consequently, furled her top-gallant-
sails, and stowed all her light stay-sails and the flying jib.
Soon after, she took a second reef in the topsails, hauled up
the courses, sent down royal-yards, cleared for action, and
beat to quarters.  At 5, the chase hoisted three English ensigns, and immediately after she opened her fire, at long gun-
shot, waring several times, to rake and prevent being raked.
The Constitution occasionally yawed as she approached, to
avoid being raked, and she fired a few guns as they bore, but
her object was not to commence the action seriously, until
quite close.

At 6 o'clock, the enemy bore up, and ran off under his three
topsails and jib, with the wind on his quarter.  As this was an
indication of a readiness to receive his antagonist, in a fair
yard-arm and yard-arm fight, the Constitution immediately set
her main-topgallant-sail and foresail, to get alongside.  At a
little after 6, the bows of the American frigate began to double
on the quarter of the English ship, when she opened with her
forward guns, drawing slowly ahead, with her greater way,
both vessels keeping up a close and heavy fire, as their guns
bore.  In about ten minutes, or just as the ships were fairly
side by side, the mizzen-mast of the Englishman was shot
away, when the American passed slowly ahead, keeping up a
tremendous fire, and luffed short round the bows of the enemy,
to prevent being raked.  In executing this manœuvre, the ship
shot into the wind, got sternway, and fell foul of her antagonist.  While in this situation, the cabin of the Constitution took
fire from the close explosion of the forward guns of the enemy,
who obtained a small, but momentary advantage from his position.  The good conduct of Mr. Hoffman, who commanded
in the cabin, soon repaired this accident, and a gun of the enemy's that threatened further injury, was disabled.

As the vessels touched, both parties prepared to board.  The

English turned all hands up from below, and mustered forward with that object, while Mr. Morris, the first lieutenant, with his own hands endeavoured to lash the ships together. Mr. Alwyn, the master, and Mr. Bush, the lieutenant of marines, were upon the taffrail of the Constitution, to be ready to spring. Both sides now suffered by the closeness of the musketry ; the English much the most, however. Mr. Morris was shot through the body, the bullet fortunately missing the vitals. Mr. Alwyn was wounded in the shoulder, and Mr. Bush fell by a bullet through the head. It being found impossible for either party to board, in the face of such a fire, and with the heavy sea that was on, the sails were filled, and just as the Constitution shot ahead, the foremast of the enemy fell, carrying down with it his mainmast, and leaving him wallowing in the trough of the sea, a helpless wreck.

The Constitution now hauled aboard her tacks, ran off a short distance, secured her masts, and rove new rigging. At 7, she wore round, and taking a favourable position for raking, a jack that had been kept flying on the stump of the mizzen-mast of the enemy, was lowered. Mr. George Campbell Read,* the third lieutenant, was sent on board the prize, and the boat soon returned with the report that the captured vessel was the Guerriere 38, Captain Dacres, one of the ships that had so lately chased the Constitution, off New York.

The Constitution kept waring to remain near her prize, and at 2 A. M., a strange sail was seen closing, when she cleared for action ; but at three, the stranger stood off. At daylight, the officer in charge hailed to say that the Guerriere had four feet water in her hold, and that there was danger of her sinking. On receiving this information, Captain Hull sent all his boats to remove the prisoners. Fortunately, the weather was moderate, and by noon this duty was nearly ended. At 3 P. M., the prize crew was recalled, having set the wreck on fire ; and in a quarter of an hour, the Guerriere blew up. Finding himself incumbered with wounded prisoners, Captain Hull now returned to Boston, where he arrived on the 30th of the same month.

It is not easy, at this distant day, to convey to the reader the full force of the moral impression created in America by this victory of one frigate over another. So deep had been the effect produced on the public mind by the constant accounts of the successes of the English over their enemies at sea, that the

---

* Commodore Read, late in command of the East India squadron.

opinion of their invincibility on that element, already mentioned, generally prevailed; and it had been publicly predicted, that before the contest had continued six months, British sloops of war would lie alongside of American frigates with comparative impunity. Perhaps the only portion of the American population that expected different results, was that which composed the little body of officers on whom the trial would fall, and even they looked forward to the struggle with a manly resolution, rather than with a very confident hope. But the termination of the combat just related, very far exceeded the expectations of the most sanguine. After making all proper allowance for the difference of force which certainly existed in favour of the Constitution, as well as for the excuses that the defeated party freely offered to the world, men on both sides of the Atlantic, who were competent to form intelligent opinions on such subjects, saw the promise of many future successes in this. The style in which the Constitution had been handled; the deliberate and yet earnest manner in which she had been carried into battle; the extraordinary execution that had been done in so short a time by her fire; the readiness and gallantry with which she had cleared for action, so soon after destroying one British frigate, in which was manifested a disposition to meet another, united to produce a deep conviction of self-reliance, coolness, and skill, that was of infinitely more weight than the transient feeling which might result from any accidental triumph.

In this combat, the Constitution suffered a good deal in her rigging and sails, but very little in her hull. Her loss was seven killed, and seven wounded. As soon as she had rove new rigging, applied the necessary stoppers, and bent a few sails, as has been seen, she was ready to engage another frigate. On the other hand, the Guerriere was completely dismasted, had seventy-nine killed and wounded, and, according to the statement of her commander in his defence, before the court which tried him for the loss of his ship, she had received no less than thirty shot as low as five sheets of copper beneath the bends! All this execution had been done between the time when the ships opened their fire abeam, and the moment when the Guerriere's masts fell; for the few shot thrown by the Constitution, previously to the first event, were virtually of no use, and, subsequently to the last, she did not discharge a gun. The whole period, between the time when the Guerriere commenced her fire at long shot, and that when she ac-

tually hauled down her jack, something like two hours was
included in the enemy's accounts of the duration of the combat;
but it is well understood by professional men, that in truth the
battle was decided in about a fourth of that time.

Captain Dacres lost no professional reputation by his defeat.
He had handled his ship in a manner to win the applause of
his enemies, fought her gallantly, and only submitted when
further resistance would have been nearly impossible.  Less
can be said in favour of the efficiency of the Guerriere's batteries, which were not equal to the mode of fighting that had
been introduced by her antagonist, and which, in fact, was
the commencement of a new era in combats between single
ships.

We have dwelt at length on the circumstances connected
with this action, not only because it was the first serious conflict of the war, but because it was characterised by features
which, though novel at the time, became identified with nearly
all the subsequent engagements of the contest, showing that
they were intimately connected with the discipline and system
of the American marine.

Captain Hull having performed the two handsome exploits
recorded, now gave up the command of his frigate, in order to
allow others an equal chance to distinguish themselves, there
being unfortunately many more captains than vessels in the
navy, at that trying moment.   Captain Bainbridge was named
to be his successor, being transferred from the Constellation
38, then fitting for sea at Washington, to the Constitution.

As Captain Bainbridge was one of the oldest officers of his
rank in the service, he was given a command consisting of his
own ship, the Essex 32, and the Hornet 18.   He hoisted his
broad pennant on board the Constitution, accordingly, on the
15th of September, at Boston.   Captain Stewart, lately returned from a furlough, was appointed to the Constellation 38,
and Mr. Charles Morris, the first lieutenant of the Constitution,
in the chase and in the battle, was shortly after promoted to
the rank of captain, passing the step of master-commandant, as
had been the case with Commodore Decatur.

## CHAPTER XXVIII.

Congress did nothing of any moment towards increasing the navy, on the ocean, during the year 1812, although war was declared in June. This neglect of so important a branch of the public service, under circumstances that would seem so imperiously to call for the fostering care and active exertions of the government, must be ascribed to the doubts that still existed as to the possibility of keeping ships at sea, in face of the British navy. It had been customary to say, that France, whenever she put a ship into the water, was merely building for her great enemy ; and an opinion was prevalent, that America would be doing the same thing, if she wasted her resources in creating a marine ; thus rendering it literally necessary for the accomplished officers who composed the germ of the service, to demonstrate, from fact to fact, their ability to maintain the honour of the country, before that country would frankly confide to them the means.

Commodore Rodgers, having refitted, sailed on a second cruise, leaving the Hornet in port; but Commodore Decatur, in the United States 44, and the Argus 16, Captain Sinclair, parted company with him, at sea, on the 12th of October, after cruising some time without falling in with any thing of importance. On the 17th, he captured the British packet Swallow, with a large amount of specie on board, and continued his cruise to the eastward. In the mean while, the United States and Argus having separated, the former stood more to the southward and eastward, with a view to get into the track of the enemy's Indiamen. Sunday, October 25th, the United States, then in lat. 29° N., long. 29° 30′ W., made a large sail to the southward and eastward. The stranger was running down a little free, while the American ship was on a wind, standing towards the chase, which was soon ascertained to be an enemy. The latter having come within a league, hauled up, and passed to windward, when, each party was enabled to see that it had a frigate to oppose. The stranger now wore and came round on the same tack as the United States, keeping away sufficiently to get within reach of her long guns, when she hauled up on an easy bowline, with her mizzen-topsail

aback. At this moment the distance between the two ships
a little exceeded a mile, when the Englishman opened his fire.
Finding the enemy on his weather quarter, Commodore Decatur delivered his larboard broadside, wore round, and came up
to the wind on the other tack, heading northerly. It was observed that all the carronade-shot fell short, the enemy doing
very little injury by his fire.

Having passed her antagonist, the United States delivered
her starboard broadside, and wore again, bringing her head
once more to the southward, or on the same tack as the enemy, both ships steering rap full, with their mizzen-topsails
aback, and keeping up a heavy cannonade. In this manner
the action continued about an hour, the English vessel suffering heavily, while her own fire inflicted very little injury on
her antagonist. At length the stranger's mizzen-mast came
down over his lee quarter, having been shot away about ten
feet above the deck. He then fell off, and let his foresail drop,
apparently with a wish to close. As the ships got near together, the shot of the American vessel did fearful execution,
the fore-course being soon in ribands, the fore and main-top-
masts over the side, the main-yard cut away in the slings, and
the foremast tottering. The United States now filled her mizzen-topsail, gathered fresh way, and tacked. As the stranger
was drifting down, nearly before the wind, and was almost unmanageable, Commodore Decatur had no difficulty in heading
up high enough to cross his wake, which he handsomely effected, with his people still manning the larboard guns. At
the time the United States filled her mizzen-topsail, in preparation for stays, it is said that the enemy, under the impression
she was about to run away, gave three cheers, and set a union
jack in his main rigging, all his other flags having come down
with the several spars. When, however, the American ship
was seen luffing up to close, the jack was lowered, and resistance ceased.

As the United States crossed the stern of the English ship,
the firing having ceased on both sides, she hailed and demanded the name of her antagonist, and whether she had submitted.
To the first interrogatory, Commodore Decatur was answered
that the ship was the Macedonian 38, Captain Carden, and to
the second, that the vessel had struck. On taking possession,
the enemy was found fearfully cut to pieces, having received
no less than a hundred round shot in his hull alone. Of three

hundred men on board him, thirty six were killed, and sixty-eight wounded.

The Macedonian was a very fine ship of her class, mounting, as usual, 49 guns ; eighteens on her gun-deck, and thirty-two-pound carronades above.  She was smaller, of lighter armament, and had fewer men than her opponent of course, but the disproportion between the force of the two vessels, was much less than that between the execution.  In this action, the advantage of position was with the British ship until she was crippled, and the combat was little more than a plain cannonade, at a distance that rendered grape or musketry of little or no use, for the greater part of the time.  The fire of the United States took effect so heavily in the waist of her antagonist, that it is said the marines of the latter were removed to the batteries, which circumstance increased the efficiency of the ship, by enabling new crews to be placed at guns that had been once cleared of their men.  On the other hand, the marines of the United States remained drawn up in the waist of that ship, most of the time quite useless, though they are understood to have shown the utmost steadiness and good conduct under the example of their gallant commander, the weight of the enemy's fire passing a short distance above their heads.

The United States suffered surprisingly little, considering the length of the cannonade, and her equal exposure.  She lost one of her top-gallant masts, received some wounds in the spars, had a good deal of rigging cut, and was otherwise injured aloft, but was hulled a very few times.  Of her officers and people 5 were killed and 7 wounded.  Of the latter, two died, one of whom was Mr. John Musser Funk, the junior lieutenant of the ship.  No other officer was hurt.

On taking possession of his prize, Commodore Decatur found her in a state that admitted of her being taken into port.  When the necessary repairs were completed, the two ships made the best of their way to America ; Commodore Decatur discontinuing the cruise, in order to convoy his prize into port.  The United States arrived off New London on the 4th of December, and about the same time the Macedonian got into Newport.  Shortly after, both ships reached New York by the Hell Gate passage.

The order and style with which the Macedonian was taken, added materially to the high reputation that Commodore Decatur already enjoyed.  His services were acknowledged in the usual manner, and he was soon after directed to cruise in the United States, with the Macedonian, Captain Jones, in company. Mr. Allen, the first lieutenant of the United States, was promoted to the rank of a master-commandant, and he received due credit for the steady discipline that the ship's company had displayed.

The Argus, under Captain Sinclair, after separating from the United States, cruised alone, making several captures of merchantmen, though she met no vessel of war, of a force proper for her to engage.

While these events were in the course of accomplishment, the Wasp 18, Captain Jones, left the Delaware on a cruise. She was one of the sloops built at the close of the Tripolitan war, and like her sister ship the Hornet, a beautiful and fast cruiser. The latter, however, which originally was a brig, had been rebuilt, or extensively repaired at Washington, on which occasion, she had been pierced for twenty guns, and rigged into a ship. The Wasp still retained her old armament and construction, having been a ship from the first, mounting 16 thirty-two pound carronades and 2 long twelves. Her complement of men varied from 130 to 160, according to circumstances. She had been to Europe with despatches before the declaration of war, and did not return home until some weeks after hostilities had commenced.

The Wasp, after refitting, sailed on a cruise to the northward. She ran off Boston, made one capture, and after an absence of three weeks, returned to the Delaware. On the 13th of October, she sailed a second time, and ran off east, southerly, to clear the coast, and to get into the track of vessels steering north. Three days' out it came on to blow very heavily, when the ship lost her jib-boom, and two men that were on it at the moment. The next day the weather moderated, and about 11 o'clock in the night of the 17th, being then in latitude 37° N., and longitude 65° W., several sail were made. Two of these vessels appeared to be large, and Captain Jones did not deem it prudent to close, until he had a better opportunity of observing them, but hauling off to a convenient distance, he steered in the same direction with the unknown vessels, with the intention of ascertaining their characters in the morning. When the day dawned, the strangers were seen ahead, and to leeward. Making sail to close, they were soon ascertained to be a small convoy of six English ships, under the charge of a heavy brig of war. Four of the merchantmen were armed, apparently, mounting, as well as could be ascertained at that

23

distance, from 12 to 18 guns. The commander of the brig, however, manifested no wish to avail himself of the assistance of any of his convoy, but shortening sail, the latter passed ahead, while he prepared to give battle.

The Wasp now sent down top-gallant-yards, close reefed her topsails, and was otherwise brought under short fighting canvass, there being a good deal of sea on. The stranger was under little sail also, and his main yard was on deck, where it had been lowered to undergo repairs. As it was the evident intention of the Englishman to cover his convoy, very little manœuvring was necessary to bring the vessels alongside of each other. At 32 minutes past 11 A. M., the Wasp ranged close up on the starboard side of the enemy, receiving her broadside, at the distance of about sixty yards, and delivering her own. The fire of the Englishman immediately became very rapid, it having been thought at the time, that he discharged three guns to the Wasp's two ; and as the main-topmast of the latter ship was shot away within five minutes after the action commenced, appearances at first, were greatly in the enemy's favour. In eight minutes, the gaff and mizzen top-gallant-mast also fell. But, if the fire of the Wasp was the most deliberate, it was much the most deadly.

In consequence of the fall of the main-topmast of the American ship, which, with the main-topsail-yard, lodged on the fore and fore-topsail braces, it became next to impossible to haul any of the yards, had circumstances required it, but the battle was continued with great spirit on both sides, until the ships had gradually closed so near, that the bends of the Wasp rubbed against her antagonist's bows. Here the ships came foul, the bowsprit of the enemy passing in over the quarter-deck of the Wasp, forcing her bows up into the wind, and enabling the latter to throw in a close raking fire.

When Captain Jones perceived the effect of the enemy's fire on his spars and rigging, he closed with a view to board ; but finding his ship in so favourable a position, he countermanded an order to that effect, and directed a fresh broadside to be delivered. The vessels were now so near that in loading some of the Wasp's guns, the rammers hit against the bows of her antagonist, and the people of the Englishman could no longer be kept at their quarters forward. The discharge of one or two of the carronades swept the enemy's decks, when the impetuosity of the Wasp's crew could no longer be restrained, and they began to leap into the rigging, and from thence on the bowsprit of the brig. As soon as Mr. Biddle, the first lieutenant of the Wasp, found that the people were not to be restrained, he sprang into the rigging, followed by Lieutenant G. Rodgers and a party of officers and men, and the attempt to board was seriously made. On the forecastle of the brig Mr. Biddle passed all his own people, but there was no enemy to oppose him. Two or three officers were standing aft, most of them bleeding. The decks were strewed with killed and wounded, but not a common hand was at his station; all those that were able having gone below, with the exception of the man at the wheel. The latter had maintained his post, with the spirit of a seaman, to the last.

The English officers threw down their swords in token of submission, as Mr. Biddle passed aft; and it ought to be added, to the credit of the conquerors, notwithstanding the excitement of such scenes are too apt to lead even the disciplined into excesses, not an enemy was injured by the boarders. Mr. Biddle sprang into the main rigging, and lowered the English flag with his own hands, when the combat ceased, after a duration of 43 minutes.

The prize turned out to be the British sloop of war Frolic 18, Captain Whinyates, homeward bound, with the vessels in the Honduras trade under convoy. The Frolic, with the exception of being a brig, was a vessel of the size and construction of the Wasp. She mounted, on her main deck, 16 thirty-two pound carronades, four long guns, differently stated to have been sixes, nines, and twelves, and had two twelve-pound carronades on a topgallant forecastle. This armament would make a force greater than that of the Wasp by four guns, a disparity that is not immaterial in vessels so small. The two crews were pretty equal in numbers, though it is probable that the Wasp may have had a few men the most; a difference that was of little moment under the circumstances, more particularly as the Frolic was a brig, and the battle was fought, by both vessels, under very short sail.*

The Wasp was cut up aloft to an unusual degree, there having been no question that her antagonist's fire was heavy and spirited. The braces and standing-rigging were nearly all shot away, and some of the spars that stood were injured. She had five men killed, and five wounded. The hull sustained no great damage.

---

* The Wasp's muster-roll, on the morning of the 18th October, contained the names of 138 persons, all told.

The Frolic was also much injured in her spars and rigging, more particularly in the former; and the two vessels were hardly separated, before both her masts fell. She had been hulled at almost every discharge, and was virtually a wreck when taken possession of by the Americans. Her loss in men was never accurately known, but her captain, first lieutenant, and master, were wounded; the two latter mortally. Mr. Biddle, who remained in charge of the prize, after so gallantly boarding her, stated, that as far as he could ascertain, she had from 70 to 80 killed and wounded. Subsequent information, however, has given reason to believe that the number was even greater. Captain Whinyates, in his official report, states that not 20 of his crew escaped unhurt, which would probably raise the casualties to a number between 90 and 100.

The Frolic had scarcely submitted, when a large sail was seen standing towards the two vessels, evidently a ship of force. Instructions were given to Mr. Biddle to make the best of his way to Charleston with the prize, and the Wasp began to make sail, with an intention to continue her cruise; but on opening her canvass, and turning the reefs out of her topsails, they were found to be nearly in ribands. The stranger, which turned out to be the enemy's ship Poictiers 74, hove a shot over the Frolic, in passing, and ranging up near the Wasp, both vessels were captured. The Poictiers proceeded with her two prizes to Bermuda, and the Americans, being paroled, soon after returned home.

As this was the first combat of the war between vessels of a force so nearly equal as to render cavilling difficult, the result occasioned much exultation in America, and greatly increased the confidence of the public, in supposing an American ship had quite as many claims to conduct, courage, and skill, as a British. Persons of reflection attached but little importance, it is true, to the mere fact that a few cruisers had been taken in single combat, but the idea of British invincibility was destroyed, and vast moral results were distinctly foreseen.

In the published account of the captain of the Frolic, much stress was laid on the crippled condition of his ship, when she went into action. It is admitted that his vessel had her mainyard on deck when she engaged, and, as little canvass was required, her after-sail was reduced to her fore-and-aft mainsail. There are circumstances in which the loss of a brig's main-topsail would be of the last importance; and there are circumstances, again, in which it would be of but little moment. On this occasion it does not appear to have materially influenced the result; and the very fact that the yard was down, may have prevented the mast from falling during the engagement, instead of falling after it. On details of this nature, it is difficult to reason accurately, so much depending on minute circumstances, that must escape the general observer.

Captain Jones was promoted shortly after this success, and he was appointed to the command of the Macedonian 38, which ship had been purchased and taken into the service. The name of Mr. Biddle, who was an old lieutenant, and whose spirited conduct in the action was much appreciated, was also included in the list of masters and commanders that was sent into the senate about the same time.

## CHAPTER XXIX.

WHEN Commodore Bainbridge took command of the three vessels that have been already mentioned, the Constitution 44, his own ship, and Hornet 18, Captain Lawrence, were lying in the port of Boston; and the Essex 32, Captain Porter, had just gone into the Delaware. Orders were sent to the latter officer, to rendezvous first at Port Praya, in the island of St. Jago; and secondly at Fernando Noronha. Other places of resort were pointed out; and he was also instructed to cruise in the track of the enemy's Indiamen, until a time mentioned, when, if he failed to fall in with his senior officer, he was at liberty to follow his own discretion. As the Essex never joined the other ships, we shall defer the account of her cruise, to another chapter.

The Constitution and Hornet sailed from Boston on the 26th of October. Touching at the different rendezvous, where they appeared in the character of British vessels of war, letters were left for Captain Porter, under the assumed name of Sir James Yeo, of the Southampton 32, according to arrangement, and the ships proceeded.

Commodore Bainbridge arrived off St. Salvador on the 13th

23 *

of December, and the Hornet was sent in to communicate with the consul. Captain Lawrence found the British sloop of war Bonne Citoyenne 18, Captain Green, in port, but about to sail for England, with a very large amount of specie on board. The presence of this vessel suggested a hope of being able to get her out. After conversing with the consul, that gentleman was empowered to inform the commander of the English ship, that Captain Lawrence was desirous of meeting him at sea, and to give the necessary pledges that the Constitution would be out of the way. A correspondence took place between the English and American consuls on the subject, and in the end, Captain Green declined acceding to the proposal.

The Constitution left the Hornet to blockade the Bonne Citoyenne alone, on the 26th, and stood to the southward, keeping the land aboard. About 9 A. M. of the 29th, when in lat. 13° 6′ S., and long. 31° W., or at a distance of ten leagues from the coast, two strange sail were made in-shore and to windward. One of these vessels continued to stand in, while the other, which was much the largest, altered her course in the direction of the American frigate, which had tacked to close with her. The day was pleasant, there was but little sea, and the wind was light at E. N. E.

At 11 A. M., being satisfied that the strange sail was an enemy's frigate, the Constitution tacked again to the southward and eastward, to draw her enemy off the land, which was plainly in sight. At the same time, she set her royals, and boarded main-tack, in order to effect this object.

At 12 M. the Constitution showed her colours, and shortly after the stranger set the English ensign. Signals were made by both ships, but proved to be mutually unintelligible. At 20 minutes past 1, P. M., believing himself far enough from the land, Commodore Bainbridge took in his main-sail and royals, and tacked towards the enemy. Soon after, both ships had their heads to the southward and eastward, the Englishman being to windward more than a mile distant, and well on the Constitution's quarter.

The enemy had now hauled down his ensign, though he kept a jack flying, and Commodore Bainbridge ordered a shot fired ahead of him, to induce him to show his colours anew. This order brought on a general fire, and the battle commenced at 2, P. M., on both sides, with a furious cannonade. The enemy sailed the best, and in the light wind that prevailed he soon forged ahead, keeping away with a view to cross the

Constitution's bow, but was foiled by the latter ship's waring, which brought the heads of the two combatants once more to the westward.  In performing these evolutions, as the enemy steered free, and the Constitution luffed, the vessels got within pistol-shot, when the former repeated the same attempt, the ships waring together, bringing their heads once more to the eastward.  The English ship fore-reaching again, now endeavoured to tack to preserve the weather-gage; but failing, she was obliged to ware, a manœuvre that the Constitution had already executed to avoid being raked, for the wheel of the latter ship had been shot away, and it was difficult to watch the vessel with the helm, as closely as was desirable.  The Constitution, notwithstanding, was the first in coming to the wind on the other tack, and she got an efficient raking fire at her opponent.

Both vessels now ran off free, with the wind on the quarter, the English ship still to windward, when the latter being greatly injured, made an attempt to close, at 55 minutes past 2, by running down on the Constitution's quarter.  Her jib-boom ran into the Constitution's mizzen rigging, in which situation she suffered severely, without being able to effect her purpose.  The head of her bowsprit was soon shot away, and in a few minutes after, her foremast came by the board.  The Constitution shot ahead, keeping away to avoid being raked; in separating, the stump of the enemy's bowsprit passed over the American frigate's taffrail.

The two ships now brought the wind abeam again, with their heads to the eastward, and the Constitution having fore-reached, in consequence of carrying the most sail, wore, passed her antagonist, luffed up under his quarter, wore again, and the Englishman having kept away, the vessels came alongside of each other, and engaged for a short time, yard-arm and yard-arm.  In a few minutes the enemy lost his mizzen-mast, leaving nothing standing but his main-mast, with the yard shot away near the slings.  As his fire had ceased, the Constitution hauled aboard her tacks, and luffed athwart her antagonist's bow; passing out of the combat to windward, at five minutes past 4, with her topsails, courses, spanker, and jib set.  In executing this manœuvre, Commodore Bainbridge was under the impression that the enemy had struck, the ensign which had been hoisted in his main-rigging being down, his ship a wreck, and his fire silenced.

Having got a favourable weatherly position, the Constitution passed some time in repairing damages, and in securing her masts; it being all-important to an American frigate so far from home, without colonies or military stations to repair to, and an ocean to traverse that was covered with enemies, to look vigilantly to these great auxiliaries. In about an hour, observing an ensign still flying on board his enemy, Commodore Bainbridge wore round, and standing directly across her fore-foot, the English vessel anticipated his fire by striking.

The Constitution immediately wore, with her head on the same tack as the captured vessel, hoisted out a boat, and sent Mr. Parker, her first lieutenant, to take possession. The prize proved to be the British frigate Java 38, Captain Lambert, bound to the East Indies, having on board as passengers Lieutenant General Hislop and staff, together with several supernumerary sea-officers, and a considerable number of men intended for other ships.

This combat lasted near two hours, from the commencement to the end of the firing, and it had been warmly contested on both sides, but with very different results. Although there was more manœuvring than common, the Java had been literally picked to pieces by shot, spar following spar, until she had not one left. Her foremast was first cut away near the cat-harpings, and afterwards, by a double-headed shot, about five-and-twenty feet from the deck. The main-topmast went early, and the main-mast fell after the Constitution hauled off. The mizzen-mast was shot out of the ship, a few feet from the deck, and the bowsprit near the cap. Her hull was also greatly injured; and her loss in men, according to the British published accounts, was 22 killed and 102 wounded; though there is good reason for supposing it was considerably greater. Commodore Bainbridge stated it at 60 killed and 101 wounded. There may have been some discrepancy in these statements, in consequence of the great number of supernumeraries on board the Java, which ship is said to have had more than 400 men in her when taken, or quite 100 more than her regular complement.* Captain Lambert, of the Java, was mortally

* The British accounts state the crew of the Java at 377 men, including supernumeraries. Commodore Bainbridge reports that he furloughed 361 officers, seamen, marines, and boys, exclusively of 8 passengers and 9 Portuguese seamen, making 378 souls. If to these be added the 22 allowed to be killed by the enemy, a total of just 400 is obtained. But it is said that a muster-list, made five days after the Java sailed, contained just 446 names.

wounded; and one of her lieutenants, the master, and many of her inferior officers, were slain, or seriously hurt.

The Constitution did not lose a spar. She went into action with her royal-yards across, and came out of it with all three of them in their places. An eighteen-pound shot passed through the mizzen-mast; the fore-mast was slightly wounded, and the main-mast was untouched. The main-topmast was also slightly wounded; a few other spars were hit, without being carried away; the running rigging was injured a good deal; several shrouds were cut, and the ship received a few round-shot in her hull. Of her crew, 9 were killed, and 25 were wounded. Among the latter were Commodore Bainbridge, and the junior lieutenant, Mr. Alwyn. The last died of his injuries, some time after the action. Commodore Bainbridge was slightly hurt in the hip, early in the engagement, by a musket-ball; and the shot that carried away the wheel, drove a small copper bolt into his thigh, inflicting a dangerous wound, though he kept the deck until midnight.

Although the injuries to the hull of the Java were not of a nature to render her being carried into port difficult, the smoothness of the sea having prevented her from receiving many shot below the water-line, there existed many objections to attempting it. In the first place, it was known that the Brazilian government was favourable to that of Great Britain, and there had been strong proof of it during the recent visit of Commodore Bainbridge to St. Salvador. That officer, therefore felt a hesitation about trusting his prize in a Brazilian port. The difficulty of obtaining masts of the necessary size, the distance from home, and the risks of recapture, on nearing the coast, united to render it expedient to destroy her. After lying by her two or three days, therefore, with a view to remove the wounded with proper care, the Java was blown up, and the Constitution made the best of her way to St. Salvador, where she immediately landed her prisoners on parole.

The same general peculiarities attended this combat, as had distinguished the two other cases of frigate actions. In all three, the American vessels were superior to their antagonists; but in all three, had the difference in execution been greatly out of proportion to the disparity in force. The Java, like the Guerriere, had been well handled, but her fire had been badly aimed. It would seem that the Constitution actually wore six times, after the action had fairly commenced; and allowing for the positions of the ships, the lightness of the wind, and the space that it was necessary to run, in order to avoid being raked while executing these evolutions, it is probable that the cannonade did not actually occupy an hour. The action must have terminated some miles to leeward of the spot where it commenced.

On reaching St. Salvador, Commodore Bainbridge found the Hornet off the port, and it was understood that the Bonne Citoyenne had hove-short, with an intention of going to sea that night. The arrival of the Constitution appears to have produced a change in this plan, if it ever existed. Remaining a few days in port to land his prisoners, and to complete his arrangements, Commodore Bainbridge sailed for America, January 6, 1813, and arrived at Boston on the 27th of February, after an absence of four months.

The Hornet was left with orders substantially discretionary. She remained off St. Salvador, blockading the Bonne Citoyenne, alone, for eighteen days, when she was chased into the harbour by the Montagu 74, which vessel had come to relieve the enemy's sloop of war from the awkward necessity of fighting with so much treasure on board, or of the still more unpleasant dilemma of appearing indisposed to meet a ship of equal force. It was late in the evening when the Montagu approached, and the Hornet availed herself of the darkness to ware and stand out again, passing into the offing without further molestation.

Captain Lawrence now hauled by the wind, to the northward and eastward, with the intention of going off Pernambuco. He made a few prizes, and continued cruising up the coast, until the 24th of February, when the ship was near the mouth of Demarara river. Here he gave chase to a brig, which drew him into quarter-less-five, when, having no pilot, he deemed it prudent to haul off shore. At this moment he supposed himself to be about two and a half leagues from the fort at the entrance of the river. Just without the bar, another brig was seen. As she had an English ensign set, and bore every appearance of being a man-of-war, it was determined to attack her. While the Hornet was beating round the Carobana bank, which lay between her and the enemy, with a view to get at him, another sail was made on her weather quarter, edging down towards her. It was now half past 3 P. M., and the Hornet continuing to turn to windward, with her original intention, by twenty minutes past 4 the second stranger

was made out to be a large man-of-war brig.   Shortly after
he showed English colours.

As soon as her captain was satisfied that the vessel approaching was an enemy, the Hornet was cleared for action,
and her people went to quarters.   The ship was kept close by
the wind, in order to gain the weather-gage, the enemy still
running free.   At 5 10, feeling certain that he could weather
the Englishman, Captain Lawrence showed his colours and
tacked.   The two vessels were now standing towards each
other, with their heads different ways, both close by the wind.
They passed within half pistol-shot at 5 25, delivering their
broadsides as the guns bore; each vessel using the larboard
battery.   As soon as they were clear, the Englishman put his
helm hard up, with the intention to ware short round, and get
a raking fire at the Hornet ; but the manœuvre was closely
watched and promptly imitated, and, firing his starboard guns,
he was obliged to right his helm, as the Hornet was coming
down on his quarter, in a perfect blaze of fire.   The latter
closed, and maintaining the admirable position she had taken,
poured in her shot with such vigour, that a little before 5 40,
the enemy not only lowered his ensign, but he hoisted it union
down, in the fore-rigging, as a signal of distress.   His main-
mast soon after fell.

Mr. J. T. Shubrick was sent on board to take possession.
This officer soon returned with the information that the prize
was the enemy's sloop of war Peacock 18, Captain Peake, and
that she was fast sinking, having already six feet of water in
her hold.   Mr. Conner, the third lieutenant of the Hornet, and
Mr. B. Cooper, one of her midshipmen, were immediately despatched with boats, to get out the wounded, and to endeavour
to save the vessel.   It was too late for the latter, though every
exertion was made.   Both vessels were immediately anchored,
guns were thrown overboard, shot-holes plugged, and recourse
was had to the pumps, and even to bailing ; but the short twi-
light of that low latitude left the prize-crew, before the prisoners
could be removed.   In the hurry and confusion of such a
scene, and while the boats of the Hornet were absent, four of
the Englishmen lowered the stern boat of the Peacock, which
had been thought too much injured to be used, jumped into it,
and pulled for the land, at the imminent risk of their lives.*

Mr. Conner became sensible that the brig was in momentary

---

\* These adventurers got ashore safely.

danger of sinking, and he endeavoured to collect the people remaining on board, in the Peacock's launch, which still stood on deck, the fall of the main-mast, and the want of time, having prevented an attempt to get it into the water. Unfortunately, a good many of the Peacock's people were below, rummaging the vessel, and when the brig gave her last wallow it was too late to save them.

The Peacock settled very easily but suddenly, in five and a half fathoms water, and the two American officers, with most of the men, and several prisoners, saved themselves in the launch, though not without great exertions. Three of the Hornet's people went down in the brig, and nine of the Peacock's were also drowned. Four more of the latter saved themselves by running up the rigging into the foretop, which remained out of water, after the hull had got to the bottom. The launch had no oars, and it was paddled by pieces of boards towards the Hornet, when it was met by one of the cutters of that ship, which was returning to the brig. The cutter immediately pulled towards the Peacock's fore-mast, in the hope of finding some one swimming; but, with the exception of those in the top, no person was saved.

In this short encounter, the Peacock had her captain and four men killed, and thirty-three wounded. The Hornet had one man killed, and two wounded, in addition to two men badly burned by the explosion of a cartridge. She suffered a good deal aloft, had one shot through the foremast, and the bowsprit was hit.

The Peacock was a vessel of the Hornet's size, being a little shorter, but having more beam. Her proper armament was thirty-twos, but, for some reason that is not known, it had been changed for lighter guns, and in the action she mounted 16 twenty-four pound carronades, 2 light long guns, a twelve pound carronade on her topgallant forecastle, and another light long gun aft. By her quarter-bill, she had 130 men on board, at the time she was taken. This force rendered her inferior to the Hornet, which ship mounted 18 thirty-two pound carronades and two long twelves. The Hornet in the action mustered 135 men fit for duty.

Notwithstanding the superiority of the Hornet, the same disparity between the execution and the difference in force, is to be seen in this action, as in those already mentioned. In allowing the Hornet to get the weather-gage, the Peacock was out-manœuvred; but, with this exception, she is understood to have been well managed, though her gunnery was defective. The only shot that touched the hull of the Hornet, was one fired as the latter ship was falling off, in waring; it merely glanced athwart her bows, indenting a plank beneath the cat-head. As this shot must have been fired from a starboard gun of the Peacock, the fact demonstrates how well she was handled; and that, in waring, her commander had rightly esti-mated and judiciously used the peculiar powers of a brig, though the quick movements of his antagonist deprived him of the result he had expected, and immediately gave the Hornet a decided advantage in position. It would be cavilling to deny that this short combat was decided by the superior gunnery and rapid handling of the Hornet.

As the brig at anchor might come out and attack her, the greatest exertions were made on board the Hornet to be in readiness to receive the enemy, and by 9 o'clock at night, new sails had been bent, her boats were stowed, the ship was cleared, and every thing was ready for another action. At 2 A. M., she got under way, and stood to the northward and westward, under easy sail. Captain Lawrence finding that he had now 277 souls on board, including the people of another prize, and that he was short of water, determined to return home. The allowance of water was reduced to three pints a man, and the ship ran through the West-Indies, anchoring at Holmes's Hole, in Martha's Vineyard, on the 19th of March; whence she came through the Vineyard and Long Island Sounds to New York without meeting an enemy.

The successes of the Constitution and Hornet, two of the vessels of Commodore Bainbridge's squadron, served greatly to increase the popularity of the navy. Their commanders were rewarded with medals, swords, and votes of thanks, by different legislatures; and Captain Lawrence was promoted, and transferred to the command of the Chesapeake.

Congress, by this time, began to feel more confidence in the ability to withstand British prowess, and a law had been passed on the 2d of January, to increase the naval force of the coun-try. By the provisions of this act, the President was empow-ered to build four ships to rate not less than seventy-four guns, and six ships to rate at forty-four guns each. This was at once multiplying the force of the navy tenfold, and it may be esteemed the first step that was ever actually put in execution, towards establishing a marine that might prove of material moment, in influencing the results of a war. Measures were

24

taken immediately to lay the keels of some of the ships of the line, and Commodore Bainbridge, being appointed to superintend the construction of one of them, relinquished the command of the Constitution.

Another law passed, on the 3d of March, directing six sloops of war to be built on the sea-board, and authorising the construction of as many vessels on the lakes as the public service required. Congress also voted handsome sums to the officers and crews of the ships that had destroyed captured vessels of war, in the way of prize-money.

## CHAPTER XXX.

WHEN Commodore Bainbridge sailed from Boston, the Essex, still under the command of Captain Porter, was lying in the Delaware. She quitted that river the 28th of October, or two days after the other ships of the squadron had got to sea.

The Essex was singularly unfortunate in not falling in with an enemy of any sort for several weeks, and on the 11th of December, she crossed the equator in longitude 30° W., the same bad luck attending her. On the 12th, however, about 2 P. M., a vessel was seen to windward, which had every appearance of an enemy's man-of-war brig. At six, the stranger began to show signals, which went to confirm the idea of his character. As the chase was still to windward, and night was coming on fast, an unsuccessful effort was made to decoy her down, by making signals in return. At sunset the brig showed English colours, and, when it was sufficiently dark, she made some night-signals. By 9 P. M. the Essex succeeded in getting within musket-shot. Captain Porter soon after hailed, and ordered the brig to settle her topsails, haul up her courses, and to heave-to to windward. At the same time orders were given to the different divisions not to fire into the stranger, as it was very desirable to get possession without doing him any injury. Instead of complying with the directions of Captain Porter, however, the brig endeavoured to cross the stern of the Essex, by keeping away, probably with an intention to rake her, and to escape to leeward. This drew a volley of mus-

ketry from the frigate, which killed one man, when the brig
struck.

The prize was the British government packet Nocton 10,
with a crew of 31 men.  On board of her were found $55,000
in specie.  The next day a crew of 17 men was put into the
Nocton, under the orders of Acting Lieutenant Finch, who was
instructed to make the best of his way to America.  This officer had got between Bermuda and the Capes of Virginia, in
the execution of his duty, when he was compelled to heave-to
in a gale.  Just as the weather moderated, a British frigate was
made to windward.  Mr. Finch tried the sailing of the brig
with the enemy, on different tacks, but finally put away dead
before the wind, as the only means of escape.  As it was not
in the power of the prize-crew to make sail with sufficient
rapidity to compete with a frigate's complement of men, the
Nocton was soon within rea h of the enemy's guns, and a few
shot were fired, which did some injury to her rigging.  Mr.
Finch, however, held on, until the enemy had got close upon
his quarter, and was about to fire a volley of musketry, when,
escape being hopeless, he struck.  Thus did the Essex lose
her first prize, though the specie had been taken out of her,
and was rendered secure by being subsequently used on account of the government.

On the 14th, the Essex made the island of Fernando de Noronha, and communicated with the land, without going in.
Here Captain Porter obtained the letter from Commodore Bainbridge, informing him that he would find the other vessels off
Cape Frio.  From this time, until the 25th, the ship was making her passage towards the coast; on the afternoon of that
day, she hove-to off the pitch of the Cape, where no signs were
to be seen of the Constitution or Hornet.  Three days afterwards, in fact, the first of these vessels captured the Java off
St. Salvador.  After cruising a short time, at this rendezvous,
the Essex was drawn a long distance to leeward in chase; and
in attempting to beat up again to her station, she was met by
heavy weather, which induced Captain Porter to change his
cruising ground.  On the morning of the 29th, the frigate captured an English merchant vessel, which proved to be one of
a convoy of six sail, in charge of a man-of-war schooner, that
had left Rio the night previously, this vessel having put back
in consequence of discovering a leak.  On obtaining this intelligence, Captain Porter followed on the track of the convoy,
and after a long and fruitless chase, he determined to go off

St. Salvador, in order to intercept it. While beating up with this intention, information was received from different Portuguese vessels, of the presence of the other ships of the squadron off the port, and renewed efforts were made to join. But strong northerly winds prevailed, and Captain Porter, after struggling with them a week, decided to run into St. Catherine's to water.

Having been disappointed in his attempts to fall in with the commodore, at three rendezvous, and ascertaining that the Montagu 74, had sailed from Rio to raise the blockade of the vessels at St. Salvador, Captain Porter was greatly at a loss which way to steer, in order to join the other ships. It was near the end of January, 1813, and, in point of fact, the Constitution had left the coast on the 6th of that month, on her way home. As the Hornet followed her on the 24th, in determining to act for himself, during the remainder of the cruise, Captain Porter came to a happy decision.

The Essex left St. Catherine's on the 26th of January, 1813, for the Pacific Ocean, and after a most tempestuous passage round the Horn, she fell in with the pleasant southwest breezes of that sea on the 5th of March, and at meridian of that day her people got a distant view of the Andes. On the 5th, she anchored at the island of Mocha.

The Essex was now fairly in the Pacific, though she had not fallen in with an enemy for two months. There was but one chart of the ocean in the ship, and that was very small and imperfect; the provisions were getting short, and the vessel was much in want of cordage. Notwithstanding these necessities, Captain Porter felt reluctant to let his arrival be known until he made a few captures, hoping to supply his ship from prizes. Anxious to obtain information of the British force, by the same means, he determined to cruise a short time before he proceeded to Valparaiso. An ill fortune, however, continued to prevail, and for many days the ship was enveloped in fogs. She continued standing along shore, to the northward; and on the 13th, while running before a stiff southerly breeze, she rounded the Point of Angels, shot into full view of the port and town of Valparaiso, and was becalmed under the guns of a battery.

As he had English colours flying, Captain Porter came to a conclusion not to go in, for, taking a survey of the shipping in port, and perceiving several Spaniards ready to sail, he thought it prudent to let them get to sea before the arrival of an American cruiser became known in the place. The ship's head was

consequently kept to the northward, and the breeze striking
her again, she ran the town out of sight in an hour or two.
On the 15th, however, the ship returned, made the Point of
Angels once more, went in, and anchored.

To the astonishment of Captain Porter, he now ascertained
that Chili had declared itself independent of Spain, and his reception was as favourable as he could have desired. He also
learned that the Viceroy of Peru had sent out cruisers against
the American shipping, and that his appearance in the Pacific
was of the greatest importance to the American trade, which
lay at the mercy of the English letters of marque, and of these
Peruvian corsairs. This was cheering intelligence, after the
fatigues and disappointments of a cruise of so many months.

For more than a week the Essex was employed in victual-
ling. During this time an American whaler came in from the
islands. According to the accounts of her master, the American whalers, which had left home during a time of peace, lay
entirely at the mercy of those of the enemy ; several of which
had sailed as regular letters of marque, and all of which were
more or less armed. Many of the American vessels, as they
often kept the sea six months at a time, were probably still ignorant of the war ; and it was known that one of them, at
least, had already fallen into the hands of the English. As
soon as imperfectly victualled, the frigate went to sea, to profit
by this intelligence.

On the 25th, the Essex fell in with the American whale
ship Charles, and learned that two other vessels, the Walker
and Barclay, had been captured a few days previously, off
Coquimbo, by a Peruvian, with an English ship in company.
Sail was made, in consequence, in the direction of Coquimbo,
and, a few hours later, a stranger was seen to the northward.
This vessel was soon ascertained to be a cruising ship, disguised as a whaler. She showed Spanish colours, when the
Essex set an English ensign, fired a gun to leeward, and the
Charles, which remained in company, hoisted the American flag
beneath an English jack. The Spaniard now ran down, and,
when about a mile distant, he fired a shot ahead of the Essex,
which that ship answered by throwing a few shot over him, to
bring him nearer. When close enough, the Spanish ship sent
an armed boat to board the Essex, and it was directed to go
back with an order for the cruiser to run under the frigate's
lee, and to send an officer to apologize for the shot she had
fired at an English man-of-war. This command was com-

24 *

plied with, and the ship was ascertained to be the Peruvian privateer Nereyda, armed with 15 guns, and with a full crew.
The lieutenant, who now came on board, informed Captain
Porter that they were cruising for Americans; that they had
already taken the Walker and the Barclay; that the English
letter of marque Nimrod had driven their prize-crew from on
board the Walker; that they were then cruising expressly to
look for the Nimrod, with the intention of obtaining redress;
and that they had mistaken the Essex for the latter ship.  It
would seem that the Peruvians cruised against the Americans,
under the impression that Spain, then so dependent on England for her existence, would declare war speedily against the
United States, in consequence of the war declared by the latter
against the King of Great Britain, which might legalise their
captures.

An interview with the master of the Walker satisfied Captain Porter that the captured ships had been illegally seized; and
hoisting American colours, he fired two shots over the Nereyda,
when that vessel struck.  Her crew were all sent on board the
Essex, and the three ships stood in-shore to look into Coquimbo,
in the hope of finding the Nimrod and the prizes, but without success.  The next morning, the entire armament of the Nereyda,
with all her ammunition, shot, small-arms, and light sails,
were thrown overboard, and she was otherwise put in a condition to do no harm, when she was released.  It is worthy of
remark, that the guns of this vessel were of iron, while her
shot of all descriptions were of copper; the abundance of the
latter material in that part of the world, rendering it cheaper
than the metal usually employed for such purposes.

From the master and crew of the Barclay, Captain Porter
obtained a list of such of the whaling vessels as they knew to
be in the Pacific.  It contained the names of twenty-three American, and of ten English ships.  The former was probably
the most correct, as his informants added that quite twenty
Englishmen were thought to be in that sea.  The latter were,
in general, fine vessels of near 400 tons burthen, and, as has
been said already, they were all more or less armed.

On the 28th of April, the ship was up with the island of
San Gallan, when she hauled off to the northward and west-
ward, with a view to cross the track of inward-bound vessels.
The next day, three sail were made, standing for Callao.
Every thing was set to cut the strangers off, particularly the
one nearest in, which had the appearance of the Barclay.  The

chase, however, would have escaped, had she not been becalmed when she doubled the point of San Lorenzo.  At this
moment the frigate was near a league distant, but, fortunately,
she kept the breeze until she had got within a hundred yards
of the enemy, when she lowered her boats, and took possession.  The prize proved to be the Barclay, as had been expected.  There was now a good opportunity of looking into
the harbour, and finding that nothing had arrived from Valparaiso to disclose his presence in the Pacific, Captain Porter
showed English colours, while the Barclay hoisted the American under the enemy's ensign.  In this manner both vessels
went into the offing, where the Barclay was given up to her
proper officers, though most of her crew having entered in the
Essex, and declining to rejoin the ship, her master preferred
keeping in company with the frigate, offering to act as a pilot
in searching for the enemy.  With this understanding, the two
vessels stretched off to the northward and westward.

From the end of March until the middle of April, the Essex,
with the Barclay in company, was standing across from the
main towards the islands, and on the 17th she made Chatham
Island; but no ship was found there.  From this place the frigate went to Charles's Island, where she had the same want of
success.  At the latter island, however, was a box called " the
post-office," in which the masters of the whalers were accustomed to leave written accounts of their luck and movements,
and much information was obtained from them, concerning the
different ships in the Pacific.

The Essex continued passing from island to island, without
meeting with any thing, until her crew was aroused by the
cheering cry of " sail ho!" on the morning of the 29th.  A
ship was made to the westward, and, soon after, two more a
little further south.  Chase was given to the first vessel, which
was spoke under English colours, about 9 A. M.  She proved
to be the British whale-ship Montezuma, with 1400 barrels of
oil on board.  Throwing a crew into the prize, the Essex next
made sail after the two other ships, which had taken the alarm,
and endeavoured to escape.  At 11 A. M., when the frigate
was about eight miles from the two strangers, it fell calm, and
the boats were hoisted out and sent against the enemy, under
Mr. Downes, the first lieutenant.  About 2 P. M. the party got
within a mile of the nearest ship, when the two strangers, who
were a quarter of a mile apart, hoisted English colours, and
fired several guns.  The boats now formed, and pulled for the

largest ship, which kept training her guns on them as they approached, but struck without firing a shot, just as the boarders were closing. The second vessel imitated her example, when attacked in the same manner.

The prizes were the Georgiana and the Policy, both whalers; and the three ships, together, furnished the Essex with many important supplies. They had bread, beef, pork, cordage, water, and among other useful things, a great number of Gallapagos tortoises.

The Georgiana had been built for the service of the English East India Company, and having the reputation of being a fast vessel, Captain Porter determined to equip her as a cruiser, with the double purpose of having an assistant in looking for the enemy, and of possessing a consort to receive his own crew in the event of any accident's occurring to the Essex. This ship was pierced for 18 guns, and had 6 mounted when taken. The Policy was also pierced for the same number, and had 10 guns mounted. The latter were now added to the armament of the Georgiana, which gave her 16 light guns. All the small-arms were collected from the prizes and put in her, her try-works were taken down, and other alterations made, when Mr. Downes was placed in command, with a crew of 41 men. By this arrangement, it was believed that the Georgiana would be fully able to capture any of the English letters of marque, known to be cruising among the islands. In consequence of these changes, and the manning of the two other prizes, notwithstanding several enlistments, the crew of the Essex was reduced to 264 souls, officers included. On the 8th of May, the Georgiana 16, Lieutenant-Commandant Downes, hoisted the American pennant, and fired a salute of 17 guns.

---

## CHAPTER XXXI.

A few trials proved that the Georgiana could not hold way with the Essex, and that her reputation, as a fast vessel, was unmerited. Still, as she had been relieved from much of her lumber, she outsailed the other ships, and hopes were entertained of her being made useful. Accordingly, on the 12th, she parted company, with orders to cruise against the enemy, and to rendezvous at different places on the coast, as well as at various islands, in a regular succession as to time. The separation was not long, however, the Georgiana looking into Charles's Island, in quest of English vessels, at a moment when the Essex happened to be there on the same errand.

The Georgiana was now sent to Albemarle Island, Captain Porter having reason to suppose that a particular ship of the enemy was in that quarter. The Essex continued in the vicinity of Charles's Island, capturing the Atlantic, of 355 tons, 24 men, and 8 guns, on the evening of the 28th of May. The same night she took the Greenwich, of 338 tons, 10 guns, and 28 men. These several captures nearly stripped the frigate of her officers, and she sailed for Tumbez, where she arrived on the 19th of June.

While cruising near James's Island, Mr. Downes had captured the British whale ships the Catherine, of 270 tons, 8 guns, and 29 men, and the Rose, of 220 tons, 8 guns, and 21 men. These two vessels were taken with no resistance, their masters having come on board the Georgiana, without suspecting her character. After manning his prizes, Mr. Downes had but 20 men and boys left in the Georgiana, when he chased and closed with a third whaler, called the Hector, a ship of 270 tons, 25 men, and 11 guns, though pierced for 20. At this time, Mr. Downes had also 50 prisoners, most of whom he was compelled to put in irons, before he brought the Hector to action. When within hail, the latter ship was ordered to haul down her colours, but refused, and the Georgiana opened a fire upon her. A sharp combat followed, when the Hector struck, with the loss of her maintopmast, having had most of her standing and running rigging shot away. She had also two men killed, and six wounded.

After manning the Hector, Mr. Downes had but 10 men left in the Georgiana; and, including the wounded, he had 73 prisoners. The Rose being a dull ship, he threw overboard her guns, and most of her cargo, and, paroling his prisoners, he gave her up to them, on condition that they should sail direct for St. Helena. As soon as this arrangement was made, he made sail for Tumbez, to join the Essex, at which port he arrived on the 24th of June.

The little fleet now amounted to nine sail, and there was an opportunity to make new arrangements. The Atlantic being nearly 100 tons larger than the Georgiana, as well as a much

faster ship, besides possessing, in a greater degree, every material quality for a cruiser, Mr. Downes and his crew were
transferred to her.  Twenty guns were mounted in this new
sloop of war; she was named the Essex Junior, and manned
with 60 men.  The Greenwich was also converted into a store-
ship, and all the spare stores of the other vessels were sent on
board her.  She was also armed with 20 guns, though her
crew was merely strong enough to work her.

On the 30th the fleet sailed, the Essex and Essex Junior
keeping in company, with all the carpenters at work at the
latter.  On the 4th of July a general salute was fired, principally with the guns and ammunition of the enemy.  On the
9th, the Essex Junior parted company, bound to Valparaiso,
with the Hector, Catherine, Policy, and Montezuma, prizes,
and the Barclay, recaptured ship, under convoy.

As soon as out of sight of the other ships, the Essex, Greenwich, and Georgiana steered to the westward, with an intention of going among the Gallapagos.  On the 13th, three sail
were made off Banks' Bay, all on a wind, and a good deal
separated.  The Essex gave chase to the one in the centre,
which led her down to leeward, leaving the Greenwich and
Georgiana a long distance astern and to windward.  While
the frigate was thus separated from her prizes, one of the
strangers tacked, and endeavoured to cut the latter off, but the
Greenwich hove-to, got a portion of the people out of the
Georgiana, and bore down boldly on her adversary; while the
Essex continued after the vessel she was chasing, which she
soon captured.  This ship was the English whaler Charlton,
of 274 tons, 10 guns, and 21 men.  Throwing a crew into
her, the frigate immediately hauled her wind.

It was now ascertained from the prisoners, that the largest
of the strange ships was the Seringapatam, of 357 tons, 14
guns, and near 40 men; and the smallest, the New Zealander,
of 259 tons, 8 guns, and 23 men.  The Seringapatam had
been built for a cruiser, and she was probably the most dangerous vessel to the American trade to the westward of Cape
Horn.  Captain Porter felt a corresponding desire to get pos
session of her, and was much gratified with the bold manner
in which the Greenwich had borne down on her.  This ship
was under the command of a very young officer, but he had
the advice of one of the sea-lieutenants, who was under suspension, and who behaved with great gallantry and spirit on
this occasion.  Closing with the Seringapatam, the Essex be-

ing a long distance to leeward, the Greenwich brought her to action, and after a few broadsides the English ship struck. Soon after, however, and before possession could be taken, she made an attempt to escape by passing to windward, in which she was frustrated by the perseverance of the Greenwich, which vessel kept close on the enemy's quarter, maintaining a spirited fire, for the number of men on board. As the Essex was coming up fast, the Seringapatam finally gave up the attempt, and running down to the frigate, again submitted.

In this affair, as in that of the boats, and in the capture of the Hector by the Georgiana, the officers and men engaged merited high encomiums for their intrepidity and coolness. The Greenwich, after obtaining the hands from the Georgiana, did not probably muster five-and-twenty men at quarters, and the Seringapatam was much the better ship. The New Zealander was taken without any difficulty.

The Seringapatam had made one prize, her master having turned his attention more to cruising than to whaling. On inquiry, notwithstanding, it was found that he had adopted this course in anticipation of a commission, having actually sailed without one. When this fact was ascertained, Captain Porter put the master in irons, and he subsequently sent him to America to be tried. Finding himself embarrassed with his prisoners, Captain Porter gave the Charlton up to them, and suffered them to proceed to Rio de Janeiro, under parole. He then took the guns out of the New Zealander, and mounted them in the Seringapatam, by which means he gave the latter ship an armament of 22 guns, though, as in the case of the Greenwich, her people were barely sufficient to work her.

On the 25th of July, the Georgiana was despatched to the United States with a full cargo of oil. As soon as the vessels separated, the Essex, with the Greenwich, Seringapatam, and New Zealander in company, shaped her course for Albemarle Island. On the morning of the 28th, another strange sail was discovered; but as she had a fresh breeze, and the frigate was becalmed, she was soon out of sight. When the wind came, however, the Essex ran in a direction to intercept the stranger; and the next morning he was again seen, from the masthead, standing across the Essex's bows, on a bowline. As the wind was light, recourse was now had to the drags, and the ship got within four miles of the chase, which was evidently an enemy's whaler. The stranger becoming alarmed, got his boats ahead to tow, when Captain Porter sent a gig and whale-

boat, with a few good marksmen in them, under Acting Lieutenant M'Knight, with orders to take a position ahead of the
chase, and to drive in her boats, but on no account to attempt
to board.  This duty was handsomely executed, though the
boats had great difficulty in maintaining their position within
musket-shot, as the enemy got two guns on his forecastle, and
kept up a warm discharge of grape.

At 4 P. M., the ships were little more than a league apart,
perfectly becalmed, and Captain Porter ordered the boats into
the water, to carry the stranger by boarding.  As the party
drew near, the enemy commenced firing, but, intimidated by
their steady and orderly approach, he soon lowered his ensign.
The boats were about to take possession, when a breeeze from
the eastward suddenly striking the English ship, she hauled
up close on a wind, hoisted her colours again, fired at the gig
and whale-boat as she passed quite near them, and went off,
at a rapid rate, to the northward.  The party attempted to follow, but it was sunset before the Essex got the wind, and, unwilling to leave her boats out in the darkness, she was compelled to heave-to, at 9, in order to hoist them in.  The next
morning the chase was out of sight.

This was the first instance, since her arrival in the Pacific,
in which the Essex had failed in getting alongside of a chase
that she did not voluntarily abandon.  It produced much mortification, though the escape of the enemy was owing to one
of those occurrences, so common in summer, that leave one
ship without a breath of air, while another, quite near her, has
a good breeze.

On the 4th of August, the ships went into James's Island
and anchored.  Here Captain Porter made the important discovery that a large portion of his powder had been damaged
in doubling Cape Horn.  Fortunately, the Seringapatam could
supply the deficiency, though, in doing so, that ship was rendered nearly defenceless.  On the 22d of August, all the vessels proceeded to Banks' Bay, where the prizes were moored,
and the Essex sailed on a short cruise, alone, on the 24th.

After passing among the islands, without meeting any thing,
a sail was discovered on the morning of the 15th of September, apparently lying-to, a long distance to the southward and
to windward.  The Essex was immediately disguised, by sending down some of the light yards, and the ship kept turning
to windward, under easy sail.  At meridian, the vessels were
so near each other, that the stranger was ascertained to be a

DEATH OF LAWRENCE.

whaler, in the act of cutting in. He was evidently drifting down fast on the frigate. At 1 P. M., when the ships were about four miles apart, the stranger cast off the whales, and made all sail to windward. As it was now evident that he had taken the alarm, the Essex threw aside all attempts at disguise, and pursued him, under every thing that would draw. By 4 P. M., the frigate had the stranger within reach of her guns; and a few shot, well thrown, brought him down under her lee. This ship was the Sir Andrew Hammond, of 301 tons, 12 guns, and 31 men; and she proved to be the vessel that had escaped, in the manner previously related. Fortunately, the prize had a large supply of excellent beef, pork, bread, wood, and water, and the Essex got out of her an ample stock of those great necessaries. On returning to Banks' Bay with her prize, the ship shortly after was joined by the Essex Junior, on her return from Valparaiso. By this arrival, Captain Porter discovered that several enemy's vessels of force had sailed in pursuit of him; and having by this time captured nearly all the English whalers of which he could obtain intelligence, he determined to proceed to the Marquesas, in order to refit, and to make his preparations for returning to America. He was urged to adopt this resolution, also, by understanding from Mr. Downes that the government of Chili no longer preserved the appearance of amity towards the United States, but was getting to be English in its predilections.

---

## CHAPTER XXXII.

On the 23d of October the group of the Marquesas was made from the mast-head of the Essex, and after passing among the islands for a few days, Captain Porter took his ships into a fine bay of Nooaheevah, where he anchored. Here he was soon after joined by the Essex Junior, which vessel had parted company to cruise, when he believed himself sufficiently secure, to commence a regular overhauling of the different ships.

The situation of the Essex was sufficiently remarkable, at this moment, to merit a brief notice. More than ten thousand

25

miles from home, without colonies, stations, or even a really
friendly port to repair to, short of stores, without a consort,
and otherwise in possession of none of the required means of
subsistence and efficiency, she had boldly steered into this distant region, where she had found all that she required, through
her own activity; and having swept the seas of her enemies,
she had now retired to these little-frequented islands to refit, with
the security of a ship at home.    It is due to the officer, who
so promptly adopted, and so successfully executed this plan,
to add, that his enterprise, self-reliance, and skill, indicated a
man of bold and masculine conception, of great resources,
and of a high degree of moral courage; qualities that are indispensable in forming a naval captain.

The island of Nooaheevah, on which Captain Porter landed
his stores, was intersected by valleys, and different tribes possessed them, forming distinct communities, which not unfrequently waged war on each other, converting this little and
retired fragment of the earth into an epitome of the passions
and struggles of the world beyond it.   In consequence of his
intimate connexion with the inhabitants of the valley in which
he was accidentally thrown, Captain Porter was compelled to
join in these hostilities, the assailants of his allies beginning to
treat him as an enemy.    After some fruitless negotiating, a
party was sent against the hostile tribe, and several conflicts
occurred, in which the armed seamen and marines prevailed,
as a matter of course, though not without a sharp resistance.
This success quieted the island; and during the remainder of
his stay, Captain Porter appears to have been unmolested.

It has been seen, that the Essex reached he Marquesas at
the close of October, and in the early part of December she
was again ready for sea.   In the course of November, the New
Zealander was filled with oil, from the other prizes, and despatched for America, under the charge of a master's mate.
Shortly after, a fort was constructed on a small conical hill,
near the water, when the Seringapatam, Sir Andrew Hammond,
and Greenwich, were warped close in, and moored under its
guns.   The command of this fort was given to Lieutenant John
M. Gamble, of the marines, a spirited and intelligent young
officer; and Messrs. Feltus and Clapp, two of the midshipmen,
with twenty-one men, were put under his orders, having volunteered to remain on the island during the contemplated
cruise of the Essex.   This arrangement was made to secure
the means of future repairs, as it was now believed that no

more whalers were to be found, and the Essex was going to sea, in the expectation of meeting one of the frigates that it was known had been sent into the Pacific, in pursuit of her.

The Essex, and Essex Junior, quitted the harbour of Nooa-heevah, on the 12th of December, 1813, bound for the coast of South America, which was made early in January.  After watering at San Maria, and looking into Concepcion, the ships proceeded to Valparaiso.  Up to this time, not a dollar had been drawn for, to meet the expenses of the frigate.  The ene-my had furnished provisions, sails, cordage, medicines, guns, anchors, cables, and slops.  A considerable amount of pay even had been given to the officers and men, by means of the money taken in the Nocton.  Thus far, the cruise had been singularly useful and fortunate, affording an instance of the perfection of naval warfare, in all that relates to distressing an enemy, with the least possible charge to the assailants ; and it remained only to terminate it with a victory, over a ship of equal force, to render it brilliant.  It is, perhaps, a higher eu-logium on the officers and crew of this memorable little frigate to add, that while her good fortune appeared at last to desert her, they gave this character to their enterprise, by the manner in which they struggled with adversity.

After the arrival at Valparaiso, it was found that the feelings of the Chilian government had taken an entirely new direction, as had been reported by Mr. Downes, favouring on all occa-sions the interests of the English, in preference to those of the Americans.  Without paying much regard to this circumstance, however, Captain Porter determined to remain in, or off, the port, in waiting for the Phœbe 36, Captain Hillyar, one of the ships sent out in quest of him, under the impression that her commander would not fail, sooner or later, to seek him at that place.  There was also the prospect of intercepting such of the English traders as might happen to touch at the port.

The Phœbe arrived as was expected, but instead of coming alone, she had the Cherub 20, Captain Tucker, in company. When these ships hove in sight, the Essex Junior was cruising off the harbour, and she came in and anchored.  As the Phœbe alone was a vessel of a heavier rate than the Essex, this addi-tion to her force put a conflict between the four ships quite out of the question.  Captain Porter, who had every opportunity of observing the armaments of the two English vessels, states, in his official communications to the department, that the Phœbe mounted 30 long eighteens, 16 thirty-two-pound carronades, with one howitzer, and 6 threes in her tops. This was a forced equipment for a ship of her rate, but she had probably taken in extra guns with a view to meet the Essex. Her crew is said to have consisted of 320 souls. The Cherub 20 mounted 18 thirty-two pound carronades below, with 8 twenty-four pound carronades and 2 long nines above, making a total of 28 guns, and her crew mustered 180 men and boys. In consequence of the number of prizes that had been manned, some deaths that had occurred, and the people placed in the Essex Junior, the American frigate could muster but 255 souls, notwithstanding the enlistments she had made from the whalers. The force of the Essex Junior was too inconsiderable to be relied on, in an action against ships of a metal as heavy as that of the enemy. She mounted 10 eighteen-pound carronades and 10 short sixes, with a crew of 60 souls. Her guns would have been of little service in a frigate action.

As the Phœbe came in, the wind was light, and she passed quite near the Essex, with her people at quarters. Captain Hillyar hailed, and inquired after the health of Captain Porter. After making the usual reply, the latter informed the English officer that if the vessels got foul, much confusion would ensue, and that he could not be answerable for the consequences. Captain Hillyar now observed that he did not meditate any attack, though the manner in which this was uttered, does not appear to have quieted the suspicions of the American officers. While the two vessels and their crews were in this novel position, the Phœbe was taken suddenly aback, and her bows payed off directly upon the Essex. Captain Porter immediately called away his boarders, and for a few minutes there was every appearance of a combat in a neutral port.

A great deal of confusion is said to have existed on board the Phœbe, and her commander was earnest in his protestations of an intention not to have recourse to hostilities, while he handled his yards in a way to get a stern-board on his ship. As she fell off, the jib-boom of the Phœbe passed over the Essex's deck, and she lay, for a short time, with her bows exposed to the whole broadside of the American frigate, and her stern to that of the Essex Junior. Captain Porter declining to profit by his advantage, the Phœbe was enabled to get out of her awkward situation, there being no doubt that she had lain entirely at the mercy of her enemies. There can be little question that this extraordinary occurrence would have fully justified the American ship in having recourse to her means of defence.

The English ships, having obtained some supplies, went outside and cruised off Valparaiso for six weeks. During this time, the Essex made several attempts to engage the Phœbe alone, sometimes by bringing her to action with the Essex Junior in company, and at others, by bringing her to action singly, having the crew of the Essex Junior on board the frigate. Captain Porter ascertained to his satisfaction, that he could easily outsail either of the enemy's vessels, but his object was not so much to escape, as to capture the Phœbe, which he had reason to think he might do, could he bring her to close action, without her consort's interference.

A short time after the blockade had commenced, Captain Porter determined to make an attempt on the Cherub by boarding. A strong party was detailed for this service, Captain Porter and Lieutenant Downes both accompanying it. The boats went out at night, and at first had strong hopes of being able to get alongside of the enemy ; but, by the subsequent movements of the Cherub, the Americans were induced to think that the English received an intimation of their intention in the course of the night.

Having heard that several other cruisers of the enemy might soon be expected, Captain Porter now determined to go to sea, on the first good occasion, and by leaving the Phœbe and Cherub off the coast, to allow the Essex Junior to follow. This plan was formed on the 27th of March. The very next day the wind came on to blow fresh from the southward, when the Essex parted her larboard bower, and dragged the other anchor directly out to sea. The harbour of Valparaiso opens to the northward, being formed by a headland on its western side, and a cove that makes to the southward within it ; the main coast sweeping round to the north and east again, affording the necessary protection. On the 28th of March, when the accident just mentioned occurred, the enemy's ships were at no great distance off the point, though far enough to allow the Essex to fetch past to windward of them, by hugging the land. The Point of Angels, however, is an exceedingly dangerous bluff to double, and most ships deem it prudent to reef before going round it, on account of the liability to sudden and violent squalls.

As there was no time to lose, sail was got on the Essex. On opening the enemy, Captain Porter took in his topgallant-

25 *

sails, hauled close by the wind, and made an attempt to pass
out, by keeping his weatherly position.  Every thing looked
promising for a short time ; and there is little question that the
ship would have gone clear, but, in doubling the headland, a
squall carried away the main-topmast, throwing several men
into the sea, all of whom were drowned.  Nothing remained,
of course, but to endeavour to regain the port, or to fight both
the enemy's ships, under the additional disadvantage of being
already crippled.

Finding it impossible to beat up to the common anchorage,
Captain Porter stood across the entrance of the harbour, to its
northeastern side, where he let go an anchor, about three miles
from the town, a mile and a half from the Castello Viego,
which, however, was concealed by a bluff, half a mile from a
detached battery of one twenty-four-pound gun, and within
pistol-shot of the shore.  Notwithstanding this position, the
enemy continued to approach, and it soon became evident, by
the motto flags and jacks he set, that it was his serious intention to engage.  The Essex, in consequence, cleared for action,
and attempted to get a spring on her cable, but had not succeeded in effecting this important object, when the Phœbe,
having obtained an advantageous position, nearly astern, about
4 P. M. opened her fire, at long shot.  At the same time, the
Cherub commenced the action on the starboard bow.  The fire
of the Phœbe, from the double advantage she possessed in her
long guns and her station, became very destructive, as scarce
a gun from the Essex could touch her.  The Cherub, however,
was soon driven off, when she ran down to leeward, and engaged from a position near that taken by the Phœbe.  Three
long twelves were got out aft, and they played with so much
effect on the enemy, that at the end of half an hour, both his
ships hauled off the land to repair damages.  This important
fact, which is affirmed by the Americans, is sufficiently corroborated by the accounts of the enemy.

During this first attack, the Essex, through the great exertions of the master and boatswain, had succeeded in getting
springs on the cable no less than three different times, but
before the ship's broadside could be sprung to bear, they were
as often shot away.  The ship also received a great deal of
injury, and several men had been killed and wounded.  Notwithstanding all the disastrous circumstances under which they
engaged, and the superior force opposed to them, the officers
and crew of the Essex were animated by the best spirit, and it

was not possible for efforts to be more coolly made, or better directed.

The enemy was not long in making his repairs, and both ships next took a position on the starboard quarter of the Essex, where it was not in the power of the latter vessel to bring a single gun to bear upon them, as they were too distant to be reached by carronades. Their fire was very galling, and it left no alternative to Captain Porter, between submission, and running down to assail them. He gallantly decided on the latter. But, by this time, the Essex had received many serious injuries, in addition to the loss of her topmast. Her topsail sheets, topsail halyards, jib and fore-topmast staysail halyards, had all been shot away. The only sail that could be got upon the ship, to make her head pay off, was the flying jib, which was hoisted, when the cable was cut, and the vessel edged away, with the intention of laying the Phœbe aboard.

The fore-topsail and foresail were now let fall, though, for want of tacks and sheets, they were nearly useless. Still the Essex drove down on her assailants, closing near enough to open with her carronades. For a few minutes, the firing on both sides was tremendous, the people of the Essex proving their discipline and gallantry, at that trying moment, in a way to justify all the high expectations that had been formed of them, though their decks were already strewed with killed, and the cockpit was crowded with the wounded. This work proved too hot for the Cherub, which hauled off a second time, nor did she come near enough to use her carronades again, during the remainder of the action, keeping up a distant fire with her long guns.

The Phœbe showed no disposition to throw away the immense advantage she possessed, in her long eighteens; and when she found the Essex's fire becoming warm, she kept edging off, throwing her shot at the same time with fatal effect, cutting down the people of her antagonist almost with impunity to herself. By this time, many of the guns of the American ship were disabled, and the crews of several had been swept away. One particular gun was a scene of carnage that is seldom witnessed in a naval combat, nearly three entire crews falling at it in the course of the action. Its captain alone escaped with a slight wound.

This scene of almost unresisted carnage had now lasted nearly two hours, and, finding it impossible to close with his adversary, who chose his distance at pleasure, Captain Porter felt the necessity of taking some prompt measure, if he would prevent the enemy from getting possession of his ship. The wind had got more to the westward, and he saw a hope of running her ashore, at a spot where he might land his people and set her on fire. For a few minutes every thing appeared to favour this design, and the Essex had drifted within musket-shot of the beach, when the wind suddenly shifted from the land, paying the ship's head broad off, in a way to leave her exposed to a dreadful raking fire. Still, as she was again closing with the Phœbe, Captain Porter indulged a hope of finally laying that ship aboard. At this moment, Lieutenant Commandant Downes came on board of the Essex, in order to receive the orders of his commanding officer, having pulled through all the fire in order to effect this object. He could be of no use, for the enemy again put his helm up, and kept away, when Mr. Downes, after remaining in the Essex ten minutes, was directed to return to his own ship, and to make preparations to defend, or, at need, to destroy her. On going away, he carried off several of the Essex's wounded, leaving three of his own men behind him, in order to make room in the boat.

The slaughter in the Essex having got to be horrible, the enemy firing with deliberation, and hulling her at almost every shot, Captain Porter, as a last resort, ordered a hawser to be bent to the sheet-anchor, and the latter let go, in order to bring the head of the ship round. This effected the object, and once more the Americans got their broadside to bear, remaining stationary themselves, while their enemy, a good deal crippled, was drifting slowly to leeward. Even in these desperate circumstances, a ray of hope gleamed through this little advantage, and Captain Porter was beginning to believe that the Phœbe would drift out of gun-shot, before she discovered his expedient, when the hawser parted with the strain.

There was no longer any chance of saving the ship. To add to her distress, she was on fire, the flames coming up both the main and forward hatchways; and for a few minutes it was thought she must consume. An explosion of powder also occurred below, to add to the horrors of the scene, and Captain Porter told his people, that in preference to being blown up, all who chose to incur the risk, might make the attempt to reach the shore by swimming. Many availed themselves of the permission, and some succeeded in effecting their escape. Others perished, while a few, after drifting about on bits of spars, were picked up by the boats of the enemy. Much the greater part of the crew, however, remained in the ship, and they set about an attempt to extinguish the flames ; the shot of the enemy committing its havoc the whole time. Fortunately, the fire was got under, when the few brave men who were left, went again to the long guns.

The moment had now arrived, when Captain Porter was to decide between submission or the destruction of the remainder of his people. In the midst of this scene of slaughter, he had himself been untouched, and it would seem that he felt himself called on to resist as long as his own strength allowed. But his remaining people entreated him to remember his wounded and he at last consented to summon his officers. Only one Acting Lieutenant M'Knight, could join him on the quarter deck ! The first lieutenant, Mr. Wilmer, had been knocked overboard by a splinter, and drowned, while getting the sheet-anchor from the bows ; Acting Lieutenant Cowell, the next in rank, was mortally wounded ; Acting Lieutenant Odenheimer had just been knocked overboard from the quarter, and did not regain the vessel for several minutes. The reports of the state of the ship were fearful. A large portion of the guns were disabled, even had there been men left to fight them. The berth-deck, steerage, ward-room, and cock-pit, were full of wounded ; and the latter were even killed by shot while under the surgeon's hands. The carpenter was sent for, and he stated that of his crew, he alone could perform any duty. He had been over the side to stop shot-holes, when his slings were cut away, and he narrowly escaped drowning. In short, seventy-five men, officers included, were all that remained for duty ; and the enemy, in perfectly smooth water, was firing his long eighteens, at a nearly unresisting ship, with as much precision as he could have discharged them at a target. It had become an imperative duty to strike, and the colours were accordingly hauled down, after one of the most remarkable combats that is to be found in the history of naval warfare.

In this bloody contest, the Essex had 58 men killed, including those who soon died of their hurts, and 66 wounded ; making a total of 124, or nearly half of all who were on board at the commencement of the action. Of the missing there were 31, most of whom were probably drowned, either in attempting to swim ashore, when the ship was on fire, or by being knocked overboard by the splinters, or pieces of the rigging. Including the missing, the entire loss was **152**, out of 255.

The Essex, with a very trifling exception while closing, fought this battle with her six long twelves, opposed by fifteen long eighteens in broadside,* the long guns of the Cherub, and, a good deal of the time, or while they lay on her quarter, by the carronades of both the enemy's ships. Captain Hillyar's published official letter makes the loss of the Phœbe 4 killed and 7 wounded; that of the Cherub, 1 killed and 3 wounded. There is no apparent reason for distrusting this account, as Captain Hillyar's official letter was singularly modest and just. Captain Tucker, of the Cherub, was wounded, and the first lieutenant of the Phœbe was killed. The English ships were cut up more than could have been expected under the circumstances, the latter having received no less than eighteen twelve-pound shot below the water-line. It would seem that the smoothness of the water rendered the fire very certain, on both sides, and it is only to be regretted that the Essex could not have engaged under her three topsails, from the commencement. The engagement lasted nearly two hours and a half, the long guns of the Essex, it is said, having been fired no less than seventy-five times each, in broadside. The enemy must have thrown, agreeably to the statements made at the time, not less than 700 eighteen-pound shot, at the Essex.

The battle was witnessed by thousands from the shore; and so near were all the ships to the land, that, at one time, many of the Phœbe's eighteen-pound shot struck the beach. This fact appears to be well authenticated, and, of itself, it settles the question of a violation of the neutrality of Chili; since even they who maintain the doctrine that jurisdiction does not properly extend three leagues to sea, substitute the greatest range of a shot, or a shell, in their place. During the action, Mr. Poinsett, the American consul, repaired to the governor's and asked the protection of the batteries in behalf of the Essex. He received the evasive answer, that, should the ship succeed in reaching the ordinary anchorage, an officer would be sent to the British commander, requesting him to cease his fire. The governor, however, declined resorting to force, un-

---

* It has been said that the Phœbe mounted but 26 long eighteens, her upper-deck long guns having been twelves. We have followed Captain Porter's account, though the difference, under the peculiar circumstances, was of no great moment.

der any circumstances.  This conduct left no doubt of a collusion between the English officers and the local authorities, and Mr. Poinsett took the first occasion to quit the country.

In the mode in which he fought his ship, though it was much criticised at the time, Captain Hillyar discovered seamanship and a strict attention to his duty; but his situation must have been in the last degree painful, while compelled to avoid meeting the Essex singly, under circumstances that admit of no other plausible construction than an obedience to the most rigid orders.

Captain Porter now entered into an arrangement with Captain Hillyar, under the provisions of which, the Essex Junior was converted into a cartel, and a passport was given, by means of which all the survivors of the Essex came home. From this arrangement, however, Acting Lieutenant M'Knight, Mr. Adams, the chaplain, and Mr. Lyman, a master's mate, were exempted; these three gentlemen, and eleven seamen, being exchanged on the spot, for a part of the people of the Sir Andrew Hammond, who were then prisoners in the Essex Junior.  Mr. M'Knight and Mr. Lyman went round to Rio de Janeiro, in the Phœbe, in order to give some testimony in behalf of the captors.  We shall have occasion to advert to the two last hereafter.

The Essex Junior left Valparaiso shortly after this arrangement, encountering no difficulty in doubling the Horn.  She was brought-to, off New York, by the Saturn rasée, Captain Nash.  This officer questioned the authority of Captain Hillyar to grant the passport, under which the Essex Junior was sailing, and he directed that ship to lie by him during the night.  After some communications, the next morning, when thirty miles from the beach, Captain Porter put off in a whaleboat, and, though chased, by pulling vigorously for the land, he got ashore on Long Island, escaping in a fog.  It does not appear, however, to have been the intention of Captain Nash seriously to detain the Essex Junior.  He probably distrusted some artifice, as he permitted the ship to proceed, after again examining her papers.

Thus terminated this enterprising and singular cruise, its end proving as disastrous as its commencement had been fortunate, though it was, at all times, highly creditable to the spirit, resources, self-reliance, and zeal of those engaged in it. Before quitting the subject, however, it remains to give a brief account of the fortunes of the officers and men left at Nooa-

heevah, with the three prizes, the Greenwich, the Sir Andrew
Hammond, and the Seringapatam, under the orders of Lieutenant Gamble of the marines.

The Essex had no sooner disappeared than the savages began to pilfer, and to betray a turbulent disposition.   Mr. Gamble was compelled to land a party, and to bring the natives to
terms by a show of force.   Fortunately this object was effected
without firing a musket.   In February, one of the small party
left was drowned, reducing their number to twenty-two, the
officers included.   Not long after this event, four of the men
deserted in a whale-boat, carrying off with them several small
articles of value.   But eighteen now remained.

On the 12th of April, Mr. Gamble began to rig the Seringapatam and the Sir Andrew Hammond, with the intention of
quitting the islands, the long absence of the Essex inducing
him to despair of her return.   Some symptoms of a mutiny
now began to show themselves, and he had all the arms and
ammunition brought on board the Greenwich, in which vessel
he lived; but having occasion to be on board the Seringapatam, on the 7th of May, a party of six men rose, and took the
ship from him.   During the time Mr. Gamble was in the hands
of these men, he was badly wounded in the foot by a pistol-
ball, and they succeeded in carrying off the Seringapatam,
sending the officer, and the people with him, on board another
vessel.

Every exertion was made to get to sea with the Sir Andrew
Hammond, but on the 9th, the natives made an attack, and
Mr. Feltus, with three men, was killed, and one other was severely wounded.   The situation of those that remained, now
became exceedingly critical, the whole party consisting of only
eight individuals, of whom two were badly wounded, one was
a cripple, and another was just recovering from a serious attack of the scurvy.   In fact, there were but four men on board
the Sir Andrew Hammond fit for duty.   The jib and spanker
were bent as fast as possible, the moorings were cut, and, under that short sail, the ship passed slowly out to sea, under
cover of the night.   When safe in the offing, but six cartridges
were left, the Seringapatam having carried off most of the
ammunition in kegs.

To add to the difficulties of his situation, Mr. Gamble had
no chart.   He made out to reach the Sandwich Islands, however, in seventeen days, where he was captured by the Cherub,
and first learned the fate of the Essex.   The Americans con-

tinued seven months in this ship, until they were landed at
Rio de Janeiro, from which port Mr. Gamble got to New York,
late in August, 1815.

---

## CHAPTER XXXIII.

It has been seen, that the declaration of war found the naval
preparations in so imperfect a condition, that the Constellation
38, Chesapeake 38, and Adams 28, were not ready even to
receive crews, while it was found necessary to rebuild entirely
the New York 36, Boston 28, and General Greene 28.　The
appropriations for the repairs of the three first ships having been
made in March, 1812, the Constellation was equipped and
manned at Washington, in the course of the season.　When
Commodore Bainbridge left her for the Constitution, the command of this ship had been given to Captain Stewart, the officer who had served as second in command under Commodore
Preble, during most of the operations of that celebrated captain, before Tripoli.　In the course of the month of January,
1813, Captain Stewart dropped down the river with an intention to get to sea, but on reaching St. Mary's, an order was
received, that induced him to go to Annapolis, in order to
examine his powder.　From this place, the ship was directed
to proceed to Norfolk.　In executing this order, the Constellation anchored in Hampton Roads, and the next morning a fleet
of the enemy, consisting of several two-decked ships, frigates
and sloops of war, came in and anchored off Willoughby's
Point, where they were becalmed.　While the English ships
were waiting for the turn of the tide, the Constellation was
kedged up until she grounded on the flats above ; and the same
night, when she floated with the tide, she was carried up, and
anchored between the forts at Norfolk.

A few days later, the Constellation dropped down abreast of
Craney Island, with a view to cover the fortifications then
erecting at that place.　At this time; the enemy was still lying
in force in Hampton Roads.

The Constellation was anchored in the middle of the channel, which is quite narrow, and on each side of her were

26

moored seven gun-boats, on board of which were placed officers and men belonging to the ship.  A circle of booms,
securely fastened, protected the gun-boats from being boarded,
which would enable them to maintain a flanking fire, on all
assailants of the frigate.  The gun-deck guns of the latter were
housed, and the ports were shut in.  Great care was taken
that no rope should be permitted to be hanging over the side
of the vessel, the stern-ladders were taken away, and even the
gangway-cleets were removed.  Boarding-nettings were made
of twenty-one thread ratlin-stuff, that had been boiled in half-
made pitch, which rendered it so hard as almost to defy the
knife.  To give greater strength, nail rods and small chains
were secured to the netting in lines about three feet apart.  Instead of tricing to the rigging, this netting was spread outboard, towards the yard-arms, rising about twenty-five feet
above the deck.  To the outer rope or ridge-line of the netting,
were secured pieces of kentledge, that by cutting the tricing
lines when the enemy should get alongside, his boats and men
might be caught beneath.  Pieces of kentledge were also suspended forward, from the spritsail-yard, bowsprit, &c. &c., to
prevent boats from lying under them, while the netting was
here hoisted to the fore stay.  The carronades were charged to
the muzzles with musket-balls, and depressed to the nearest
range, in order to sweep around the ship.  As the frigate was
light, and unusually high out of the water, it was the opinion
of the best judges, that defended as she would certainly have
been, under the officers who were in her, she could not have
been carried without a loss of several hundred men to the enemy, if she could have been taken by boats at all.

It would appear, notwithstanding, that the enemy was disposed to make the attempt.  A large force of British ships
having collected in the Roads, the admirals in command seriously contemplated an assault on the Constellation.  Fortunately, Captain Stewart received notice of their intentions.  A
Portuguese had been stopped by the fleet, on his way to sea,
and his ship was anchored at the upper part of the Roads, just
out of gun-shot of the frigate.  On board of this vessel, the
Admiral kept a guard and a look-out, to signal the movements
above.  An American passenger, on board the Portuguese,
learned from the conversation of different officers, their designs
on the Constellation, and he found means to get on board the
frigate in order to apprise her commander of the enemy's plan,
handsomely volunteering to remain in the ship to help defend

her.* Of course the guard-boats were enjoined to be more than usually vigilant, and every thing was got ready to receive the enemy.

The night succeeding the notice was starlight, and nothing was attempted. The next morning, the master of the Portuguese stopped alongside of the frigate, on his way to Norfolk, and stated that a large number of boats had collected at his ship the previous evening, but that the expedition had been deferred until that night, which promised to be dark and drizzling. Accordingly the guard-boat was on the look-out, and it fell in with a division of boats, that was supposed to contain from 1500 to 2000 men. As soon as the enemy was seen, the officer in the boat showed two lanterns on the off-side of his cutter, and all hands were called in the ship. It would seem the enemy ascertained that his approach was discovered, and he retired.

The following night, the attempt was renewed, with the same want of success. A few nights later, it again proved dark and drizzling, and a third expedition came up. On this occasion, Mr. B. J. Neale, the second lieutenant of the Constellation, was in the guard-boat, and he edged close in with the enemy, who discovered him. As soon as the word of " a stranger," was given, the people of the cutter sprang to their oars, and pulled out of sight ; but finding he was not pursued, Mr. Neale returned and kept company with the brigade of boats, which passed up on the inside of the flats, above the mouth of Tanner's creek, and anchored at no great distance below the forts. Here many of the officers landed and walked about to keep themselves warm, the guard-boat anchoring also. When the ebb tide made, the brigade returned, the Constellation's boat quitting them only when they had got below the frigate.

Shortly after, the fortifications being sufficiently advanced, and block ships being ready for sinking in the channel, the Constellation was carried up again to a place of security. About this time Captain Stewart was transferred to the command of the Constitution 44, and Captain Tarbell received a temporary appointment to the Constellation, though, the enemy

---

* The name of this gentleman deserves to be honourably mentioned. It was Mr. Francis March, of the mercantile firm of J. Howard, March & Co., of Madeira.

always maintaining a strong force in the waters of the Chesapeake, the ship continued to be blockaded until the peace.

The Chesapeake, lying at Boston, had less difficulty in getting to sea, for the enemy did not keep any force before that port, during the first few months of the war; most probably under the false impression that such was the disaffection of the eastern states, that it would virtually be annoying friends. She sailed at the close of February, 1813, under the orders of Captain Evans, and passing by the Canary Isles and the Cape de Verds, she crossed the equator, and remained for six weeks near the line. She then made the coast of South America, passed the spot where the Hornet sunk the Peacock, the day after that action had occurred, and went through the West-Indies, and along the American coast, to the port from which she had sailed. During this long run, Captain Evans saw but three men-of-war, a ship of the line and a frigate, near the Western Islands, and a sloop of war, off the Capes of Virginia. The latter escaped in the night, after a chase of two days. The Chesapeake captured four merchant vessels.

Captain Evans gave up the command of his ship on his return, on account of ill health, and was succeeded by Captain James Lawrence.

By this time, the enemy had changed his policy as regards the eastern states, and he kept a few frigates in the vicinity of Massachusetts Bay, with a view to intercept the American ships of war that passed in and out. Two of these cruisers, the Shannon 38, and Tenedos 38, had been off Boston, it was said, in waiting for the President 44, and Congress 38 to come out, but these ships had sailed without encountering them, and it was by no means probable that the English seriously wished a meeting. When it was understood, however, that the Chesapeake was ready to sail, the Shannon, Captain Broke, appeared alone in the offing, and as the ships were fairly matched, a combat appeared much more probable. It is now known, that Captain Broke, that very day, sent in an invitation to Captain Lawrence, to meet him in any latitude and longitude that might be agreed on. Unfortunately, this letter was not written until about the moment the Chesapeake was getting under way, and the advantage of having officers and men accustomed to act a little together, was lost. The Chesapeake's contemplated cruise was to the northward and eastward, with a view to intercept the store-ships and troop-ships that were steering for the St. Lawrence. The Hornet 18, Captain Biddle, had

been put under the orders of Captain Lawrence, and it was
intended that the two ships should cruise in company.   The
Greenland whale-fishery was the ultimate object of these
vessels.

In the forenoon of June 1st, 1813, the Shannon appeared in
the bay.   The Chesapeake was then lying in President Roads,
ready for sea ; though some disaffection existed among the
crew, on account of the prize-money of the last cruise, which
was still unpaid.   The ship had an unusual number of merce-
naries in her ; and among others, was a boatswain's mate, a
Portuguese, who was found to be particularly troublesome.
Under the extraordinary circumstances in which the vessel
was placed, it was thought prudent to temporise, and the people were addressed, and some promises were made to them,
which apparently had the effect of putting them in a better
humour.

At 12, meridian, the Chesapeake lifted her anchor, and stood
out, with a pleasant breeze from the southward and westward.
As the Shannon was then in plain sight, the ship was cleared
for action, and the best appearances were assumed, although
it is known that Captain Lawrence went into this engagement
with strong reluctance, on account of the peculiar state of his
crew.   He had himself only joined the vessel a few days before ; her proper first lieutenant, Mr. O. A. Page, of Virginia,
an officer of experience, was ill on shore, and died soon after,
in Boston ; the acting first lieutenant, Mr. Augustus Ludlow,
of New York, though an officer of merit, was a very young
man, and was in an entirely novel situation ; and there was but
one other commissioned sea-officer in the ship, two of the midshipmen acting as third and fourth lieutenants, and now performing this duty for the first time.   One, if not both of these
young gentlemen, had also just joined the ship, following the
captain from the Hornet.   In addition, the Chesapeake had an
unusual number of landsmen in her.

The Shannon stood off under easy sail, when Captain Lawrence fired a gun, about half-past 4, which induced her to heave
to, with her head to the southward and eastward.   By this
time the wind had freshened, and at 5, the Chesapeake took in
her royals and topgallant-sails, and half an hour later, she
hauled up her courses.   The two ships were now about 30
miles from the light, the Shannon under single-reefed topsails
and jib, and the Chesapeake under her whole topsails and jib,
coming down fast.   As the Shannon was running with the

26 *

wind a little free, there was an anxious moment on board of her, during which it was uncertain on which side the Chesapeake was about to close, or whether she might not be disposed to commence the action on her quarter. But Captain Lawrence chose to lay his enemy fairly alongside, yard-arm and yard-arm; and he luffed, and ranged up abeam, on the Shannon's starboard side. When the Chesapeake's foremast was in a line with the Shannon's mizzen-mast, the latter ship discharged her cabin guns, and the others in succession, from aft forward. The Chesapeake did not fire until all her guns bore, when she delivered a very destructive broadside. For six or eight minutes the cannonading was fierce, and the best of the action, so far as the general effect of the fire was concerned, is said to have been with the American frigate, though it was much in favour of the enemy, in its particular and accidental consequences. While passing the Shannon's broadside, the Chesapeake had her fore-topsail tie and jib sheet shot away. Her spanker-brails also were loosened, and the sail blew out. These accidents occurring nearly at the same instant, they brought the ship up into the wind, when, taking aback, she got sternway, and fell aboard of the enemy, with her mizzen-rigging foul of the Shannon's fore-chains. By some accounts, the fluke of an anchor on board the Shannon hooked in the rigging of the Chesapeake. Whatever may have served to keep the ships together, it appears to be certain, that the American frigate lay exposed to a raking fire from the enemy, who poured into her the contents of one or two carronades, that nearly swept her upper deck. At the few first discharges of the Shannon, Captain Lawrence had received a wound in the leg; Mr. Broom, the marine officer, Mr. Ballard, the acting fourth lieutenant, and the boatswain, were mortally wounded; Mr. White, the master, was killed; and Mr. Ludlow, the first lieutenant, was twice wounded by grape and musketry. Such was the state of the upper deck, as the accidents mentioned, brought the vessels in contact. When Captain Lawrence perceived that the ships were likely to fall foul of each other, he directed the boarders to be called; but unfortunately, a bugleman had been substituted for the drummer, and this man, a negro, was so much alarmed at the effects of the conflict, that he had concealed himself under the stern of the launch; when found he was completely paralysed by fear, and was totally unable to sound a note. Verbal orders were consequently s nt below, by the captain's aids, for the boarders to come on deck. At this critical moment Captain Lawrence fell with a ball through the body.

The upper deck was now left without an officer above the rank of a midshipman.  It was the practice of the service, in that day, to keep the arms of the boarders on the quarter-deck, and about the masts ; and even when the boarders had been summoned in the slow and imperfect manner that, in the confusion of a combat, was allowed by the voice, they were without arms ; for, by this time, the enemy was in possession of the Chesapeake's quarter-deck.

As soon as the ships were foul, Captain Broke passed forward in the Shannon, and, to use his own language, " seeing that the enemy were flinching from his guns," he gave the order to board.  Finding that all their officers had fallen, and exposed to a raking fire, without the means of returning a shot, the men on the Chesapeake's quarter-deck had indeed left their guns.  The marines had suffered severely, and having lost their officer, were undecided what to do, and the entire upper deck was left virtually without any defence.

When the enemy entered the ship, from his fore-channels, it was with great caution, and so slowly, that twenty resolute men would have repulsed him.  The boarders had not yet appeared from below, and meeting with no resistance, he began to move forward.  This critical moment lost the ship, for the English, encouraged by the state of the Chesapeake's upper deck, now rushed forward in numbers, and soon had entire command above board.  The remaining officers appeared on deck, and endeavoured to make a rally, but it was altogether too late, for the boatswain's mate mentioned, had removed the gratings of the berth-deck, and had run below, followed by a great many men.*  Soon after, the Chesapeake's colours were hauled down by the enemy, who got complete possession of the ship, with very little resistance.

Captain Broke, in his official report of this action, observes that after he had boarded, " the enemy fought desperately, but in disorder."  The first part of this statement is probably true, as regards a few gallant individuals on the upper deck, but there was no regular resistance to the boarders of the Shannon at all.  The people of the Chesapeake had not the means to resist, neither were they collected, nor commanded in the mode in which they had been trained to act.  The enemy fired down

* As this man performed this act of treachery, he is said to have cried out, " so much for not having paid the men their prize-money."

the hatches, and killed and wounded a great many men, in this manner, but it does not appear that their fire was returned. Although the English lost a few men when they boarded, it is understood that the slaughter was principally on the side of the Americans, as might be expected, after the assault was made.*

Few naval battles have been more sanguinary than this. It lasted altogether not more than 15 minutes, and yet both ships were charnel-houses. The Chesapeake had 48 men killed, and 98 wounded, a large portion of whom fell by the raking fire of the Shannon, after the Chesapeake was taken aback, and by the fire of the boarders. The Shannon had 23 killed and 56 wounded, principally by the Chesapeake's broadsides. It was impossible for ships of that size to approach so near, in tolerably smooth water, and to fire with so much steadiness, without committing great havoc. On board the Chesapeake fell, or died of their wounds shortly after the combat, Captain Lawrence, Lieutenants Ludlow, Ballard, and Broom, (of the marines,) Mr. White, the master, Mr. Adams, the boatswain, and three midshipmen. All but the midshipmen, fell before the enemy boarded. Mr. Budd second, and Mr. Cox third lieutenant, were wounded after the enemy had got on the Chesapeake's decks. Several midshipmen were also wounded. The Shannon lost her first lieutenant, and one or two inferior officers, and Captain Broke was badly wounded; the boatswain lost an arm, and one midshipman was wounded, mostly after the boarding.

As soon as the ships were clear of each other, they both made sail for Halifax, where they soon after arrived. Captain Lawrence died of his wounds on the 6th of June, and, with Mr. Ludlow, was buried by the enemy with military honours.

Perhaps the capture of no single ship ever produced so much exultation on the side of the victors, or so much depression on that of the beaten party, as that of the Chesapeake. The American nation had fallen into the error of their enemy, and had begun to imagine themselves invincible on the ocean, and this without any better reason than having been successful in

---

* The fact that the English met with no resistance in coming on board the Chesapeake, is fully confirmed by the official account of Captain Broke. This officer, who appears to have behaved with great personal gallantry, was among the first to board, and he says, " having received a sabre wound, *at the first onset,* while charging a part of the enemy, who had rallied *on their forecastle,*" &c. &c. The enemy came in *astern,* and the *first onset* occurring on the *forecastle,* it follows that there was no resistance aft.

a few detached combats, and its mortification was in proportion to the magnitude of its delusion; while England hailed the success of the Shannon as a proof that its ancient renown was about to be regained.

In America reflection soon caused the mortification in a great measure to subside, as it was seen that the capture of the Chesapeake was owing to a concurrence of circumstances that was not likely again to happen.  It was soon understood that the closeness and short duration of this combat were actually owing to their own officer, who brought his ship so near that the battle was necessarily soon decided, while its succeeding incidents were altogether the results of the chances of war. At the moment when the English boarded, the total loss of the Shannon in men, is believed to have been at least equal to that of the Chesapeake; yet the former vessel was deprived of the services of no important officer but the boatswain, while the Chesapeake had lost those of her captain, two of her lieutenants, master, marine officer, and boatswain, including every one in any authority on the upper deck.  These fortuitous events are as unconnected with any particular merit on the one side, as with any particular demerit on the other; and the feeling of the Americans gradually settled down into a sentiment of sincere respect for the high-spirited Lawrence, and of deep regret for his loss.  When told of their defeat, and called on to acknowledge that their enemy was victorious in one of the most extraordinary combats of the age, they have generally given all the credit to the conquerors that they deserved; and while they frankly admit that the victory was remarkable, they may be excused for believing it quite as much so for standing alone in such a war, as for any other distinguishing characteristic.

## CHAPTER XXXIV.

WHILE these different events were occurring among the frigates and larger sloops of war, the lighter cruisers of the navy
had not been idle.   The fate of the Nautilus has been already
mentioned ; the Argus's cruises have also been alluded to ;
but nothing has been said of the Siren, Enterprise, and Vixen,
the other three little vessels, which were so distinguished in the
Tripolitan contest.   The latter, like her sister the Nautilus, had
but a short career after the declaration of war.   During the
first few months, she was on the southern coast, under the
command of Captain Gadsden, but that officer dying, she was
given to Captain Washington Reed, who went on a cruise
among the Islands.   A few days out, he was fallen in with
and chased by the Southampton 32, Captain Sir James Lucas
Yeo, which ship succeeded in getting alongside of the Vixen,
after a short but severe trial of speed, and of course captured
her.   Both vessels were soon after wrecked on one of the Ba-
hama Islands, when, it is said, that the American crew set an
example of subordination, sobriety, and order, that produced
a strong impression on the British officers.

The Siren cruised a short time in the Gulf of Mexico without meeting with any thing, under Lieutenant Commandant
Joseph Bainbridge, and then came north, going into Boston.
Here Mr. Bainbridge, who had been promoted, was transferred
to the Frolic, one of the new sloops built under the late laws ;
and Mr. George Parker, who had been the first lieutenant of
the Constitution, in her action with the Java, having been promoted, was attached to the brig in his place.   The future history of this little cruiser being brief, it may be given here.
She sailed from Boston in the summer of 1814, and, shortly
after she got to sea, Captain Parker died ; when Lieutenant N.
Nicholson succeeded to the command.   On the 12th of July,
the Siren fell in with the Medway 74, Captain Brine, and,
after a vigorous chase of eleven hours, during which the brig
threw her guns overboard, she was captured, and taken into
the Cape of Good Hope.

The fortune of the Enterprise was better.   Her first commander was Mr. Johnston Blakely, who kept her on the east-

ern coast, where she was of great service, in driving off the small privateers that were sent out of the adjacent English ports. In August, she captured the Fly privateer; and soon after, Mr. Blakely, having risen to the rank of master and commander, was given the command of a new sloop called the Wasp. His successor in the Enterprise was Mr. William Burrows. The service of the vessel, under this officer, was not changed; but she was still kept to watch the enemy's privateers, between Cape Ann and the Bay of Fundy.

The Enterprise left Portsmouth, N. H., on the 1st of September, 1813, and steering to the eastward, was led into Portland, in chase of a schooner, on the 3d. On the 4th, she swept out to sea again, and pursued her course to the eastward in quest of several privateers that were reported to be off Manhagan. While opening the bay, near Penguin Point, a brig was seen getting under way, that had every appearance of being a vessel of war. The character of the stranger was soon put out of all doubt, by her setting four British ensigns, firing several guns, which are since known to have been signals of recall to a boat that had gone to the shore, and her making sail to close with the Enterprise. Being satisfied that he had an enemy and a vessel of war to deal with, Lieutenant Commandant Burrows hauled up, in order to clear the land.

While the two vessels were standing out, the Enterprise leading, some preparations were making on board the latter that produced uneasiness in a portion of her crew. This little brig had a small poop-cabin on deck, and Mr. Burrows had directed a long gun from forward to be brought aft, and to be run out of one of the windows. Owing to the rake of the stern-frame, and to the fixtures of the cabin, this arrangement could not be completed without cutting away some of the wood. On observing this, the impression became general among the men that it was the intention of their commander, who was almost a stranger to them, to keep off, and to use the gun as a stern-chaser. This was an unpleasant idea to the forecastle-men in particular, who were burning with a desire to be carried alongside of the enemy. The forecastle was commanded by a young officer of great promise, and the seamen at length urged him to go aft and state their anxiety to engage, as well as their entire confidence of success. This gentleman so far complied as to speak privately to the first lieutenant, who explained the intention of Mr. Burrows, and fully satisfied the people.

At 3 P. M., believing himself far enough from the land, and

having completed his preparations, Lieutenant Commandant
Burrows shortened sail and edged away towards his enemy,
who seemed equally willing to engage.  The two brigs approached on contrary tacks.  As they neared each other, or
at 20 minutes past 3, they kept away together; and as they
came side by side, both delivered their fire, within pistol-shot.
The Enterprise opened with her larboard, and the enemy
with his starboard guns.  The former brig drew ahead, keeping up an animated fire, and finding himself well forward of
the English vessel's bow, Mr. Burrows put his helm a-starboard, and sheered across his antagonist's forefoot, firing the
gun that had been run out of the cabin window once or twice
with great effect in passing.  The enemy was now allowed to
come up again on the Enterprise's quarter, when the two vessels engaged with their opposite guns; the American brig continuing to keep well on the enemy's bow.  In this situation the
English vessel lost her main-topmast, when the Enterprise
again sheered athwart her forefoot, raked her once or twice
more with the long gun aft, which proved to be the most serviceable piece in the vessel, and resumed her position on the
enemy's starboard bow, maintaining an animated fire.  While
lying in this favourable situation, the enemy struck.

In this hot and vigorous combat, the Enterprise was singularly well handled, manœuvring on the bows of her enemy
with effect, while she was kept perfectly in command, and was
ready at any moment to meet any change of position on the
part of her antagonist.  That it was the original intention of
her commander to fight her in this novel manner, was apparent by the forethought he discovered in shifting the bow gun
aft.

The fire of the enemy ceased about 4, though his colours
were still flying.  He now hailed to say he had struck; and
when ordered to haul down his ensign, an answer was given
that it had been nailed aloft, and could not be lowered until
the fire of the Enterprise should cease.  After this awkward
explanation, the Enterprise stopped firing, and took possession.
The prize proved to be H. B. M. brig Boxer 14, Captain
Blythe, an officer of merit, who had been cut nearly in two
by an eighteen-pound shot.  The loss of the Boxer in killed
has never been accurately ascertained, though it is thought to
have been relatively heavy.  She had 14 men wounded.  The
Enterprise had 1 man killed, and 13 wounded, of whom 3
subsequently died.  Among the latter, unhappily, was her gal-

lant commander. Although the disparity in the casualties of this action was not so striking as in some of the previous engagements, that in the injuries received by the two vessels was very great. But one eighteen-pound shot hulled the Enterprise; one passed through her mainmast, and another through her foremast. She was much cut up aloft, particularly by grape; and a great many shot of the latter description had struck her hull. Nearly all of the casualties were received from grape or canister shot. On the other hand, the Boxer had been repeatedly hulled, had no less than three eighteen-pound shot through her foremast alone; several of her guns were dismounted, her topgallant-forecastle was nearly cut away, and her sails, spars, and rigging generally, were much torn to pieces. The water being quite smooth, neither vessel was dismasted. The Enterprise returned to Portland on the 7th, with the Boxer, where Lieutenant Commandant Burrows, and Captain Blythe, were both buried with the honours of war.

After the death of Mr. Burrows, Lieutenant James Renshaw was appointed to the command of the Enterprise, under which officer, during the following winter, she made a cruise to the southward, as far as the West-Indies. Here her usual good fortune accompanied her; for though she sailed badly, and was three times hard chased, she always escaped. The Rattlesnake 16, a fast-sailing brig, bought into the service, was in company, under the orders of Lieutenant Commandant Creighton, who was the senior officer of the two vessels. Mr. Creighton went on cruising ground much frequented by the enemy, and yet fell in with no man-of-war he could engage. He was chased by heavy ships, and, to use his own expression, " in every instance, the good fortune of the Enterprise has been wonderfully manifest." The Rattlesnake outsailed her consort with so much ease, that most of the cruise she was under her topsails.

While off the coast of Florida, the Enterprise got alongside of the Mars 14, a British privateer, with a crew of 75 men. When the two brigs appeared, near half the people of the Mars took to the boats and went ashore, to escape impressment; but her master, notwithstanding this reduction of his force, ranged up under the broadside of the Enterprise, with his tompions out and guns trained. Lieutenant Renshaw, being ignorant of the strength of the crew of the Mars, fired into her, when she struck, having had 4 men killed and wounded. On the 25th of April, the brigs separated while

27

chased by a frigate.  The enemy pursued the Enterprise, and for 70 hours pressed her very hard.  Lieutenant Commandant Renshaw was compelled to throw all his guns but one over-board, and yet the enemy frequently came within the range of shot.  On the morning of the 27th, it was perfectly calm, and the frigate, then at long gun-shot, began to hoist out her boats, when a light breeze sprang up, and brought this lucky little brig again dead to windward.  Nothing but this favourable shift of wind saved the Enterprise from capture.

Shortly after, Mr. Creighton was promoted, and appointed to the command of a new sloop of war just launched at Wash-ington, and Mr. Renshaw was transferred to the Rattlesnake. The two vessels being in a southern port, the Enterprise was sent to Charleston, where she became the guard-vessel, her sailing being too indifferent to allow of her being sent to sea again, in such a war.  When cruising in the Rattlesnake, in lat. 40° N., long. 33° W., Lieutenant Commandant Renshaw was chased by a frigate, and compelled to throw overboard all his armament but the two long guns.  By this means he es-caped.  June 22d, near the same spot, however, he fell in with the Leander 50, a new ship, constructed on the most approved modern plan, which vessel captured him ; the Rattlesnake hav-ing been unfortunately placed between an enemy that had the advantage of the wind, and the land.  On this occasion, Lieu-tenant Commandant Renshaw kept his colours flying in a very steady and officer-like manner, until the Leander threw her shot into the Rattlesnake with precision and effect.

CHAPTER XXXV.

In addition to the law of January 2d, 1813, which authorised the construction of four ships of the line and six heavy frigates, it will be remembered that the executive was also empowered to cause several sloops of war to be laid down.  These ships were of the class of the Hornet and Wasp, but were a little larger than the old vessels of the same rate ; and they all mounted 20 thirty-two-pound carronades, besides the two bow guns.  Most of them were got into the water in the course of

the year 1813, though their preparations were in different de-
grees of forwardness.  They were called the Wasp, the Frolic,
the Peacock, the Erie, the Ontario, and the Argus.  As there
had been a brig in the navy of the latter name, however, with
which the reader has long been acquainted, it is now necessary
to allude to her fate.

After the return of the Argus from her cruise under Lieutenant Commandant Sinclair, as has been already stated, Mr.
William Henry Allen, who had been the first lieutenant of the
United States 44, in her action with the Macedonian, was
appointed to command her.  Lieutenant Allen first obtained
the Argus by an order from Commodore Decatur ; and there
was a moment when it was uncertain whether Captain Biddle,
or this gentleman, should go to sea in the brig, but the former
was put into the Hornet.  Mr. Allen was shortly after promoted, when his new station was confirmed by the department.
June 18th, 1813, the Argus sailed from New York, with Mr.
Crawford, then recently appointed minister to France, on
board; and after a passage of 23 days, she arrived safe at
l'Orient.  Remaining but three days in the port, Captain Allen
proceeded on a cruise.

The Argus sailed from l'Orient about the middle of July,
and her exploits for the next few weeks, revive the recollections
of those of Captains Jones, Wickes, and Conyngham, during
the Revolution.  Captain Allen kept his brig for some time in
the chops of the English Channel, then went round the Land's
End, and shifted his cruising ground to the Irish Channel.  He
captured twenty sail of merchantmen, while passing, as it
might be, through the very centre of the enemy, most of which
were destroyed.  The appearance of this vessel so near the
British coast, excited much interest in the English commercial
world, and several cruisers were immediately sent in chase of
her.

It will readily be understood, that the duty on board the
Argus, was of the most harassing and fatiguing nature, the
feelings of Captain Allen inducing him to allow the masters
and passengers of the different vessels he took, to remove every
thing of value, that belonged to themselves, before he caused
the prizes to be burned.  Indeed, in so honourable and chivalrous a spirit did this excellent officer conduct the peculiar warfare in which he was engaged, that even the enemy did ample
justice to his liberality.

On the night of the 13th of August, the Argus fell in with

a vessel from Oporto, loaded with wine.   It has been said, and
apparently on authority entitled to credit, that a good deal of
the liquor was brought on board the brig, clandestinely, as the
boats passed to and fro, and that many of the people, who had
been over-worked and kept from their rest, partook of the re-
freshment it afforded too freely.   A little before daylight the
prize was set on fire, when the Argus left her, under easy sail.
Shortly after, a large brig of war was seen standing down upon
the American vessel, under a cloud of canvass ; and finding it
impossible to gain the wind of his enemy, Captain Allen shortened sail to allow him to close.   At 6, the Argus wore, and
fired her larboard broadside, the English vessel being then
within good grape and canister range.   The fire was immediately returned, the brigs fast drawing nearer.   Within four
minutes after the commencement of the action, Captain Allen
was mortally wounded, by a round shot's carrying off a leg.
He refused to be taken below, but fainting from loss of blood,
he was carried off the deck at 8 minutes past 6.   At 12 minutes past 6, Mr. Watson, the first lieutenant, was severely
wounded in the head by a grape-shot, which stunned him, and
he was also taken below.   But one lieutenant remained, Mr.
W. H. Allen, who continued to fight the brig, in a very gallant
manner, under the most discouraging circumstances.   At this
juncture, the Argus was beautifully handled, an attempt of the
enemy to cross her stern, by keeping away, having been frustrated, by the American brig's luffing into the wind, making a
half-board and throwing in a completely raking broadside herself.   But all the braces aft having been shot away, the Argus
broke round off, in filling again, when the enemy succeeded in
crossing her stern and raking.   At 25 minutes past 6, the
wheel-ropes and nearly all the running rigging being gone, the
Argus became unmanageable, and the enemy chose his position
at pleasure.   At half-past 6, Mr. Watson returned to the deck,
when he found the enemy lying under the Argus's stern, pouring in his fire without resistance.   An attempt was made to
get alongside, with a view to board, but it was found impracticable to move the American brig, while the enemy kept on her
quarter, or bow, throwing in a cross or raking fire with impunity, the Argus seldom being able to bring a gun to bear.
At 47 minutes past 6, the colours were ordered to be hauled
down ; the enemy, at the same moment, falling on board, and
taking possession over the bow.

The English brig was the Pelican 18, Captain Maples,

mounting 16 thirty-two-pound carronades, four long guns, and one twelve-pound carronade. The armament of the Argus, by crowding guns into the bridle ports, was 18 twenty-four-pound carronades and two chase guns. The enemy was so much heavier, that it may be doubted whether the Argus could have captured her antagonist under any ordinary circumstances, but it has been usual, in the service, to impute this defeat to a want of officers, and to the fact that the people of the Argus were not in a fit condition to go into action. The American vessel was particularly well officered, so far as quality was concerned, though her batteries were necessarily left without a proper supervision, after Mr. Watson was taken below. It is not easy to believe that Captain Allen would have engaged with his people under any very obvious influence from a free use of wine, but nothing is more probable than that the crew of the Argus should have been overworked, in the peculiar situation in which they were placed ; and they may have been exposed to the particular influence mentioned, without the circumstance having come to the knowledge of the superior officers. They have, indeed, been described as " nodding at their guns," from excessive fatigue. One thing would seem to be certain, that, while the brig was beautifully handled, so long as she was at all manageable, the fire of no other American cruiser in this war, was as little destructive as that of the Argus.* This has been attributed to the fatigue of the crew, and it is reasonable to suppose that the circumstance of the two lieutenants having been so early taken from the batteries, did not contribute to the accuracy of the fire. It ought, moreover, to be added, that the Pelican was about a fourth larger than her antagonist.

On the other hand, the fire of the enemy, when its length, closeness, and want of resistance, are considered, does not appear to have been remarkable. The Argus had two midshipmen, and four men killed, and 17 men wounded, in an action of three quarters of an hour. The Pelican, notwithstanding,

---

* It is one tradition of the service that the Argus was lost by double shotting the carronades. It is certain that a carronade will not bear two shot to advantage. In her first cruise, the Essex, which vessel had an armament of carronades, took a merchant-brig, on which Captain Porter determined to try the effect of his broadside. The frigate ranged fairly alongside of her prize, and fired a whole broadside into her, each gun being double-shotted. Nearly every shot struck, and but two or three, with the exception of those from the long twelves, penetrated the brig's sides.

27 *

was extremely well managed, and was very gallantly fought. She lost 7 men in killed and wounded, but appears to have suffered very little in her hull, or even aloft.

Captain Allen died of his wound in the hospital of Mill Prison, and was buried by the enemy with the honours of war. Mr. Watson recovered of his hurts.

Thus the navy lost all but the Enterprise, of the five little cruisers that had figured before Tripoli, and which had become endeared to the service by its traditions and recollections. The Argus alone, had been taken under circumstances that allowed a gun to be fired.

---

## CHAPTER XXXVI.

Shortly after the commencement of the war, a hundred British pennants were assembled in the American seas. A considerable force collected in the Chesapeake, a part of which was kept to watch the Constellation, in the manner mentioned, while the small vessels made descents on the coast, or entered the rivers and creeks, with which those waters abound.

In the early part of June, 1813, the enemy was thought to have had more than twenty sail of cruisers in and about the Chesapeake, of which several were ships of the line. The flags of two admirals were flying among them. On the 18th, three frigates came into Hampton Roads, and one of them went up nearly to the quarantine ground, sending her boats to destroy some small vessels in the James. The next day the flotilla of gun-boats descended to attack her, under the orders of Captain Tarbell, then temporarily in command of the Constellation. There were fifteen boats in all, acting in two divisions, one of which was directed by Lieutenant Gardner, and the other by Lieutenant Robert Henley. Officers and men were taken from the frigate to man them, including nearly all her lieutenants and midshipmen. A company of riflemen volunteered to join the seamen, and were also distributed among the boats. The weather prevented Captain Tarbell from approaching the enemy, until Sunday, the 20th, when it fell calm, and the gunboats dropped down within a good range for shot, and opened

on the upper frigate, about 4, A. M.  At this time the two
other frigates were still lying in the Roads.

The gun-boats formed in a crescent, and a brisk cannonade
was commenced on the part of the Americans.  It was some
time before the enemy returned it, the approach in the dark
and mist having taken him completely by surprise.  The
flotilla began the action at anchor, but it was soon found impossible to keep the boats steady, and most of them weighed,
and got out their sweeps, by means of which the guns were
kept bearing in the right direction.  The defence of the frigate
was very feeble, and after discharging two or three broadsides,
she got under way, but the wind was too light to enable her
either to close, or to haul off.  This vessel was in a very
critical situation, and owed her escape in a great measure to
her consorts ; for, after a severe cannonade of more than an
hour, one of the ships below was enabled to close, when a much
sharper contest occurred.  But the wind increasing, and the
third ship drawing near, Captain Tarbell made a signal for the
flotilla to retire.

In this affair, most of the boats were conducted with spirit.
Their fire was well directed, and they treated the upper ship
quite roughly.  The fire of this vessel was extremely feeble,
and it appears to have done no execution whatever.  That of
the second ship, however, was very animated, and it was particularly well directed.  Although the loss of the Americans in
men was small, consisting of only one master's mate killed,
and two men wounded, the enemy's grape flew around them
in great numbers.  One boat received a bad shot between wind
and water, and several had their sweeps shot away, or were
otherwise injured.  The gun-boat commanded by Mr. Nantz,
the sailing-master, was crippled, and in danger of being captured by the enemy, when, by order of Captain Tarbell, she
was taken in tow by the boat commanded by Lieutenant W.
B. Shubrick, of the Constellation, and brought off.

The frigate first engaged was thought to be the Narcissus
32, and the vessel that came to her relief, the Junon 38, Captain Saunders.  This experiment had the effect to convince
most of the sea-officers engaged on board the gun-boats, of the
bad qualities of that description of vessel, they having been
very generally found wanting in a sufficient degree of steadiness to render their fire certain, even in smooth water.  The
recoils of the guns caused them to roll to a degree that rendered

the aim uncertain, and it has been seen that they could only be kept in the proper positions by the aid of sweeps.

The next flood, a large force of the enemy, consisting of fourteen sail, came into the Roads, and an attack was expected. On the 20th, the enemy's ships weighed, and ascended with the tide to the mouth of James river, where, in the afternoon, they were seen making preparations to send up a large force in boats. As so much depended on the defence of the batteries of Craney Island, Captain Cassin, who commanded the naval force at Norfolk, sent three of the lieutenants of the Constellation, Messrs. Neale, W. Branford Shubrick, and Sanders, on shore, with 100 seamen, to take charge of the principal guns. This party was sustained by Lieutenant Breckenridge, of the marines, and about 50 men of that gallant corps. Most of the officers of the navy then at Norfolk, and who did not belong to the frigate, were also employed in the gun-boats, or about the island.

Early on the morning of the 22d, the enemy was discovered landing a large force round the point of the Nansemond ; and about 8 A. M., the barges of the vessels of war attempted to land in front of Craney Island, at a point where they were safe from the fire of the gun-boats, though exposed to that of the seamen's battery. Mr. Neale now opened his fire, which was directed with great coolness and precision ; and, after having three of his boats sunk, the enemy abandoned the attempt. The narrative of the remainder of the operations of this day, belongs to the general history of the war, rather than to a work of this character.

The officers, seamen, and marines of the Constellation, as well as the other portions of the navy employed on this occasion, gained great credit for their steadiness, discipline, and spirit. One of the barges sunk was said to have been a peculiar boat, called, from the great number of oars she rowed, the Centipede. She was described as having been fifty feet long, and as having contained 75 men. About 40 prisoners were made from the boats that were sunk, though the total loss of the enemy who were opposed to the seamen and marines, is not known. Captain Cassin, in describing the fire of the seamen's battery, observed that it resembled the shooting of riflemen. There is no doubt that the enemy found it much too cool and direct to be faced.

The government had fitted out several small vessels for the defence of the bays and rivers, and among others were the

ENTERPRISE AND BOXER.

Scorpion and Asp.  On the 14th, these two little cruisers got under way from the Yeocomico, and stood out into the river, when, at 10 A. M., a considerable force of the enemy was seen in chase.  The Scorpion, on board of which was the senior officer, immediately made a signal for the Asp to act at discretion, and began to beat up the river.  The Asp being a dull sailer, her commander, Mr. Sigourney, thought it expedient to re-enter the creek.  He was followed by two brigs, which anchored off the bar, and hoisted out their boats.  Mr. Sigourney now deemed it more prudent to run higher up the Yeocomico; and as the enemy was already pulling in, he cut his cable and made sail.  Three boats soon after attacked the Asp, which made a very gallant defence, and handsomely beat them off.  The enemy, however, reinforced, and renewed the attack with five boats, when Mr. Sigourney ran the Asp on shore, and was boarded by about 50 men, who succeeded in carrying her.  She was set on fire and abandoned, but Mr. M'Clintock, the officer second in command, got on board her again, and succeeded in extinguishing the flames.  In this affair, Mr. Sigourney was killed, dying sword in hand in defence of his vessel, in a manner to reflect the highest credit on his professional training and personal gallantry.  The Asp had but two or three light guns, and a crew of 21 souls.  Of the latter, 10 were killed, wounded, and missing : facts that attest the gallantry of the defence.

While these events were occurring at the south, some movements farther north brought a part of the enemy's force within the waters of Long Island Sound, where, with occasional changes of ships, it continued to the close of the war.  After the United States had refitted at New York, on her return from the cruise in which she had captured the Macedonian, Commodore Decatur prepared to sail again, with the latter frigate in company.  The Hornet being about to go to sea, at the same time, in order to join the Chesapeake, Captain Lawrence, the three vessels got under way, and passed Hell Gate on the 27th of May, with a view to run off the coast between Montauk and Block Island.  It was June the 1st before the ships found an opportunity to pass through the Race : but they were met near the end of the island by a greatly superior force, and were chased into New London.  Here all three of the vessels were closely blockaded, nor was either of the frigates able to get to sea during the remainder of the war, though opportunities were long and anxiously sought.  In the end, their officers and people were transferred to other vessels. It will give an idea of the great importance that ought to be attached to the means of raising blockades, when it is remembered that, while watching the three American vessels which then lay in the Thames above New London, the enemy also had it in his power to blockade the most important point on the continent connected with the coasting trade.

About this time, also, a small brig called the Viper, which had been put into the service under the orders of Lieutenant John D. Henley, was taken by the Narcissus 32, under circumstances that require no particular description.

In January, 1814, the Alligator, another small schooner, commanded by Mr. Basset, a sailing-master, was lying at anchor off the coast, abreast of Cole's Island, and observing an enemy's frigate and brig, just without the breakers, Mr. Basset suspected that an attempt would be made on him in the course of the night. Preparations to receive the enemy were made accordingly. About half-past 7 in the evening, six boats were discovered, under cover of the marsh grass, pulling up with muffled oars. When near enough, they were hailed, and a musket was fired at them. The boats now made a general discharge of musketry and grape, which the Alligator immediately returned. The schooner then cut her cable, and availing herself of a light breeze, she was immediately brought under command of her helm. By this promptitude, Mr. Basset succeeded in beating off his assailants, notwithstanding the schooner soon after grounded. The Alligator had 2 men killed, and 2 wounded, while the loss of the enemy was never known. The schooner had but 40 men on board, while the boats are thought to have contained about 100. Of the latter, the loss must have been severe, or they would not have abandoned the attack after the Alligator had grounded. The firing continued half an hour, and the schooner was a good deal cut up in her sails and rigging. A large cutter, that was supposed to have been one of the boats of the enemy on this occasion, was shortly after picked up on the North Edisto, much injured by shot. The bodies of one officer and of a common seaman were also found near by. The former had lost an arm, besides receiving a musket-shot wound. Mr. Basset was promoted for his gallantry.

The in-shore war at the south was distinguished by many other little exploits, resembling those already related; one of which, performed under the eyes of Captain Dent, who commanded at Charleston, is deserving of particular notice. Although it will be advancing the time to a period near the close of the war, it may be related here, with a view to present to the reader most of these isolated instances of gallantry in one picture.

In January, 1815, while Captain Dent was at the North Edisto, he obtained information that a party of officers and men, belonging to the Hebrus, Captain Palmer, was watering on one of the islands of the vicinity, and he directed Mr. Lawrence Kearny to proceed outside, with three barges, to cut them off, while a party of militia endeavoured to assail them by land. The frigate was at anchor, out of gun-shot; but as soon as she perceived the design of the Americans, she fired guns, and made other signals of recall, when two of the boats pulled towards her, and a tender, that contained a strong party, attempted to run out also. Fortunately the wind shifted, bringing the Hebrus to windward of the American barges, but the tender to leeward of them. Discovering his advantage, Mr. Kearny determined to make a dash at the latter, regardless of the frigate and of the two boats that were pulling off. The Hebrus, perceiving the danger in which her tender was placed, now made the greatest exertions to save her. Shot were fired at her own cutters, to drive them back to the assistance of the tender ; and a third boat was sent from the frigate with the same object. She also opened her fire on the American barges with some effect, one of her shot taking off the head of a man at Mr. Kearny's side. But this gallant officer, disregarding every thing but his object, laid the tender aboard in the steadiest manner, and carried her off, directly under the guns of the frigate to which she belonged. The Hebrus's launch was also taken, her people having hurried on board the tender when the alarm was given. The latter had a carronade and six brass swivels in her, besides other arms.

Mr. Kearny took about 40 prisoners on this occasion. The Hebrus intercepting his return, by the way he had come out, he carried his prize to the South Edisto.

A few days later, Mr. Kearny, in the launch of the Hebrus, with a crew of 25 men, went out and captured a tender belonging to the Severn, having on board between 30 and 40 men. Handsomer exploits of the sort were not performed in the war.

To this list of the minor conflicts, may be added an attack on gun-boat No. 160, commanded by Mr. Paine. This officer, who then held the rank of sailing-master, was convoying a number of coasters from Savannah to St. Mary's, when an expedition, consisting of a tender full of men, and ten boats, attacked him in St. Andrew's Sound, about 3 A. M. of the 6th of October, 1814. After a short cannonading and a sharp discharge of musketry, that lasted about 20 minutes, the enemy closed, and carried the boat by boarding. There were but 16 men fit for duty in No. 160 at the time; her entire complement consisting of 30 souls. Mr. Paine was badly wounded, as were two of his people. The enemy suffered severely, the defence having been spirited and obstinate.

A short notice of the warfare in the Delaware properly occurs next. This bay had no longer the importance it possessed in the war of 1775. Philadelphia had now lost the distinction of being the commercial and political capital of the country; and in the way of shipping, several ports were fast outstripping it. The enemy, consequently, paid much less attention to these waters than to those of the Chesapeake, and to other points of more interest. The length of the river, too, added to the security of the places that lie on its banks, and there was little apprehension of any serious descent. Still a flotilla consisting of gun-boats and block-sloops had been equipped, and it was put under the orders of Lieutenant Angus, an officer of tried spirit.

On the 29th of July, 1813, Mr. Angus had an affair with the Junon 38, and Martin 16, in which No. 121, Mr. Shead, was taken, after a handsome resistance.

The loss of the enemy's ships was 7 killed and 12 wounded. No. 121 had 7 men wounded.

CHAPTER XXXVII.

In the summer of 1814, several of the new ships were put into the water: among them were the Independence 74, the Guerriere and Java, 44 each, and the Wasp, Frolic and Peacock, sloops of war. The Frolic 18, Captain Bainbridge, had a short career, having been chased and captured, on the 20th of April, 1814, by the Orpheus 36, Captain Pigot, soon after she got out. There was no action, the Frolic having thrown most of her guns overboard in the chase.

The Adams 28 had been cut down to a sloop of war and lengthened, at Washington, so as to mount 28 guns on one deck, under the law of 1812. She succeeded in passing the enemy's ships in Lynnhaven Bay, on the night of the 18th of January, 1814, under the command of Captain Morris, and made a cruise in the track of the enemy's East Indiamen; returning to Savannah in April. Quitting this port early in May, she went off the coast of Ireland, when she was hard chased, on different occasions, by heavy frigates.

The ship had now been near two months in a cold, foggy, damp atmosphere, and the scurvy made its appearance on board. So many men were laid up with this terrible disease, that Captain Morris deemed it prudent to go into port. At 4 A. M. on the 17th of August, in very thick weather, the Adams ran ashore on the Isle of Haute, but was got off by lightening. It was found, however, that she made nine feet of water in an hour, and Captain Morris succeeded in getting her into the Penobscot, in Maine, as high up as Hampden, which is several miles above Castine.

While the Adams lay ready to be hove out, with nothing in her, a strong expedition of the enemy, consisting of troops and vessels of war, entered the river, and ascended as high as Hampden. A small force of militia was assembled, and a battery was mounted with the guns of the ship, in order to protect her; but the irregular troops giving way, and leaving the seamen and marines exposed in the rear, the first without muskets, nothing remained but to set the vessel on fire, and to make a retreat. All the service connected with the ship was performed in the most orderly and creditable manner, until a part of the country was reached where it was found impossible to subsist the men in a body, on account of the distance between the inhabitants, when the people were directed to break up into small parties, and to make the best of their way to Portland. It is a fact worthy of being recorded, that every man rejoined his commander, though a fatiguing march of two hundred miles was necessary to do so.

The ship had made many prizes during this cruise, most of which were destroyed.

While the Adams was thus running the chances of chases and shipwreck, the Wasp 18, Captain Blakely, sailed from Portsmouth, N. H., on a cruise. A letter from Captain Blakely

28

announced that he was in the offing, on the 1st of May, 1814, with a fine breeze at N. W.  He ran off the coast without molestation, and soon appeared near the chops of the English Channel, where he began to repeat the ravages caused by the Argus.  The position of the ship now exacted the utmost vigilance, as she was in the very track of the enemy.  At a quarter past 4 A. M., on the 28th of June, 1814, the Wasp, then cruising in lat. 48° 36′ N., long. 11° 15′ W., made two sail, a little forward of the lee-beam.  The weather was fine, the wind light, and the water exceedingly smooth for that sea.  After keeping away in chase, another stranger was discovered on the weather-beam, when the ship was immediately brought by the wind, in order to close with her, it being obviously expedient for the American vessel to select the antagonist that had the most weatherly position.  At 10 the chase showed English colours, and began to make signals.  At noon her signals were repeated, and she fired a gun.  The Wasp did not go to quarters until 15 minutes past 1 ; and soon after, believing he could weather the chase, Captain Blakely tacked.  The stranger also tacked, and stood off, no doubt to preserve the weather-gage.  The Wasp now showed her ensign, and fired a gun to windward.  The enemy, a large man-of-war brig, gallantly answered this defiance.  The Wasp immediately set her light canvass to close, when, at 32 minutes past 2, the enemy tacked, and began to draw near.  The American now took in her light sails, and tacked in her turn ; the English vessel still maintaining her weatherly position, and making sail to close.

At 17 minutes past 3, the enemy was on the weather-quarter of the Wasp, distant about sixty yards, when he fired his shifting-gun, a twelve-pound carronade mounted on a topgallant forecastle.  Two minutes later he fired again ; and the discharges were repeated until the gun had been deliberately fired five times into the Wasp, at that short distance, and in unusually smooth water.  All this time the Wasp could not bring a gun to bear ; and finding that the enemy drew ahead very slowly, Captain Blakely put his helm down, and made a half-board, firing from aft forward, as the guns bore.  He now hauled up the mainsail, and the two ships being necessarily very near, every shot told.  But the fire of the Wasp was too heavy to be borne, and the brig ran her aboard, on her starboard-quarter, at 40 minutes past 3, her larboard bow coming foul.  The English now made several trials to enter the Wasp, led by their commander in person, but were repulsed with steadiness and without confusion. Two or three desperate efforts were repeated, but with the same want of success, when, at 44 minutes past 3, Captain Blakely gave the order in turn, to go on board the Englishman, and in one minute the flag of the latter was lowered. On the part of the enemy, this action lasted 28 minutes; on the part of the Wasp, 19 minutes, including the time employed in boarding.

The prize was his Britannic Majesty's sloop of war Reindeer 18, Captain Manners. The Reindeer was an ordinary thirty-two-pounder brig, but, like the Peacock, her armament, when taken, was of twenty-four-pound carronades. She mounted 18 guns, besides the shifting carronade, and had a complement on board of 118 souls. Her loss was 25 killed, and 42 wounded; 10 of the latter dangerously. Among the slain was Captain Manners; and the first lieutenant and master were wounded. The Wasp had 5 men killed, and 22 wounded. Two midshipmen, both of whom subsequently died, were among the latter. The Reindeer was literally cut to pieces, in a line with her ports; her upper works, boats, and spare spars being one entire wreck. A breeze springing up next day, her foremast fell. The Wasp was hulled six times, and she was filled with grape. The principal loss she sustained in men, however, was in repelling the attempt to board.

Captain Blakely put a portion of his wounded prisoners on board a neutral, and proceeded himself to l'Orient, where he arrived on the 8th of July, with the remainder. The prize was burned, on account of the great danger of recapture.

After a detention in port until the 27th of August, the Wasp sailed on another cruise. Two prizes were made when a few days out; and on the 1st of September she cut a vessel, loaded with guns and military stores, out of a convoy of ten sail, that was under the care of the Armada 74; but was chased off by the enemy, in an attempt to seize another. On the evening of the same day, while running free, four sail were seen nearly at the same time, of which two were on the larboard, and two on the starboard bow. The latter being farthest to windward, the Wasp hauled up for the most weatherly. At 7 P. M., the chase began to make signals, with flags, lanterns, rockets, and guns. These the Wasp disregarded, but kept steadily approaching. At 20 minutes past 9, she had the enemy on her lee bow, within hail, and a gun was fired into him. The shot was returned, when Captain Blakely put his helm

up, and passed to leeward, under an apprehension that the enemy might attempt to escape, for it was blowing fresh, and the
ship was running ten knots.   This was easily effected, the enemy being still in doubt as to the character of the Wasp, both
vessels hailing.   As soon as she had got the desired position,
however, the American ship poured in a broadside, and a warm
engagement commenced at 29 minutes past 9.   The firing was
close and severe, though the combat had the usual embarrassments of a night action.   By 10 o'clock, notwithstanding the
darkness and the swell that was on at the time, the fire of the
enemy had ceased, and Captain Blakely hailed to ascertain if
he had surrendered.   Receiving no answer, and a few guns
being fired on board the English vessel, the Wasp poured in a
fresh broadside; but at 12 minutes past 10, perceiving that the
enemy did not fire any longer, he was again hailed, with a demand to know if he had surrendered.   The answer was in the
affirmative, and the Wasp lowered a boat to take possession.
Before the latter reached the water, however, the smoke having
blown away, another vessel was seen astern, coming up fast,
when the boat was run up, the people were again sent to the
guns, and the Wasp was brought under command, in readiness to
receive this second antagonist.   At 36 minutes past 10, two
more sail were seen astern, and it became necessary to abandon the prize.

The helm of the Wasp was now put up, and the ship ran
off dead before the wind, in order to reeve new braces, and in
the hope of drawing the nearest vessel farther from her consorts.   This vessel continued the chase, until she got quite
near, when she hauled her wind across the stern of the Wasp,
delivered a broadside, and made stretches to rejoin the captured vessel, which, by this time, was firing guns of distress.
It would have been easy for the second vessel to run alongside
of the Wasp, but the urgent situation of her consort, probably,
prevented the experiment.

As the Wasp left her prize so suddenly, she had no means
of learning her name or loss.   She had herself but two men
killed, and one wounded, the latter by a wad; a circumstance
that proves the closeness of the combat.   She was hulled four
times, had a good many grape in her, and was much cut up
aloft.   All that Captain Blakely could state concerning his
enemy, was his impression that she was one of the largest
brigs in the British navy.  The four shot that hulled the Wasp,

weighed each just 32 pounds.  She had many hands in her tops, and otherwise appeared to be strongly manned.

It is now known that the vessel captured by the Wasp, was the Avon 18, Captain Arbuthnot.  The brig that followed the Wasp, and fired into her, was the Castilian 18.  The Avon was so much injured that she sunk, and it was with great difficulty that the other vessel saved her people.  By some accounts indeed, a few of the wounded were lost.  The loss of men on board the Avon is not accurately known, the statements varying from 30 to 50.  The vessel was cut up in an extraordinary manner.  She is believed to have mounted 18 thirty-two-pound carronades, with the usual chase guns, and to have had a crew of 120 men in her.

The action between the Wasp and the Avon occurred on the 1st of September, 1814, (sea-time,) in lat. 47° 30′, N. long. 11° W.  September the 12th, in lat. 38° 2′, N., and long. 14° 58′, W., the former ship took the brig Three Brothers, and scuttled her.  September 14th, in lat. 37° 22′, N., long. 14° 33′, W., she took the brig Bacchus, and scuttled her.  September the 21st, in lat. 33° 12′, N., long. 14° 56′ W., she took the brig Atalanta 8, with 19 men.  As this was a valuable prize, Mr. Geisinger, one of the midshipmen of the Wasp, was put on board her, and she was sent to America.  The Atalanta arrived safely at Savannah, Nov. 4th, and brought the last direct intelligence that was ever received from the regretted Blakely and the Wasp.  Various accounts have been given of the manner in which she was probably lost, but nothing that can be deemed authentic has ever been ascertained.

An incident occurred a few years after the last direct intelligence was received from this gallant ship, that suddenly and keenly revived the interest of the public in her fate, which had begun to settle into a saddened sympathy with the friends of those who had perished.  It will be remembered that Acting Lieutenant M'Knight, and Mr. Lyman, a master's mate, both of the Essex, had been exchanged by Captain Hillyar, and taken to Rio de Janeiro, in the Phœbe, with a view to make certain affidavits necessary to the condemnation of the American frigate.  These gentlemen, after remaining some time in Brazil, took passage in a Swedish brig bound to England, as the only means of getting home.  A long time passing without any intelligence from Mr. M'Knight and his companion, inquiries were set on foot, which terminated in ascertaining this fact, and, subsequently, in finding the master of the Swedish

28 *

brig, who proved by his log-book and other documents, that he had fallen in with the Wasp 18, Captain Blakely, when his two passengers seized the occasion to put themselves under the flag.*

The Peacock 18, Captain Warrington, went to sea from New York, in March, 1814, and proceeded to the southward, as far as the Great Isaacs, cruising in that vicinity and along the Florida shore, to Cape Carnaveral. On the 29th of April, in lat. 27° 47', N., long. 80° 9', W., three sail were made to windward, under convoy of a large brig of war. The merchantmen hauled up to E. N. E., and the sloop of war edged away for the American ship. The two vessels were soon alongside of each other, when a close action commenced. The Peacock received two thirty-two-pound shot in the quarter of her fore-yard, from the first broadside of the enemy, which rendered the head-sails nearly useless. This injury compelled the Peacock to fight running large, and prevented much ma-

---

* *Extracts from the Journal kept on board the Swedish brig Adonis, during a voyage from Rio de Janeiro towards Falmouth, in the year* 1814.

"August 23.—Left Rio de Janeiro; Stephen Decatur M'Knight, and James Lyman, passengers for England.

"October 9th.—In lat. 18° 35' N., long. 30° 10' W., sea account, at 8 o'clock in the morning, discovered a strange sail giving chase to us, and fired several guns; she gaining very fast. At half-past 10 o'clock hove to, and was boarded by an officer dressed in an English doctor's uniform, the vessel also hoisted an English ensign. The officer proceeded to examine my ship's papers, &c. &c., likewise the letter-bags, and took from one of them a letter to the victualling-office, London. Finding I had two American officers as passengers, he immediately left the ship, and went on board the sloop of war; he shortly after returned, took the American gentlemen with him, and went a second time on board the sloop. In about half an hour, he returned again with Messrs. M'Knight and Lyman, and they informed me that the vessel was the United States sloop of war the Wasp, commanded by Captain Bleaky, or Blake, last from France, where she had refitted; had lately sunk the Reindeer, English sloop of war, and another vessel which sunk without their being able to save a single person, or learn the vessel's name, — that Messrs. M'Knight and Lyman had now determined to leave me, and go on board the Wasp—paid me their passages in dollars, at 5s. 9d., and having taken their luggage on board the Wasp, they made sail to the southward. Shortly after they had left, I found that Lieutenant M'Knight had left his writing-desk behind; and I immediately made signal for the Wasp to return, and stood towards her; they, observing my signals, stood back, came alongside, and sent their boat on board for the writing-desk; after which they sent me a log-line and some other presents, and made all sail in a direction for the line; and I have reason to suppose for the convoy that passed on Thursday previous."

nœuvring, the combat being effectually decided by gunnery.
At the end of 42 minutes, the enemy struck.

The prize was H. B. M. brig Epervier 18, Captain Wales.
The Epervier was extensively injured, having received no less
than 45 shot in her hull, and had 22 men killed and wounded.
Her main-topmast was over the side, her main boom was shot
away, her foremast tottering, her bowsprit badly wounded,
standing rigging much cut, and she had five feet water in her
hold.   The Peacock received very little injury ; that done the
fore-yard being the principal ; while her hull escaped almost
entirely, not a round shot touching it.   No person was killed,
and only two men were wounded.

The Peacock was a heavier vessel than the Epervier, while,
as usual, the disparity in the loss was infinitely greater than
that in the force.   The metal was nominally the same ; but, if
the shot of the Peacock were as short of weight as those of the
Wasp are known to have been, she threw at a broadside only
twenty pounds of metal more than her antagonist.   The Epervier mounted 18 thirty-two-pound carronades, and it would
seem had no chase guns; her crew consisted of 128 men.
On board this vessel were found $118,000 in specie.

In one hour after the retreat from quarters was beat, the
Peacock had her fore-yard fished, and in all respects was
ready again to engage.   The Epervier struck about 11 A. M.,
and by sunset she was in a condition to carry sail.   It was
only by the greatest exertions, however, that she was, at first,
kept from sinking.

Mr. J. B. Nicolson, the first lieutenant of the Peacock, was
put in charge of the prize, with directions to make the best of
his way to Savannah.   The southern coast was then much
infested by the enemy, and, as Captain Warrington knew that
she was liable to be brought to action at any moment, he determined to convoy his prize into port.   On the evening of the
29th of April, or the day of the capture, the vessels made sail,
and the next afternoon they were abreast of Amelia Island,
when two frigates were discovered at the northward, and to
leeward.   At Mr. Nicolson's request, Captain Warrington
now took all the prize crew from the Epervier but that gentleman and sixteen officers and men, intending to send the prize
into St. Mary's, and to haul to the southward with the Peacock, to lead the enemy off the coast.   This plan succeeded,
the Peacock getting rid of the frigate that chased her next day.
The Epervier, while subsequently running along the coast, on

her way to Savannah, however, fell in with the other frigate, and keeping close in, in shoal water, the wind being light, the enemy manned his boats, and sent them in chase.  There was a moment when the prize was in great danger of falling into the hands of her pursuers, for the boats got quite near, in her wake. In this critical situation, Mr. Nicolson had recourse to a stratagem to keep them off.  He used the trumpet as if full of men, and when the boats were the nearest, he issued an order, in a very loud voice, to make a yaw, in order to fire a broadside.  This appearance of a readiness to engage intimidated the enemy, who abandoned his attempt at a moment when he might have carried the Epervier with little or no loss.  On the 1st of May the brig arrived safely at Savannah, and, on the 4th, the Peacock came in also.  Mr. Nicolson's steadiness and ingenuity were much applauded.

Shortly after, the Peacock sailed on a cruise for the enemy's seas, the Bay of Biscay, the coast of Portugal, and among the Islands, constantly changing her position to elude the English squadrons.  After passing over some of the best cruising ground in the Atlantic, the ship returned to New York, at the end of October, without having fallen in with an enemy of a force proper for her to engage.  She captured, however, 14 sail of merchantmen.

The President 44 continued to cruise under the orders of Commodore Rodgers, and the Congress 38 under those of Captain Smith, with a similar want of success, when the merits of their commanders were considered.  These two fine frigates traversed the Northern Atlantic, in a variety of directions, in company and singly, and yet it was never the good fortune of either to fall in with an enemy, that could be brought to action.  The latter ship even went south of the equator, and one of her cruises extended to eight months ; but her luck did not vary.

In one of his cruises Commodore Rodgers captured an enemy's man-of-war schooner, called the Highflyer, drawing her under his guns by an artifice, and this was the only English man-of-war that he took during his command of this ship.

## CHAPTER XXXVIII.

It would exceed the limits of a work of this nature, to enter into a minute relation of all the skirmishes to which the predatory warfare of the English, in the Chesapeake, gave rise ; but it is due to the officers and men employed against them, to furnish an outline of their services.  On various occasions, parties from the ships had conflicts with the detached militia, or armed citizens, who were frequently successful.  Although it is a little anticipating events, it may be mentioned here, that in one of these skirmishes, Captain Sir Peter Parker, of the Menelaus, was killed, and his party driven off to its ship.  In several other instances, captures were made of boats and their crews ; the people of the country frequently displaying a coolness and gallantry that were worthy of trained soldiers.  On the whole, however, the vast superiority of the enemy in numbers, and his ability to choose his time and place of attack, gave the English the advantage, and their success was usually in proportion.

The government had equipped a large flotilla, to protect those waters, the command of which was given to Capt. Josh. Barney, the officer who so much distinguished himself by the capture of the Monk, during the war of the revolution.

The presence of Captain Barney's flotilla compelled the enemy to be more guarded, and his small vessels became cautious about approaching the shallow waters in calms, or in light winds.  On the 1st of June, this active and bold officer left the Patuxent, with the Scorpion, two gun-boats, and several large barges, in chase of two schooners.  He was closing fast, by means of sweeps, when a large ship was discovered to the southward.  Just at this moment the wind shifted, bringing the enemy to windward, blowing fresh and becoming squally. Signal was made for the flotilla to return to the Patuxent, as the weather was particularly unfavourable for that description of force, and the ship proved to be a two-decker.  On re-entering the river, the wind came ahead, when the gun-boats began to sweep up under the weather shore.  One of the latter being in some danger, Captain Barney anchored with the Scorpion and the other boats, and opened a fire, which immediately drove the enemy's schooners out of the river.   On this occasion, the English pushed a barge in front which began to throw Congreve rockets.   By this essay, it was found that the rockets could be thrown farther than shot, but that they could not be directed with any certainty.   The ship of the line anchored at the mouth of the Patuxent; the enemy's barges kept hovering about it, and the American flotilla was anchored about three miles within the river.

Between the 4th and 8th of June, the enemy was joined by a rasée and a sloop of war, when Captain Barney removed his flotilla up the river, to the mouth of St. Leonard's creek. On the morning of the 8th, the British were seen coming up the river, the wind being fair, with a ship, a brig, two schooners, and fifteen barges, which induced Captain Barney to move up the St. Leonard's about two miles, when he anchored in a line abreast, and prepared to receive an attack.   At 8 A. M. the ship, brig, and schooners anchored at the mouth of the creek, and the barges entered it, with the rocket-boat in advance.

Captain Barney now left the Scorpion and the two gun-boats at anchor, and got his barges, 13 in number, under way, when the enemy retreated towards their vessels outside.   In the afternoon, the same manœuvre was repeated, the enemy throwing a few rockets without effect.

On the afternoon of the 9th, the ship of the line having sent up a party of men, the enemy entered the creek again, with 20 barges, but after a sharp skirmish he retired.   The object of these demonstrations was probably to induce the Americans to burn their vessels, or to venture out within reach of the guns of the ships ; but the flotilla was commanded by an officer much too experienced and steady to be forced into either measure without sufficient reason.   On the 11th, a still more serious attempt was made, with 21 barges, having the two schooners in tow.   Captain Barney met them again, and, after a sharper encounter than before, drove them down upon their larger vessels.   On this occasion, the pursuit was continued, until the rasée, which, by this time, had ascended the Patuxent, and the brig, opened a fire on the Americans.   In this affair, the English are thought to have suffered materially, especially one of the schooners.   A shot also struck the rocket-boat.

Some small works were now thrown up on the shore, to protect the American flotilla, and the blockade continued.   In the mean time, Captain Miller, of the marine corps, joined the flotilla, and a considerable force of militia was collected under Colonel Wadsworth, of the ordnance service. The enemy had also brought a frigate, in addition to the rasée, off the mouth of the creek. The largest of these vessels was believed to be the Severn, and the smallest the Narcissus 32. On the 26th, an attempt was made by the united force of the Americans to raise the blockade. The cannonade was close, for the species of force employed, and it lasted two hours, when the Severn cut, and was run on a sand-bank to prevent her sinking.* It is said that a raking shot ripped a plank from her bow, and placed her in imminent danger. Shortly after, in company with the Narcissus, she dropped down the river, and went into the bay. In this handsome affair, the flotilla lost 13 men in killed and wounded; but it effectually raised the blockade, and induced the enemy to be more cautious.

The portion of the flotilla that was in the Patuxent, remained in that river until the middle of August, when the enemy commenced that series of movements, which terminated in his advance upon Washington. On the 16th, Captain Barney received intelligence that the British were coming up the Patuxent in force, when he sent an express to the navy department for instructions. The answer was to land the men, and join the army that was hurriedly assembling for the defence of the coast, under General Winder, and, if pressed, to burn the flotilla.

On the 21st, the news was received that the enemy had landed a force of four or five thousand men at Benedict, and that he was marching in the direction of the capital. Captain Barney immediately landed 400 of his party, leaving the vessels in charge of Mr. Frazier, with orders to set fire to them, if attacked, and to join the main body with as little delay as possible. The next day this order was executed, a strong detachment of seamen and marines approaching the flotilla to attack it.

On the 22d, Captain Barney joined the assemblage of armed citizens, that was called an army, at the Wood-Yard. The next day he marched into Washington, and took up his quarters in the marine barracks.

After a good deal of uncertainty concerning the movements of the enemy, it was understood he was marching directly os Washington, and that it was intended to fight him at Bladenn

---

* By some accounts this ship was the Loire.

burgh.   The flotilla-men and marines left the Yard on the
morning of the 24th; they arrived at the battle-ground on a
trot, and were immediately drawn up about a mile to the west
of Bladensburgh, holding the centre of General Winder's position.   After a short skirmish in front, where the enemy suffered severely in crossing a bridge, the militia fell back, and
the British columns appeared, following the line of the public
road.   The entire force of the flotilla-men and marines, was
about 500 men; and they had two eighteens, and three twelve-
pounders, ship's guns, mounted on travelling carriages.   Captain Barney took command of the artillery in person, while
Captain Miller had the disposition of the remainder of the two
parties, who were armed as infantry.   The marines, 78 men
in all, formed a line immediately on the right of the guns,
while 370 of the seamen were drawn up a little in the rear,
and on the right flank of the marines, on ground that permitted them to fire over the heads of the latter.   Although the
troops that were falling back did not halt, Captain Barney held
his position; and as soon as the enemy began to throw rockets,
he opened on him with a sharp discharge of round and grape.
The column was staggered, and it immediately gave ground.
A second attempt to advance was repulsed in the same manner, when the enemy, who, as yet, had been able to look down
resistance by advancing steadily in column, was obliged to
make an oblique movement to his left, into some open fields,
and to display.   Here he threw out a brigade of light troops,
in open order, and advanced in beautiful style upon the command of Captain Barney, while the head of a strong column
was seen in reserve in a copse in its rear.   Captain Miller,
with the marines, and that portion of the seamen who acted as
infantry, met the charge in the most steady and gallant manner, and after a short conflict, drove the British light troops
back upon their supporting column.   In this conflict the English commanding officer, in advance, Colonel Thornton, with
his second and third in rank, Lieutenant Colonel Wood, and
Major Brown, were all wounded, and left on the field.   The
marines and seamen manifested the utmost steadiness, though
it was afterwards ascertained that the light troops brought up
in their front, amounted to about 600 men.

There can be no question, that a couple of regular regiments would now have given the Americans the day; but no
troops remained in line, except the party under Captain Barney, and two detachments on his right, that were well posted.

Having been so roughly handled, the enemy made no new attempt to advance directly in front of the seamen and marines, but, after forcing the troops on their right from the field, by a demonstration in that direction, they prepared to turn the rear of Captain Barney, in order to surround him. While these movements were going on in front, and on the right of the Americans, a party of light troops had been thrown out on the enemy's right, and the militia having abandoned the ground, they were also beginning to close upon the Americans that stood. By this time, Captain Barney, Captain Miller, and several other officers were wounded; and victory being impossible, against odds so great, an order was given to commence a retreat. The defence had been too obstinate to admit of carrying off the guns, which were necessarily abandoned. All the men retired, with the exception of the badly wounded; among the latter, however, were Captain Barney and Captain Miller, who both fell into the enemy's hands. The loss of the latter in front of the seamen and marines, was near 300 men, in killed and wounded. Of the marines, nearly one-third were among the casualties; and the flotilla-men suffered considerably, though in a smaller proportion.

The people of the flotilla, under the orders of Captain Barney, and the marines, were justly applauded for their excellent conduct on this occasion. No troops could have stood better; and the fire of both artillery and musketry has been described as to the last degree severe. Captain Barney himself, and Captain Miller, of the marine corps, in particular, gained much additional reputation; and their conspicuous gallantry caused a deep and general regret, that their efforts could not have been sustained by the rest of the army.

As the enemy took possession of Washington, a perfectly defenceless straggling town of some eight or nine thousand inhabitants, that evening, and a considerable force in ships was ascending the Potomac, it was thought necessary to destroy the public property at the navy yard. At that time, a frigate, of the first class, called the Columbia, was on the stocks; and the Argus 18, and Lynx 12, had not long been launched. A small quantity of stores and ammunition had been removed, but on the night of the 24th, fire was communicated to the remainder. It is difficult to say why the vessels afloat were not scuttled, a measure that would have allowed of their being raised, as it would have been impossible for the enemy to injure ships in that state, and equally so to

29

remove them. Indeed the expediency of setting fire to any
thing has been questioned, since the enemy himself could not
very easily have done more. It is, however, just to remember, that
the sudden retreat of the English could not have been foreseen,
and that they had a commanding naval force in the Potomac.
The loss in vessels was not great; the Columbia 44, on the
stocks, and the Argus 18, being the only two destroyed that
were of any value. The Lynx escaped; and it would seem
that the enemy was in too great a hurry to do her any injury.
On this occasion, the Boston 28 was burned; but the ship
had been previously condemned. The hulk of the New York
36 escaped; but all the naval stores were consumed.

To aid in resisting these descents which were believed, at
the time, to be made by a force greatly exceeding that actually
employed, the officers and men of the navy, who were in the
vicinity, were collected on the shores of the Chesapeake.
Commodore Rodgers, with the crew of the Guerriere 44, then
nearly ready for sea, was withdrawn from Philadelphia; Captain Perry, of the Java 44, which ship was fitting at Baltimore,
and Captain Porter, with other gentlemen of the service, had
been actively employed on the banks of the Potomac, in endeavouring to intercept the return of the British ships that had
ascended to Alexandria; a duty that could not be effected,
however, for want of means and time. The guns at command
were altogether too light. Some fighting occurred. Several
gallant attempts with fire-ships were made, but the enemy's
movements were too rapid, to allow of the necessary preparations in a country so thinly settled, and almost destitute of
military supplies. In the course of this service, Commodore
Rodgers repelled an attack on a small party of less than 50
men, that was made by the enemy in an attempt to cut off a
lighter and a fire-vessel, on which occasion, Mr. Newcomb,
Mr. Ramage, Mr. Forrest, and Mr. Stockton, of the Guerriere,
were conspicuously useful. These gentlemen were also active
in endeavouring to fire the enemy's ships, though unsuccessful.
Most of these officers, and all their men, were ordered to Baltimore, when that town was threatened.

Baltimore was a much more formidable place to assail than
Washington, being compact, and containing, at that time, more
than 40,000 souls. Its water defences were respectable,
though it had no other fortifications on the side of the land,
than temporary breastworks of earth. The seamen, both
of the ships of war and of the flotilla, with the marines pre-

sent, were all under the command of Commodore Rodgers, who made a judicious disposition of his force.

The enemy landed early on the 12th of September, near a place called North Point. While this was effecting, the British frigates, sloops, and bomb-vessels, under the command of Captain Nourse, of the Severn, proceeded up the Patapsco, with a view to cannonade and bombard the water defences of the town. Vice-Admiral Cochrane, and Rear-Admiral Malcolm, were with this squadron. A brigade of seamen accompanied the army, under Captain Crofton. With this party Rear-Admiral Cockburn landed in person. The troops, as at Washington, were led by Major General Ross.

After proceeding about five miles, a small advanced party of the local militia momentarily checked the march of the enemy, falling back, agreeably to orders, when it found itself about to be surrounded. In the trifling skirmish that occurred at this spot, Major General Ross was killed. A sharper encounter took place shortly after, in which the Americans had about 1500 men engaged. On this occasion, the militia had 24 men killed, and 129 wounded. They lost also, 1 officer and 49 privates, prisoners. According to the accounts of the enemy, he lost in both affairs, 290 in killed and wounded. Shortly after the second skirmish, the English retreated to the place of debarkation, and abandoned the enterprise. The armed citizens of Baltimore and its vicinity, composed the force that met the enemy on this occasion.

The attack by water was equally unsuccessful. Fort M'Henry was bombarded for twenty-four hours, without making any serious impression on it. A small battery in advance, manned by officers and men of the flotilla, although much exposed, returned the fire to the last. In the course of the night, a strong brigade of boats pushed into the Ferry Branch, and would have gained the harbour, had it not been received by a warm fire from Forts Covington and Babcock, as well as from the barges of the flotilla. The defence was found to be toc obstinate, and the enemy retreated. Fort Covington was manned by 80 seamen of the Guerriere, under Mr. Newcomb, a very excellent young officer of that ship ; and Mr. Webster, a sailing-master, with 50 men of the flotilla, was in the six-gun battery called Babcock. The barges were under the orders of Lieutenant Rutter, the senior officer present, in that branch of the service. All these gentlemen, and their several commands, distinguished themselves by their steadiness and efficiency.

The barges, in particular, though exposed for nearly a day and a night to the shells and rockets of the enemy, maintained their position with unflinching firmness, and when more closely attacked, repelled the attempt with ease.  At a most critical moment, several vessels were sunk in the channel, which would have completely prevented the enemy from bringing up his heavy ships, had he seen fit to attempt it.  The duty was performed with coolness and expedition by Captain Spence.

This failure virtually terminated the warfare in the Chesapeake, the enemy shortly after collecting most of his forces at the south, with a view to make a still more serious attempt on New Orleans.  Small predatory expeditions, however, continued in this quarter, to the close of the war, though they led to no results of sufficient importance to be mentioned.  This warfare was generally beneficial to the American government; the excesses into which the enemy were led, whether intentionally or not, having the effect to disgust that portion of the population which had been seriously averse to the conflict; and the administration was probably never stronger, than after the wanton destruction of the public buildings at Washington. About this time, Captain Barney was exchanged, and he resumed his former command, less than half of his flotilla having been destroyed in the Patuxent.

# CHAPTER XXXIX.

THE movements in the Chesapeake were made by a force that was assembled for other and greater objects.  The principal expedition of the year was not commenced until near the close of the season, when Admiral Cochrane, after collecting, in the different islands, a large number of ships of war, transports, and store-vessels, suddenly appeared off the mouth of the Mississippi.  This was at the commencement of December, 1814, and left no doubt, of a design to make a formidable attempt on the important town of New Orleans.

The defences of the place, with the exception of some respectable fortifications that commanded the river, were of a very trifling nature. The latter were formidable, and they rendered it necessary to make either a descent in some of the bayoux, by means of boats, or to destroy the works by bombardment. As the latter required time, which would allow the Americans to assemble a force to resist the invasion, and was of doubtful issue, the former project was adopted.

On the 12th of December, when the enemy's fleet first made its appearance off the entrance of Lake Borgne, a division of five gun-boats was in that bay, under the command of Mr. Thomas Ap Catesby Jones, then a young sea-lieutenant. As soon as apprised of the appearance of the enemy, Mr. Jones reconnoitred his force, and, having ascertained its strength, he retired higher into the bay, with a view to take a position to command the approaches towards the town. There were several small forts, either at the entrance of Lake Ponchartrain, or at the mouth of different bayous, or creeks, that put up into the low swampy grounds below New Orleans, and it was the intention of Mr. Jones to anchor near one of them, at a place called les Petites Coquilles. His vessels consisted merely of gun-boats, No. 5, commanded by Mr. Ferris, a sailing-master, and mounting 5 guns, with a crew of 36 men; No. 23, Acting Lieutenant M'Keever, 5 guns and 39 men; No. 156, Lieutenant Commandant Jones, 5 guns and 41 men; No. 162, Acting Lieutenant Spedden, 5 guns and 35 men; and No. 163, Mr. Ulrick, a sailing-master, 3 guns and 21 men; making a united force of 23 guns and 183 men. The metal varied, some of the boats having two long heavy guns, others but one, and all having two or three short lighter pieces. The vessels themselves, like all gun-boats, were low, easy of entrance, slow in their movements, and totally without quarters.

Some movements of the enemy, who appeared with a large flotilla of barges and boats in the bay, induced Mr. Jones to expect an attack, on the 13th, and he got under way from the position he then held, at 3 30 P. M., to attain les Petites Coquilles, as mentioned. A small tender, called the Seahorse, had been despatched into the Bay of St. Louis, a short time previously, to destroy some stores; and about 4 o'clock the enemy sent three boats in after her, to cut her out. The Seahorse carried one light six-pounder, and had but 14 men. She was commanded by Mr. Johnson, a sailing-master. A few discharges of grape drove back the boats, which were soon reinforced, however, by four more, when a spirited engagement ensued. This was the

29 *

commencement of actual hostilities, in the celebrated expedition against New Orleans.  Mr. Johnson having got a position, where he was sustained by two sixes on the shore, made a handsome resistance, and the barges retired with some loss. A few hours later, however, the Seahorse and stores were set on fire by the Americans themselves, as it was not possible to prevent them from eventually falling into the hands of a force as formidable as that brought up by the enemy.  Not long after, another tender, called the Alligator, armed with a four-pounder, and with a crew of only 8 men, fell into the hands of the English.

About 1 A. M. on the 14th, the flotilla, which had been endeavouring to gain a better position, was compelled to anchor in the west end of the passage of Malhereux Island, on account of a failure of wind and the strength of the current.  At daylight the boats of the enemy were seen, having brought up about three leagues to the eastward.  It was a perfect calm, and a strong ebb tide setting through the Pass, no alternative was left Mr. Jones, but to prepare obstinately to defend, or to abandon his vessels.  He gallantly determined on the first, although the force that would be brought against him was known to be overwhelming.  Arrangements were accordingly made to resist the expected attack to the utmost.  It had been the intention to form the five gun-boats with springs on their cables, directly across the channel, in a close line abreast, but the force of the current deranged the plan; Nos. 156 and 163 having been forced about a hundred yards down the Pass, and that much in advance of the three other boats.  The approach of the enemy prevented an attempt to repair this great disadvantage, which exposed the vessels mentioned to being assailed while, in a measure, unsupported by their consorts.  When the character of the resistance is considered, it appears probable that this accident alone prevented a victory from having been obtained.

The English flotilla consisted of between 40 and 50 barges and boats, the former expressly constructed for the purposes of the invasion, and they are said to have mounted 42 guns, principally carronades of the calibers of 12, 18, and 24 pounds. The number of men embarked in these boats has been computed as high as 1200 by some accounts, while by others it has been put as low as 400.  The size and number of the barges, however, render the latter account improbable, ten men to a boat being altogether too few. The truth would most probably lie between the extremes.

At 10 39, A. M., the enemy raised his grapnels and kedges, and forming in open order, in a line abreast, he pulled up steadily to the attack. When near enough to be reached by shot, the gun-boats opened a deliberate fire on the approaching barges, though with little effect, as they presented objects too small to be aimed at with any accuracy. At 11 10, however, the enemy opened a fire through his whole line, and the action immediately became general and destructive. At 11 49, the enemy was near enough to make an attempt to board 156, which vessel was much exposed by her advanced position. Three boats dashed at her, but two were sunk, and the attack was repulsed. It was renewed by four boats, which were also beaten off with a heavy loss. In repelling this last attack, Mr. Jones was unfortunately shot down, when the command devolved on Mr. Parker, a young midshipman, who defended his vessel until he was severely wounded himself, and was overpowered by numbers. The enemy got possession of No. 156 at 12 10, and he immediately turned her guns on the other American boats. No. 163 was next carried, after a very gallant resistance; and No. 162 followed, but not until Mr. Spedden was severely wounded. The twenty-four-pounder of No. 5 had been dismounted by the recoil, and the fire of the captured boats having been turned on her, she was also compelled to submit. No. 23, Mr. M'Keever, was the last vessel taken, hauling down her flag about 12 30, when under the fire of the captured boats, and all the enemy's remaining force. Captain Lockyer of the Sophie commanded the English flotilla on this occasion, assisted by Captain Montresor of the Manley, and Captain Roberts of the Meteor.

Although the loss of this division of gun-boats was a serious impediment to the defence of New Orleans, both the country and the service looked upon the result of the combat as a triumph. On the latter, in particular, the resistance made by Mr. Jones, and the officers and men under his orders, reflected great honour, for it was known to have been made almost without hope. Circumstances compelled the assailed to fight to great disadvantage, and it would seem that they struggled to render their chances more equal by a desperate but cool gallantry. In consequence of the character of this defence, it is usually thought, in the service, to bestow as much credit on an officer to have been present at the defeat of Lake Borgne, as to have been present at a signal victory.

There is the same disagreement in the published accounts of the loss of the British on this occasion, as in the published accounts of their force. It was the opinion of Lieutenant Commandant Jones, who was carried on board the enemy's fleet, that their killed and wounded amounted to nearly 400 ; while other prisoners, who, from not having been wounded, had perhaps better opportunities for ascertaining facts of this nature, have never placed it lower than between 200 and 300 men. By the official statement of the enemy, as published, his loss was 94. As even this was more than half the number of the Americans engaged, it proves the gallantry of the resistance, but it is believed that the true account was varied for the purposes of effect. The American loss, though severe, was comparatively trifling.

The command of the naval force at New Orleans had been given to Captain Patterson, one of the young officers who had been a prisoner at Tripoli with Captain Bainbridge. Captain Patterson was a master commandant, and he was assisted by many excellent officers ; but his force was merely intended to command the river and the shallow waters in the vicinity of the town. A ship called the Louisiana had been purchased and armed with 16 long twenty-fours. Men were pressed in the streets for the emergency, under a law of the state, and the command of the vessel was given to Lieutenant C. B. Thompson.

The enemy finding himself in command of Lake Borgne, by the capture of the gun-boats, sent up a brigade of troops, under Major General Keane, which succeeded in entering a bayou, and in landing but a few miles below the town. Here he encamped, after advancing to some hard ground, on the night of the 23d of December, with his left flank resting on the Mississippi. No sooner was the position of the British known to the Americans, than General Jackson marched against them with all the disposable force he could assemble, making a total of about 1500 men, and by a prompt and spirited night attack he saved New Orleans. The movements of the troops on this occasion, were preceded by Captain Patterson's dropping down abreast of the English bivouac, in the U. S. schooner Carolina 14, and opening a most galling fire. The excellent use made of this little vessel, on the 23d, as well as her continuing to threaten the left flank of the enemy, materially con-

tributed to the general success of the campaign, there being
no question that the check received by the English in the action just mentioned, alone prevented them from marching into
New Orleans, from which town they were distant only a few
miles.   It had been intended that the Louisiana should join in
this attack, but the ship could not be got ready in time.

A few days later, however, the Carolina was very critically
placed.   The enemy had landed some guns, and the wind having blown fresh for some time at N. N. W., it had been found
impossible to ascend the stream against a current that was
even too strong for warping.   The armament of the schooner
consisted only of twelve-pound carronades, and one long gun
of the same calibre.   On the morning of the 27th, the wind
being quite light at the northward, the enemy opened upon the
Carolina with hot shot and shells, from a five-gun battery.
The cannonade was returned from the long twelve, the only
piece that could be used, but the schooner was soon set on
fire, beneath her cable tiers, and a little after sunrise Captain
Henley was compelled to give orders to abandon her.   Before
this could be effected, 7 men were killed and wounded, and the
vessel was much injured by shot.   Shortly after the crew had
got on shore, the Carolina blew up.   During four or five of
the most critical days of the campaign, this little vessel rendered signal service, and the enemy have always paid a just
tribute to the spirit, judgment, and intrepidity with which she
was managed.   Her behaviour on the night of the 23d, reflected great credit on Captain Patterson, and on all under his
orders.

The Louisiana was now the only vessel in the river, and
she covered the flank of the American lines.   On board this
ship Captain Patterson repaired, after the loss of the Carolina.
On the morning of the 28th, an advance of the enemy against
the American troops, drew a fire from and upon the ship, which
was maintained for seven hours.   In the course of this long
cannonade, the Louisiana threw 800 shot among the enemy,
suffering very little in return.

After the destruction of the Carolina, her officers and people
volunteered to man some of the heavy guns that were mounted
on the American lines, and they had a share in all the subsequent successes obtained on shore.   Captain Patterson also erected a battery on the right bank of the river, which was put up
under the orders of Captain Henley, and was of material use.
On the 8th of January the English made their grand assault,
and were defeated with dreadful slaughter.   In this extraordi-

nary battle, the loss of the enemy was computed at from two
to three thousand men ; more than two thousand having been
killed and wounded.   The seamen's battery on the right bank
of the river was temporarily abandoned, but the Louisiana was
of great use, and the officers and men of the service distinguished themselves by their activity, zeal, and courage.   On
this occasion Captain Henley was wounded.   One gun in particular, commanded by Mr. Philibert, a midshipman, was served in a manner to attract general attention.   The Louisiana
continued to assist in annoying the enemy, until the night of
the 18th, when the English retreated to their boats, and embarked, abandoning their attempt altogether.

Captain Patterson immediately despatched several officers,
in command of expeditions, to intercept and annoy the enemy
on their retreat, though the want of a direct communication
between the river and the lakes, prevented the employment of
any vessels larger than boats, on this service.   Mr. Thomas
Shields, a purser, who had previously been a sea-officer, and
who had 6 boats and 50 men under his orders, was so fortunate as to capture one of the enemy's large boats, with 40 officers and men of the 14th light dragoons, and 14 seamen on
board.   After securing these prisoners, Mr. Shields captured
a barge and a transport schooner, and subsequently five other
boats, making in all 83 more prisoners.   Some skirmishing
occurred, and Mr. Shields lost one or two of his prizes and a
few of his prisoners ; but he succeeded in bringing in with him
78 of the latter, besides destroying several boats.   Mr. Johnson, a sailing-master, also performed some service of the same
nature with credit, destroying a transport and capturing a party
of men.

In all the important service performed in front of New Orleans, during this short but arduous campaign, the navy had
a full share, though its means were necessarily limited.   Captain Patterson, Captain Henley, Lieutenants Jones, Thompson,
M'Keever, Spedden, Cunningham, Norris, Crowley, with several sailing-masters and midshipmen, distinguished themselves
on different occasions.   The service also witnessed with particular satisfaction the intelligence and spirited conduct of Mr.
Shields, an officer who had received his training in its own
school.   The marine corps had its share, too, in the honour
of this glorious campaign, a small detachment of it having
acted with its usual good conduct, under the command of Major Carmick, who was wounded in the affair of the 28th of
December.

## CHAPTER XL.

We have now reached a period when it has become proper to advert to events on the different lakes, which were the scenes of some of the most important, as well as of the most interesting incidents of the war. In order to do this, it will be necessary to return to the commencement of hostilities, for the whole of this portion of the subject has been reserved, in order to lay it before the reader in a continued narrative, having no immediate connexion with the war on the ocean.

The English government had long maintained a small naval force on the great lakes ; though much the larger portion of Champlain being within the jurisdiction of the United States, it had kept no cruiser on that water. On Lake Ontario, however, there were several vessels, as early as the commencement of the century, one of which was a ship called the Earl of Moira. When the American government caused the Oneida 16 to be built, that of the Canadas laid down the keel of a ship called the Royal George, which was pierced for 22 guns, and which was about one-half larger than the American vessel.

The Oneida was manned and equipped at the declaration of the war, and was still under the command of Mr. Woolsey, who had built her four years previously. The naval station on the American side of the lake, was at Sackett's Harbour, a beautiful and safe basin, not far from the commencement of the St. Lawrence ; while that of the British was nearly opposite, at Kingston. The enemy, however, had greatly the advantage in ports, those of the north shore of this lake being generally the most commodious and easy of entrance, though probably not as numerous as those of the south. The English also possessed a material advantage over the Americans, in all the warfare of this region of country, whether on the water, or on the land, in the age and more advanced civilisation, and, consequently, in the greater resources of the settlements on their southern frontier, over those on the northern frontier of the United States.

The great superiority of the enemy in force, notwithstanding his known inferiority in discipline and comparative efficiency,

prevented Lieutenant Commandant Woolsey from inviting hostilities, which were permitted to come from the enemy. On
the 19th of July, or about a month after war was declared, five
sail were discovered from the fort at Sackett's Harbour, a few
leagues in the offing ; and shortly after, they captured a boat
belonging to the custom-house, which they sent in, with a demand that the Oneida should be surrendered to them, as well
as a schooner called the Lord Nelson, that had been captured
not long before by the brig.   The Oneida now got under way,
and ran down, to windward of the enemy's squadron, to try
her sailing, and, if possible, to pass it, with a view to escape.
Finding the latter impracticable, however, Lieutenant Commandant Woolsey beat back into the harbour, and anchored
his brig close under a bank, where she could rake the entrance.
All the guns of her off side were landed and mounted on the
shore, presenting a force of 16 twenty-four-pound carronades
in battery.   On a height that commanded the offing, as well
as the entrance, was a small fort ; and here a long thirty-two-
pounder, that had been originally intended for the Oneida, in
her legal character of a gun-boat, was mounted ; and the
enemy still remaining outside, Mr. Woolsey repaired to the
spot, and took charge of the piece in person.

The enemy kept turning to windward, and having got
within gun-shot, he opened a slow, irregular, and ill-directed
fire on the fort, brig, and batteries.   His fire was returned ;
and, after a cannonade of about two hours, the English vessels
bore up, and stood back towards Kingston.   This was the
commencement of hostilities on the lakes, and it fully proved
the incompetency of the officers in charge of the enemy's force,
for the duty with which they had been entrusted.   The English
vessels consisted of the Royal George 22, Prince Regent 16,
Earl of Moira 14, Duke of Gloucester, Seneca, and the Simcoe.
On the part of the Americans, no harm was done ; while the
enemy is believed to have received some trifling injuries.

It is probable that the government of Canada was itself dis-
satisfied with the result of this first experiment of its naval
forces, for soon after arrangements were made to send officers
and men who belonged to the royal navy, upon the lakes.   It
was apparent to both nations, that the command of the inland
waters was of great importance in carrying on the war of the
frontiers, and each of the belligerents commenced systematic
operations to obtain it.   As the enemy was already much the
strongest on Ontario, it was incumbent on the American go-

vernment to take the first measures, and it set about them in earnest, very shortly after the beginning of hostilities.  It being evident that the command was one of the most important that had ever been confided to an American officer, great care was necessary in the selection of the individual to whom this highly responsible and arduous duty was to be entrusted.  The choice of the department fell on Captain Isaac Chauncey, then at the head of the New York navy-yard.  His orders were dated August 31st, 1812, and on the 6th of October, he arrived at Sackett's Harbour in person.  Forty ship-carpenters left New York in the first week of September, and more followed immediately.  Instructions were sent to Mr. Woolsey, to purchase sundry small merchant vessels ; and on the 18th of September, 100 officers and seamen left New York for Sackett's Harbour, with guns, shot, stores, &c.

The vessels used by the Americans in the navigation of Lake Ontario, were schooners, varying in size from 30 to 100 tons ; and the first measure of Commodore Chauncey was to purchase a sufficient number of these craft to obtain the command of the lake, until others better fitted for war could be constructed.  A selection of the most eligible was accordingly made by Mr. Woolsey ; they were bought, armed, equipped, manned, and put into the service, under the names of the Hamilton, Governor Tompkins, Conquest, Growler, Julia, Pert, &c., &c.  Neither of these schooners had the construction or the qualities requisite for a vessel of war, but they were the best for the service contemplated that could then be found on those waters.  Without quarters, their armaments consisted principally of long guns, mounted on circles, with a few of a lighter description, that could be of no material service, except in repelling boarders.  The keel of a ship to mount 24 thirty-two-pound carronades, however, was laid down in September, or before the commanding officer reached the station.

In conjunction with the Oneida, the entire flotilla that could be made immediately available mounted 40 guns, and it was manned with 430 men, the marines included.  As the armament of the Oneida was just 16 guns, it follows that there was an average of 4 guns each, among the six other vessels.  At this time, the enemy was said to possess on Ontario, the Royal George 22, Earl of Moira 14, both ships ; and the schooners Prince Regent 16, Duke of Gloucester 14, Simcoe 12, and Seneca 4 ; making a force in guns, more than double that of the Americans, with a proportionate disparity in the number of the men.  As cruising vessels, the enemy's squadron possessed an advantage in their size and construction, that greatly increased their superiority.

Previously to the war of 1812, there was no vessel on the upper lakes, that properly belonged to the American marine. A brig, called the Adams, however, had been constructed on these waters, for the convenience of the war department, which, under its own officers, had long found it useful in the transportation of stores and military supplies.  By the capture of Michigan, the Adams fell into the hands of the enemy, who changed her name to the Detroit, and took her into their service.  At this time, the enemy possessed two or three other vessels on the upper lakes, and of course, this capture, for the moment, gave them complete command of the waters between the outlet of Lake Erie and the head of Lake Michigan.

With a view to counteract this ascendency, Lieutenant J. D. Elliot was sent by Commodore Chauncey to the upper lakes, about the time that the latter officer appeared at Sackett's Harbour, with directions to purchase any suitable vessels that might be found, and to make preparations also for the creation of the necessary force in that quarter.  While Mr. Elliot was thus employed, a fortunate concurrence of circumstances, put it in the power of this officer to plan a blow at the enemy, of which he availed himself with a spirit and promptitude that were highly creditable.  On the morning of the 7th of October, the Detroit came down the lake, in company with another brig, called the Caledonia, and anchored under Fort Erie; and that very day intelligence was received that the first party of seamen intended for the lake, was within a short march of the Niagara frontier.  Orders were accordingly sent to hasten their arrival, which actually took place about noon of the same day.

Finding that the men were without arms, Mr. Elliot applied to Brigadier General Smythe, the officer in command of the troops on that frontier, who not only furnished the necessary means, but who permitted about fifty soldiers to volunteer to aid in the enterprise.

Two of the large boats used in those waters, containing about 50 men each, partly seamen and partly soldiers, were prepared for the service, and a small boat, or two, were manned by a few citizens.  The party attempted to pull out of Buffalo Creek, early in the evening of the 7th ; but the large boats grounded on the bar. Here some delay occurred, it being found necessary for most on board to get into the water, before they could make the boats float again. It was consequently much later when the adventurers reached the stream.

As the enemy lay near their own shore, the party pulled some distance up the lake in order to get above his vessels, before they edged away. It was past midnight when they got near the two brigs, the Detroit lying highest up stream, and farthest from the land. The boat destined to attack the Caledonia was directed to lead, in order that both vessels might be assaulted as nearly as possible at the same moment. This boat was under the orders of Mr. Watts, a sailing-master, supported by Captain Towson of the artillery ; while Mr. Elliott, in person, had charge of the other boat, in which were Lieutenant Roach of the artillery, and Ensign Pressman of the infantry.

As the leading boat crossed the bow of the Detroit, the enemy took the alarm, and the party of Mr. Elliott, as it approached, received two volleys of musketry. Without regarding this, both boats pulled steadily on, that which led reaching the Caledonia in proper time, but it would seem that one of the grapnels missed, and she fell so far astern as to allow the enemy to make a stout resistance. Here the decision and spirit of Captain Towson were of material service, and the vessel was captured. Lieutenant Roach of the army, who was accustomed to the duty, steered the boat of Mr. Elliott, which was laid alongside of the Detroit with great steadiness and accuracy, when the party went aboard of the enemy, Lieutenants Elliott and Roach leading. The former had a narrow escape, his hat having been struck from his head, and at the same instant he nearly cleft the skull of the English commander, who discovered the greatest resolution. Being well supported, this brig was carried with great rapidity.

In this handsome affair one man was killed, and a few were wounded, including Mr. Cummings a midshipman, in the boat of Mr. Elliott ; while that of Mr. Watts, owing to the circumstance mentioned, sustained rather more loss. Mr. Elliott reported the Detroit as carrying six long nines, and to have had a crew of fifty-six souls. The Caledonia mounted but two guns, and had a much smaller complement of men. About thirty American prisoners were found in the former vessel, and ten in the latter.

The Caledonia was brought successfully over to the Ameri-

can side, but the Detroit met with greater difficulty. Mr. Elliott found himself obliged to drop down the river, passing the
forts under a brisk fire, and anchoring within reach of their
guns. Here a cannonade took place, during which fruitless
efforts were made to get lines to the American shore, in order
to warp the brig across. Finding himself assailed by the guns
of the enemy's works, as well as by some light artillery, Mr.
Elliott determined to cut, and drop out of the reach of the first,
believing himself able to resist the last. This plan succeeded
in part, but the pilot having left the vessel, she brought up on
Squaw Island. The prisoners were now sent on shore, and
shortly after Mr. Elliott left her, with a view to obtain assistance. About this time the enemy boarded the prize, but were
soon driven out of her, by the artillery of Lieutenant Colonel
Scott, the Detroit being commanded equally by the guns on
both sides of the Niagara. Under such circumstances, the
vessel was effectually rendered unfit for service, and in the end,
after removing most of her stores, she was burned by the
Americans.

This was the first naval success obtained by either nation,
in the warfare on the lakes, and it was deemed a fortunate
commencement for the Americans, on waters where they might
hope to contend with their powerful foes on an equality. The
conduct of Mr. Elliott was much applauded, and Congress
voted him a sword. His promptitude and decision were of
great service, and it adds to the merit of all engaged, that the
Caledonia was thought to be a brig of a force much superior
to what she proved to be, when they left the shore. The army
had an equal share, in the credit of this dashing little enterprise, Captain Towson, who, in effect, commanded one of the
boats, though it was necessarily managed by a sea-officer, having particularly shown decision and conduct. The names of
Lieutenant Roach of the artillery, Ensign Pressman of the
infantry, and of several volunteers from Buffalo, were also
included in the eulogies of the commanding officer.

Not long after this successful exploit, part of the crew of
the John Adams 28, which had been laid up at New York,
reached Buffalo, to help man the vessels government intended to
equip on Lake Erie. Mr. Angus, his senior officer, accompanying this party, and there being a want of lieutenants on the
other lake, Mr. Elliott now went below to join the force immediately under the orders of Commodore Chauncey. Before
quitting this station, however, this officer had contracted for

several schooners, that lay in the Niagara, but which it was subsequently found difficult to get into the lake on account of the enemy's batteries.

Commodore Chauncey first appeared on the lake on the 8th of November, with his broad pennant flying on board the Onei-da 16, Lieutenant Commandant Woolsey, and having in com-pany the Conquest, Lieutenant Elliott; Hamilton, Lieutenant M'Pherson; Governor Tompkins, Lieutenant Brown; Pert, Mr. Arundel; Julia, Mr. Trant; and Growler, Mr. Mix; the three last named officers holding the rank of sailing-masters. The object in going out, was to intercept the return of the en-emy's vessels, most of which were known to have been to the westward, conveying supplies to the army at Kingston. In order to effect this purpose, the American squadron, or flotilla, for it scarcely merited the former term, went off the False Ducks, some small islands that lie in the track of vessels keep-ing the north shore aboard. As it approached the intended station, a ship was made in-shore. She was soon ascertained to be the Royal George, then much the largest vessel that had ever been constructed on the inland waters of America. That a ship of her force should feel it necessary to retire before the Oneida, must be attributed to the circumstance of her not be-ing properly officered, the enemy not having yet made their drafts from the royal navy for the service on the lakes. Com-modore Chauncey chased the Royal George into the Bay of Quinté, and lost sight of her in the night. The next morning, however, she was seen again, lying in the narrow passage that leads down to Kingston. Signal was immediately made for a general chase, which was vigorously kept up, with alternate squalls and light airs, until the enemy was fairly driven in under the protection of his own batteries.

Although the wind blew directly in, and made a retreat dif-ficult, Commodore Chauncey decided to follow the enemy, and feel his means of defence, with an intention of laying the ship aboard, should it be found practicable. Arrangements for that purpose were accordingly made, and a little before 3 P. M. the vessels that were up, got into their stations, and stood to-wards the mouth of the harbour. The Conquest, Lieutenant Elliott, led in handsome style, followed by the Julia, Mr. Trant, Pert, Mr. Arundel, and Growler, Mr. Mix, in the order named. The Oneida brought up the rear, it being intended to give time for the heavy guns of the schooners to open the way for a closer attack by the brig. The Hamilton and Governor Tompkins were a considerable distance astern, having been sent to chase, and did not close for some time.

At five minutes past 3, the batteries on India and Navy Points opened on the Conquest, but their fire was not returned until seven minutes later.   In three minutes after the Conquest commenced firing, she was joined by the other three schooners in advance.   The gun of the Pert bursted at the third discharge.   By this accident, Mr. Arundel, her commander, was badly, and a midshipman and three men were slightly wounded.   The vessel was rendered, in a great degree, useless for the remainder of the day.   The Oneida, though under fire for some time previously, did not open with her carronades on the Royal George, until forty minutes past 3 ; but when she did commence, the enemy was soon thrown into confusion, and at 4 P. M. he cut his cables, ran deeper into the bay, and made fast to a wharf, directly under the protection of the muskets of the troops.   Here, a part of her people actually deserted her, though they subsequently returned on board.   Soon after, the Governor Tompkins, Lieutenant Brown, bore up off the harbour in a beautiful manner, and engaged, having been preceded some time, with equal gallantry, by the Hamilton, Lieutenant M'Pherson.   The action became warm and general, and was maintained with spirit for half an hour, the enemy firing from five batteries, the ship, and some moveable guns.   It was now so near night, the wind blew so directly in, and the weather looked so threatening, that the pilots declared their unwillingness to be responsible any longer for the vessels ; and Commodore Chauncey, who found the enemy much stronger on shore than he had been taught to believe, made the signal for the flotilla to haul off.   When an offing of about two miles had been gained, the squadron anchored, with an intention to renew the attack in the morning.

In this spirited affair, which partook of the character of the assaults on Tripoli, and which, after a due allowance is made for the difference in the force employed, was probably inferior to none of the cannonades on that town, for gallantry and vigour, the Americans suffered much less than might have been expected.   The Oneida had one man killed and three wounded, and she received some damage aloft.   The other vessels escaped even better, the audacity of the attack, as is so often the case, producing a sort of impunity.   Mr. Arundel, of the Pert, however, who had refused to quit the deck, though badly wounded, was unfortunately knocked overboard and drowned, while the vessel was beating up to her anchorage.

The vessels shortly after returned to port, bringing in with them two or three small prizes.

Intelligence reaching Commodore Chauncey that the Earl of Moira was off the Ducks, he sailed on the 13th with the Oneida, in a snow storm, to capture her; but the enemy was too much on the alert to be caught by surprise, and the distances on the lake were too short to admit of his being easily overtaken in chase. The Oneida saw the Royal George and two schooners, but even these three vessels were not disposed to engage the American brig singly. The two schooners in company with the Royal George on this occasion, were supposed to be the Prince Regent and the Duke of Gloucester. Commodore Chauncey then went off Oswego to cover some stores expected by water. During this short cruise the Oneida narrowly escaped shipwreck, and the ice made so fast, that at one time, it would have been impossible to work the carronades had there been a necessity for it. The Conquest, Tompkins, Growler, and Hamilton, notwithstanding, continued to cruise off Kingston, until the 17th of November. On the 19th the Commodore attempted to go to the head of the lake, but was driven back by a gale, during which so much ice was made as to endanger the vessels. The Growler was dismasted. Early in December the navigation closed for the season.

While these events were occurring on the lower lake, the navy was not altogether unemployed on the upper waters. Towards the close of November, it was believed that the arrangements were in a sufficient degree of forwardness to admit of an attempt to drive the enemy from the batteries that lined the opposite shore of the Niagara in order to clear the way for the landing of a brigade of troops. To aid it in executing this important service, the army naturally turned its eyes for professional assistance towards the body of seamen collected at this point.

The men of the John Adams had encamped in the woods, near the river, and finding the enemy in the practice of cannonading across the Niagara, shortly after their arrival they dove into the wreck of the Detroit, at night, made fast to, and succeeded in raising four of that vessel's guns, with a large quantity of shot. These pieces were mounted in battery, and a desultory cannonading was maintained, by both parties, until the arrival of some heavy guns from the seaboard, when the

Americans got a force in battery, that enabled them completely
to maintain their ground against their adversaries. In this
manner, more than a month had passed, when the application
was made to Mr. Angus, for some officers and seamen to assist
in carrying and silencing the batteries opposite, in order to
favour the intended descent. The arrangements were soon
completed, and the morning of the 28th of November was
chosen for the undertaking.

The contemplated invasion having separate points in view,
the expedition was divided into two parties. One, commanded
by Captain King of the 15th infantry, was directed to ascend
the current a little, in order to reach its point of attack, while
the other was instructed to descend it, in about an equal proportion. The first being much the most arduous at the oars,
the seamen were wanted especially for this service. Mr.
Angus accordingly embarked in 10 boats, with 70 men, exclusively of officers, and accompanied by Captain King, at the
head of a detachment of 150 soldiers. With this party went
Mr. Samuel Swartwout of New York, as a volunteer. Lieutenant Colonel Boerstler commanded 10 more boats, which
conveyed the detachment, about 200 strong, that was to descend with the current.

The division containing the seamen left the American shore
about 1 A. M. with muffled oars, and pulled deliberately,
and in beautiful order into the stream. That the enemy was
ready to meet them is certain, and it is probable he was
aware of an intention to cross that very night. Still all was
quiet on the Canada side, until the boats had passed out of the
shadows of the forest into a stronger light, when they were
met with a discharge of musketry and a fire from two field-pieces,
that were placed in front of some barracks known by the name
of the Red House. The effect of this reception was to produce
a little confusion and disorder, and some of the officers and a
good many men being killed or wounded, all the boats did not
gain the shore. Those in which efficient officers remained,
however, dashed on, in the handsomest manner, and the seamen
in them landed in an instant. A body of the enemy was
drawn up in front of the barracks, with their left flank covered
by the two guns. As soon as the troops could be formed, the
enemy's fire was returned and a short conflict occurred. At
this juncture a small party of seamen armed with pikes and
pistols, headed by Mr. Watts, a sailing-master, and Mr. Holdup, made a détour round the foot of the hill, and charging the

artillerists, took the guns in the most gallant manner, mortally wounding and capturing Lieutenant King, who commanded them. At the same instant the remaining seamen and the troops charged in front, when the enemy broke and took refuge in the barracks.

The enemy's fire was now very destructive, and it became indispensable to dislodge him. Several spirited young mid-shipmen were with the party ; and three of them, Messrs. Wragg, Holdup, and Dudley, with a few men, succeeded in bursting open a window, through which they made an entrance. This gallant little party unbarred an outer door, when Mr. Angus and the seamen rushed in. In an instant, the straw on which the soldiers slept was on fire, and the barracks were immediately wrapt in flames. The enemy, a party of grena-diers, was on the upper floor, and finding it necessary to re-treat, he made a vigorous charge, and escaped by the rear of the building. Here he rallied, and was attacked by Captain King, who had formed outside.

The party of seamen and soldiers now got separated, in con-sequence of an order having been given to retreat, though it is not known from what quarter it proceeded, and a portion of both the seamen and the soldiers fell back upon the boats and re-embarked. Mr. Angus, finding every effort useless to stop this retreat, retired with his men. But Captain King, with a party of the troops, still remained engaged, and with him were a few seamen, with Messrs. Wragg, Dudley, and Holdup at their head. These young officers fell in with the soldiers, and a charge being ordered, the enemy again broke and fled into a battery. He was followed, and driven from place to place, until, entirely routed, he left Captain King in complete com-mand of all the batteries at that point.

Believing that their part of the duty was performed, the young sea-officers who had remained, now retired to the shore, and crossed to the American side, in the best manner they could. Most of the seamen, who were not killed, got back, by means of their professional knowledge ; but Captain King, and several officers of the army, with 60 men, fell into the enemy's hands, in consequence of not having the means of retreat. The attack of Colonel Boerstler succeeded, in a great degree, and his party was brought off.

Although this affair appears to have been very confused, the fighting was of the most desperate character. The impression made by the seamen with their pikes, was long remembered, and their loss was equal to their gallantry. The enemy was effectually beaten, and nothing but a misunderstanding, which is said to have grown out of the fact that the boats which did not come ashore at all, were supposed to have landed and then retreated, prevented the attack from being completely successful. Still, the batteries were carried, guns spiked, barracks burned, and caissons destroyed.

Owing to the nature of the service and the great steadiness of the enemy, who behaved extremely well, this struggle was exceedingly sanguinary. Of twelve sea-officers engaged, eight were wounded, two of them mortally. The entire loss of the party was about 30 in killed and wounded, which was quite half of all who landed, though some were hurt who did not reach the shore. The troops behaved in the most gallant manner also, and many of their officers were wounded. Both Mr. Angus and Captain King, gained great credit for their intrepidity.

As none of the great lakes are safe to navigate in December, this closed the naval warfare for the year, though both nations prepared to turn the winter months to the best account, while the coasts were ice-bound.

---

## CHAPTER XLI.

BOTH parties employed the winter of **1812–13** in building. In the course of the autumn, the Americans had increased their force to eleven sail, ten of which were the small schooners bought from the merchants, and fitted with gun-boat armaments, without quarters. In addition to the vessels already named, were the Ontario, Scourge, Fair American and Asp. Neither of the ten was fit to cruise; and an ordinary eighteen-gun brig ought to have been able to cope with them all, in a good working breeze, at close quarters. At long shot, however, and in smooth water, they were not without a certain efficiency. As was proved in the end, in attacking batteries, and in covering descents, they were found to be exceedingly serviceable.

On the 26th of November, the new ship was launched at

Sackett's Harbour, and was called the Madison.   She was pierced for 24 guns, and her metal was composed of thirty-two-pound carronades, rendering her a little superior to the Royal George.   Nine weeks before this ship was put into the water, her timber was growing in the forest.   This unusual expedition, under so many unfavourable circumstances, is to be ascribed to the excellent dispositions of the commanding officer, and to the clear head, and extraordinary resources of Mr. Henry Eckford, the builder employed, whose professional qualities proved to be of the highest order.

On the other hand, the enemy laid the keel of a ship a little larger than the Madison, which would have effectually secured the command of the lake, notwithstanding the launching of the latter, as their small vessels were altogether superior to those of the Americans ; and the Royal George was perhaps strong enough to engage two brigs of the force of the Oneida.   It became necessary, therefore, to lay down a new ship at Sackett's Harbour, and for this purpose a fresh gang of shipwrights went up in February.

About this time, the enemy made choice of Captain Sir James Lucas Yeo, to command on the American lakes.

In the meantime, preparations were made for constructing a force on Lake Erie, two brigs having been laid down at Presque Isle, (now Erie,) during the month of March.

Fresh parties of seamen began to arrive at Kingston in March, where the new ship was fast getting ready.

On the 6th of April Mr. Eckford put into the water, on the American side, a beautiful little pilot-boat schooner, that was intended for a look-out and despatch vessel.   She was armed with merely one long brass nine on a pivot, and was called the Lady of the Lake.   Two days later, the keel of the new ship was laid.   She was considerably larger than the Madison.

About the middle of the month, the lake was considered safe to navigate, and on the 19th, the squadron was reported ready for active service.   On the 22d, accordingly, General Dearborn caused a body of 1700 men to be embarked, and on the 24th, owing to the impatience of the army, which suffered much by being crowded into small vessels, an attempt was made to get out.   The commodore, however, agreeably to his own expectations, was obliged to return, it blowing a gale. These few days had a very injurious effect on the health of both branches of the service, as there was not sufficient room for the men to remain below, and on deck they were exposed

to the inclemency of the season.    The Madison alone, a mere
sloop of war, had 600 souls in her, including her own people.
On the 25th, however, the squadron, consisting of the Madi-
son, Lieutenant Commandant Elliott, Commodore Chauncey;
Oneida, Lieutenant Commandant Woolsey; Fair American,
Lieutenant Chauncey; Hamilton, Lieutenant M'Pherson; Governor Tompkins, Lieutenant Brown; Conquest, Mr. Mallaby;
Asp, Lieutenant Smith; Pert, Lieutenant Adams; Julia, Mr.
Trant; Growler, Mr. Mix; Ontario, Mr. Stevens; Scourge,
Mr. Osgood; Lady of the Lake, Mr. Flinn; and Raven, transport, got out, and it arrived off York, on the morning of the
26th, without loss of any sort.    All the vessels ran in and anchored about a mile from the shore, to the southward and westward of the principal fort.

   Great steadiness and promptitude were displayed in effecting
a landing.    The wind was blowing fresh from the eastward,
but the boats were hoisted out, manned, and received the
troops, with so much order, that in two hours from the commencement of the disembarkation, the whole brigade was on
shore, under the command of Brigadier General Pike.    The
wind drove the boats to leeward of the place that had been
selected for the landing, which was a clear field, to a point
where the Indians and sharp-shooters of the enemy had a cover; but the advance party was thrown ashore with great gallantry, and it soon cleared the bank and thickets, with a loss
of about 40 men.    This movement was covered by a rapid
discharge of grape from the vessels.    As soon as a sufficient
number of troops had got ashore, they were formed by General
Pike in person, who moved on to the assault.    The small vessels now beat up, under a brisk fire from the fort and batteries,
until they had got within six hundred yards of the principal
work, when they opened with effect on the enemy, and contributed largely to the success of the day.    The commodore
directed the movements in person, pulling in in his gig, and
encouraging his officers by the coolness with which he moved
about, under the enemy's fire.    There never was a disembarkation more successfully, or more spiritedly made, considering the state of the weather, and the limited means of the
assailants.    In effecting this service, the squadron had two
midshipmen slain, and 15 men killed and wounded, mostly
while employed in the boats.    After sustaining some loss by
an explosion that killed Brigadier General Pike, the troops so
far carried the place, that it capitulated.    It remained in peace-

able possession of the Americans until the 1st of May, when it was evacuated to proceed on other duty.

The capture of York was attended with many important results, that fully established the wisdom of the enterprise. Although the Prince Regent, the third vessel of the enemy, escaped, by having sailed on the 24th for Kingston, the Duke of Gloucester, which had been undergoing repairs, fell into the hands of the Americans. A vessel of twenty guns, that was nearly finished, was burnt, and a large amount of naval and military stores was also destroyed. A very considerable quantity of the latter, however, was saved, shipped, and sent to Sackett's Harbour. Many boats that had been built for the transportation of troops were also taken. In the entire management of this handsome exploit, the different vessels appear to have been well conducted, and they contributed largely to the complete success which crowned the enterprise.

Although the brigade re-embarked on the 1st of May, the squadron was detained at York until the 8th, by a heavy adverse gale of wind. The men were kept much on deck for more than a week, and the exposure produced many cases of fever, in both branches of the service. More than a hundred of the sailors were reported ill, and the brigade, which had lost 269 men in the attack, the wounded included, was now reduced by disease to about 1000 effectives. As soon as the weather permitted, the commanding naval and army officers crossed in the Lady of the Lake, and selected a place for an encampment about four miles to the eastward of Fort Niagara, when the vessels immediately followed and the troops disembarked.

As soon as released from this great incumbrance on his movements, Commodore Chauncey sailed for the Harbour, with a view to obtain supplies, and to bring up reinforcements for the army. A few of the schooners remained near the head of the lake, but the greater part of the squadron went below, where it arrived on the 11th. The small vessels were now employed in conveying stores and troops to the division under General Dearborn, which was reinforcing fast by arrivals from different directions.

On the 15th of this month the enemy had advanced so far with his new ship, which was called the Wolfe, as to have got in her lower masts, and expedition became necessary, an action for the command of the lake being expected, as soon as this vessel was ready to come out. On the 16th, 100 men

31

were sent to the upper lakes, where Captain Perry, then a
young master and commander, had been ordered to assume
the command, some months previously.  On the 22d, the Madison, with the commodore's pennant still flying in her, embarked 350 troops, and sailed for the camp to the eastward of
the mouth of the Niagara, where she arrived and disembarked
the men on the 25th.  The Fair American, Lieutenant Chauncey, and Pert, Acting Lieutenant Adams, were immediately
ordered down to watch the movements of the enemy at Kingston, and preparations were made, without delay, for a descent
on Fort George.  On the 26th Commodore Chauncey reconnoitred the enemy's coast, and his position ; and that night he
sounded his shore, in person, laying buoys for the government
of the movements of the small vessels, which it was intended
to send close in.  The weather being more favourable, the
Madison, Oneida, and Lady of the Lake, which could be of
no use in the meditated attack, on account of their armaments,
received on board all the heavy artillery of the army, and as
many troops as they could carry, while the rest of the soldiers
embarked in boats.

At 3 A. M., on the 27th of May, the signal was made to
weigh, and the army having previously embarked, at 4 the
squadron stood towards the Niagara.  As the vessels approached the point of disembarkation, the wind so far failed,
as to compel the small vessels to employ their sweeps.  The
Growler, Mr. Mix, and Julia, Mr. Trant, swept into the mouth
of the river, and opened on a battery near the lighthouse.
The Ontario, Mr. Stevens, anchored more to the northward to
cross their fire.  The Hamilton, Lieutenant M'Pherson, the
Asp, Lieutenant Smith, and the Scourge, Mr. Osgood, were directed to stand close in, to cover the landing, to scour the
woods, or any point where the enemy might show himself,
with grape-shot; while the Governor Tompkins, Lieutenant
Brown, and Conquest, Lieutenant Pettigrew, were sent farther
to the westward to attack a battery that mounted one heavy
gun.

Captain Perry had come down from the upper lake on the
evening of the 25th, and on this occasion was the sea-officer
second in rank, present.  Commodore Chauncey confided to
him the duty of attending to the disembarkation of the troops.
The marines of the squadron were embodied with the regiment
of Colonel Macomb, and 400 seamen held in reserve, to land,

if necessary, under the immediate orders of the commodore in person.

When all was ready, the schooners swept into their stations, in the handsomest manner, opening their fire with effect. The boats that contained the advance party, under Colonel Scott, were soon in motion, taking a direction towards the battery near Two Mile Creek, against which the Governor Tompkins and Conquest had been ordered to proceed. The admirable man-ner in which the first of these two little vessels was conducted, drew the applause of all who witnessed it, on Mr. Brown and his people. This officer swept into his station, under fire, in the steadiest manner, anchored, furled his sails, cleared his decks, and prepared to engage, with as much coolness and method, as if coming-to in a friendly port. He then opened with his long gun, with a precision that, in about ten minutes, literally drove the enemy from the battery, leaving the place to his dead. The boats dashed in, under Captain Perry, and Colonel Scott effected a landing with the steadiness and gal-lantry for which that officer is so distinguished. The enemy had concealed a strong party in a ravine, and he advanced to repel the boats ; but the grape and the canister of the schooners, and the steady conduct of the troops, soon drove him back. The moment the command of Colonel Scott got ashore, the suc-cess of the day was assured. He was sustained by the re-mainder of the brigade to which he belonged, then commanded by Brigadier General Boyd, and after a short but sharp con-flict, the enemy was driven from the field. The landing was made about 9 A. M., and by 12 M. the town and fort were in quiet possession of the Americans, the British blowing up and evacuating the latter, and retreating towards Queenston.

In this handsome affair, in which the duty of the vessels was performed with coolness and method, the navy had but one man killed and two wounded. So spirited, indeed, was the manner in which the whole duty was conducted, that the assailants generally suffered much less than the assailed, a circumstance that is, in a great measure, to be ascribed to the good conduct of the covering vessels. General Dearborn reported his loss, on this occasion, at only 17 killed and 45 wounded, while he puts that of the enemy at 90 killed, and 160 wounded, most of whom were regular troops. One hundred prisoners were also made.

Both the commanding general, and the commanding sea-officer, spoke in the highest terms of the conduct of the naval force employed in the descent on Fort George. General Dearborn admitted the extent of his obligations to Commodore Chauncey for the excellent dispositions he had made for landing the troops, always a service of delicacy and hazard, and his judicious arrangements for silencing the batteries, under the fire of which it was necessary to approach the shore. The trifling amount of the loss, is the best evidence how much these thanks were merited. Commodore Chauncey himself commended all under his orders, though he felt it due to their especial services, particularly to mention Captain Perry, and Lieutenant M'Pherson. Lieutenant Brown, of the Governor Tompkins, was signally distinguished, though his name, from some accident, was omitted in the despatches.

The occupation of Fort George brought with it an evacuation by the British of the whole Niagara frontier. Lieutenant Colonel Preston took possession of Fort Erie on the evening of the 28th, and the entire river, for the moment, was left at the command of the Americans. By this success, the squadron obtained the temporary use of another port, Commodore Chauncey running into the Niagara and anchoring, on the afternoon of the 27th. Captain Perry was immediately despatched above the falls, with a small party of seamen, to carry up five vessels that had been purchased, or captured, and which it had not been practicable, hitherto, to get past the enemy's batteries. This duty was performed during the first days of June, though not without infinite labour, as it was found necessary to track the different vessels by the aid of oxen, every inch of the way, against the strong current of the Niagara, a party of soldiers lending their assistance. By the close of the month, that zealous officer had got them all across the lake to Presque Isle, where the two brigs, laid down early in the spring, were launched in the course of May, though their equipment proceeded very slowly, from the state of the roads and a want of men.

## CHAPTER XLII.

WHILE these important movements were in the course of execution near the western end of the lake, others of equal magnitude were attempted near its eastern. The descent on Fort George took place on the 27th of May, and almost at the same moment, Sir George Prevost, the British Commander-in-chief and Commodore Sir J. L. Yeo, meditated a *coup de main* against Sackett's Harbour, in revenge for the blow they had received at York. By destroying the new ship, Commodore Yeo would most probably secure a superiority on the lake for the remainder of the season, the Americans having no cruising vessel but the Madison, fit to lie against the Wolfe or Royal George.

On the morning of the 28th of May, the Wolfe, Royal George, Moira, Prince Regent, Simcoe, and Seneca, with two gun-boats, and a strong brigade of barges and flat-bottomed boats, appeared off Sackett's Harbour. When about two leagues from the shore, a considerable party of troops was placed in the boats, and the whole squadron bore up, with a view to land; but their attention was diverted by the appearance to the westward of a brigade containing nineteen boats, which were transporting troops to the Harbour. The enemy immediately sent his own barges in pursuit, and succeeded in driving twelve boats on shore, and in capturing them, though not until they had been abandoned by the Americans. The remaining seven got into the Harbour. Hoping to intercept another party, the enemy now hauled to the westward, and sent his boats ahead to lie in wait, and the intention to disembark that afternoon was abandoned.

As the day dawned, on the morning of the 29th, a strong division of barges, filled with troops, and covered by the two gun-boats, was seen advancing upon Horse Island, a peninsula at a short distance from the village of Sackett's Harbour. A body of about 800 men effected a landing, accompanied by Sir George Prevost in person, and an irregular and desultory, but spirited engagement took place. At first, the enemy drove all before him, and he advanced quite near the town, but being

31 *

met by a detachment of regulars, he was driven back with loss, and compelled to abandon his enterprise.

In this affair, had the enemy's vessels done as good service as the American vessels performed near the Niagara, the result might have been different; but, though some of them swept up pretty near the shore, they were of no assistance to the troops. Unfortunately false information was given to the sea-officer in charge of the store-houses, and he set fire to them, by which mistake, not only most of the stores taken at York, but many that had come from the sea-board, were consumed. But for this accident, the enemy would have had no consolation for his defeat.

Information reached Commodore Chauncey on the 30th of May, that the enemy was out, and he immediately got under way from the Niagara, looked into York, then ran off Kingston, but falling in with nothing, he crossed to the Harbour, where he anchored; being satisfied that the English squadron had returned to port.

Every exertion was now made to get the new ship afloat, Commodore Chauncey rightly thinking he should not be justified in venturing an action with his present force. Although he had fourteen sail of vessels, which mounted altogether 82 guns, only two had quarters, or were at all suited to close action. As both the Madison and Oneida had been constructed for a very light draught of water, neither was weatherly, though the former acquitted herself respectably; but the latter was dull on all tacks, and what might not have been expected from her construction, particularly so before the wind. The schooners were borne down with metal, and could be of no great service except at long shot. On the other hand, all the enemy's vessels had quarters, most of them drew more water, relatively, and held a better wind than the Americans, and as a whole they were believed to mount about the same number of guns. In the way of metal the English large ships were decidedly superior to the two largest American vessels, mounting several sixty-eight-pound carronades among their other guns.

The keel of the new ship had been laid on the 9th of April, and she was got into the water June 12th. This ship was a large corvette, and was pierced for 26 guns, long twenty-fours, and she mounted two more on circles; one on a topgallant forecastle, and the other on the poop. The day before the launch, Captain Sinclair arrived and was appointed to this ves-

sel, which was called the General Pike. Lieutenant Trenchard, who arrived at the same time, received the command
of the Madison.

Although the Pike was so near completion, there were neither officers nor men for her, on the station ; and the canvass
intended for her sails had been principally burned during the
late attack on the Harbour.    At this time, moreover, while the
service pressed, only 120 men had been sent on lake Erie,
Commodore Chauncey having entertained hopes of being able
to reinforce that station from below, after defeating the enemy.

Lake Champlain had attracted but little of the attention of
either of the belligerents until this summer, as it did not come
in the line of the military operations of the day.    Some small
vessels, however, had been fitted out, on each side of the frontier ; and on the 3d of June, Lieutenant Sidney Smith, who
then commanded on the lake, ventured down into the narrow
part of that water, with two armed sloops called the Eagle and
the Growler, where he was completely exposed to the fire of
musketry from a body of troops on the land.    It appears that
the Eagle sunk, her seams having opened by the discharges
of her guns, and the Growler was compelled to strike, the
wind being fresh at south, rendering a retreat impossible.    On
this occasion, near a hundred prisoners were made by the
enemy, a considerable portion of whom were volunteers from
the army.

After this loss, the government turned its attention towards
the construction of a naval force on that lake, but its movements were slow, the state of the warfare not appearing to
require much exertion in that quarter.    After the capture of
Mr. Smith, however, Lieutenant Thomas M'Donough, an officer who had distinguished himself as the associate of Decatur,
in his chivalrous exploits before Tripoli, was detached for this
service, and appointed to the command of the lake.    Shortly
after, Mr. M'Donough was raised to the rank of a master and
commander ; but so few men were attached to this station, that
when this gallant officer first reached it, and even for some
time afterwards, he actually worked with his own hands, strap-
ping blocks, and performing other similar duties, in order to
prepare some small vessels for service.    An inroad made by
the enemy, about this time, a little quickened the efforts of the
government, however ; for on the 1st of August, Captain Ever-
ard, of the British navy, at the head of a force consisting of
the two captured sloops, three gun-boats, and several batteaux,

made an incursion as far as Plattsburgh, where he destroyed
a considerable amount of stores. He also captured several
small trading vessels before he returned. As Captain M'Donough had no force equal to resisting such inroads, exertions
were made to equip one that should prevent their repetition;
for, in consequence of the territorial division of this lake, its
warfare, on the part of the Americans, was principally defensive.

In the mean time, the efforts on Ontario continued. Early
in June, the British squadron went up the lake, most probably
to carry troops, quitting port in the night; but Commodore
Chauncey very properly decided that the important interests
confided to his discretion required that he should not follow it,
until his squadron was reinforced by the accession of the
Pike, to get which vessel ready, every possible exertion was
making.

On the 14th of June, the Lady of the Lake, Lieutenant W.
Chauncey, left the harbour to cruise off Presque Isle, to intercept the stores of the enemy; and on the 16th, she captured
the schooner Lady Murray, loaded with provisions, shot, and
fixed ammunition. This vessel was in charge of an ensign
and 15 men, the prisoners amounting, in all, to twenty-one.
Mr. Chauncey carried his prize into the harbour on the 18th,
passing quite near the enemy's squadron. The prisoners
reported the launch of a new brig at Kingston.

About this time, the enemy's squadron, consisting of the
Wolfe, Royal George, Moira, Melville, Berresford, Sidney
Smith, and one or two gun-boats, appeared off Oswego. Preparations were made to disembark a party of troops, but the
weather becoming threatening, Sir James Yeo was induced to
defer the descent, and stood to the westward. He then went
off the Genesee, where some provisions were seized and carried away, and a descent was made at Great Sodus, with a
similar object, but which failed, though several buildings were
burned, and some flour was captured. Shortly before, he had
appeared off the coast, to the westward of Niagara, seizing
some boats belonging to the army, loaded with stores. Two
vessels, similarly employed, were also captured.

On the 23d of June, 14 of the guns, and a quantity of the
rigging for the Pike, reached the harbour; and the next day,
Commodore Chauncey advised the government to commence
building a fast-sailing schooner. This recommendation was
followed, and the keel of a vessel that was subsequently called

PEACOCK AND L'EPERVIER.

the Sylph, was soon after laid, her size being determined by
the nature of the materials necessary for her equipment, which
were principally on the spot.

It was the last of June before the people began to arrive for
the Pike; the first draft, consisting of only 35 men, reaching
the harbour on the 29th of that month.   These were followed,
on the 1st of July, by 94 more, from Boston.   It was thought,
by the assistance of the army, that the ship might be got out,
with the aid of these men.   In estimating the embarrassments
of the lake service, in general, the reluctance of the sailors
to serve on those inland waters should not be overlooked.
The stations were known to be sickly, the service was exceedingly arduous, several winter months were to be passed, under
a rigorous climate, in harbours that had none of the ordinary
attractions of a seaport, and the chances for prize-money were
too insignificant to enter into the account.   At this period in
the history of the navy, the men were entered for particular
ships, and not for the general service, as at present; and it
would have been nearly impossible to procure able seamen for
this unpopular duty, had not the means been found to induce
parts of crews to follow their officers from the Atlantic coast,
as volunteers.   A considerable party had been sent from the
Constitution, to Lake Ontario, after her return from the coast
of Brazil; and the arrival of a portion of the crew of the John
Adams, on Lake Erie, has already been mentioned.   On the
8th of July, Captain Crane arrived from the same ship; and
two days later, he was followed by all the officers and men of
that vessel, for which a new crew had been enlisted.   This
timely reinforcement was assigned, in a body, to the Madison,
that ship being nearly of the size and force of the vessel from
which they came.

On the afternoon of the 1st of July, however, or previously
to this important accession to his force, a deserter came in and
reported that Sir James Yeo had left Kingston the previous
night, in 20 large boats, with a body of 800 or 1000 men, with
which he had crossed and landed in Chaumont Bay, about
seven miles from the Harbour.   Here he had encamped in the
woods, concealing his boats with the branches of trees, with an
intention to make an attack on the American squadron, in the
course of the approaching night.   Preparations were accordingly made to receive the expected assault, but the enemy did
not appear.   On the following morning, Commodore Chauncey
went out with the vessels that were ready, and examined the

shore, but the enemy could not be found.  At sunset he returned, and moored the vessels in readiness for the attack.
Still no enemy appeared.  That night and the succeeding day,
five more deserters came in, all corroborating each other's account, by which it would seem that the expedition was abandoned on the night of the 1st, in consequence of the desertion
of the man who had first come in.  At this time, the Pike had
16 of her guns mounted ; and there is little doubt that Commodore Yeo would have been defeated, had he persisted in his
original intention.  By July 3d, the remainder of her armament had reached the Harbour.

On the 21st of July, the Madison, Captain Crane, went off
Kingston, communicating with the commodore by signal, who
remained at anchor in the Pike, which ship was getting ready
as fast as possible.  The same evening the latter went out, accompanied by the squadron, running over to the north shore,
and then steered to the westward.  The winds were light, and
the vessels did not arrive off the mouth of the Niagara, until
the 27th.  Here a small body of troops was embarked under
Colonel Scott, and the squadron proceeded to the head of the
lake, with a view to make a descent at Burlington Bay.  After
landing the troops and marines, and reconnoitring, Colonel
Scott believed the enemy to be too strong, and too well posted,
for the force under his command ; and on the 30th, the vessels weighed and ran down to York.  Here Colonel Scott
landed without opposition, and got possession of the place.
A considerable quantity of provisions, particularly flour, was
seized, five pieces of cannon were found, some shot and powder were brought off, and 11 boats, built to transport troops,
were destroyed.  Some barracks, and other public buildings, were burned.  The troops re-embarked on the 1st of
August, and on the 3d they were disembarked again, in the
Niagara.

At daylight, on the morning of the 7th, while at anchor off
the mouth of the Niagara, the enemy's squadron, consisting
of two ships, two brigs, and two large schooners, were seen to
the northwest, and to windward, distant about six miles.  The
American vessels immediately weighed, and endeavoured to
obtain the weather-gage, the construction of a large portion of
the force rendering this advantage important in a general action.
At this time, Commodore Chauncey had present, the Pike,
Madison, Oneida, Hamilton, Scourge, Ontario, Fair American,
Governor Tompkins, Conquest, Julia, Growler, Asp, and Pert,

or thirteen sail. The size of the lake, which at first view might seem to render it difficult to avoid a combat, was in truth in favour of such a design; the distances being so small, that the retiring party, under ordinary circumstances, would have it in his power to gain a harbour, before its enemy could close. Both commanders, it is now understood, acted under very rigid instructions, it being known that the fortune of the northern war, in a great measure, depended on the command of this lake, and neither party was disposed to incur any undue risks of losing the chance to obtain it.

On the present occasion, however, Commodore Chauncey was anxious to bring the enemy to battle, feeling a sufficient confidence in his officers and men to believe they would render his mixed and greatly divided force sufficiently available. The principal advantage of the enemy was in the identity of character that belonged to his squadron, which enabled him to keep it in compact order, and to give it concentrated and simultaneous evolutions, while the movements of the best of the American vessels, were necessarily controlled by those of their worst. In short, the manœuvring of the American squadron, throughout this entire summer, furnishes an illustration of that nautical principle to which there has elsewhere been an allusion, in an attempt to point out the vast importance of preserving an equality in the properties of ships. Indeed the Pike and Madison alone could compete with vessels of ordinary qualities, the Oneida proving to be so dull, that the Pike was frequently compelled to take her in tow.

At 9 A. M. the Pike, having got abreast of the Wolfe, the leading vessel of the enemy, hoisted her ensign, and fired a few guns to try the range of her shot. Finding that the latter fell short, she wore and hauled to the wind on the other tack, the sternmost of the small schooners being then six miles distant. The enemy wore in succession, also, and got upon the same tack as the American squadron, but ascertaining that the leading vessels of the latter would weather upon him, he soon tacked, and hauled off to the northward. As soon as the rear of the American line was far enough ahead to fetch his wake, signal was made to the squadron to tack once more, and to crowd sail in chase. The wind now gradually fell, and about sunset it was calm, the schooners using their sweeps to close. As night approached, the signal of recall was made, in order to collect the squadron, there being an apprehension that some of the small vessels might be cut off.

In the night the wind came from the westward, and it blew in squalls. All the vessels were at quarters, carrying sail to gain the wind of the enemy, with a view to engage him in the morning. Not long after midnight, a rushing sound was heard ; and several of the vessels felt more or less of a squall; but the strength of the gust passed astern. Soon after, it was ascertained that the Hamilton, Lieutenant Winter, and Scourge, Mr. Osgood, had disappeared. The Pike now spoke the Governor Tompkins, which informed the commodore that the missing schooners had capsized in the squall, and that the whole of their officers and men, with the exception of sixteen of the latter, had been drowned. It is supposed, as all the crews were at quarters, and the guns were loose, that when the gust struck the vessels, their heavy pieces, which worked on slides, with all the shot on deck, went to leeward, and helped to carry the two schooners over. This accident showed how unsuited these vessels were to the service on which they were employed, those lost having been two of the very best in the squadron, mounting between them 19 guns.

The American squadron now hove-to, and soon after daylight the enemy set studding-sails and stood down upon it, apparently with an intention to engage. When a little more than a league distant, however, he brought by the wind, and the signal was made from the Pike to ware and to bring-to on the same tack. After waiting some time for the English ships to come down, Commodore Chauncey edged away for the land, hoping, by getting the breeze which, at that season, usually came off the southern shore, in the afternoon, to obtain the weather-gage. It fell calm, however, and the schooners were ordered to sweep up towards the enemy, and to bring him to action. While the latter were attempting to execute this order, the wind came out light at the eastward, when the Pike took the Oneida in tow, and stood down towards the enemy. The van of the schooners had got within two miles of the English squadron, when the breeze suddenly shifted to the westward, giving the latter the advantage of the wind. Sir James Yeo now bore up, in the expectation of cutting off the American small vessels, before the ships could cover them; but the former, by freely using their sweeps, soon got into their stations again, when the enemy hauled by the wind and hove-to.

It now became squally, and the people having been at quarters nearly two days and nights, and the enemy, who was evidently indisposed to engage, unless on his own terms, pos-

sessing a great advantage in such weather, as the late accident
sufficiently proved, Commodore Chauncey ran in, and anchored
at the mouth of the Niagara.  It blew heavy in squalls
throughout the night, but the enemy being in sight to the northward, at daylight, the squadron weighed and stood out after
him.  Throughout the whole of this day, and of the succeeding
night, under a succession of squalls, light airs, and calms, and
constant changes in the direction of the winds, the American
vessels were endeavouring to close with the enemy, without
success.  At daylight, however, on the morning of the 10th,
Commodore Chauncey, having taken the precaution to get
under the north shore, found himself to windward, with the
enemy bearing S. W.  The Pike now took the Asp, and the
Madison the Fair American in tow, and the whole squadron
kept away, with every prospect of forcing the English to engage.  About noon, and before the squadrons were within
gun-shot of each other, the wind shifted to W. S. W., giving
the enemy the weather-gage.  Throughout the day, there was
a series of unsuccessful manœuvres to close and to gain the
wind, but, about 5 P. M., the enemy was becalmed under the
south shore, and the American squadron got a breeze from
N. N. W., nearing him fast.  At 6, being then distant about
four miles, the line of battle was formed, though the wind had
become very light.  The vessels continued to close until 7,
when a fresh breeze came out at S. W., placing the enemy
once more to windward.  After some manœuvring, the two
squadrons were standing to the northward, with their larboard
tacks aboard, under easy canvass, the enemy astern and to
windward.  It being now pretty certain that with vessels of
qualities so unequal, he could not get the wind of the English,
while the latter were disposed to avoid it, Commodore Chauncey adopted an order of battle that was singularly well adapted
to draw them down, and which was admirable for its advantages and ingenuity.  The American squadron formed in two
lines, one to windward of the other.  The weather line consisted altogether of the smallest of the schooners, having in it,
in the order in which they are named, from the van to the
rear, the Julia, Growler, Pert, Asp, Ontario, and Fair American.  The line to leeward contained, in the same order, the
Pike, Oneida, Madison, Governor Tompkins, and Conquest.
It was hoped that Sir James Yeo would close with the weather
line in the course of the night, and, with a view to bring him
down, the Julia, Growler, Pert, and Asp were directed, after

32

engaging as long as was prudent, to edge away, and to pass
through the intervals left between the leading vessels of the
line to leeward, forming again under their protection, while
the Ontario and Fair American were directed to run into the
leeward line, and form astern of the Conquest.

At half-past 10 P. M. the enemy tacked and stood after the
American squadron, keeping to windward of the weather line.
At 11, the Fair American, the sternmost of the schooners in
this line, began to fire; and the enemy continuing to draw
ahead, in about fifteen minutes the action became general between him and the weather line. At half-past 11 all the
schooners engaged bore up, according to orders, with the exception of the two in the van, which tacked in the hope of
gaining the wind of the English ships, instead of waring, or
bearing up. This unfortunate departure from the order of
battle, entirely changed the state of things; Sir James Yeo,
instead of following the schooners down, as had been expected,
keeping his wind with a view to cut off the two that had separated. Commodore Chauncey now filled, and kept away two
points, in the hope of drawing the enemy from the vessels to
windward, but the English exchanged a few shots with the Pike
in passing, and continued in pursuit of the two schooners. The
American squadron immediately tacked, and endeavoured to
close, with the double view of covering their consorts, and of
engaging. As the chase was to windward, it was impossible to
protect the vessels that had separated, the English ships easily
getting them under their guns, when the former struck, of course.

The vessels captured were the Growler, Lieutenant Deacon;
and the Julia, Mr. Trant. They sustained a small loss before
they surrendered, having, in some measure, repaired the fault
they had committed, by the handsome manner in which they
held on to the last. It was the opinion of Commodore Chauncey, that these schooners were lost through excess of zeal in
their commanders, who thought that a general action was
about to take place, and that by gaining the wind, they might
be of more service, than if stationed to leeward. The result
showed the necessity of complete concert in naval evolutions,
and the virtue of implicit obedience.

Each of the vessels taken by the enemy, carried two guns,
and had a crew of about 40 souls. Some damage was done
to the sails and rigging of the enemy, by the fire of the
schooners; but the American squadron, the Julia and Growler
excepted, received no injury worth mentioning. The Growler

had a man killed, lost her bowsprit, and was a good deal damaged before she struck.

The Pike, after carrying sail hard for some time, finding that she was separating from the rest of the squadron, and that there was no hope of saving the two schooners, rejoined the other vessels, and formed the line again. At daylight, the enemy was seen a long way to windward, it blowing fresh. The small vessels beginning to labour excessively, it became necessary to send two of the dullest of them into the Niagara for security.

The gale continuing, the commodore now determined to run for the Genesee, with the rest of the vessels; but the wind increasing, and the Madison and Oneida not having a day's provisions on board, he stood for the Harbour, where he did not arrive until the 13th, the wind failing before he got in.

---

## CHAPTER XLIII.

WITHOUT waiting for his new vessel, Commodore Chauncey took in provisions for five weeks, and sailed on another cruise the very day of his arrival. On the 16th, the squadron was off the Niagara, and the same day the enemy was made, being eight sail in all. Some manœuvring to obtain the wind followed, but it coming on to blow, the vessels ran into the mouth of the Genesee, and anchored. This was another of the evil consequences of having vessels like the small schooners in the squadron, a sea little heavier than common causing them to labour to a degree that rendered it unsafe to keep the lake. The wind, however, freshened so much as to compel the whole squadron to weigh and bear up, forcing them down the lake under easy canvass. The enemy, it would seem, was also driven to leeward, for he was seen at anchor under the False Ducks, as those islands came in sight. The Fair American and Asp having been sent into the Niagara on duty, the vessels present in the American squadron, on this occasion, were the Pike, Madison, Oneida, Tompkins, Conquest, Ontario, Pert, and Lady of the Lake; the latter having no armament fit for a general engagement. It was now expected that the enemy would be willing to engage, and the vessels were cleared for action. The wind again shifted, however, bringing the English squadron to windward; but by carrying sail hard, the American vessels were weathering on the enemy when the latter ran behind the islands, and was believed to have stood into Kingston. The gale increasing, and the schooners being actually in danger of foundering, Commodore Chauncey bore up for the Harbour, where he arrived on the 19th of the month.

The new vessel had been launched on the 18th, and she was immediately rigged and named the Sylph. Her armament was peculiar, for, in that comparative wilderness, the materials that could be had were frequently taken, in the place of those that were desired. Four long thirty-twos were mounted on circles between her masts, and six sixes were placed in broadside. As this vessel was expected to be weatherly, it was hoped these heavy guns might cut away some of the enemy's spars, and bring on a general action. It is due to the extraordinary capacity of the builder, to say that this schooner was put into the water in twenty-one working days after her keel had been laid.

A promotion had been made previously, and the new commissions were now found at the Harbour. Lieutenant Commandant Woolsey was transferred to the Sylph, with his new rank; Lieutenant Thomas Brown, the officer who had so much distinguished himself at the landing before Fort George, succeeding him in the Oneida.

On the 28th of August, Commodore Chauncey sailed again, with the Pike, Madison, Sylph, Oneida, Tompkins, Conquest, Ontario, Pert, and Lady of the Lake. The enemy was not seen until the 7th of September, when the squadron lying at anchor in, and off, the Niagara, his ships were made out at daylight, close in and to leeward. The signal to weigh was instantly shown, and the Pike, Madison, and Sylph, each taking a schooner in tow, sail was made in chase. The enemy bore up to the northward, and for six days the American squadron followed the English, endeavouring to bring it to action, without success. On the 11th of September, the enemy was becalmed off the Genesee, when the American vessels got a breeze and ran within gun-shot, before the English squadron took the wind. A running fight, that lasted more than three hours, was the result; but the enemy escaped in consequence of his better sailing, it being out of the power of

the American commander to close with more than two of his
vessels, the Sylph being totally unfitted for that species of combat.   As the Pike succeeded in getting several broadsides at
the enemy, he did not escape without being a good deal cut
up, having, according to his own report, an officer and ten
men killed and wounded.   The Pike was hulled a few times,
and other trifling injuries were received, though no person was
hurt.   Previously to this affair, Commodore Chauncey had
been joined by the Fair American and Asp.   On the 12th, Sir
James Yeo ran into Amherst Bay, where the Americans were
unable to follow him, on account of their ignorance of the
shoals.   It was supposed that the English Commodore declined
engaging on this occasion, in consequence of the smoothness
of the water, it being his policy to bring his enemy to action
in blowing weather, when the American schooners would be
nearly useless.

Commodore Chauncey remained off the Ducks until the
17th, when the English squadron succeeded in getting into
Kingston, after which he went into port for despatches and
supplies.   The next day, however, he came out again, and on
the 19th, the enemy was seen in the vicinity of the Ducks.
No notice was now taken of him, but the squadron stood up
the lake, in the hope that the English would follow, and also
with a view of bringing down a brigade of troops, a division
of the army being about to concentrate at Sackett's Harbour,
preparatory to descending the St. Lawrence with a view to
attack Kingston or Montreal.

In a day or two, the squadron got off the Niagara, and anchored.   On the 26th of September, information was received
that Sir James Yeo was at York, with all his squadron.   The
Lady of the Lake was sent across to ascertain the fact, on the
morning of the 27th, and returning the same evening with a
confirmation of the report, the squadron instantly got under
way.   Owing to the wind, the darkness of the night, and the
bad sailing of so many of the vessels, the squadron was not got
into line, until 8 A. M., on the morning of the 28th, when the
Pike, Madison, and Sylph, each took a schooner in tow, as
usual, and sail was made for the north shore.

The English squadron was soon discovered under canvass,
in York Bay, and the American vessels immediately edged
away for it.   Fortunately, the Americans had the weather-
gage, the wind being at the eastward, blowing a good breeze.
As soon as the enemy perceived the American ships approach-

ing, he tacked and stretched out into the lake, in order to get room to manœuvre; Commodore Chauncey forming his line, and 'steering directly for his centre. When the American squadron was about a league distant, the English ships made all sail, on a wind, to the southward. The former now wore in succession, to get on the same tack with the enemy; and as soon as this object was effected, it began to edge away again in order to close.

The enemy had now no alternative between putting up his helm, and running off before the wind, thus satisfactorily demonstrating which party sought, and which avoided a general action, or in allowing the Americans to commence the engagement. Notwithstanding the wariness with which Sir James Yeo had hitherto manœuvred to prevent a decisive combat, he had always maintained the pretension of seeking a conflict, probably with a view to encourage the colonies; and a retreat, at this moment, would have been too unequivocally a flight to admit of palliation. The American squadron was a good deal extended, in consequence of the great difference in the sailing of its vessels, the Pike being considerably ahead of most of her consorts. As the signal was flying for close action, the Governor Tompkins had passed several of the larger vessels, and was next astern of the commodore, while the Madison, which had one of the heaviest of the schooners in tow, was prevented from getting as near as was desirable. The Oneida, too, now showed her worst qualities, no exertions of her gallant commander, Lieutenant Commandant Brown, being able to urge her into the conflict. In this state of things, Sir James Yeo, perceiving that his two sternmost vessels were in danger, and that there was some little chance of cutting off the rear of the American line, determined to tack, and to hazard an engagement.

At ten minutes past meridian, accordingly, the English ships began to tack in succession, while the Pike made a yaw to leeward, edging away rapidly, to get nearer to the enemy's centre. As soon as the two or three leading vessels of the enemy, among which were the Wolfe and Royal George, got round, they opened on the Pike, which ship received their fire for several minutes without returning it. When near enough, she opened in her turn. The Pike, on this occasion, was not only beautifully handled, but her fire was probably as severe as ever came out of the broadside of a ship of her force. For twenty minutes she lay opposed to all the heaviest vessels of the enemy, receiving little or no support from any of her own squadron, with the exception of the Asp, the schooner she had in tow, and the Governor Tompkins. The latter vessel, commanded for the occasion by Lieutenant W. C. B. Finch,* of the Madison, was handled with a gallantry that reflected high credit on that young officer, steadily keeping the station into which she had been so spiritedly carried, and maintaining a warm fire until crippled by the enemy, and unavoidably left astern. When the smoke blew away, during a pause in this sharp combat, it was found that the Wolfe had lost her main and mizzen topmasts and her main-yard, besides receiving other injuries. Cut up so seriously, she put away dead before the wind, crowding all the canvass she could carry on her forward spars. At this moment, the Royal George luffed up in noble style, across her stern, to cover the English commodore, who ran off to leeward, passing through his own line, in order to effect his retreat.

When the English squadron bore up, the American vessels followed, maintaining a heavy fire with as many of their circle and chase guns as could reach the enemy. It was now found that the armament of the Sylph was not suited to service, the guns between her masts being so crowded as not to allow of their being used with freedom, or rapidity, more especially when in chase. This circumstance, notwithstanding her size and sailing, rendered her of little more use than one of the smaller schooners.

After pursuing the enemy about two hours, during which time the squadron had run nearly up to the head of the lake, where the former had a post at Burlington Bay, and finding that the English ships outsailed most of his vessels, Commodore Chauncey made the signal to haul off with a view to stand in for the Niagara. As the enemy was effectually beaten, and there is scarcely a doubt, would have been destroyed, had he been pressed, this order has been much criticised, as uncalled for, and unfortunate. The motives which influenced the American commander, however, were marked by that discretion and thoughtfulness, which are among the highest attributes of an officer, and which distinguished his whole career, while entrusted with the arduous and responsible service over which he presided during the war.

The wind was increasing, and it shortly after came on to

---

* Now Captain W. C. Bolton.

blow an easterly gale, and an action, under such circumstances, would probably have caused both squadrons to be thrown ashore, there being nothing but a roadstead, under Burlington heights, which the wind that then blew swept. As the enemy was known to have a considerable land force at this point, all who were driven ashore, would necessarily have fallen into his hands ; and had he succeeded in getting off one or two of the smaller vessels, he would effectually have obtained the command of the lake. By going into the Niagara, on the other hand, the American squadron was in a position to intercept the retreat of the enemy, who was in a *cul de sac ;* and after waiting for more moderate weather, he might be attacked even at anchor, should it be deemed expedient, under much more favourable circumstances. In addition to these reasons, which were weighty, and worthy of a commander of reflection and judgment, the Pike had received a shot or two beneath her water line, which required that her pumps should be kept going, a toil, that united to the labour of an action, would have finally exhausted the strength of the ship's company. The enemy had batteries to command the anchorage, too ; and no doubt he would have established more, had the Americans gone in.

In the action of the 28th of September, the Pike suffered a good deal, both in her hull and aloft, bearing the weight of the enemy's fire for most of the time. Her main-top-gallant-mast was shot away early in the engagement, and her bowsprit, foremast, and mainmast were all wounded. Her rigging and sails were much cut up, and she had been repeatedly hulled ; two or three times below the water line, as already stated. Five of her men, only, were killed and wounded by shot. While bearing up in chase, however, the starboard bow gun bursted, by which accident twenty-two men were either slain, or seriously injured. The topgallant forecastle was torn up by this explosion, rendering its circle gun useless during the remainder of the day. Four of the other guns also cracked in the muzzles, producing great distrust about using them. The Madison received some slight injuries, and the Oneida had her main-topmast badly wounded. But no person was hurt in either of these vessels. The Governor Tompkins lost her foremast. On the part of the enemy, the Wolfe and Royal George suffered most ; and it is believed that the former vessel sustained a very heavy loss in men. It is also understood, that one, if not two, of the enemy's smallest vessels struck ; but the

Pike declining to take possession, in the eagerness to close with the Wolfe, they eventually escaped.

On the 2d, the wind coming round light to the westward, and the last transport having been sent down the lake with troops, the squadron weighed, and stretched out to look for the enemy. At 10 A. M. he was seen standing down, under studding sails. The instant the American vessels were made, however, the enemy came by the wind and carried sail to keep off. During the remainder of this day, the English ships gained on the American, and at daylight on the 3d they were seen at anchor, close in under an island between Twelve and Twenty Mile Creeks. It blew quite heavily in gusts throughout the day, both squadrons turning to windward, the enemy being nearly up with the head of the lake at sunset. The night proved dark and squally, with a good deal of rain, and every precaution was taken to prevent the enemy from getting past, as he was now caught, as it might be, in a net.

The next morning the weather was thick, and nothing could be seen of the English squadron. It falling calm at noon, the Lady of the Lake was ordered to the westward, to sweep up to ascertain the position of the enemy, or whether he had not anchored again in Burlington Bay. At 9 P. M. that schooner returned, and reported that the English squadron was not to be seen, only two gun-boats being visible. As a discreet and experienced officer had been sent on this service, Commodore Chauncey immediately inferred that the enemy had got past him, during the darkness of the preceding night, and that he had gone down the lake, either to cut off the American transports, or to get into Kingston. Sail was immediately made to run off the Ducks, with a view to intercept Sir James Yeo, or any prizes he might have taken. It is now known that the officers of the Lady of the Lake were deceived, the British fleet actually lying at anchor so close under the heights that their hulls and spars were confounded with objects on the shore ; the gentleman sent to ascertain the fact being too eager to report the supposed escape of the enemy, to go near enough in to make certain of the truth.

That night and the succeeding day the American squadron made a great run, the wind blowing heavily from the N. W. At 3 P. M., on the 5th, seven sail were seen ahead, near the False Ducks, and no doubts were entertained that they were the British squadron. All sail was carried to close, but at 4 the chases were made out to be schooners and sloops. Signals

were now shown for the Sylph and Lady of the Lake to cast
off their tows, and to chase to the N. E. This induced the
strangers to separate, when the Pike cast off the Governor
Tompkins, and past ahead also. The strangers now set fire
to one of their vessels, the other six crowding sail to escape.
At sunset, when opposite the Real Ducks, the British vessels
the Confiance, Hamilton, and Mary, struck to the Pike. The
Sylph soon after joined, bringing down with her another prize,
the Drummond cutter, and early next morning the same schooner brought out of the Ducks the Lady Gore. The Enterprise,
the seventh vessel, escaped.

The prizes were gun-vessels, carrying from one to three
guns each, and were employed as transports; a part of one of
the German regiments in the British service being on board at
the time. The whole number of prisoners made amounted to
264, including officers. Among the latter were a lieutenant
and two master's mates of the British Royal Navy, and four
masters of the provincial marine. Ten officers of the army
were also taken. The Confiance and Hamilton, two of the
prizes, were the schooners Growler and Julia, taken on the
night of the 8th of August, which, the enemy had rightly
judged, would prove an incumbrance rather than an accession
to their squadron, and had declined receiving them in it. This
circumstance, of itself, sufficiently proves the equivocal advantage enjoyed by the possession of these craft, which formed so
conspicuous a part of Commodore Chauncey's force on paper,
the enemy being unwilling to injure the manœuvring of his
vessels by using them.

Early in November, Commodore Chauncey was lying at the
outlet of the St. Lawrence, below the east end of Long Island,
when Sir James Yeo came out with his ships, and anchored
within two leagues of him, the squadrons being separated by
a chain of small islands. There was but one passage by
which this chain could be passed, and the Americans sent
boats to sound it, intending to lighten and go through, when
the enemy lifted his anchors and returned to port. On the
11th, the army having gone down the river, the American
squadron went into the Harbour.

Two days later, Commodore Chauncey, who had now an almost undisturbed possession of the lake, went to the Genesee,
where, on the 16th of the month, he took on board 1100 men,
belonging to the army of General Harrison. A severe gale
came on, by which the vessels were separated, some being

driven as far west as the head of the lake.   The transports, into which most of the small schooners were now converted, having been finally despatched, the commodore went off Kingston again, to occupy the enemy, and to cover the passage of the troops.   All the transports had arrived on the 21st but the Julia, which did not get in until a few days later.   The Fair American had gone ashore near the Niagara, during the gale, but was got off, and reached the Harbour on the 27th.   By this time, the navigation of the lake was virtually closed, and it being too late to attempt any naval operations, while the duty of transporting the troops and stores had been successfully performed, preparations were made to lay the vessels up for the winter.

## CHAPTER XLIV.

In the course of the winter of 1812–13, Captain O. H. Perry, then a young master and commander at the head of the flotilla of gun-boats, at Newport, Rhode Island, finding no immediate prospect of getting to sea in a sloop of war, volunteered for the lake service.   Captain Perry brought on with him a number of officers, and a few men, and Commodore Chauncey gladly availed himself of the presence of an officer of his rank, known spirit, and zeal, to send him on the upper lakes, in command, where he arrived in the course of the winter.   From this time, until the navigation opened, Captain Perry was actively employed, under all the embarrassments of his frontier position, in organising and creating a force, with which he might contend with the enemy for the mastery of those important waters. Two large brigs, to mount 20 guns each, were laid down at Presque Isle, and a few gun-vessels, or schooners, were also commenced.   The spring passed in procuring guns, shot, and other supplies ; and, as circumstances allowed, a draft of men would arrive from below, to aid in equipping the different vessels.   As soon as the squadron of Commodore Chauncey appeared off the mouth of Niagara, Captain Perry, with some of his officers, went to join it, and the former was efficiently employed in superintending the disembarkation of the troops, as has been already related.  The fall of Fort George produced that of Fort Erie, when the whole of the Niagara frontier came under the control of the American army.

Captain Perry now repaired to his own command, and with infinite labour, he succeeded in getting the vessels that had so long been detained in the Niagara, by the enemy's batteries, out of the river.  This important service was effected by the 12th of June, and preparations were immediately commenced for appearing on the lake.  These vessels consisted of the brig Caledonia, (a prize,) and the schooners Catherine, Ohio, and Amelia; with the sloop Contractor.  The Catherine was named the Somers, the Amelia the Tigress, and the Contractor the Trippe.  At this time, the enemy had a cruising force under the orders of Captain Finnis, which consisted of the Queen Charlotte, a ship of between three and four hundred tons, and mounting 17 guns; the Lady Prevost, a fine warlike schooner, of about two hundred tons, that mounted 13 guns; the brig Hunter, a vessel a little smaller, of 10 guns, and three or four lighter cruisers.  He was also building, at Malden, a ship of near five hundred tons measurement, that was to mount 19 guns, and which was subsequently called the Detroit.

It was near the middle of June before Captain Perry was ready to sail from the outlet of Lake Erie, for Presque Isle.  There being no intention to engage the enemy, and little dread of meeting him in so short a run, as she came in sight of her port each vessel made the best of her way.  The enemy had chosen this moment to look into Presque Isle, and both squadrons were in view from the shore, at the same time, though, fortunately for the Americans, the English did not get a sight of them, until they were too near the land to be intercepted.  As the last vessel got in, the enemy hove in sight, in the offing.

The two brigs laid down in the winter, under the directions of Commodore Chauncey, had been launched towards the close of May, and were now in a state of forwardness.  They were called the Lawrence and the Niagara.  The schooners also were in the water, and Captain Perry, having all his vessels in one port, employed himself in getting them ready for service, as fast as possible.  Still various stores were wanting.  There was a great deficiency of men, particularly of seamen, and Captain Perry, and Mr. D. Turner, were, as yet, the only commissioned sea-officers on the lake.  The latter, moreover, was quite young in years, as well as in rank.

Presque Isle, or, as the place is now called, Erie, was a

good and spacious harbour; but it had a bar on which there was less than seven feet of water.   This bar, which had hitherto answered the purposes of a fortification, now offered a serious obstruction to getting the brigs on the lake.   It lay about half a mile outside, and offered great advantages to the enemy for attacking the Americans while employed in passing it.   So sensible was Captain Perry of this disadvantage, that he adopted the utmost secresy in order to conceal his intentions, for it was known that the enemy had spies closely watching his movements.

Captain Barclay had lately superseded Captain Finnis in the command of the English force, and for near a week he had been blockading the American vessels, evidently with an intention to prevent their getting out, it being known that this bar could be crossed only in smooth water.   On Friday, the 2d of August, he suddenly disappeared in the northern board.

The next day but one was Sunday, and the officers were ashore seeking the customary relaxation.   Without any appearances of unusual preparation, Captain Perry privately gave the order to repair on board the respective vessels and to drop down to the bar.   This command was immediately obeyed; and at about 2 P. M., the Lawrence had been towed to the point where the deepest water was to be found.   Her guns were whipped out, loaded and shotted as they were, and landed on the beach; two large scows, prepared for the purpose, were hauled alongside, and the work of lifting the brig proceeded as fast as possible.   Pieces of massive timber had been run through the forward and after ports, and when the scows were sunk to the water's edge, the ends of the timbers were blocked up, supported by these floating foundations.   The plugs were now put in the scows, and the water was pumped out of them.   By this process, the brig was lifted quite two feet, though, when she was got on the bar, it was found that she still drew too much water.   It became necessary, in consequence, to come-up every thing, to sink the scows anew, and to block up the timbers afresh.   This duty occupied the night.

The schooners had crossed the bar, and were moored outside, and preparations were hurriedly made to receive an attack.   About 8 A. M., the enemy re-appeared.   At this time, the Lawrence was just passing the bar.   A distant, short, and harmless cannonade ensued, though it had the effect to keep the enemy from running in.   As soon as the Lawrence was

33

in deep water, her guns were hoisted in, manned as fast as mounted, and the brig's broadside was sprung to bear on the English squadron. Fortunately, the Niagara crossed on the first trial ; and before night, all the vessels were as ready for service, as circumstances would then allow. The enemy remained with his topsails to the mast half an hour, sullenly reconnoitring ; he then filled, and went up the lake under a press of canvass.

This occurred on the 4th of August, and on the 5th, Captain Perry sailed in quest of the enemy, having received on board a number of soldiers and volunteers. He ran off Long Point, and sweeping the Canada shore for some distance, returned to Erie on the 8th. Taking in some supplies, he was about to proceed up the lake again, when intelligence arrived that a party sent from below, under Lieutenant Elliott, was at Cattaraugus, on its way to join the squadron. A vessel was immediately sent for this acceptable reinforcement. Shortly after its arrival, the commissions that had been made out some time previously, were received from below. By these changes, Mr. Elliott became a master and commander, and Messrs. Holdup, Packett, Yarnall, Edwards, and Conklin, were raised to the rank of lieutenants. Most of these gentlemen, however, had been acting for some months.

The American squadron now consisted of the Lawrence 20, Captain Perry ; Niagara 20, Captain Elliott ; Caledonia 3, Mr. M'Grath, a purser ; Ariel 4, Lieutenant Packett ; Trippe 1, Lieutenant Smith ; Tigress 1, Lieutenant Conklin ; Somers 2, Mr. Alney ; Scorpion 2, Mr. Champlin ; Ohio 1, Mr. Dobbins ; and Porcupine 1, Mr. Senatt. On the 18th of August, this force sailed from Erie, and off Sandusky, a few days later, it chased, and was near capturing one of the enemy's schooners.

The squadron cruised for several days, near the entrance of the strait, when Captain Perry was taken ill with the fever peculiar to these waters, and shortly after the vessels went into Put-in Bay, a harbour, among some islands that lay at no great distance.

Here a few changes occurred, Mr. Smith going to the Niagara, and Mr. Holdup to the Trippe ; Mr. M'Grath went also to the Niagara, and Mr. Turner took command of the Caledonia. The Ohio was sent down the lake on duty.

While in port, on this occasion, Captain Perry contemplated an attack on the enemy's vessels, by means of boats ; and

orders were issued, accordingly, to drill the people with muffled oars.

The squadron was still lying at Put-in Bay on the morning
of the 10th of September, when, at daylight, the enemy's ships
were discovered at the N. W. from the mast-head of the Lawrence.   A signal was immediately made for all the vessels to
get under way.   The wind was light at S. W., and there was
no mode of obtaining the weather-gage of the enemy, a very
important measure with the peculiar armament of the largest
of the American vessels, but by beating round some small
islands that lay in the way.   It being thought there was not
sufficient time for this, though the boats were got ahead to tow,
a signal was about to be made for the vessels to ware, and to
pass to leeward of the islands, with an intention of giving the
enemy this great advantage, when the wind shifted to S. E.
By this change the American squadron was enabled to pass in
the desired direction, and to gain the wind.   When he perceived the American vessels clearing the land, or about 10
A. M., the enemy hove-to, in a line, with his ships' heads to
the southward and westward.   At this time the two squadrons
were about three leagues asunder, the breeze being still at S.
E., and sufficient to work with.   After standing down, until
about a league from the English, where a better view was got
of the manner in which the enemy had formed his line, the
leading vessels of his own squadron being within hail, Captain
Perry communicated a new order of attack.   It had been expected that the Queen Charlotte, the second of the English
vessels, in regard to force, would be at the head of their line,
and the Niagara had been destined to lead in, and to lie against
her, Captain Perry having reserved for himself a commander's
privilege of engaging the principal vessel of the opposing
squadron ; but, it now appearing that the anticipated arrangement had not been made, the plan was promptly altered.
Captain Barclay had formed his line with the Chippeway, Mr.
Campbell, armed with one gun on a pivot, in the van ; the
Detroit, his own vessel, next ; and the Hunter, Lieutenant
Bignall ; Queen Charlotte, Captain Finnis ; Lady Prevost,
Lieutenant Commandant Buchan ; and Little Belt astern, in
the order named.   To oppose this line, the Ariel, of four long
twelves, was stationed in the van, and the Scorpion, of one
long and one short gun on circles, next her.   The Lawrence,
Captain Perry, came next ; the two schooners just mentioned
keeping on her weather bow, having no quarters.   The Cale-

donia, Lieutenant Turner, was the next astern, and the Niagara, Captain Elliot, was placed next to the Caledonia. These vessels were all up at the time, but the other light craft were more or less distant, each endeavouring to get into her berth. The order of battle for the remaining vessels, directed the Tigress to fall in astern of the Niagara, the Somers next, and then the Porcupine and Trippe, in the order named.

By this time the wind had got to be very light, but the leading vessels were all in their stations, and the remainder were endeavouring to get in as fast as possible. The English vessels presented a very gallant array, and their appearance was beautiful and imposing. Their line was compact, with the heads of the vessels still to the southward and westward; their ensigns were just opening to the air; their vessels were freshly painted, and their canvass was new and perfect. The American line was more straggling. The order of battle required them to form within half a cable's length of each other, but the schooners astern could not close with the vessels ahead, which sailed faster, and had more light canvass, until some considerable time had elapsed.

A few minutes before twelve, the Detroit threw a twenty-four-pound shot at the Lawrence, then on her weather quarter, distant between one and two miles. Captain Perry now passed an order by trumpet, through the vessels astern, for the line to close to the prescribed order; and soon after, the Scorpion was hailed, and directed to begin with her long gun. At this moment, the American vessels in line were edging down upon the English, those in front being necessarily nearer to the enemy than those more astern, with the exception of the Ariel and Scorpion, which two schooners had been ordered to keep well to windward of the Lawrence. As the Detroit had an armament of long guns, Captain Barclay manifested his judgment in commencing the action in this manner; and in a short time, the firing between that ship, the Lawrence, and the two schooners at the head of the American line, got to be very animated. The Lawrence now showed a signal for the squadron to close, each vessel in her station, as previously designated. A few minutes later the vessels astern began to fire, and the action became general but distant. The Lawrence, however, appeared to be the principal aim of the enemy, and before the firing had lasted any material time, the Detroit, Hunter, and Queen Charlotte, were directing most of their efforts against her. The American brig endeavoured to close,

and did succeed in getting within reach of canister, though
not without suffering materially, as she fanned down upon the
enemy.　At this time, the support of the two schooners ahead,
which were well commanded and fought, was of the greatest
moment to her ; for the vessels astern, though in the line, could
be of little use n diverting the fire, on account of their positions
and the distance.　After the firing had lasted some time, the
Niagara hailed the Caledonia, and directed the latter to make
room for the former to pass ahead.　Mr. Turner put his helm
up in the most dashing manner, and continued to near the
enemy, until he was closer to his line, perhaps, than the commanding vessel ; keeping up as warm a fire as his small armament would allow.　The Niagara now became the vessel next
astern of the Lawrence.

The cannonade had the usual effect of deadening the wind,
and for two hours there was very little air.　During all this
time, the weight of the enemy's fire was directed against the
Lawrence ; the Queen Charlotte having filled, passed the Hunter, and closed with the Detroit, where she kept up a destructive cannonading on this devoted vessel.　These united attacks
dismantled the American brig, besides producing great slaughter on board her.　At the end of two hours and a half, agreeably to the report of Captain Perry, the enemy having filled,
and the wind increasing, the two squadrons drew slowly ahead,
the Lawrence necessarily falling astern and partially out of the
combat.　At this moment the Niagara passed to the southward
and westward, a short distance to windward of the Lawrence,
steering for the head of the enemy's line, and the Caledonia
followed to leeward.

The vessels astern had not been idle, but, by dint of sweeping and sailing, they had all got within reach of their guns,
and had been gradually closing, though not in the prescribed
order.　The rear of the line would seem to have inclined down
towards the enemy, bringing the Trippe, Lieutenant Holdup,
so near the Caledonia, that the latter sent a boat to her for a
supply of cartridges.

Captain Perry, finding himself in a vessel that had been
rendered nearly useless by the injuries she had received, and
which was dropping out of the combat, got into his boat, and
pulled after the Niagara, on board of which vessel he arrived
at about half-past 2.　Soon after, the colours of the Lawrence
were hauled down, that vessel being literally a wreck.

After a short consultation between Captains Perry and

33 *

Elliott, the latter volunteered to take the boat of the former, and to proceed and bring the small vessels astern, which were already briskly engaged, into still closer action. This proposal being accepted, Captain Elliott pulled down the line, passing within hail of all the small vessels astern, directing them to close within half pistol-shot of the enemy, and to throw in grape and canister, as soon as they could get the desired positions. He then repaired on board the Somers, and took charge of that schooner in person.

When the enemy saw the colours of the Lawrence come down, he confidently believed that he had gained the day. His men appeared over the bulwarks of the different vessels and gave three cheers. For a few minutes, indeed, there appears to have been, as if by common consent, nearly a general cessation in the firing, during which both parties were preparing for a desperate and final effort. The wind had freshened, and the position of the Niagara, which brig was now abeam of the leading English vessel, was commanding; while the gun-vessels astern, in consequence of the increasing breeze, were enabled to close very fast.

At 45 minutes past 2, or when time had been given to the gun-vessels to receive the order mentioned, Captain Perry showed the signal from the Niagara, for close action, and immediately bore up, under his foresail, topsails, and topgallant-sail. As the American vessels hoisted their answering flags, this order was received with three cheers, and it was obeyed with alacrity and spirit. The enemy had attempted to ware round, to get fresh broadsides to bear, in doing which his line got into confusion, and the two ships for a short time, were foul of each other, while the Lady Prevost had so far shifted her berth, as to be both to the westward and to the leeward of the Detroit. At this critical moment, the Niagara came steadily down, within half pistol-shot of the enemy, standing between the Chippeway and Lady Prevost, on one side, and the Detroit, Queen Charlotte, and Hunter, on the other. In passing, she poured in her broadsides, starboard and larboard, ranged ahead of the ships, luffed athwart their bows, and continued delivering a close and deadly fire. The shrieks from the Detroit, proclaimed that the tide of battle had turned. At the same moment, the gun-vessels and Caledonia were throwing in close discharges of grape and canister astern. A conflict so fearfully close, and so deadly, was necessarily short. In fifteen or twenty minutes after the Niagara bore up, a hail was passed among the small vessels, to say that the enemy had struck, and an officer of the Queen Charlotte appeared on the taffrail of that ship, waving a white handkerchief, bent to a boarding-pike.

As soon as the smoke cleared away, the two squadrons were found partly intermingled. The Niagara lay to leeward of the Detroit, Queen Charlotte, and Hunter; and the Caledonia, with one or two of the gun-vessels, was between the latter and the Lady Prevost. On board the Niagara, the signal for close action was still abroad, while the small vessels were sternly wearing their answering flags. The Little Belt and Chippeway were endeavouring to escape to leeward, but they were shortly after brought-to by the Scorpion and Trippe; while the Lawrence was lying astern and to windward, with the American colours again flying. The battle had commenced about noon, and it terminated at 3, with the exception of a few shots fired at the two vessels that attempted to escape, which were not overtaken until an hour later.

In this decisive action, so far as their people were concerned, the two squadrons suffered in nearly an equal degree, the manner in which the Lawrence was cut up, being almost without an example in naval warfare. It is understood that when Captain Perry left her, she had but one gun on her starboard side, or that on which she was engaged, which could be used, and that gallant officer is said to have aided in firing it in person the last time it was discharged. Of her crew, 22 were killed, and 61 were wounded, most of the latter severely. When Captain Perry left her, taking with him his own brother and six of his people, there remained on board but 14 sound men. The Niagara had 2 killed, and 25 wounded, or about one-fourth of all at quarters. This was the official report; but, according to the statement of her surgeon, her loss was 5 killed, and 27 wounded. The other vessels suffered relatively less. The Caledonia, Lieutenant Turner, though carried into the hottest of the action, and entirely without quarters, had 3 men wounded; the Trippe, Lieutenant Holdup, which, for some time, was quite as closely engaged, and was equally without quarters, had 2 men wounded; the Somers, Mr. Almy, the same; the Ariel, Lieutenant Packett, had 1 man killed, and 3 wounded; the Scorpion, Mr. Champlin, had 2 killed, one of whom was a midshipman; the Tigress, Lieutenant Conklin, and Porcupine, Mr. Senatt, had no one hurt. The total loss of the squadron was 27 killed, and 96 wounded, or altogether 123 men; of whom 12 were quarter-deck officers. More than a hundred men were unfit for duty, among the different vessels, previously to the action, cholera morbus and dysentery prevailing in the squadron. Captain Perry himself was labouring under debility, from a recent attack of the lake fever, and could hardly be said to be in a proper condition for service, when he met the enemy; a circumstance that greatly enhances the estimate of his personal exertions on this memorable occasion. Among the Americans slain, were Lieutenant Brooks, the commanding marine officer, and Messrs. Laub and Clark, midshipmen; and among the wounded, Messrs. Yarnall and Forrest, the first and second lieutenants of the Lawrence, Mr. Taylor, her master, Mr. Hambleton, her purser, and Messrs. Swartwout and Claxton, two of her midshipmen. Mr. Edwards, second lieutenant of the Niagara, and Mr. Cummings, one of her midshipmen, were also wounded.

For two hours the weight of the enemy's fire had been thrown into the Lawrence; and the water being perfectly smooth, his long guns had committed great havoc, before the carronades of the American vessels could be made available. For much of this period, it is believed that the efforts of the enemy were little diverted, except by the fire of the two leading schooners, a gun of one of which (the Ariel) had early bursted, the two long guns of the large brigs, and the two long guns of the Caledonia. Although the enemy undoubtedly suffered by this fire, it was not directed at a single object, as was the case with that of the English, who appeared to think that by destroying the American commanding vessel they would conquer. It is true that carronades were used on both sides, at an earlier stage of the action than that mentioned, but there is good reason for thinking that they did but little execution for the first hour. When they did tell, the Lawrence, the vessel nearest to the enemy, if the Caledonia be excepted, necessarily became their object, and, by this time, the efficiency of her own battery was much lessened. As a consequence of these peculiar circumstances, her starboad bulwarks were nearly beaten in; and even her larboard were greatly injured, many of the enemy's heavy shot passing through both sides; while every gun was finally disabled in the batteries fought. Although much has been justly said of the manner in which the Bon Homme Richard and the Essex were injured, neither of those ships suffered, relatively, in a degree proportioned to the Lawrence. Distinguished as were the two former vessels,

for the indomitable resolution with which they withstood the
destructive fire directed against them, it did not surpass that
manifested on board the latter ; and it ought to be mentioned,
that throughout the whole of this trying day, her people, who
had been so short a time acting together, manifested a steadiness and a discipline worthy of veterans.

Although the Niagara suffered in a much less degree, 27
men killed and wounded, in a ship's company that mustered
little more than 100 souls at quarters, under ordinary circumstances, would be thought a large proportion.  Neither the
Niagara nor any of the smaller vessels were injured in an
unusual manner in their hulls, spars, and sails, the enemy having expended so much of his efforts against the Lawrence, and
being so soon silenced when that brig and the gun-vessels got
their raking positions, at the close of the conflict.

The injuries sustained by the English were more divided,
but were necessarily great.  According to the official report
of Captain Barclay, his vessels lost 41 killed, and 94 wounded, making a total of 135, including twelve officers, the precise number lost by the Americans.  No report has been published, in which the loss of the respective vessels was given ;
but the Detroit had her first lieutenant killed, and her commander, Captain Barclay, with her purser, wounded.  Captain
Finnis, of the Queen Charlotte, was also slain, and her first
lieutenant was wounded.  The commanding officer and first
lieutenant of the Lady Prevost were among the wounded, as
were the commanding officers of the Hunter and Chippeway.
All the vessels were a good deal injured in their sails and hulls ;
the Queen Charlotte suffering most in proportion.  Both the
Detroit and Queen Charlotte rolled the masts out of them, at
anchor at Put-in Bay, in a gale of wind, two days after the
action.

It is not easy to make a just comparison between the forces
of the hostile squadrons on this occasion.  In certain situations
the Americans would have been materially superior, while in
others the enemy might possess the advantage in perhaps an
equal degree.  In the circumstances under which the action
was actually fought, the peculiar advantages and disadvantages
were nearly equalized, the lightness of the wind peventing
either of the two largest of the American vessels from profiting by its peculiar mode of efficiency, until quite near the
close of the engagement, and particularly favouring the armament of the Detroit ; while the smoothness of the water ren-

dered the light vessels of the Americans very destructive as
soon as they could be got within a proper range.  The Detroit has been represented on good authority, to have been both
a heavier and stronger ship, than either of the American brigs,
and the Queen Charlotte proved to be a much finer vessel than
had been expected ; while the Lady Prevost was found to be
a large, warlike schooner.  It was, perhaps, unfortunate for
the enemy, that the armaments of the two last were not available under the circumstances which rendered the Detroit so
efficient, as it destroyed the unity of his efforts.  In short, the
battle, for near half its duration, appears to have been fought,
so far as efficiency was concerned, by the long guns of the
two squadrons.  This was particularly favourable to the Detroit and to the American gun-vessels ; while the latter fought
under the advantages of smooth water, and the disadvantages
of having no quarters.  The sides of the Detroit, which were
unusually stout, were filled with shot that did not penetrate.

In the number of men at quarters, there could have been no
great disparity in the two squadrons.  Mr. Yarnall, the first
lieutenant of the Lawrence, testified before a court of inquiry,
in 1815, that the brig to which he belonged had but " 131 men
and boys, of every description" on board her, and that of these
but 103 were fit for duty in the action.  The Niagara was
nearly in the same state.  A part of the crews of all the vessels belonged to the militia.  Indeed, without a large proportion of volunteers from the army, the battle could not have
been fought.  The British were no better off, having a considerable proportion of soldiers on board their vessels, though
men of that description were probably as efficient in smooth
water, and under the actual circumstances, as ordinary sailors.

Captain Perry, in his report of the action, eulogised the conduct of his second in command, Captain Elliott ; that of Mr.
Turner, who commanded the Caledonia ; and that of the officers
of his own vessel.  He also commended the officers of the
Niagara, Mr. Packett of the Ariel, and Mr. Champlin of the
Scorpion.  It is now believed that the omission of the names
of the commanders of the gun-vessels astern, was accidental.
It would seem that these vessels, in general, were conducted
with great gallantry.  Towards the close of the action, indeed,
the Caledonia, and some of the gun-vessels, would appear to
have been handled with a boldness, considering their total
want of quarters, bordering on temerity.  They are known to
have been within hail of the enemy, at the moment he struck,
and to have been hailed by him.  The grape and canister

thrown by the Niagara and the schooners, during the last ten minutes of the battle, and which missed the enemy, rattled through the spars of the friendly vessels, as they lay opposite to each other, raking the English ahead and astern.

Captain Perry was criticised, at the time, for the manner in which he had brought his squadron into action, it being thought he should have waited until his line was more compactly formed, and his small vessels could have closed. It has been said, that " an officer seldom went into action worse, or got out of it better." Truth is too often made the sacrifice of antithesis. The mode of attack appears to have been deemed by the enemy judicious, an opinion that speaks in its favour. The lightness of the wind, in edging down, was the only circumstance that was particularly adverse to the American vessels, but its total failure could not have been foreseen. The shortness of the distances on the lake rendered escape so easy, when an officer was disposed to avoid a battle, that no commander, who desired an action, would have been pardonable for permitting a delay on such a plea. The line of battle was highly judicious, the manner in which the Lawrence was supported by the Ariel and Scorpion being simple and ingenious. By steering for the head of the enemy's line, the latter was prevented from gaining the wind by tacking, and when Captain Elliott imitated this manœuvre in the Niagara, the American squadron had a very commanding position, of which Captain Perry promptly availed himself. In a word, the American commander appears to have laid his plan with skill and judgment, and, in all in which it was frustrated, it would seem to have been the effect of accident. There has never been but one opinion of the manner in which he redeemed his error, even admitting that a fault was made at the outset ; the united movements of the Niagara and of the small vessels, at the close of the action, having been as judicious as they were gallant and decisive. The personal deportment of Captain Perry, throughout the day, was worthy of all praise. He did not quit his own vessel when she became useless, to retire from the battle, but to gain it ; an end that was fully obtained, and an effort which resulted in a triumph.

The British vessels appear to have been gallantly fought, and were surrendered only when the battle was hopelessly lost. The fall of their different commanders was materially against them, though it is not probable the day could have been recovered after the Niagara gained the head of their line and the gun-vessels had closed.  If the enemy made an error, it was in not tacking when he attempted to ware, but it is quite probable that the condition of his vessels did not admit of the former manœuvre.  There was an instant when the enemy believed himself the conqueror, and a few minutes even, when the Americans doubted ; but the latter never despaired ; a moment sufficed to change their feelings, teaching the successful the fickleness of fortune, and admonishing the depressed of the virtue of perseverance.

For his conduct in this battle, Captain Perry received a gold medal from Congress.  Captain Elliott also received a gold medal.  Rewards were bestowed on the officers and men generally, and the nation has long considered this action one of its proudest achievements on the water.

On the 23d of October, the squadron transported the army of General Harrison to Buffalo; and on the 25th, Captain Perry resigned the command of the upper lakes to Captain Elliott, repairing himself to the sea-board.  November 29th, this gallant and successful officer received the commission of a captain, which was dated on the day of the victory, and soon after he was appointed to the command of the Java 44, a new frigate, then fitting for sea at Baltimore.

## CHAPTER XLV.

In February, 1814, three vessels were laid down at the Harbour, a frigate of 50 guns, and two large brigs, pierced for 22 guns each.  As the English were known to be building extensively, the timber was also got out for a second frigate.  Early in March many deserters came in, who agreed in stating that the largest of the enemy's new ships, which had been laid down the previous autumn, was caulked and decked, and that she was pierced for 60 guns.  A third ship was also said to be in preparation.  In consequence of this intelligence, the size of the first American frigate was materially increased.  March 26th, the important information was obtained that the enemy had actually laid down a two-decked vessel of unusual dimensions.  Thus did those inland waters, on which, until quite lately, nothing had ever floated larger than a sloop of war, bid fair to witness the evolutions of fleets!

On the 7th of April one of the new brigs was launched. She was called the Jefferson. Still the guns which had left New York two months previously, had not even reached Albany. The other brig was launched on the 10th, and was called the Jones. Not a man or gun, however, had yet arrived. April the 11th, the enemy was ascertained to be in the stream, with all his vessels of the previous year; and on the 14th, he put his two frigates into the water. The Lady of the Lake was sent out to watch the motions of the English, as soon as the state of the ice permitted.

April 25th, while rowing guard, Lieutenant Dudley detected three boats in the offing, and immediately fired into them. The strangers did not return the fire, but pulled swiftly away. Obtaining a reinforcement, Mr. Dudley gave chase, but could not again fall in with the suspicious party. The next day there was a close search, and at the spot where the strangers received the fire of the guard-boat, six barrels of gunpowder were found in the lake, slung in such a manner, that one man might carry two at a time, across his shoulders. They had fuse-holes, and were, no doubt, intended to blow up the frigate.

On the 2d of May, the American frigate was launched. She was called the Superior. Another of less size, was immediately laid down on her blocks. The guns began to arrive at the Harbour about the beginning of May, though the heaviest were still working their way through the imperfect navigation of the Mohawk and Wood Creek, towards Oswego. On the 4th, the Lady of the Lake, Lieutenant Gregory, saw six sail of the enemy coming out of Kingston, about dusk, steering towards Amherst Bay; and on the 5th, the latter appeared off Oswego, with seven sail. The greatest exertions were now made to get the Pike, Madison, Jefferson, Sylph, and Oneida, ready to follow him; these being all the vessels that had their armaments, the small schooners being pretty generally abandoned as cruisers, and converted into transports. But a report was received from Captain Woolsey, then on duty at Oswego, that one of the new frigates was certainly in the enemy's squadron; and Mr. Gregory brought in information that he had seen the other off the Ducks the same day: when Commodore Chauncey abandoned the intention to go out, the great superiority of the English putting a battle out of the question.

The active cruising force under Sir James Yeo, consisted of the Prince Regent 58, Captain O'Conner, the flag-ship, armed with heavy long guns, sixty-eight and thirty-two-pound carronades, and containing near 500 men; the Princess Charlotte 42, Captain Mulcaster, having guns nearly or quite as heavy, and between 300 and 400 men; the Montreal, (late Wolfe,) Captain Downie; the Niagara, (late Royal George,) Captain Popham; the Charwell, (late Moira,) Lieutenant Dobbs; Magnet, (late Sidney Smith;) the Star, (late Melville,) Captain Clover; and the Netley, (late Beresford,) Lieutenant Owen. It was evident that nothing less than unusually heavy frigates could lie against the largest of these vessels.

Captain Woolsey had been sent to Oswego, to transport the heavy guns, cables, &c., of the two new frigates, most of which had reached the falls, twelve miles above that town, where they were kept for the sake of security, until the schooners could be loaded, and despatched singly. The Growler was in the river with that object, when Sir James Yeo appeared in the offing. He was about to make a descent, with a body of troops, on the 5th, but the weather induced him to defer the enterprise. On this occasion, there was some firing, and the enemy abandoned an empty boat or two. The succeeding day, however, every thing being favourable, the original design was resumed.

At the moment when Sir James Yeo appeared, a battalion of the light artillery, consisting of 290 effectives, under Lieutenant Colonel Mitchell, was at Fort Oswego, and but a few militia had been called in, the adjacent country being little more than a wilderness. It would trespass on another branch of the subject, minutely to relate the affair that followed. Lieutenant General Drummond landed, and carried the place after a sharp resistance; the Americans having too small a force to repel him.

The enemy remained two days at Oswego, when they raised the Growler, and carried her off; this making the third time that vessel had been taken during the last year. But few stores were found in the village, the orders of Commodore Chauncey having required that they should be kept at the falls, until vessels were ready to receive them.

Sir James Yeo now returned to Kingston, landed the troops, and on the 19th, he came out and chased the Lady of the Lake into the Harbour, off which place he appeared with four ships and three brigs, blockading the port, for the first and only time during the war. At this moment, many of the stores, and some of the lighter guns, were coming in by land, though the heavy guns and cables still remained in the Oswego river.

About the middle of May, reinforcements of officers and men began to arrive from the seaboard. The Macedonian had been laid up in the Thames, and Mr. Rodgers, her first lieutenant, came in with her crew, between the 11th and the 21st. Captain Elliott rejoined the station on the 12th, and Captain Trenchard on the 15th. The Erie, a new sloop of war, then blockaded at Baltimore, had also been laid up, and her commander, Captain Ridgely, with his people, arrrived some time before, and were put on board the Jefferson.

Notwithstanding all the exertions that had been made in building, the ships were useless without guns and cables, and most of those intended for the two frigates, had yet to be transported to the Harbour by water, their weight and the state of the roads rendering other means too costly and difficult. Captain Woolsey, who was still entrusted with this duty, caused reports to be circulated that the heavy articles were to be sent back to the Oneida lake; and when time had been allowed for the enemy to receive this false information, he ran the guns over the falls, and at sunset, on the 28th of May, he reached Oswego with 19 boats loaded with 21 long thirty-two-pounders, 18 twenty-four pounders, 3 forty-two-pound carronades, and 10 cables. The look-outs having reported the coast clear, the brigade of boats rowed out of the river, at dusk, and after passing a dark and rainy night at the oars, reached the mouth of Big Salmon River, at sunrise on the 29th, one boat having unaccountably disappeared.

Captain Woolsey was accompanied by a detachment of 130 riflemen, under Major Appling, and at the Big Salmon he also met a party of Oneida Indians, which had been directed to follow on the shore. The brigade now proceeded, entered the Big Sandy Creek, and ascended about two miles to its place of destination; the blockade rendering it necessary to convey the supplies by land the remainder of the distance.

At this time, the English squadron lay at anchor, a few miles from the Harbour, and the missing boat had gone ahead, in the professed hope of making the whole distance by water. Seeing the English ships, either by mistake or treachery it pulled directly for them, under a belief, real or pretended, that they were Americans. It is thought, however, that the people in the boat were deceived.

From the prisoners, Sir James Yeo learned the situation of

the remainder of the brigade. He had gun-boats on the station, and Captain Popham of the Montreal, was put into one, and Captain Spilsbury into another having three cutters and a gig in company. After cruising without success, separately, the two parties joined, and having ascertained that the brigade had entered Sandy Creek, they followed on the 30th, with the expectation of capturing it. Major Appling, being apprised of the approach of the enemy, placed his riflemen, supported by the Indians, in ambush, about half a mile below the place where Captain Woolsey was discharging the stores. The enemy had a party of marines on board, under two lieutenants of that corps. These, in conjunction with a body of seamen, were landed, and the gun-boats approached, throwing grape and canister into the bushes, with a view to feel their way. Major Appling permitted the enemy to get quite near, when he threw in a close discharge of the rifle. The resistance was trifling, and in ten minutes the whole of the English demanded quarter. The enemy had a midshipman and 13 seamen and marines killed, and 2 lieutenants of marines, with 26 common men wounded. In addition to the wounded, there was a sufficient number of prisoners made to raise his total loss to 186. All the boats were taken, the three gun-vessels carrying 68, 24, 18 and 12 pound carronades. Among the prisoners were Captains Popham and Spilsbury, 4 sea-lieutenants, and 2 midshipmen. Although there was a considerable force a short distance above, without the range of the rifle, the command of Major Appling, which effected this handsome exploit, was scarcely equal to the enemy in numbers, and yet he had but a single man wounded. This little success was the effect of a surprise and an ambush.

Most of the Superior's guns having now arrived, the enemy raised the blockade on the 6th of June. Two days later the last of the guns actually reached Sackett's Harbour. The frigate which had been laid down on the blocks of the Superior, was launched on the 11th of June, having been put into the water in 34 working days, from the time her keel was laid. She was called the Mohawk. Still the squadron was 500 men short of its complements, though the crew of the Congress 38, which was undergoing extensive repairs, at Portsmouth, N. H., had been ordered to this service. About the middle of the month, the latter began to arrive. The enemy also continued to reinforce both his army and his marine, 200 boats at a time having been observed passing up the St. Lawrence.

BATTLE OF LAKE CHAMPLAIN.

About the middle of the month, Commodore Chauncey sent Acting Lieutenant Gregory, with three gigs, into the St. Lawrence, where the enemy had a line of gun-boats, to cover the passage of his supplies and reinforcements, with directions to surprise some of his boats loaded with stores, and, if possible, to destroy them. For this purpose Mr. Gregory lay in ambush on one of the islands, but was discovered by the look-outs of the enemy, who immediately despatched a gun-boat in chase. Instead of retiring before this force, Mr. Gregory determined to become the assailant, and he dashed at the gun-boat, carrying her without the loss of a man. This vessel had an eighteen-pound carronade, and a crew of 18 men. While proceeding up the river with his prize, Mr. Gregory was chased by a much larger boat, mounting 2 guns, and pulling a great number of oars, which compelled him to scuttle and abandon her. On this occasion Mr. Gregory was accompanied by Messrs. Vaughan and Dixon, two gallant mariners of the lake, and he brought in nearly as many prisoners as he had men.

Ten days later, Mr. Gregory was sent with two gigs, accompanied as before by Messrs. Vaughan and Dixon, to Nicholas Island, near Presque Isle, where the enemy had a cruiser, intended to mount 14 guns, nearly ready to launch, and to endeavour to destroy her. This duty, after running much risk, and suffering greatly from hunger, was effectually performed by the party, which was absent near a week. The day after his return from this expedition, Mr. Gregory received the commission of a lieutenant, which had been conferred on him for the handsome manner in which he had captured the gun-boat.

On the afternoon of the 31st of July, Commodore Chauncey, who had been very ill, was carried on board the Superior, and the American squadron sailed. Its force consisted of the Superior 62, Lieutenant Elton, Commodore Chauncey; Mohawk 42, Captain Jones; Pike 28, Captain Crane; Madison 24, Captain Trenchard; Jefferson 22, Captain Ridgely; Jones 22, Captain Woolsey; Sylph 14, Captain Elliott; Oneida 14, Lieutenant Commandant Brown, and the Lady of the Lake, look-out vessel. There is no question that this force, which, with the exception of the Oneida, was composed of efficient vessels, was superior to that of the English, who were striving to regain the ascendency, by constructing, as fast as possible, the two-decker already mentioned.

Commodore Chauncey, whose health rapidly improved in

34 *

the pure air of the lake, appeared off the Niagara, now by the vicissitudes of war again in the possession of the English, on the 5th of August.   As the American vessels approached, they intercepted one of the English brigs, which was convoying troops from York to Niagara, and she was chased ashore about two leagues to the westward of Fort George.

Commodore Chauncey left the Jefferson, Sylph, and Oneida to watch two brigs of the enemy, who were then lying in the Niagara, and went off Kingston, where he arrived on the 9th. One of the English ships was in the offing, and was chased into port by the American squadron.   The next day, the Jones, Captain Woolsey, was sent to cruise between Oswego and the Harbour; and the Conquest, Lieutenant Reid, one of the best of the schooners, which had been kept armed for any light ser-vice that might offer, was employed on the same duty, the enemy having intercepted some flour that was passing, by means of boats.

From this time, until the month of October, Commodore Chauncey continued a close blockade of Sir James Yeo, in Kingston, having undisputed command of the entire lake. With a view to tempt the English to come out, he kept only four vessels in the offing, and as the enemy had an equal number, it was thought the provocation might induce him to risk a battle.   Some guns were also sent ashore, with a view to bring the vessels as near as possible to an equality.   The American ships were the Superior 58,* Mohawk 42, Pike 28, and Madison 24; the British, the Prince Regent 58, Princess Charlotte 42, Wolfe 25, and Niagara 24.   There was also a large schooner at Kingston, and several gun-boats and smaller vessels.   It is probable that there was a trifling superiority on the part of the Americans, notwithstanding; for in a conflict between vessels of so much force, the smaller craft could be of no great moment; but it was such a superiority as the enemy had long been accustomed to disregard; and the result showed that the American marine commanded his respect to a degree which rendered the minutest calculations of force necessary.

On the 20th of August, the blockading ships were driven off by a gale; and on regaining their station on the 25th, the enemy could not be seen in port.   Lieutenant Gregory, with Mr. Hart, a midshipman, was immediately sent in, in a gig, to reconnoitre.   While on this duty, Mr. Gregory landed to set

---

* Four guns having been landed

fire to a raft of picket-timber that he accidentally passed. This deviation from the direct route, brought the gig so near in-shore, that two barges of the enemy, carrying 30 men, were enabled to head it, as it doubled a point. A chase, and a sharp fire of musketry ensued, Mr. Gregory persevering in his attempt to escape, until Mr. Hart was killed, and five men out of eight were wounded, when this enterprising officer was obliged to surrender.

On the 11th of September, the wind came from the northward, when Commodore Chauncey stood in towards Kingston, and brought-to, just without the drop of the shot from the batteries ; and the ships hoisted their ensigns, as a challenge for the enemy to come out. The English sprung their broadsides to bear, set their colours, but did not accept the defiance. It was now seen that the two-decker was launched, and she was ascertained to be very large. After remaining close in, for a considerable time, the American ships filled and gained an offing.

The next day it came on to blow, and the squadron was compelled to make an offing. The gale lasted until the 15th, when the Lady of the Lake joined, to say that General Izard had reached the Harbour. The ships now went in, for the first time, since the 2d of August, having kept the lake 45 days ; much of the time under canvass. On the 16th, the look-out vessel was sent to order in the different brigs.

The division of General Izard was landed at the mouth of the Genesee, on the 22d. As soon as this duty was performed, Commodore Chauncey went off Kingston again, where he appeared on the 28th. Two of the enemy's ships were coming out under a press of sail, but were driven back. The 29th, the wind being fair, the squadron looked into Kingston again, and the Lady was sent close in, when it was found that the large ship, which had been called the St. Lawrence, was completely rigged, but had no sails bent. As this vessel was pierced for 112 guns, and was intended for metal in proportion, she was more than equal to meeting the whole American force. On the 5th of October, the Sylph looked in again, and found her sails bent and topgallant-yards crossed, when Commodore Chauncey ran over to the Harbour, where he anchored on the 7th, and prepared to receive an attack.

Sir James Yeo sailed in the St. Lawrence, with four other ships, two brigs, and a schooner, on the 15th of October, and he continued in command of the lake for the remainder of the

season.  He is said to have had more than 1100 men in his
flag-ship ; and it was understood that the enemy had become
so wary, that a captain was stationed on each deck.  Other
duty probably occupied him, for no attempt was made on the
Harbour, nor did the enemy even blockade it ; the necessities
of the Niagara frontier calling his attention in that quarter.
At the end of the month of November, the navigation closed.

## CHAPTER XLVI.

In the autumn of 1814, the enemy contemplated an invasion of the northern and least populous counties of New York,
with a large force, following the route laid down for General
Burgoyne, in his unfortunate expedition of 1777.  It was most
probably intended to occupy a portion of the northern frontier,
with the expectation of turning the circumstance to account
in the pending negotiations, the English commissioners soon
after advancing a claim to drive the Americans back from
their ancient boundaries, with a view to leave Great Britain
the entire possession of the lakes.  In such an expedition, the
command of Champlain became of great importance, as it
flanked the march of the invading army for more than a hundred miles, and offered so many facilities for forwarding supplies, as well as for annoyance and defence.  Until this season, neither nation had a force of any moment on that water,
but the Americans had built a ship and a schooner, during the
winter and spring ; and when it was found that the enemy
was preparing for a serious effort, the keel of a brig was laid.
Many galleys, or gun-boats, were also constructed.

The American squadron lay in Otter Creek, at the commencement of the season ; and near the middle of May, as
the vessels then launched were about to quit port, the enemy
appeared off the mouth of the creek, with a force consisting
of the Linnet brig, and eight or ten galleys, under the orders
of Captain Pring, with a view to fill the channel.  For this
purpose two sloops loaded with stones were in company.  A
small work had been thrown up at the mouth of the creek
some time previously, by Captain Thornton of the artillery,

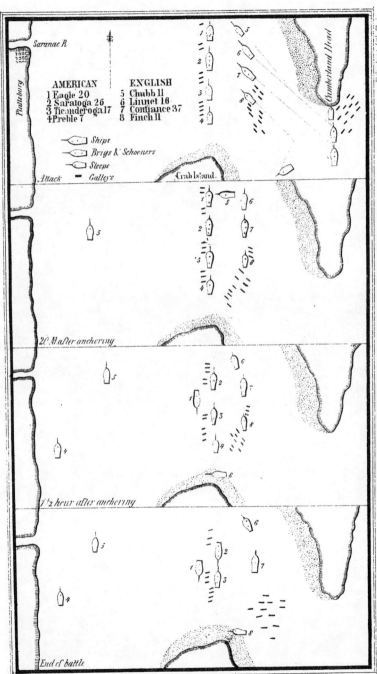

**BATTLE OF PLATTSBURG BAY**

*The distances are not accurate, the intention being to give an idea of the positions of the vessels. ——*

T. Sinclair's lith. Phila.

*Within the figure:*

Saranac R.

Plattsburg

**AMERICAN**
1 Eagle 20
2 Saratoga 26
3 Ticonderoga 17
4 Preble 7

**ENGLISH**
5 Chubb 11
6 Linnet 16
7 Confiance 37
8 Finch 11

Ships
Brigs & Schooners
Sloops
Galleys

Attack

Crab Island.

Cumberland Head

20 M. after anchoring

1½ hour after anchoring

End of battle

and Lieutenant Cassin was despatched with a party of seamen, to aid that officer in defending the pass.  After a cannonading of some duration, the enemy retired without effecting
his object, and the vessels got out.  In this affair, no one was
hurt on the side of the Americans, although shells were thrown
from one of the galleys.

On the other hand, the English were not idle.  In addition
to the small vessels they had possessed the previous year, they
had built the brig just mentioned, or the Linnet, and as soon
as the last American vessel was in frame, they laid the keel
of a ship.  By constructing the latter, a great advantage was
secured, care being taken, as a matter of course, to make her
of a size sufficient to be certain of possessing the greatest
force.  The American brig, which was called the Eagle, was
launched about the middle of August; and the English ship,
which was named the Confiance, on the 25th of the same
month.  As the English army was already collecting on the
frontier, the utmost exertions were made by both sides, and
each appeared on the lake as he got ready.  Captain M'Donough, who still commanded the American force, was enabled
to get out a few days before his adversary; and cruising being
almost out of the question on this long and narrow body of
water, he advanced as far as Plattsburg, the point selected for
the defence, and anchored, the 3d of September, on the flank
of the troops which occupied the entrenchments at that place.

About this time, Sir George Prevost, the English commander-
in-chief, advanced against Plattsburg, then held by Brigadier
General Macomb at the head of only 1500 effectives, with a
force that probably amounted to 12,000 men.  A good deal
of skirmishing ensued; and from the 7th to the 11th, the enemy was employed in bringing up his battering train, stores,
and reinforcements.  Captain Downie, late of the Montreal,
on Lake Ontario, had been sent by Sir James Yeo, to command on this lake.

On the 6th, Captain M'Donough ordered the galleys to the
head of the bay, to annoy the English army, and a cannonading occurred which lasted two hours.  The wind coming on
to blow a gale that menaced the galleys with shipwreck, Mr.
Duncan, a midshipman of the Saratoga, was sent in a gig to
order them to retire.  It is supposed that the appearance of the
boat induced the enemy to think that Captain M'Donough himself had joined his galleys; for he concentrated a fire on the
galley Mr. Duncan was in, and that young officer received a

severe wound, by which he lost the use of his arm.  Afterwards one of the galleys drifted in, under the guns of the enemy, and she also sustained some loss, but was eventually brought off.

Captain M'Donough had chosen an anchorage a little to the south of the outlet of the Saranac.  His vessels lay in a line parallel to the coast, extending north and south, and distant from the western shore near two miles.  The last vessel at the southward was so near the shoal, as to prevent the English from passing that end of the line, while all the ships lay so far out towards Cumberland Head, as to bring the enemy within reach of carronades, should he enter the bay on that side. The Eagle, Captain Henley, lay at the northern extremity of the American line, and what might, during the battle, have been called its head, the wind being at the northward and eastward; the Saratoga, Captain M'Donough's own vessel, was second; the Ticonderoga, Lieutenant Commandant Cassin, third; and the Preble, Lieutenant Charles Budd, last.   The Preble lay a little farther south than the pitch of Cumberland Head.   The first of these vessels just mentioned was a brig of 20 guns, and 150 men, all told; the second a ship of 26 guns, and 212 men; the third a schooner of 17 guns and 110 men; the last a sloop, or cutter, of 7 guns and 30 men.   The metal of all these vessels, as well as those of the enemy, was unusually heavy, there being no swell in the lake to render it dangerous.   The Saratoga mounted 8 long twenty-fours, 6 forty-two, and 12 thirty-two-pound carronades; the Eagle, 8 long eighteens, and 12 thirty-two-pound carronades; the Ticonderoga, 4 long eighteens, 8 long twelves, and 4 thirty-two-pound carronades, and one eighteen-pound columbiad; the Preble, 7 long nines.   In addition to these four vessels, the Americans had 10 galleys, or gun-boats, six large and four small.   Each of the former mounted a long twenty-four, and an eighteen pound columbiad; each of the latter one long twelve.   The galleys, on an average, had about 35 men each.   The total force of the Americans present consisted, consequently, of 14 vessels, mounting 86 guns, and containing about 850 men, including officers and a small detachment of soldiers, who did duty as marines, none of the corps having been sent on Lake Champlain.   To complete his order of battle, Captain M'Donough directed two of the galleys to keep in-shore of the Eagle, and a little to windward of her, to sustain the head of the line; one or two more to lie opposite to the interval between the

Eagle and Saratoga ; a few opposite to the interval between the Saratoga and Ticonderoga ; and two or three opposite the interval between the Ticonderoga and Preble.

The Americans were, consequently, formed in two lines, distant from each other about 40 yards ; the large vessels at anchor, and the galleys under their sweeps.

The force of the enemy was materially greater than that of the Americans. His largest vessel, the Confiance, commanded by Captain Downie in person, had the gun-deck of a heavy frigate, mounting on it an armament similar to that of the Constitution or United States, or 30 long twenty-fours. She had no spar-deck, but there was a spacious top-gallant forecastle, and a poop that came no farther forward than the mizzen-mast. On the first were a long twenty-four on a circle, and 4 heavy carronades ; and on the last 2 heavy carronades, making an armament of 37 guns in all. Her complement of men is supposed to have been considerably more than 300. The next vessel of the enemy was the Linnet, Captain Pring, a brig of 16 long twelves, with a crew of from 80 to 100 men. There were two sloops, the Chubb, Lieutenant M'Ghee, and the Finch, Lieutenant Hicks, the former carrying 10 eighteen-pound carronades, and 1 long six, and the latter 6 eighteen-pound carronades, 1 eighteen-pound columbiad, and 4 long sixes. Each of these sloops had about 40 men. To these four vessels were added a force in galleys, or gun-boats, which Sir George Prevost, in his published accounts, states at twelve in number, and Captain M'Donough at thirteen. These vessels were similarly constructed to the American galleys, eight mounting two, and the remainder but one gun each. Thus the whole force of Captain Downie consisted of sixteen or seventeen vessels, as the case may have been, mounting in all, 95 or 96 guns, and carrying about 1000 men.

On the 3d of September, the British gun-boats sailed from Isle aux Noix, under the orders of Captain Pring, to cover the left flank of their army. On the 4th that officer took possession of Isle au Motte, where he constructed a battery, and landed some supplies for the troops. On the 8th, the four larger vessels arrived under Captain Downie, but remained at anchor until the 11th, waiting to receive some necessaries. At daylight, on the morning just mentioned, the whole force weighed, and moved forward in a body.

The guard-boat of the Americans pulled in shortly after the sun had risen, and announced the approach of the enemy. As

the wind was fair, a good working breeze at the northward
and eastward, Captain M'Donough ordered the vessels cleared,
and preparations made to fight at anchor.  Eight bells were
striking in the American squadron, as the upper sails of the
English vessels were seen passing along the land, in the main
lake, on their way to double Cumberland Head.  The enemy
had the wind rather on his larboard quarter.  The Finch led,
succeeded by the Confiance, Linnet, and Chubb; while the gun-
boats, all of which, as well as those of the Americans, had two
latine sails, followed without much order, keeping just clear of
the shore.

The first vessel that came round the Head was a sloop,
which is said to have carried a company of amateurs, and
which took no part in the engagement.  She kept well to leeward, stood down towards Crab Island, and was soon un-
observed.  The Finch came next, and soon after the other
large vessels of the enemy opened from behind the land, and
hauled up to the wind in a line abreast, lying-to until their
galleys could join.  The latter passed to leeward, and formed
in the same manner as their consorts.  The two squadrons
were now in plain view of each other, distant about a league.
As soon as the gun-boats were in their stations, and the different commanders had received their orders, the English
filled, with their starboard tacks aboard, and headed in towards
the American vessels, in a line abreast, the Chubb to windward, and the Finch to leeward, most of the gun-boats, however, being to leeward of the latter.  The movements of the
Finch had been a little singular ever since she led round the
Head, for she is said not to have hove-to, but to have run off,
half-way to Crab Island with the wind abeam, then to have
tacked and got into her station, after the other vessels had
filled.  This movement was probably intended to reconnoitre,
or to menace the rear of the Americans.  The enemy was now
standing in, close-hauled, the Chubb looking well to windward
of the Eagle, the vessel that lay at the head of the American
line, the Linnet laying her course for the bows of the same
brig, the Confiance intending to fetch far enough ahead of the
Saratoga to lay that ship athwart hawse, and the Finch, with
the gun-boats, standing for the Ticonderoga and Preble.

As a matter of course, the Americans were anchored with
springs.  But not content with this customary arrangement,
Captain M'Donough had laid a kedge broad off on each bow
of the Saratoga, and brought their hawsers in, upon the two

quarters, letting them hang in bights, under water. This timely precaution gained the victory.

As the enemy filled, the American vessels sprung their broadsides to bear, and a few minutes were passed in the solemn and silent expectation, that, in a disciplined ship, precedes a battle. Suddenly the Eagle discharged, in quick succession, her four long eighteens. In clearing the decks of the Saratoga, some hen-coops were thrown overboard, and the poultry had been permitted to run at large. Startled by the reports of the guns, a young cock flew upon a gun-slide, clapped his wings and crowed. At this animating sound, the men spontaneously gave three cheers. This little occurrence relieved the usual breathing time between preparation and the combat, and it had a powerful influence on the known tendencies of the seamen. Still Captain M'Donough did not give the order to commence, although the enemy's galleys now opened ; for it was apparent that the fire of the Eagle, which vessel continued to engage, was useless. As soon, however, as it was seen that her shot told, Captain M'Donough, himself, sighted a long twenty-four, and the gun was fired. This shot is said to have struck the Confiance near the outer hawse-hole, and to have passed the length of her deck, killing and wounding several men, and carrying away the wheel. It was a signal for all the American long guns to open, and it was soon seen that the English commanding ship, in particular, was suffering heavily. Still the enemy advanced, and in the most gallant manner, confident if he could get the desired position, that the great weight of the Confiance would at once decide the fate of the day. But he had miscalculated his own powers of endurance. The anchors of the Confiance were hanging by the stoppers, in readiness to be let go, and the larboard bower was soon cut away, as well as a spare anchor in the larboard fore-chains. In short, after bearing the fire of the American vessels as long as possible, and the wind beginning to baffle, Captain Downie found himself reduced to the necessity of anchoring while still at the distance of about a quarter of a mile from the American line. The helm was put a-port, the ship shot into the wind, and a kedge was let go, while the vessel took a sheer, and brought up with her starboard bower. In doing the latter, however, the kedge was fouled and became of no use. In coming-to, the halyards were let run, and the ship hauled up her courses. At this time the Linnet and Chubb were still standing in, farther to windward ; and the former, as her guns

35

bore, fired a broadside at the Saratoga. The Linnet soon after anchored, somewhat nearer than the Confiance, getting a very favourable position forward of the Eagle's beam. The Chubb kept under way, intending, if possible, to rake the American line. The Finch got abreast of the Ticonderoga, under her sweeps, supported by the gun-boats.

The English vessels came to in very handsome style, nor did the Confiance fire a single gun until secured; although the American line was now engaged with all its force. As soon as Captain Downie had performed this duty, in a seaman-like manner, his ship appeared a sheet of fire, discharging all her guns at nearly the same instant, pointed principally at the Saratoga. The effect of this broadside was terrible in the little ship that received it. After the crash had subsided, Captain M'Donough saw that near half his crew was on the deck, for many had been knocked down who sustained no real injuries. It is supposed, however, that about 40 men, or near one-fifth of her complement, were killed and wounded on board the Saratoga, by this single discharge. The hatches had been fastened down, as usual, but the bodies so cumbered the deck, that it was found necessary to remove the fastenings and to pass them below. The effect continued but a moment, when the ship resumed her fire as gallantly as ever. Among the slain, was Mr. Peter Gamble, the first lieutenant. By this early loss, but one officer of that rank, Acting Lieutenant Lavallette, was left in the Saratoga. Shortly after, Captain Downie, the English commanding officer, fell also.

On the part of the principal vessels, the battle now became a steady, animated, but as guns were injured, a gradually decreasing cannonade. Still the character of the battle was relieved by several little incidents that merit notice. The Chubb, while manœuvring near the head of the American line, received a broadside from the Eagle that crippled her, and she drifted down between the opposing vessels, until near the Saratoga, which ship fired a shot into her, and she immediately struck. Mr. Platt, one of the Saratoga's midshipmen, was sent with a boat to take possession. This young officer threw the prize a line, and towed her down astern of the Saratoga, and in-shore, anchoring her near the mouth of the Saranac. This little success occurred within a quarter of an hour after the enemy had anchored, and was considered a favourable omen, though all well knew that on the Confiance alone depended the fate of the day. The Chubb had suffered materially, nearly half of her people having been killed and wounded.

About an hour later, the Finch was also driven out of her berth, by the Ticonderoga; and being crippled, she drifted down upon Crab Island Shoal, where, receiving a shot or two from the gun mounted in the battery, she struck, and was taken possession of by the invalids belonging to the hospital. At this end of the line, the British galleys early made several desperate efforts to close; and soon after the Finch had drifted away, they forced the Preble out of the American line, that vessel cutting her cable, and shifting her anchorage to a station considerably in-shore, where she was of no more service throughout the day. The rear of the American line was certainly its weakest point; and having compelled the little Preble to retreat, the enemy's galleys were emboldened to renew their efforts against the vessel ahead of her, which was the Ticonderoga. This schooner was better able to resist them, and she was very nobly fought. Her spirited commander, Lieutenant Commandant Cassin, walked the taffrail, where he could watch the movements of the enemy's galleys, amidst showers of canister and grape, directing discharges of bags of musket-balls, and other light missiles, effectually keeping the British at bay. Several times the English galleys, of which many were very gallantly fought, closed quite near, with an intent to board; but the great steadiness on board the Ticonderoga beat them back, and completely covered the rear of the line for the remainder of the day. So desperate were some of the assaults, notwithstanding, that the galleys have been described as several times getting nearly within a boat-hook's length of the schooner, and their people as rising from the sweeps in readiness to spring.

While these reverses and successes were occurring in the rear of the two lines, the Americans were suffering heavily at the other extremity. The Linnet had got a very commanding position, and she was admirably fought; while the Eagle, which received all her fire, and part of that of the Confiance, having lost her springs, found herself so situated, as not to be able to bring her guns fairly to bear on either of the enemy's vessels. Captain Henley had run his topsail-yards, with the sails stopped, to the mast-heads, previously to engaging, and he now cut his cable, sheeted home his topsails, cast the brig, and running down, anchored by the stern, between the Saratoga and Ticonderoga, necessarily a little in-shore of both.

Here he opened afresh, and with better effect, on the Confiance and galleys, using his larboard guns. But this movement left the Saratoga exposed to nearly the whole fire of the Linnet, which brig now sprung her broadside in a manner to rake the American ship on her bows.

Shortly after this important change had occurred at the head of the lines, the fire of the two ships began materially to lessen, as gun after gun became disabled; the Saratoga, in particular, having had all her long pieces rendered useless by shot, while most of the carronades were dismounted, either in the same manner, or in consequence of a disposition in the men to overcharge them. At length but a single carronade remained in the starboard batteries, and on firing it, the navel-bolt broke, the gun flew off the carriage, and it actually fell down the main hatch. By this accident, the American commanding vessel was left in the middle of the battle, without a single available gun. Nothing remained, but to make an immediate attempt to wind the ship.

The stream anchor suspended astern, was let go accordingly. The men then clapped on the hawser that led to the starboard quarter, and brought the ship's stern up over the kedge; but here she hung, there not being sufficient wind, or current, to force her bows round. A line had been bent to a bight in the stream cable, with a view to help wind the ship, and she now rode by the kedge and this line, with her stern under the raking broadside of the Linnet, which brig kept up a steady and well-directed fire. The larboard batteries having been manned and got ready, Captain M'Donough ordered all the men from the guns, where they were uselessly suffering, telling them to go forward. By rowsing on the line, the ship was at length got so far round, that the aftermost gun would bear on the Confiance, when it was instantly manned, and began to play. The next gun was used in the same manner, but it was soon apparent that the ship could be got no farther round, for she was now nearly end-on to the wind. At this critical moment, Mr. Brum, the master, bethought him of the hawser that had led to the larboard quarter. It was got forward under the bows, and passed aft to the starboard quarter, when the ship's stern was immediately sprung to the westward, so as to bring all her larboard guns to bear on the English ship, with fatal effect.

As soon as the preparations were made to wind the Saratoga, the Confiance attempted to perform the same evolution.

Her springs were hauled on, but they merely forced the ship ahead, and having borne the fresh broadside of the Americans, until she had scarcely a gun with which to return the fire, and failing in all her efforts to get round, about two hours and a quarter after the commencement of the action, her command- ing officer lowered his flag.   By hauling again upon the star- board hawser, the Saratoga's broadside was immediately sprung to bear on the Linnet, which brig struck about fifteen minutes after her consort.   The enemy's galleys had been driven back, nearly or quite half a mile, and they lay irregularly scattered, and setting to leeward, keeping up a desultory firing.   As soon as they found that the large vessels had submitted, they ceased the combat, and lowered their colours.   At this proud moment, it is believed, on authority entitled to the highest respect, there was not a single English ensign, out of sixteen or seventeen, that had so lately been flying, left abroad in the bay !

In this long and bloody conflict, the Saratoga had 28 men killed, and 29 wounded, or more than a fourth of all on board her ; the Eagle 13 killed, and 20 wounded, which was sus- taining a loss in nearly an equal proportion ; the Ticonderoga 6 killed, and 6 wounded ; the Preble 2 killed ; while on board the 10 galleys, only 3 were killed, and 3 wounded.   The Saratoga was hulled fifty-five times, principally by twenty- four-pound shot ; and the Eagle, thirty-nine times.

According to the report of Captain Pring, of the Linnet, dated on the 12th of September, the Confiance lost 41 killed, and 40 wounded.   It was admitted, however, that no good opportunity had then existed to ascertain the casualties.   At a later day, the English themselves enumerated her wounded at 83.   This would make the total loss of that ship 124 ; but even this number is supposed to be materially short of the truth. The Linnet is reported to have had 10 killed, and 14 wounded. This loss is also believed to be considerably below the fact. The Chubb had 6 killed, and 10 wounded.   The Finch was reported by the enemy, to have had but 2 men wounded.   No American official report of the casualties in the English vessels has been published ; but by an estimate made on the best data that could be found, the Linnet was thought to have lost 50 men, and the two smaller vessels taken, about 30 between them.   No account whatever has been published of the casual- ties on board the English galleys, though the slaughter in them is believed to have been very heavy.

As soon as the Linnet struck, a lieutenant was sent to take
    35 *

possession of the Confiance. Bad as was the situation of the Saratoga, that of this prize was much worse. She had been hulled 105 times; had probably near, if not quite, half her people killed and wounded; and this formidable floating battery was reduced to helpless impotency.

As the boarding officer was passing along the deck of the prize, he accidentally ran against a lock-string, and fired one of the Confiance's starboard guns. Up to this moment, the English galleys had been slowly drifting to leeward, with their colours down, apparently waiting to be taken possession of; but at the discharge of this gun, which may have been understood as a signal, one or two of them began to move slowly off, and soon after the others followed, pulling but a very few sweeps. It is not known that one of them hoisted her ensign. Captain M'Donough made a signal for the American galleys to follow, but it was discovered that their men were wanted at the pumps of some of the larger vessels, to keep them from sinking, the water being found over the berth-deck of the Linnet; and the signal was revoked. As there was not a mast that would bear any canvass among all the larger vessels, the English galleys escaped, though they went off slowly and irregularly, as if distrusting their own liberty.

Captain M'Donough applauded the conduct of all the officers of the Saratoga. Mr. Gamble died at his post, fighting bravely; Mr. Lavallette, the only lieutenant left, displayed the cool discretion that marks the character of this highly respectable and firm officer; and Mr. Brum, the master, who was entrusted with the important duty of winding the ship, never lost his self-possession for an instant. Captain Henley praised the conduct of his officers, as did Lieutenant Commandant Cassin. The galleys behaved very unequally; but the Borer, Mr. Conover;* Netley, Mr. Breese;† one under the orders of Mr. Robins, a master, and one or two more, were considered to have been very gallantly handled.

There was a common feeling of admiration at the manner in which the Ticonderoga, Lieutenant Commandant Cassin, defended the rear of the line, and at the noble conduct of all on board her.

The Saratoga was twice on fire by hot shot thrown from the Confiance, her spanker having been nearly consumed. No battery from the American shore, with the exception of the

---

* Now Commander Conover.                    † Now Capt. Breese.

gun or two fired at the Finch from Crab Island, took any part in the naval encounter; nor could any, without endangering the American vessels equally with the enemy. Indeed the distance renders it questionable whether shot would have reached with effect, as Captain M'Donough had anchored far off the land, in order to compel the enemy to come within range of his short guns.

The Americans found a furnace on board the Confiance, with eight or ten heated shot in it, though the fact is not stated with any view to attribute it to the enemy as a fault. It was an advantage that he possessed, most probably, in consequence of the presence of a party of artillerists.

Captain M'Donough, who was already very favourably known to the service for his personal intrepidity, obtained a vast accession of reputation by the results of this day. His dispositions for receiving the attacks, were highly judicious and seaman-like. By the manner in which he anchored his vessels, with the shoal so near the rear of his line as to cover that extremity, and the land of Cumberland Head so near his broadside as necessarily to bring the enemy within reach of his short guns, he made all his force completely available. The English were not near enough, perhaps, to give to carronades their full effect; but this disadvantage was unavoidable, the assailing party having, of course, a choice in the distance. All that could be obtained, under the circumstances, appears to have been secured, and the result proved the wisdom of the actual arrangement. The personal deportment of Captain M'Donough in this engagement, like that of Captain Perry in the battle of Lake Erie, was the subject of general admiration in his little squadron. His coolness was undisturbed throughout all the trying scenes on board his own ship, and although lying against a vessel of double the force, and nearly double the tonnage of the Saratoga, he met and resisted her attack with a constancy that seemed to set defeat at defiance. The winding of the Saratoga, under such circumstances, exposed as she was to the raking broadsides of the Confiance and Linnet, especially the latter, was a bold, seaman-like, and masterly measure, that required unusual decision and fortitude to imagine and execute. Most men would have believed that, without a single gun on the side engaged, a fourth of their people cut down, and their ship a wreck, enough injury had been received to justify submission; but Captain M'Donough found the means to secure a victory in the desperate condition of his own vessel.

The deportment of Lieutenant Commandant Cassin* was also the subject of general applause in the American squadron.

Although many of the American officers were wounded, only two that belonged to the quarterdeck were killed. These were Mr. Gamble, the first lieutenant of the Saratoga, and Mr. Stansbury, the first lieutenant of the Ticonderoga.† Mr. Smith,‡ a very valuable officer, and the first lieutenant of the Eagle, received a severe wound, but returned to his quarters during the action. On the part of the enemy, besides Captain Downie, several officers were killed, and three or four were wounded.

Captain M'Donough, besides the usual medal from Congress, and various compliments and gifts from different states and

---

* Now Commodore Cassin.

† The manner in which Mr. Gamble met his death, has been mentioned. Mr. Stansbury suddenly disappeared from the bulwarks forward, while superintending some duty with the springs. Two days after the action, his body rose to the surface of the water, near the vessel to which he had belonged, and it was found that it had been cut in two by a round shot. Both these gentlemen showed great coolness and spirit, until they fell. Many officers were knocked down in the engagement, without having blood drawn. At one moment, there was a cry in the Saratoga that Captain M'Donough, or as he was usually called, the commodore, was killed. He was thrown on his face, on the quarter deck, nearly if not quite senseless, and it was two or three minutes before he came to his recollection. He pointed a favourite gun most of the action, and while standing in the middle of the deck bending his body to sight it, a shot had cut in two the spanker-boom, letting the spar fall on his back, a blow that might easily have proved fatal. A few minutes after this accident, the cry that the commodore was killed was heard again. This time, Captain M'Donough was lying on the off-side of the deck, between two of the guns, covered with blood, and again nearly senseless. A shot had driven the head of the captain of his favourite gun in upon him, and knocked him into the scuppers. Mr. Brum the master, a venerable old seaman, while winding the ship, had a large splinter driven so near his body, as actually to strip off his clothes. For a minute he was thought to be dead, but, on gaining his feet, he made an apron of his pocket handkerchief, and coolly went to work again with the springs ! A few months later this veteran died, as is thought of the injury. Mr. Lavallette had a shot-box, on which he was standing, knocked from under his feet, and he too, was once knocked down by the head of a seaman. He also received a severe splinter wound, though not reported. In short, very few escaped altogether ; and in this desperate fight, it appears to have been agreed on both sides, to call no man wounded who could keep out of the hospital. Many who were not included among the wounded, feel the effects of their hurts to this day. It is said, that scarecly an individual escaped on board of either the Confiance or Saratoga, without some injury.

‡ Now Captain Smith.

towns, was promoted for his services.   Captain Henley also received a medal.   The legislature of Vermont presented the former with a small estate on Cumberland Head, which over-looked the scene of his triumph.   The officers and crews met with the customary acknowledgments, and the country ge-nerally placed the victory by the side of that of Lake Erie.   In the navy, which is better qualified to enter into just estimates of force, and all the other circumstances that enhance the me-rits of nautical exploits, the battle of Plattsburg Bay is justly ranked among the very highest of its claims to glory.

The consequences of this victory were immediate and im-portant.   During the action, Sir George Prevost had skir-mished sharply in front of the American works, and was busy in making demonstrations for a more serious attack.   As soon, however, as the fate of the British squadron was ascertained, he made a precipitate and unmilitary retreat, abandoning much of his heavy artillery, stores, and supplies, and from that mo-ment to the end of the war, the northern frontier was cleared of the enemy.

## CHAPTER XLVII.

AFTER the success of Captain Perry on Lake Erie, the En-glish made no serious effort to recover the ascendency on the upper waters.   During the winter of 1813–14, they are be-lieved to have contemplated an attempt against a portion of the American vessels, which were lying in Put-in Bay, but the en-terprise was abandoned.   When Commodore Sinclair hoisted his pennant, as commander on this station, an expedition sailed against Michilimackinac, which was repulsed.   He made some captures of vessels belonging to the Northwest Company, blew up a block-house in the Nautauwassauga, and compelled the enemy to destroy a schooner, called the Nancy, commanded by Lieutenant Worsley.

While these movements were in the course of occurrence on Lakes Superior and Huron, several of the small vessels were kept at the foot of Lake Erie, to co-operate with the army then besieged in the fort of the same name.   On the night of the

12th of August, the Somers, Ohio, and Porcupine, all of which were under Lieutenant Conklin, were anchored just at the outlet of the lake, to cover the left flank of the American works. The enemy brought up a party of seamen from below, with a view to cut them off, and about midnight he made an attack, under Captain Dobbs, in six or eight boats, most of which were large batteaux. The Ohio and Somers were surprised, the last being captured without any resistance, but the Porcupine taking the alarm, easily effected her escape. The enemy drifted down the rapids with their two prizes, and secured them below.

In this sudden and handsome affair, the Americans had 1 man killed and 10 wounded. The enemy lost about the same number, by the resistance on board the Ohio, among whom was Lieutenant Radcliffe, of the Netley, slain. The Porcupine had no part in the action. This surprise was the result of excess of confidence, it being thought that the enemy had no force on Lake Erie with which to make such an attack. The manner in which the men and boats were brought up from Lake Ontario, for this purpose, and the neatness with which the enterprise was executed, reflected great credit on the enemy.

Nor was this the only successful attempt of the same nature, made by the English on the upper lakes, during this season. Lieutenant Worsley, the officer who commanded the schooner destroyed by Commodore Sinclair, had escaped with all his men, and obtaining a party of soldiers from Michilimackinac, and a strong body of Indians, he planned a surprise upon the Tigress and Scorpion, two schooners that had been left in Lake Huron after the repulse on the post just mentioned. The Tigress mounted a twenty-four, had a crew of 28 men, officers included, and was commanded by Mr. Champlin. She was lying at St. Joseph's, on the night of the 3d of September, when Mr. Worsley made his attack in five large boats, one of which mounted a six, and another a three-pounder, accompanied by nineteen canoes, containing more than 200 men. The night was so dark that the enemy got very near before they were discovered, but Mr. Champlin* and his officers made a very gallant resistance. The schoooner was not captured until all her officers had been shot down. The guns of the enemy were transferred to the Tigress, and while she still con-

* Now Commander Champlin.

tinued in her berth, the evening of the next day, the Scorpion, Lieutenant Turner, which had been cruising, came in and anchored about five miles from her. Neither vessel had signals, and there was no attempt to communicate that night. The next morning, at daylight, the Tigress was seen standing down towards the Scorpion, with American colours flying, and there not being the slightest apparent motive to suspect her change of character, she was permittted to come alongside, when she fired all her guns, ran the Scorpion aboard, and carried her without difficulty. This surprise was wholly attributed to the want of signals, and Mr. Turner was honourably acquitted for the loss of his vessels. In carrying the Tigress, the enemy had a lieutenant and 2 men killed, and 7 men wounded. On board the Tigress 3 men were killed, and all the officers and 3 seamen were wounded. The Scorpion, being surprised, made but a trifling resistance.

These little captures, which were very creditable to the enterprise of the enemy, terminated the war on the upper lakes, the vessels being shortly after laid up. During the winter of 1814–15 both belligerents were building, the enemy having laid down a second two-decker at Kingston, while the Americans prepared to build two at the Harbour. Mr. Eckford engaged to put into the water two ships, to carry 102 guns each, within sixty days from the time he commenced, the timber then standing in the forest. The order was given, and the work commenced in January. The news that a treaty of peace had been signed, was received when the work on one of these vessels, called the New Orleans, had been commenced but twenty-nine days. She was then nearly planked in, and it was thought would have been in the water in twenty-seven days more. The second vessel was but little behind her, and there is no doubt that Commodore Chauncey would have taken the lake, as soon as the navigation opened, with a force consisting of 2 sail of the line, 2 frigates, 2 corvettes, 4 brigs, and as many small craft as the service could possibly have required. As the enemy had received the frames of one or two frigates from England, and had already begun to set them up, it is probable that a frigate would have been added to this force, by building her of the timber found too small for the heavier ships.

The peace put a stop to the strife in ship-building, and terminated the war on the lakes. In this inland contest, while the enemy had been active, bold, and full of resources, impartial judges must award the palm to the Americans.  On the upper lakes and on Champlain, the English had sought general actions, and decisive victories placed the republic in nearly undisputed command of those waters.  The important results that had been expected, fully rewarded this success.  On Lake Ontario, the English pursued a different policy, cautiously avoiding any conflict that might prove final, unless under circumstances that would ensure victory.

On Lake Champlain the enemy captured in the course of the war, the Eagle and Growler, by means of their army.  These two vessels were subsequently retaken, under the names of the Chubb and the Finch, and the whole English force was defeated.  On Lake Erie, the success of the enemy was limited to the surprise of the four schooners mentioned in this chapter ; while they lost equally by surprise, the Detroit and Caledonia, their whole squadron in action, and a schooner on Lake Huron blown up.  On Lake Ontario, the success of the enemy was limited to the capture of the Julia and Growler, in the affair of the 10th of August, and the re-capture of the latter vessel at Oswego.  On no other occasion, with the exception of the gig of Mr. Gregory, and one boat carrying a gun and two cables, did any man, or thing, belonging to the navy fall into his hands.  He made one exceedingly impotent attack on the Harbour, (previously to the arrival of Commodore Yeo,) was beaten in a subsequent attempt on the same place, succeeded in taking Oswego, and committed some ravages at Sodus, and at the mouth of the Genesee.  For a few days he also co-operated with his army.  On the part of the Americans, a spirited attack was made on Kingston in 1812 ; York was twice captured in 1813, as was Fort George once ; a brig was brought off from York, and a vessel of 20 guns burned at the same place ; another of 14 guns at Presque Isle ; a third was driven ashore, and blown up, to the westward of Niagara ; six gun-vessels and three gun-boats, and many smaller craft were captured ; and, at different times, two captains, many other officers, and several hundred seamen and marines were taken.  Kingston was often long and closely blockaded, and, with short and few exceptions, the Americans had the command of the lake.  The greater age of the English frontier, as a settled country, gave the enemy material advantages, of which he fully availed himself.

No officer of the American navy ever filled a station of the responsibility and importance of that which Commodore Chaun-

cey occupied ; and it may be justly questioned if any officer
could have acquitted himself better, of the high trust that had
been reposed in him.   He commanded the profound respect of
the vigilant, bold, and skilful commander to whom he was
opposed, and to the last, retained the entire confidence of his
own government.

---

## CHAPTER  XLVIII.

WHEN Commodore Bainbridge gave up the command of the
Constitution 44, in 1813, that ship was found to be so decayed
as to require extensive repairs.   Her crew was principally sent
upon the lakes, a new one entered, and the command of her
was given to Captain Charles Stewart.   The ship, however,
was not able to get to sea  until the winter of 1814, when she
made a cruise to the southward, passing down  the coast, and
running through the West Indies, on her way home, where she
fell in with La Pique 36, which ship made her escape by going through the Mona passage in the night.   Previously to her
return the Constitution captured the Pictou 14, a man-of-war
schooner of the enemy.   Reaching the American coast, she
was chased into Marblehead by two English frigates, the Junon and Tenedos.   Shortly after she went to Boston.   In this
cruise, the Constitution made a few prizes, in addition to the
schooner.

On the 17th of December, the Constitution again left Boston, and ran off Bermuda ; thence to the vicinity of Madeira,
and into the Bay of Biscay.   After this, she cruised some time
in sight of the  Rock of Lisbon, making  two prizes, one of
which was destroyed, and the other sent in.    While in the vicinity of Lisbon, she made a large ship and gave chase, but
before her courses were raised, one of the prizes just mentioned, was fallen in with, and while securing it, the strange sail
disappeared.   This vessel is understood to have been the Eli-
zabeth 74, which, on her arrival at Lisbon, hearing that the
Constitution was off the coast, immediately came out in pursuit of her ; but Captain Stewart had stood to the southward
and westward, in quest of an enemy said to be in that direction.
36

On the morning of the 20th of February, the wind blowing a light Levanter, finding nothing where he was, Captain Stewart ordered the helm put up, and the ship ran off southwest, varying her position, in that direction, fifty or sixty miles. At 1 P. M., a stranger was seen on the larboard bow, when the ship hauled up two or three points, and made sail in chase. In about twenty minutes the stranger was made out to be a ship; and half an hour later, a second vessel was seen farther to leeward, which at two was also ascertained to be a ship. The Constitution kept standing on, all three vessels on bowlines, until four, when the nearest of the strangers made a signal to the ship to leeward, and shortly after he kept away and ran down towards his consort, then about three leagues under his lee. The Constitution immediately squared away, and set her studding-sails, alow and aloft. No doubt was now entertained of the strangers being enemies; the nearest ship having the appearance of a small frigate, and the vessel to leeward that of a large sloop of war. The first was carrying studding-sails on both sides, while the last was running off under short canvass, to allow her consort to close. Captain Stewart believed it was their intention to keep away, on their best mode of sailing, until night, in the hope of escaping; and he crowded every thing that would draw, with a view to get the nearest vessel under his guns. About half-past four, the spar proving defective, the main royal-mast was carried away, and the chase gained. A few guns were now fired, but finding that the shot fell short, the attempt to cripple the stranger was abandoned.

Perceiving, at half-past five, that it was impossible to prevent the enemy from effecting a junction, the Constitution, then a little more than a league distant from the farthest ship, cleared for action. Ten minutes later, the two chases passed within hail of each other, came by the wind with their heads to the northward, hauled up their courses, and were evidently clearing to engage. In a few minutes both ships suddenly made sail, close by the wind, in order to weather upon the American frigate, but perceiving that the latter was closing too fast, they again hauled up their courses, and formed on the wind, the smallest ship ahead.

At 6 P. M., the Constitution had the enemy completely under her guns, and she showed her ensign. The strangers answered this defiance, by setting English colours, and five minutes later, the American ship ranged up abeam of the stern-

most vessel, at the distance of a cable's length, passing ahead
with her sails lifting, until the three ships formed nearly an
equilateral triangle, the Constitution to windward.   In this
masterly position the action commenced, the three vessels keeping up a hot and unceasing fire for about a quarter of an hour,
when that of the enemy sensibly slackened.   The sea being
covered with an immense cloud of smoke, and it being now
moonlight, Captain Stewart ordered the cannonading to cease.
In three minutes the smoke had blown away, when the leading ship of the enemy was seen under the lee-beam of the
Constitution, while the sternmost was luffing, as if she intended to tack and cross her wake.   Giving a broadside to the
ship abreast of her, the American frigate threw her main and
mizzen-topsails with topgallant-sails set, flat aback, shook all
forward, let fly her jib-sheet, and backed swiftly astern, compelling the enemy to fill again to avoid being raked.   The
leading ship now attempted to tack, to cross the Constitution's
fore-foot, when the latter filled, boarded her fore-tack, shot
ahead, forced her antagonist to ware under a raking broadside,
and to run off to leeward to escape from the weight of her
fire.

The Constitution perceiving that the largest ship was waring also, wore on her keel, and crossing her stern, raked her
with effect, though the enemy came by the wind immediately,
and delivered his larboard broadside ; but as the Constitution
ranged up close on his weather quarter, he struck.   Mr. Hoffman, the second lieutenant of the Constitution, was immediately sent to take possession ; the prize proving to be the British ship Cyane 24, Captain Falcon.

In the mean time, the ship that had run to leeward had been
forced out of the combat by the crippled condition of her running rigging, and to avoid the weight of the Constitution's fire.
She was ignorant of the fate of the Cyane, but at the end of
about an hour, having repaired damages, she hauled up, and
met the Constitution coming down in quest of her.   It was
near nine before the two ships crossed each other on opposite
tacks, the Constitution to windward, and exchanged broadsides.   The English ship finding her antagonist too heavy,
immediately bore up, in doing which she got a raking discharge, when the Constitution boarded fore-tack and made sail,
keeping up a most effective chasing fire, from her two bow
guns, nearly every shot of which told.   The two ships were
so near each other, that the ripping of the enemy's planks was

heard on board the American frigate. The former was unable to support this long, and at 10 P. M. he came by the wind, fired a gun to leeward, and lowered his ensign. Mr. W. B. Shubrick, the third lieutenant, was sent on board to take possession, when it was found that the prize was the Levant 18, the Honourable Captain Douglas.

During this cruise, the Constitution mounted 52 guns; and she had a complement of about 470 men, all told; a few of whom were absent in a prize. The Cyane was a frigate-buil ship, that properly rated 24 guns, though she appeared as only a 20 in Steele's list, mounting 22 thirty-two-pound carronades on her gun-deck, and 10 eighteen-pound carronades, with two chase guns, on her quarterdeck and forecastle; making 34 in all. The Levant was a new ship, rating 18, and mounting 18 thirty-two-pound carronades, a shifting eighteen on her topgallant forecastle, and two chase guns; or 21 in all. There were found in the Cyane, 168 prisoners, of whom 26 were wounded. The precise number slain on board her is not known; Captain Stewart, probably judging from an examination of the muster-book, computing it at 12, while the accounts given by the English publications differ, some putting the killed at only 4 and others at 6. It was probably between the two estimates. Her regular crew was about 185, all told; and there is no reason to believe that it was not nearly, if not absolutely full. Captain Stewart supposes it to have been 180 in the action, which was probably about the truth. The Levant's regular complement is said to have been 130, all told; but it appears by a statement published in Barbadoes, where some of her officers shortly after went, that there were a good many supernumeraries in the two vessels, who were going to the Western Islands, to bring away a ship that was building there. Captain Stewart supposes the Levant to have had 156 men in the action, of whom he believed 23 to have been killed, and 16 wounded. The first estimate may have been too high, though the truth can probably never be known. It is believed that no English official account of this action has ever been published, but the Barbadoes statement makes the joint loss of the two ships, 10 killed, and 28 wounded; other English accounts raise it as high as 41 in all. It may have been a little less than the estimate of Captain Stewart, (although his account of the wounded must have been accurate,) but was probably considerably more than that of the English statements. The Constitution had 3 killed, and 12 wounded, or she sustained a total loss of 15

men.  By 1 A. M., of the 21st, she was ready for another
action.  Although it was more than three hours and a half,
from the time this combat commenced, before the Levant
struck, the actual fighting did not occupy three-quarters of an
hour.  For a night action, the execution on both sides was
unusual, the enemy firing much better than common.  The
Constitution was hulled oftener in this engagement, than in
both her previous battles, though she suffered less in her crew,
than in the combat with the Java.  She had not an officer
hurt.

The manner in which Captain Stewart handled his ship, on
this occasion, excited much admiration among nautical men,
it being an unusual thing for a single vessel to engage two
enemies, and escape being raked.  So far from this occurring
to the Constitution, however, she actually raked both her op-
ponents, and the manner in which she backed and filled in the
smoke, forcing her two antagonists down to leeward, when
they were endeavouring to cross her stern or fore-foot, is among
the most brilliant manœuvring in naval annals.

It is due to a gallant enemy to say, that Captain Douglas
commanded the respect of the Americans, by his intrepid perseverance in standing by his consort.  Although the attempt
might not have succeeded, the time necessarily lost in securing
the Cyane, gave him an opportunity to endeavour to escape,
that he nobly refused to improve.

Captain Stewart proceeded with his two prizes to Port Praya,
where he arrived on the 10th of March.  Here a vessel was
engaged as a cartel, and more than a hundred of the prisoners
were landed with a view to help fit her for sea.  Saturday,
March 11th, 1815, a little after meridian, while the cutter was
absent to bring the cartel under the stern of the frigate, the
sea was covered with a heavy fog, near the water, and there
was a good deal of haze above, but in the latter, the sails of a
large ship were visible.  She was on a wind, looking in-shore,
and evidently stretching towards the roads.  The first lieutenant, Mr. Shubrick, reported the circumstance to Captain
Stewart.  This officer believing that the strange sail would
prove to be an English frigate or an Indiaman, directed the
lieutenant to return on deck, call all hands, and get ready to
go out and attack her.  As soon as this order was given, the
officer took a new look at the stranger, when he discovered
the canvass of two other ships rising above the bank of fog,
in the same direction.  These vessels were evidently heavy

36 *

men-of-war, and Captain Stewart was immediately apprised of
the fresh discovery. That prompt and decided officer did not
hesitate an instant concerning the course he ought to take.
Well knowing that the English would disregard the neutrality
of any port that had not sufficient force to resist them, or
which did not belong to a nation they were obliged to respect,
he immediately made a signal for the prizes to follow, and ordered the Constitution's cable to be cut. In 10 minutes after
this order was issued, and in 14 after the first ship had been
seen, the American frigate was standing out of the roads,
under her three topsails.

The cool and officer-like manner in which sail was made
and the ship cast, on this occasion, has been much extolled,
not an instant having been lost by hurry or confusion. The
prizes followed with promptitude. The northeast trades were
blowing, and the three vessels passed out to sea about gun-shot
to windward of the hostile squadron, just clearing East Point.
As the Constitution cleared the land, she crossed topgallant-
yards, boarded her tacks, and set all the light sails that would
draw. The English prisoners on shore, took possession of a
battery, and fired at her as she went out. As soon as the
American ships had gained the weather beam of the enemy,
the latter tacked, and the six vessels stood off to the southward and eastward, carrying every thing that would draw, and
going about ten knots.

The fog still lay so thick upon the water as to conceal the
hulls of the strangers, but they were supposed to be two line-
of-battle ships, and a large frigate, the vessel most astern and
to leeward, being the commodore. The frigate weathered on
all the American ships, gaining on the Levant and Cyane, but
falling astern of the Constitution; while the two larger vessels,
on the latter's lee quarter, held way with her. As soon as
clear of the land, the Constitution cut adrift two of her boats,
the enemy pressing her too hard to allow of their being hoisted
in. The Cyane was gradually dropping astern and to leeward,
rendering it certain, if she stood on, that the most weatherly
of the enemy's vessels would soon be alongside of her; and
at 10 minutes past one, Captain Stewart made a signal for her
to tack. This order was obeyed by Mr. Hoffman, the prize-
master; and it was now expected that one of the enemy's
ships would go about, and follow him; a hope that was disappointed. The Cyane finding that she was not pursued, stood
on until she was lost in the fog, when Mr. Hoffman tacked

again, anticipating that the enemy might chase him to leeward. This prudent officer improved his advantage, by keeping to windward long enough to allow the enemy to get ahead, should they pursue him, when he squared away for America, arriving safely at New York on the 10th of April following.

The three ships of the enemy continued to chase the Constitution and Levant. As the vessels left the land the fog lessened, though it still lay so dense on the immediate surface of the ocean, as to leave Captain Stewart in doubt as to the force of his pursuers. The English officers on board the Constitution affirmed that the vessel that was getting into her wake was the Acasta 40, Captain Kerr, a twenty-four-pounder ship, and it was thought that the three were a squadron that was cruising for the President, Peacock, and Hornet, consisting of the Leander 50, Sir George Collier, Newcastle 50, Lord George Stuart, and the Acasta; the ships that they subsequently proved to be. The Newcastle was the vessel on the lee-quarter of the Constitution, and by half-past two the fog had got so low, that her officers were seen standing on the hammock-cloths, though the line of her ports was not visible. She now began to fire by divisions, and some opinion could be formed of her armament, by the flashes of her guns, through the fog. Her shot struck the water within a hundred yards of the American ship, but did not rise again. By 3 P. M., the Levant had fallen so far astern, that she was in the very danger from which the Cyane had so lately been extricated, and Captain Stewart made her signal to tack also. Mr. Ballard immediately complied, and 7 minutes later the three English ships tacked, by signal, and chased the prize, leaving the Constitution standing on in a different direction, and going at the rate of eleven knots.

Mr. Ballard finding the enemy bent on following the Levant, with the Acasta already to windward of his wake, ran back into Port Praya, and anchored, at 4 o'clock, within 150 yards of the shore, under a strong battery. The enemy's ships had commenced firing, as soon as it was seen that the Levant would gain the anchorage, and all three now opened on the prize. After bearing the fire for a considerable time, the colours of the Levant were hauled down. No one was hurt in the prize, Mr. Ballard causing his men to lie on the deck, as soon as the ship was anchored. The English prisoners in the battery, also fired at the Levant.

Sir George Collier was much criticised for the course he pursued on this occasion. It was certainly a mistake to call off' more than one ship to chase the Levant, though the position of the Leander in the fog, so far to leeward and astern, did not give the senior officer the best opportunities for observing the course of events. There was certainly every prospect of the Acasta's bringing the Constitution to action in the course of the night, though the other vessels might have been left so far astern, as still to render the result doubtful.

Whatever may be thought of the management of the enemy, there can be but one opinion as to that of Captain Stewart. The promptitude with which he decided on his course, the judgment with which he ordered the prizes to vary their courses, and the steadiness with which the Constitution was commanded, aided in elevating a professional reputation that was already very high.

This terminated the exploits of the gallant Constitution, or Old Ironsides, as she was affectionately called in the navy; Captain Stewart, after landing his prisoners at Maranham, and learning at Porto Rico, that peace had been made, carried her into New York, about the middle of May. In the course of two years and nine months, this ship had been in three actions, had been twice critically chased, and had captured five vessels of war, two of which were frigates, and a third frigate-built. In all her service, as well before Tripoli, as in this war, her good fortune was remarkable. She never was dismasted, never got ashore, or scarcely ever suffered any of the usual accidents of the sea. Though so often in battle, no very serious slaughter ever took place on board her. One of her commanders was wounded, and four of her lieutenants had been killed; two on her own decks, and two in the Intrepid; but, on the whole, her entire career had been that of what is usually called a "lucky ship." Her fortune, however, may perhaps be explained in the simple fact, that she had always been well commanded. In her two last cruises she had probably possessed as fine a crew as ever manned a frigate. They were principally New England men, and it has been said of them, that they were almost qualified to fight the ship without her officers.

## CHAPTER XLIX.

When Commodore Rodgers left the President, in the summer of 1814, to take command of the Guerriere, Commodore Decatur was transferred to the former ship; the United States and Macedonian, then blockaded in the Thames, having been laid up, and the Hornet, Captain Biddle, left to protect them. This service was particularly irksome to an officer of the spirit of the last-named gentleman; and persevering in his applications to be released from it, he finally received an order to join Commodore Decatur at New York, where the President had been some time detained to make part of the defence of the port, while the enemy was committing his depredations on the coast, during the mild weather. No sooner did Captain Biddle receive this welcome command, than he took the first favourable occasion to pass out, leaving the blockading squadron to the eastward, and ran down to New York. This was in the month of November, 1814, and Commodore Decatur had now a force consisting of the President 44, his own ship, Peacock 18, Captain Warrington, Hornet 18, Captain Biddle, and Tom Bowline store-vessel. His destination was the East Indies, where it was thought great havoc might be made with the valuable trade of the English.

Owing to different causes, but principally to the wish of the government to keep a force at New York to resist the depredations of the enemy, Commodore Decatur did not get to sea until the middle of January, 1815. The President dropped down to Sandy Hook alone, leaving the other vessels lying at Staten Island, and on the night of the 14th, she made an attempt to cross the bar. In consequence of the darkness, the pilots missed the channel and the ship struck; beating heavily on the sands, for an hour and a half. About 10 o'clock the tide had risen to its height, and she was forced into deep water. Although the vessel had received considerable injury, it was impossible to return, and a strong blockading force being in the offing, it became necessary to carry sail to get off the coast before morning. It had blown a gale the previous day, and Commodore Decatur, rightly judging that the enemy had been driven to leeward, decided to run along the land to the northward and eastward, as the best means of avoiding a greatly superior force. This determination was judicious, and, had not the detention occurred on the bar, it would have been completely successful. After running off in a northeastern direction for about 5 hours, the course of the ship was altered to S. E. by E. Two hours later, a strange sail was discovered ahead, within gun-shot, and two others being soon after seen, the President hauled up and passed to the northward of them all. At daylight, four ships were seen in chase, one on each quarter and two astern. The nearest vessel was believed to be the Majectic rasée, which fired a broadside or two, in the hope of crippling the American frigate as she passed, but without effect. It is now known, that the enemy had been driven down to the southward by the gale, and that he was just returning to his station, when this unlucky encounter occurred.

The chase continued throughout the forenoon, the wind becoming lighter and baffling. The rasée was dropped materially, but the next nearest ship, the Endymion, 40, a twenty-four-pounder frigate, had closed, and as the President was very deep, being filled with stores for a long cruise, Commodore Decatur commenced lightening her. Unfortunately the commander, all the lieutenants, and the master were strangers, in one sense, to the ship ; most of them never having been at sea in her at all, and neither in any responsible situation. The duty of lightening a ship in chase, is one of the most delicate operations in seamanship, and it ought never to be attempted except by those perfectly acquainted with her lines, trim, and stowage. Half-a-dozen more water-casks emptied at one end of the vessel than at the other may injure her sailing ; and the utmost care is to be observed lest the indiscretion of inferiors in the hold, defeat the calculations of the commander on deck. On the other hand, Commodore Decatur decided to undertake this delicate operation under the most favourable circumstances that a want of familiarity with his ship would allow, as the wind was getting to be light, and was nearly aft.

It is not certain, however, that the sailing of the President was injured by the process of lightening, for she is supposed to have suffered materially while on the bar, and the enemy obtained a material advantage by a change in the wind. While it was still light with the American ship, the British, about 3 P. M., were bringing down with them a fresh breeze. Soon after, the Endymion, the nearest vessel, having got within reach of shot, opened with her bow guns, the President returning the fire with her stern-chasers. The object of each, was to cripple the spars of the other. It is said, that on this occasion, the shot of the American ship were observed to be thrown with a momentum so unusually small, as to have since excited a distrust of the quality of her powder. It is even added, that many of these shot were distinctly seen, when clear of the smoke, until they struck.

By 5 P. M., the Endymion had got so far on the starboard, or lee quarter of the President, that no gun of the latter would bear on her without altering the course. The fire of the English ship now became exceedingly annoying, for she was materially within point-blank range, and every shot cut away something aloft. Still it was borne, in the hope that she would range up alongside, and give the President an opportunity of laying her aboard. Finding, however, that the enemy warily kept his position by yawing, in the hope of gradually crippling the American ship, Commodore Decatur decided on a course that singularly partook of the daring chivalry of his character.

It was now evident that the sailing of the President was much impaired by some cause or other; either by injuries received on the bar, or by the manner in which she had been lightened, and escape by flight had become nearly hopeless. Commodore Decatur, therefore, decided to make an effort to exchange ships, by carrying the Endymion, hand to hand, and to go off in the prize, abandoning his own vessel to the enemy. With this object in view, he determined to keep away, lay the enemy aboard if possible, and put every thing on the success of the experiment. The plan was communicated to the people, who received it cheerfully, and just at dusk, the helm of the President was put up, bringing the wind over the taffrail, the ship heading south. But she was so closely watched, that the Endymion kept away at the same moment, and the two ships soon came abeam of each other, when both delivered their broadsides. All the President's attempts to close, were defeated, for the vessels were about a quarter of a mile apart, and as she hauled nearer to the enemy, the latter sheered away from her. Without a superiority in sailing, it was impossible for Commodore Decatur to get any nearer, and he was now reduced to the necessity of attempting to get rid of the Endymion by dismantling her. The two frigates, consequently continued running off dead before the wind, keeping up a heavy cannonade for two hours and a half, when the enemy's vessel was so far injured that she fell astern, most of her sails having been cut from the yards.  The President, at this moment, was under her royal studding-sails, and there is no doubt, by choosing her position, she might easily have compelled her adversary to strike; but, by this time, though the night was dark, the vessels astern were in sight, and she was obliged to resume her original course to avoid them.  In doing this, the President hauled up under the broadside of her late antagonist, without receiving any fire to injure her.

It was now half-past eight, and the President continued to run off southeast, repairing damages, but it was found impossible to prevent the other vessels of the enemy from closing. At 11 P. M., the Pomona 38 got on the weather bow of the American ship, and poured in a broadside ; and as the Tenedos, of the same force, was fast closing on the quarter, and the Majestic was within gun-shot astern, further resistance was useless.   Commodore Decatur had ordered his people below, when he saw the two last frigates closing, but finding that his signal of submission was not at first understood, the Pomona continuing to fire, an order had been given for them to return to their guns, just as the enemy ceased.  The Majestic coming up before the removal of Commodore Decatur, that gentleman delivered his sword to her captain, who was the senior English officer present.

In this long and close cannonade, agreeably to the official reports, the President lost 24 men killed, and 56 wounded. She was a good deal injured in her hull, and most of her important spars were badly damaged.   By one of those chances which decide the fortunes of men, among the slain were the first, fourth, and fifth lieutenants.

The Endymion had 11 killed, and 14 wounded, according to the published reports.  As it is known that an order was given to aim at the rigging and spars of this ship, with a view to cripple her, it is probable this statement was accurate.  It is believed, however, on respectable authority, that a great many shot hulled the Endymion, which did not penetrate ; a fact which, coupled with other observations made during the day, has induced the distrust of the quality of the President's powder. Owing to one, or to both, the circumstances named, the English ship lost but about a third as many men as the American, though a considerable number of the President's people were killed and wounded by the unresisted fire of the Pomona, having been ordered back to the guns before the latter ceased.

The President was carried to Bermuda, and both she and

CONSTITUTION, CYANE AND LEVANT.

the Endymion were dismasted in a gale, before reaching port. The latter also threw overboard her upper-deck guns. Commodore Decatur was shortly after paroled, and he and all his surviving officers and men, were subsequently acquitted, with honour, for the loss of the ship.

The commanders of the Peacock, Hornet, and Tom Bowline brig, ignorant of the capture of the President, followed her to sea, about the 22d, taking advantage of a strong northwester, to pass the bar by daylight. The enemy was seen lying-to at the southward and eastward, but was disregarded. A few days out the Hornet parted company in chase of a neutral, when all three vessels made the best of their way to the island of Tristan d'Acunha, the place of rendezvous appointed by Commodore Decatur. The Peacock and Tom Bowline arrived about the middle of March, but bad weather coming on, they were driven off the land. On the morning of the 23d of the same month, the Hornet came in, with the wind fresh at S. S. W., and was about to anchor, having let go her topsail-sheets to clew up, when the men aloft discovered a sail to windward. The stranger was standing to the westward, and was soon shut in by the land. Captain Biddle immediately sheeted home his topsails again, and made a stretch to windward and towards the chase, which was shortly after seen running down before the wind. There being little doubt as to the character of the stranger, the Hornet hove-to, waiting for him to come down, and when he had got near enough to render it prudent, the main-topsail was filled, and the ship was kept yawing, occasionally waring, both to allow him to close and to prevent his giving a raking fire.

At 1 40 P. M., the stranger having got within musket-shot, came by the wind, set English colours and fired a gun. On this challenge, the Hornet luffed up, showed her ensign, and returned a broadside. For 15 minutes both vessels kept up a sharp cannonade, that of the American ship, in particular, being very animated and destructive, the enemy gradually drifting nearer, when the latter, finding it impossible to stand the Hornet's fire, put his helm up and ran down directly on the starboard broadside of the latter, to lay her aboard. The enemy's bowsprit came in between the main and mizzen rigging of the Hornet, affording a perfectly good opportunity to attempt effecting his purpose, but, though his first lieutenant made a gallant effort to lead on his men, the latter could not be induced to follow. Captain Biddle had called away boarders

37

to repel boarders, and his people now manifested a strong wish to go into the English vessel, but perceiving his great advantage at the guns, that intrepid officer, who had been so free to adopt this expedient, when it was his duty to lead in his own person, judiciously refused his permission.

The vessels lay in this position but a minute or two, the American raking, when the sea lifted the Hornet ahead, carrying-away her mizzen rigging, davits, and spanker-boom, the enemy swinging round and hanging on the larboard quarter. At this moment, Captain Biddle sent the master forward to set the foresail, with a view to part the vessels, when an officer on board the English ship called out that she surrendered. The positions prevented any other firing than that of small-arms; this was ordered to cease, and Captain Biddle sprang upon the taffrail to inquire if the enemy submitted. While putting this question, he was within thirty feet of the forecastle of the English vessel, and two marines on board discharged their muskets at him. The ball of one just missed the chin and passing through the skin of the neck, inflicted a severe, but fortunately not a dangerous wound. This incident drew a discharge of muskets from the Hornet, which killed the two marines; the American ship forged ahead at that instant, and the enemy lost his bowsprit and foremast as the vessels separated.

The Hornet now wore round, bringing a fresh broadside to bear, and was about to throw in a raking fire, when twenty men appeared at the side and on the forecastle of the enemy, raising their hands for quarter, and eagerly calling out that they had struck. The excitement on board the American ship, however, was so great, in consequence of the manner in which their gallant captain had received his wound, that it was with the utmost difficulty Captain Biddle and his officers could prevent the people from pouring in another broadside.

The prize was H. B. Majesty's brig the Penguin 18, mounting 19 carriage guns; viz., 16 thirty-two-pound carronades, two chase guns, and a shifting carronade on the topgallant forecastle. She was a vessel of the Hornet's class, size, and metal, and is represented as having had a spare port forward, by means of which she could fight ten guns in broadside.* Her

---

* On an accurate computation of the real (not nominal) metal of the two vessels, the Hornet would appear to have thrown, at a broadside, about nine pounds more shot than the Penguin; the latter not using her spare port. As respects the crews, the American ship had some ten or fifteen the most men at quarters. In tonnage the vessels were very nearly equal.

complement of men was 132, of whom 12 had been put on
board her for the express purpose of engaging a very heavy
American privateer called the Young Wasp, a fact that is
known by a letter found in her, from the Admiral at the Cape
of Good Hope, to which station the Penguin belonged. Captain Biddle stated the loss of his prize at 14 killed and 28
wounded. As respects the latter, there could be no mistake,
though it was the opinion of the officer in charge of the English
vessel, that more men had been slain. Some time previously
to this capture, the enemy had ceased to publish the official
accounts of his nautical defeats, but a letter purporting to be
the one written on this occasion, has found its way before the
world, in which the English loss is stated at only 10 killed and
28 wounded. The Penguin was completely riddled with the
Hornet's shot, lost her foremast and bowsprit, and her main-
mast was too much injured to be secured. Among her slain
was her commander, Captain Dickenson, and the boatswain;
and among the wounded a lieutenant, two midshipmen, and the
purser.

The Hornet had but 1 man killed, and 10 wounded. Among
the latter, in addition to Captain Biddle, was the first lieutenant,
Mr. Conner,* a young officer of high promise, whose life was
considered in great danger for some time. Not a round shot
touched the Hornet's hull, nor did her spars receive any material injury, though she was a good deal cut up in her rigging
and sails.

The combat between the Hornet and the Penguin was one
of the most creditable to the character of the American marine
that occurred in the course of the war. The vessels were very
fairly matched, and when it is remembered that an English
flag-officer had sent the Penguin on especial service against a
ship believed to be materially heavier than the vessel she actually encountered, it is fair to presume she was thought to be,
in every respect, an efficient cruiser. Yet, with the advantage
of the wind, this ship was taken in 22 minutes, including the
time lost while she hung on the Hornet's quarter, and while
the latter was waring. The neatness and despatch with which
the American sloop did her work, the coolness with which she
met the attempt to board, and the accuracy of her fire and
handling, are all proofs of her having been a disciplined man-
of-war, and of the high condition of that service in which she

---

* Now Captain Conner

was one of the favourites. It is by such exploits that the character of a marine is most effectually proved.

A few hours after the action, a strange and suspiciously look-ing sail heaving in sight, a cable was taken from the Penguin, and the Hornet towed her some distance off the land. After thoroughly examining the prize, and getting out of her all the stores and provisions that were wanted, before daylight, on the morning of the 25th, Captain Biddle scuttled her. The Hornet then stood in towards the island to look for the strange sail, which was found to be the Peacock, having the Tom Bowline in company. An arrangement was now made, by which the latter was converted into a cartel, and was sent into St. Salva-dor with the prisoners.

As soon as he was released from this encumbrance, and from the great drain on his supplies, Captain Biddle was ready to continue his cruise. This spirited officer did not consider the capture of a vessel of the same class as his own, a reason of itself for returning to port; but, it having been ascertained, by means of the Macedonian, a brig which sailed with the President, that the latter ship was probably captured, Captain Warrington determined to proceed on the original cruise, with the remaining vessels. They sailed, accordingly, on the 13th of April, having remained at the island the time directed in the instructions of Commodore Decatur.

While making the best of their way towards the Indian seas, on the morning of the 27th of April, the two ships then being in lat. 38° 30' S., long. 33° E., the Peacock made the signal of a stranger to the southward and eastward. Both the sloops of war made sail in chase. Though the wind was light, before evening it was found that the stranger was materially nearer. It now fell calm, and the chase was in sight in the morning. The wind coming out at N. W., the ships ran down before it, with studding-sails on both sides, the stranger hauling up, appa-rently, to look at them. The Peacock was the fastest vessel, and being two leagues ahead at half past 2, P. M., she was ob-served to manifest some caution about approaching the stranger, when the Hornet took in her starboard light sails, and hauled up for her consort. It was now thought, on board the latter ship, that the stranger was a large Indiaman, and that the Peacock was merely waiting for the Hornet to come up, in order to attack her. But an hour later Captain Warrington made a signal that the vessel in sight was a line-of-battle ship, and an enemy. The Hornet immediately hauled close upon the wind, the stranger then on her lee quarter, distant not quite two leagues, the Peacock passing ahead and soon getting clear of him.

It was now seen that the English ship sailed very fast, and was unusually weatherly. The Hornet being more particularly in danger, about 9 P. M., Captain Biddle felt it necessary to begin to lighten, his vessel being crowded with stores taken from the Penguin. Twelve tons of kentledge, a quantity of shot, some heavy spars, and the sheet-anchor and cable, were thrown overboard. By 2 A. M., the enemy had drawn forward of the lee-beam, when the Hornet tacked to the westward, the enemy immediately following. At daylight on the 29th, the English ship was on the lee quarter of the American, and within gun-shot. At 7 o'clock she had English colours set with a rear-admiral's flag flying, and she commenced firing. The shot passing over the Hornet, the launch was cut up and gotten rid of, the other anchors and cables, more shot, as many heavy articles as could be come at, and six of the guns were also thrown overboard. By 9 o'clock, the enemy had dropped so far astern that he ceased firing, the concussion produced by his guns having deadened the wind.

By 11 A. M., however, it was found that the enemy was again closing, when the Hornet threw overboard all the remaining guns but one, the boats, most of her shot, all the spare spars, and as many other articles off deck and from below, as could be got at. She also cut up her topgallant forecastle, and threw the pieces into the ocean. At meridian, the enemy had got within a mile, and he began again to fire, his shot flying far beyond the ship. Fortunately but three struck her. One passed through her jib, another plunged on her deck, glancing and lodging forward, and a third also hulled her. Still Captain Biddle held on, determined not to give up his ship while there was a ray of hope, for it was seen that the enemy was dropped while firing. About 2 P. M. the breeze freshened, and got more to the westward. Previously to this, the wind, by backing to the southeast, had greatly favoured the chase, but it now brought the Hornet more to windward, and she began to get brisk way on her. At sunset the stranger was more than a league astern, and the ship was running nine knots throughout the night, the wind blowing in squalls. The enemy was seen at intervals, carrying sail in chase, but at daylight he was nearly hull down astern. At half-past 9 A. M., he took in his studding-sails, reefed his top-

37 *

sails and hauled off to the eastward; and two hours later, his upper sails had dipped. The Hornet had now no anchor, cable, nor boat, and but one gun, and she made the best of her way to St. Salvador, for the relief of the wounded. Here Captain Biddle heard of the peace, when he sailed for New York, which port he reached on the 30th of July.

The vessel that chased the Hornet was the Cornwallis 74 bearing the flag of an officer proceeding to the East Indies.

The Peacock continued her cruise, and on the 30th of June in the Straits of Sunda, she fell in with the East India Company's cruiser, Nautilus 14, Captain Boyce. In consequence of Captain Warrington's having no knowledge of the peace, broadsides were exchanged, when the Nautilus struck. This unfortunate mistake occurred a few days after the period set for the termination of hostilities, and having ascertained that a treaty of peace had been ratified in March, Captain Warrington gave up the Nautilus the next day. The latter vessel had 6 killed and 8 wounded, but no person was hurt on board the Peacock, which ship immediately returned home.

The combat between the Hornet and Penguin was the last regular action of the war, and the rencontre between the Peacock and Nautilus, the last instance of hostilities between the belligerents. When the Peacock got in, every cruiser that had been out against the English had returned to port.

The burning of the frigate Columbia, at Washington, and the blockade of the Java in the Chesapeake, had induced the government, in the autumn of 1814, to purchase or build two squadrons of small vessels, one of which was to be commanded by Captain Porter, and the other by Captain Perry. The former succeeded in buying five brigantines, or schooners, and he was about to sail with them, when the news of peace reached the country. The vessels, which formed one of these flying squadrons, were the Firefly, Spark, Torch, Spitfire, and Flambeau. The first destination of this force was the West Indies, and it was understood that it was to sail with orders to burn, sink, and destroy, without attempting, except in very extraordinary cases, to get any thing in.

Captain Perry was less successful in finding suitable vessels, and three stout brigs, called the Boxer, Saranac, and Chippewa, were laid down, though built with green timber. Another, called the Escape, was purchased and named the Prometheus; but it would seem that a fifth vessel had not been found when peace was proclaimed.

Thus terminated the war of 1812, so far as it was connected with the American marine. The navy came out of this struggle with a vast increase of reputation. The brilliant style in which the ships had been carried into action, the steadiness and rapidity with which they had been handled, and the fatal accuracy of their fire, on nearly every occasion, produced a new era in naval warfare. Most of the frigate actions had been as soon decided as circumstances would at all allow, and in no instance was it found necessary to keep up the fire of a sloop of war an hour, when singly engaged. Most of the combats of the latter, indeed, were decided in about half that time. The execution done in these short conflicts was often equal to that made by the largest vessels of Europe, in general actions; and in some of them, the slain and wounded comprised a very large proportion of the crews.

It is not easy to say in which nation this unlooked-for result created the most surprise; America or England. In the first it produced a confidence in itself that had been greatly wanted, but which, in the end, perhaps, degenerated to a feeling of self-esteem and security that was not without danger, or entirely without exaggeration. The last was induced to alter its mode of rating, adopting one by no means as free from the imputation of a want of consistency as that which it abandoned, and it altogether changed its estimate of the force of single ships, as well as of the armaments of frigates. The ablest and bravest captains of the English fleet were ready to admit that a new power was about to appear on the ocean, and that it was not improbable the battle for the mastery of the seas would have to be fought over again. In short, while some of the ignorant, presuming, and boastful were disposed to find excuses for the unexpected nautical reverses which Great Britain had met with in this short war, the sagacious and reflecting saw in them matter for serious apprehension and alarm. They knew that the former triumphs of their admirals had not so much grown out of an unusual ability to manœuvre fleets, as in the national aptitude to manage single ships; and they saw the proofs of the same aptitude, in the conduct of the Americans during this struggle, improved on by a skill in gunnery, that had never before been so uniformly manifested in naval warfare. In a word, it may be questioned if all the great victories of the last European conflicts caused more exultation among the uninstructed of that nation, than the defeats of this gave rise to misgivings and apprehensions among those who were able to appreciate causes and to antici pate consequences in a matter so purely professional as the construction, powers, and handling of ships. Many false modes of accounting for the novel character that had been given to naval battles was resorted to. Among other reasons, it was affirmed that the American vessels of war sailed with crews of picked seamen. It is not known that a single vessel left the country, the case of the Constitution on her two last cruises excepted, with a crew that could be deemed extraordinary. No American man-of-war ever sailed with a complement composed of nothing but able seamen; and some of the hardest fought battles that occurred during this war, were fought by ships' companies that were materially worse than common. The people of the vessels on Lake Champlain, in particular, were of a quality much inferior to those usually found in ships of war. Neither were the officers, in general, old or very experienced. The navy itself had existed but fourteen years, when the war commenced; and some of the commanders began their professional careers, several years after the first appointments had been made. Perhaps one half of the lieutenants, in the service at the peace of 1815, had gone on board ship, for the first time, within six years from the declaration of the war, and very many of them within three or four. So far from the midshipmen having been masters and mates of merchantmen, as was reported at the time, they were generally youths that first quitted the ease and comforts of the paternal home, when they appeared on the quarter-deck of a man-of-war.

That the tone and discipline of the service were high, is true; but it must be ascribed to moral, and not to physical causes; to that aptitude in the American character for the sea, which has been so constantly manifested from the day the first pinnace sailed along the coast on the trading voyages of the seventeenth century, down to the present moment.

## CHAPTER L.

AGREEABLY to the policy of the Barbary powers, the Dey of Algiers no sooner found the republican cruisers excluded from the Mediterranean, by the English war, than he began to commit his depredations on the little American commerce that remained in or near that sea. During the late conflict, there was little leisure, and no great motive, to attend to this new enemy, but peace was no sooner made with England, than Congress, on the 2d of March, 1815, passed an Act authorizing hostilities against Algiers. This was at a moment when extensive preparations had been making to continue the more serious contest, and, as several thousand mariners were at once withdrawn from the lakes, the government was enabled to strike an early and important blow at its new enemy. Crews were thrown into the Guerriere, Macedonian and Congress frigates, the light squadrons mentioned in the last chapter furnished several efficient vessels for such service, and various sloops were already prepared to go to sea. A force consisting of the Guerriere 44, Capt. Lewis; the Constellation 38, Capt. Gordon; the Macedonian 38, Capt. Jones; the Ontario 18, Capt. Elliott; Epervier 18, Capt. Downes; Firefly 12, Lt. Com. Rodgers; Spark 12, Lt. Com. Gamble; Flambeau 12, Lt. Com. Nicolson; Torch 12, Lt. Com. Chauncey, and Spitfire 12, Lt. Com. Dallas, assembled in the port of New York in the course of the spring. May the 21st, this squadron sailed for the Mediterranean, under the orders of Commodore Decatur, whose pennant was flying in the Guerriere.

The Torch, Spitfire and Firefly separated in a gale, on the 26th of May, the Firefly being obliged to return in consequence of springing her masts. The Ontario also lost the squadron on the 31st. Commodore Decatur reached Tangiers on the 15th of June, and had some communications with the consul. From this gentleman he learned that the Algerine Admiral Hammida, had been off the port the previous day, in a frigate, and that he had sailed again on his way to Carthagena, in company with a heavy brig. The squadron entered the Straits immediately, called the Ontario, Spitfire and Torch out of Gibraltar by signal, in passing, and shaped its course for Cape de Gatt. On the 17th of June, it fell in with the Algerine frigate Mishouri 46, Rais Hammida, when the Constellation, Capt. Gordon, the leading vessel, succeeded in bringing her to action. In a few minutes the Guerriere, Capt. Lewis, bearing the Commodore's pennant, passed between the two vessels, and poured in a broadside. Unfortunately one of the twenty-fours burst, at this discharge, blew up the spar deck, and killed and wounded from 30 to 45 men. The effect of her broadside, notwithstanding, was to drive the enemy from his guns, a few musketmen alone continuing the action on the part of the Algerines. The Ontario pressing the Mishouri on her quarter, the Macedonian coming up on her beam, and the small vessels closing also, there was no possibility of escape, and the enemy struck. The Algerine Admiral was among the slain.

Com. Decatur reported this affair as a running fight of 25 minutes, in which the enemy had 30 men killed, besides a great many wounded. The prisoners amounted to 406. No vessel sustained any loss but the Guerriere, on board of which ship 4 men were wounded by musket-balls, in addition to those who suffered by the explosion.

Two days later, or on the 19th of June, the squadron chased an enemy's brig of 22 guns, and 180 men, into shoal water, off Cape Palos. The Epervier, Spark, Torch and Spitfire were ordered in to destroy her, and they compelled her to strike after a short resistance. No less than 23 dead were found on board this vessel, and 80 prisoners were received from her, though many of her people escaped to the shore. It was thought that many of those who had left the prize, perished by the fire of the assailants, and it was known that one boat was sunk. No injury was sustained by the Americans, nor was either of the vessels injured. The brig was called the Estedio.

Commodore Decatur sent his prizes into Carthagena, and proceeded to Algiers with most of his vessels, where he arrived on the 28th. Here the Dey was offered the choice of war or peace, and he wisely accepted the latter. A treaty was concluded June 30th, or just 40 days after the American squadron left New York. This treaty is memorable from the circumstance that it was made on the terms of reciprocity acknowledged among civilised nations. By this treaty, tribute was for ever abolished, as between the United States and Algiers; there was a mutual delivery of prisoners; a restitution of property taken from American citizens was made; nor were slaves to be made, in the event of any future war.   In other respects, this arrangement was acceptable to the republic and humiliating to the regency.

There can be no doubt that the Dey was induced to sign this treaty thus promptly, on account of the critical condition of the remainder of his fleet; portions of which were expected hourly off the place.   An attempt had been made to procure a suspension of hostilities, pending the negotiation; but to this proposition, the American commissioners, Com. Decatur and Mr. William Shaler, absolutely declined acceding.   A sloop of war did actually heave in sight before the treaty was received, signed by the Dey; and had she appeared an hour sooner, she would have been captured.   The Dey asked, as a personal favour, to have the frigate and brig restored, and to this the Commissioners consented, though they refused to allow an article to that effect to be inserted in the treaty.

After dictating terms to the Dey of Algiers, in the manner mentioned, Commodore Decatur transferred Captain Downes of the Epervier to his own ship, gave the command of the former to the Guerriere's first lieutenant, Mr. John Templar Shubrick, and ordered the latter home with the treaty.   The Epervier left the squadron a few days after the prisoners were released, and passed the Straits about the 10th of July.   It is said that she was seen early in August, and that a tremendous gale succeeded on the following day; but nothing certain is known of her fate.   Twenty-six years have elapsed, and no occurrence has transpired to throw any light on the nature of the disaster.   Like the Saratoga, l'Insurgente, the Pickering, the Wasp, and gun-boat No. 7, this unfortunate vessel has disappeared, leaving behind her no traces of the manner in which she was lost.*

---

* There were several passengers on board the Epervier, some of whom had been prisoners in Algiers.   Among others were Captain Lewis, late of the Guerriere, and Mr. Benedict J. Neale, late first lieutenant of the Constellation.   These gentlemen had married sisters, a short time before the squadron left home, and having seen the war at an end, were returning to their brides, with the feelings of men who had the consciousness of having temporarily sacrificed the best affections to duty.   Of course they were lost in the vessel.

Mr. John Templar Shubrick was a son of Col. Richard Shubrick of South Carolina, who had served with credit in the war of the revolution, and was allied by blood to the Draytons, Hamiltons, Haynes', and other patriotic and distinguished families of that State.   Mr. Shubrick had been singularly fortunate in seeing service.   He was on board the Con-

Peace was no sooner signed with Algiers, than Commodore
Decatur proceeded first to Tunis and then to Tripoli, with
reclamations on those governments, for injuries done American
commerce, during the late English war.   In both instances
redress was obtained in the promptest manner.   Commodore
Decatur says, in one of his official letters, in reference to these
demands,—" During the progress of our negotiations with the
States of Barbary, now brought to a conclusion, there has appeared a disposition, on the part of each of them, to grant as
far as we were disposed to demand."   No better illustration
can be given of the change that had been effected by the services of the Navy, within twelve or fifteen years, than is to be
found in this simple but memorable declaration.   The facts
fully warranted it ; and from the summer of 1815, dates the
fall of a system of piratical depredations that had rendered the
high seas in that quarter of the world insecure for several centuries, and which existed a disgrace to European civilization.

As the prompt submission of the Dey of Algiers could not
be foreseen, vessels were constantly quitting the United States
for the Mediterranean, as they got ready, in order to reinforce
the squadron, in anticipation of an attack upon the town.
Among others, the Independence 74 sailed, under the orders
of Commodore Bainbridge, who was to assume the chief command, on arriving out.   This was the first two-decked ship
that ever went to sea under the American flag.   She arrived
too late for active service ; but collecting several ships, Com-

---

stitution in her actions with the Guerriere and Java.   He was then transferred to the Hornet, and acted as her first lieutenant when she took the
Peacock.   He sailed in the President, Commodore Decatur, as her second
lieutenant, but became first in the action, Mr. Babbit having been killed
at the first broadside of the Endymion.   He then went to the Guerriere,
as first, and was near being destroyed by the bursting of the gun, in the
action with the Algerine, a large piece of the metal actually hitting his
hat.   After all his escapes, Mr. Shubrick perished in the manner mentioned.   He was an officer of not only high promise, but of high performance, his conduct on every occasion eliciting praise from his supe-
riors.   He had not long been married when he was lost, leaving an only
son.   Four brothers of this family have served in the navy with reputation.   The second in years, is Commodore Wm. Branford Shubrick, late
of the West-India squadron, and now commanding at Norfolk ; Captain
Edward Shubrick is the third ; and Commander Irvine Shubrick is the
youngest.   The son of Mr. John Templar Shubrick, is also a lieutenant
in the navy.

On board the Epervier also perished Lieutenant Yarnall, who had been
first in the Lawrence, in her bloody conflict on Lake Erie.

modore Bainbridge made a great impression on the different Barbary powers, by showing this fresh force off their ports, just after Commodere Decatur had left them. In this manner a squadron was soon assembled, that greatly exceeded in numbers and guns, any force that the republic had then sent to sea. It is believed that the following vessels appeared in the Mediterranean at, or quite near, the same time, viz :—

Independence ... 74 .... Com. Bainbridge.
Guerriere ...... 44 .... Capt. Downes, Com. Decatur.
United States ... 44 .... Capt. Shaw.
Constellation ... 38 .... Capt. Gordon.
Congress ...... 38 .... Capt. Morris.
Macedonian .... 38 .... Capt. Jones.
Ontario........ 18 .... Capt. Elliott.
Erie .......... 18 .... Capt. Ridgely.
Epervier....... 18 .... Lt. Com. Shubrick.
Boxer ......... 16 .... Lt. Com. Porter.
Saranac ....... 16 .... Lt. Com. Elton.
Chippewa ...... 16 .... Lt. Com. Reid.
Spark ......... 12 .... Lt. Com. Gamble.
Enterprise...... 12 .... Lt. Com. Kearny.
Firefly ........ 12 .... Lt. Com. Rodgers.
Spitfire ........ 12 .... Lt. Com. Dallas.
Torch......... 12 .... Lt. Com. Chauncey.
Flambeau...... 12 .... Lt. Com. Nicolson.
Lynx ......... 12 .... Lt. Com. Storer.

The Java 44, Captain Perry, appeared a little later. Commodore Decatur returned home with the Guerriere and one or two other vessels, as soon as the service was completed; and Commodore Bainbridge arrived at Newport in November, with thirteen vessels of the squadron, viz : one ship of the line, two frigates, seven brigs, and three schooners. This is the largest American force that ever crossed the Atlantic in company.

Commodore Shaw was left in command, in the Mediterranean, with the United States 44, Constellation 38, Ontario 18, and Erie 18. The Java 44, joined him shortly after.

Thus terminated the last Barbary war, the impression left by which promises to be lasting, and which may be said, indeed, to have changed the policy of Europe, as regards those States, which had so long existed as nuisances to all legal

38

navigation, and exceptions to the laws that regulated inter-
course between civilized nations.

The misunderstanding in the Mediterranean being arranged,
the country had no longer any pressing service for its marine.
Nevertheless, it now offered the singular spectacle of a country
increasing its naval armaments, in a time of profound peace.
The views of the government would seem to have enlarged
with the late events, and the necessity of keeping afloat a force
sufficient to protect a navigation that extended to the remotest
corners of the earth, was now generally admitted. The foreign
stations were no longer limited to the Mediterranean, but ships
from this time forward were periodically sent to the Pacific
and the coast of Brazil. Not long after, the East and West
Indies, and the coast of Africa attracted notice; and for many
years, squadrons have been employed in the Mediterranean,
on the coast of Brazil, in the West Indies, and in the East
Indies, the latter, however, regularly proceeding round the
world, touching at all such points as the public interests have
required. It is worthy of remark that all the active cruisers
have been employed on this foreign service, leaving the home
coast, with few and transient exceptions, quite without protection. A recent law (1841) has remedied this signal defect in
the nautical policy of the country, and henceforth, it is to be
hoped, the nation will possess an active home squadron.

Attention was paid, soon after the peace of 1815, to the
regular increase of the navy, and a great improvement has been
made in the construction of dry docks. The following two-
decked ships have been put into the water, and all of them
have been used on foreign stations, viz:

| | |
|---|---|
| Independence | 74 |
| Washington | 74 |
| Franklin | 74 |
| Columbus | 80 |
| North Carolina | 80 |
| Delaware | 80 |
| Ohio | 80 |

Most of these ships have been found to be good vessels of
their class, and two or three of them quite superior to ordinary
ships of the line. They have never been tried in squadron,
an experiment that is necessary to a just appreciation of their
respective qualities. It remains yet to assemble the first
American fleet. A strong force of this character is indispen-

sable to forming a perfect and efficient marine, since in war great results can only be obtained by an exhibition of great power.

One three-decker, the Pennsylvania 120, has been launched. Several ships of the line and frigates are also on the stocks.

The navy has also been increased, within the last twenty-five years, by the addition of many heavy frigates and sloops of war: although still far from having reached the point necessary to a complete defence of the nation, it is probably, to-day, a hundred-fold stronger than it was at the declaration of war in 1812. Timber and other materials have been collected in considerable quantities, for the construction of new ships on an emergency; and there is little doubt that another contest would develope the nautical resources of the nation to an extent never anticipated by the last generation.

As the ships of the navy are constantly changing, a list would be of little permanent use. The officers form the essential feature of the service, and of these there are now, between—

                60  and   70  Captains,
                90  and  100  Commanders,
               350  and  400  Lieutenants, &c. &c.

Unfortunately, Congress has not yet established any higher grade than that first named, thereby neglecting the calls of justice, and the lofty considerations which are inseparable from the incentives connected with professional rank, as well as one of the most certain means of maintaining discipline. All military experience shows that rank and authority are correlatives; and all nautical practice has gone to prove that fleets are never thoroughly efficient, until animated and controlled by the feeling connected with a perfect submission to orders.

There is no longer any question concerning the expediency of the republic's maintaining a powerful marine. Experience has shown there is no security without one, and the gallant service, whose exploits have here been recorded, has got to be so necessary to, and so general a favourite with, the nation, that it scarcely exceeds the bounds of truth to say that their existence is inseparable.

**THE END.**

# CLASSICS OF NAVAL LITERATURE

## JACK SWEETMAN, SERIES EDITOR